WITHDRAWN

Memory's Daughters

Memory's

Daughters

The Material Culture of Remembrance
in Eighteenth-Century America

SUSAN M. STABILE

CORNELL UNIVERSITY PRESS   ITHACA AND LONDON

First published 2004 by Cornell University Press
Printed in the United States of America

Library of Congress Cataloging-in-Publication Data

Stabile, Susan M., 1966–
    Memory's daughters : the material culture of remembrance in eighteenth-century
America / Susan M. Stabile—1st ed.
        p. cm.
Includes bibliographical references and index.
    ISBN 0-8014-4031-9 (alk. paper)
1. Philadelphia (Pa.)—Intellectual life—18th century.   2. Philadelphia (Pa.)—
Biography.   3. Women—Pennsylvania—Philadelphia—Intellectual life—18th
century.   4. Women poets, American—Pennsylvania—Philadelphia—Biography.
5. American poetry—Women authors—History and criticism.   6. Memory—
Social aspects—Pennsylvania—Philadelphia—History—18th century.   7. Material
culture—Pennsylvania—Philadelphia—History—18th century.   8. Architecture,
Domestic—Social aspects—Pennsylvania—Philadelphia—History—18th century.
9. Commonplace books.   10. Souvenirs (Keepsakes)—Pennsylvania—Philadelphia—
History—18th century.   I. Title.
    F158.44.S73 2004
        974.8'1102—dc22

                                                            2003020313

Cornell University Press strives to use environmentally responsible suppliers and
materials to the fullest extent possible in the publishing of its books. Such materials
include vegetable-based, low-VOC inks and acid-free papers that are recycled,
totally chlorine-free, or partly composed of nonwood fibers. For further information,
visit our website at www.cornellpress.cornell.edu.

Cloth printing   10 9 8 7 6 5 4 3 2 1

But words are things, and a small drop of ink
Falling like dew upon a thought

—Lord Byron, *Don Juan,* canto 3

CONTENTS

Preface: Mnemosyne's Gift   ix

Introduction: The Genealogy of Memory   1

PART ONE: MEMORY

Chapter One: The Architecture of Memory   19

Chapter Two: Pen, Ink, and Memory   74

PART TWO: COLLECTIVE REMINISCENCE

Chapter Three: Among Her Souvenirs   129

Chapter Four: In Memoriam   178

Conclusion: The Ruins of Time   228

Notes   235

Index   277

Thomas Rowlandson, "Four Generations," n.d. Copyright Tate Gallery, London / Art Resource, New York. Reproduced with permission.

Mnemosyne's Gift

> Let us call it the gift of the Muses' Mother, Mnemosyne, and say
> that whenever we wish to remember something we see or hear or
> conceive in our own minds, we hold this wax under the percep-
> tions or ideas and imprint them on it.
>
> —Plato, *Phaedrus*

I lost my maternal grandmother in increments. Slowly succumbing to the
oblivion of dementia, she faded before my eyes, forgetting her name, my
name, and our shared past. She died—my heart's darling—the day I began this
book. Six months later my paternal grandmother entered an assisted-living
home, leaving behind her house of forty-five years and its heirlooms. Suddenly enveloped by the same degenerative forgetfulness that would bring her
both frustration and peace of mind, she was transferred to a nursing home.
Last month, as I worked through the copyedited text of *Memory's Daughters*,
she died quietly in her sleep. Mourning these losses, I have felt the burden of
memory, longing for one grandmother and remembering for the other.

But inheriting my grandmothers' belongings, I treasure the family history embodied in their things. The old sideboard and wobbly table that
now stand in my dining room hosted two decades of Saturday night dinners
at the Cunninghams. Even now a weekend rarely passes without bringing
nostalgia for the warm smells of Nana's kitchen: savory pot roast; buttery,
lumpy noodles; crispy green beans; and some sugary confection. Her misty-
painted secretary, which I have restored to its original oak finish, houses a

blotter graffitied by my mother's adolescent inscriptions to a long forgotten beau. Nana's dresser, previously filled with wonderfully disorganized envelopes of old photographs, now holds my own effects. Best of all is the rusty cookie tin filled with her old buttons. Plunging my hands into such an unlikely treasure chest, I trickle the buttons through my fingers like coins—but only for a few indulgent moments. Closing the tin, I covetously preserve Nana's distinctive scent to discover again another time.

Two summers ago I traveled to the Catskills to help my paternal grandmother select the few personal objects she would bring to the assisted-living home. I drove back to Texas, hauling my guilty treasures across the country, wondering how they would fit in our small house and distressed that Dambi no longer lived in her own. Now every nook and cranny of our home is filled with her gifts, placed beside and among Nana's bequests.

The sturdy oak kitchen table standing on its enormous claw feet recalls schooldays begun with a lively breakfast, along with my siblings and cousins, at Dambi and Opah's house. As we shouted our food orders from the table, my grandmother, like a patient short-order cook, catered to each of our persnickety palates. The large sideboard, still filled with her starched holiday linens, sits in my dining room, embodying the many festive Christmas celebrations at the Stabile house, which ended in sing-alongs around the piano and trap set. The piano now adorns my living room, quietly reminding me of the lessons I have promised to take in order to keep alive her old favorites by Cole Porter, Henry Mancini, Johnny Mercer, and Dorothy Fields. The oak rolltop desk at which I wrote this book lovingly preserves the miscellaneous residue of my grandmother's years as the school tax collector, as well as two leather-bound daguerreotypes of unidentifiable yet curiously familiar ancestors. Now that her house is kept by strangers, I maintain Dambi's old-fashioned cottage garden from afar, planting brightly colored trumpet vines, sweet Williams, black-eyed Susans, and tiger lilies in my own garden. Tending to the flowers revives the childhood summers at her house that will never return: the dribbling brook and grove of enormous pines, whose carpet of needles welcomed our sun-kissed feet; the jars of dandelions transforming into wine; and the pollywogs that were the envy of other show-and-tellers at school. Never thinking of growing older myself, I imagined she would live there forever.

More than through their material possessions, I remember and perpetuate my grandmothers through my hands. Polishing their furniture, I trace their handprints layered beneath decades of lemon oil. Wearing their shawls, scarves, gloves, and jewelry, I imaginatively wrap their arms around me. I also cherish what remains of my grandmothers' various handcrafts, which their arthritic fingers eventually laid aside: Dambi's oil paintings and pieced quilts, Nana's handkerchiefs and elaborate afghans. Tenderly passed from their hands to mine, these miscellaneous metonyms seem to me to embody my grandmothers, preserving their unique imprints, talents, faults. Such permanent impressions are the gifts of memory.

Like Mnemosyne, the classical goddess of memory and mother of the Muses, my grandmothers initiated a genealogy of remembrance, which I continue with this modest tribute. This book is dedicated to my grandmothers, Dorothy Waldyer Cunningham and Lillian von Kampen Stabile, for the fond memories they continue to inspire.

Though my grandmothers unwittingly prompted this project, countless others have encouraged me along the way. I give my warmest thanks to my indescribable editor, Sheri Englund, who made this book possible. I am deeply grateful for her support and friendship.

I have benefited from the generosity of several national and private institutions for funding my research, including the National Endowment for the Humanities, the Huntington Library, the Winterthur Museum, and the Mellon Foundation. Thanks are due also to Texas A&M University for numerous research grants. I am especially indebted to Texas A&M's Center for Humanities Research and its predecessor, the Interdisciplinary Group for Literary and Historical Studies, for providing research support, course relief, and the welcome opportunity to present my developing work.

It is a pleasure to thank the many wonderful people who encouraged and forwarded my work on this book. At the Winterthur Museum and Library, I am grateful to professors Gary Kulik and Gretchen Buggeln for fostering a collegial and intellectually stimulating environment between resident graduate students and visiting scholars. I greatly profited from conversations with Professor Bernie Herman on architectural history and the history of privacy. My thanks also go to librarians Neville Thompson and Jeanne Solensky for their capable assistance and to curators Linda Eaton, Don Fenimore, and Wendy Cooper for sharing their expertise in early American textiles, metals, and furniture. Finally, the camaraderie I experienced with other research fellows continues today: cheers to Janet Theophano for our rich discussions of colonial cookbooks and handwriting, to Lewis Nelson for introducing me to architectural theory, and to Charlotte Smith for helping me interpret historic houses with her undaunted spatial skills and for making Foulsham House feel like home.

To the many other archivists, librarians, and curators who offered their assistance, I owe a special debt of thanks, particularly to Jordan Rockford

and Laura Beardsley at the Historical Society of Pennsylvania, Karie Diet-
horn with Independence National Historical Park, Jeff Cohen of Bryn
Mawr College, Jim Green and John Van Horne at the Library Company of
Philadelphia, and Martha Slotten (formerly at Dickinson College's Archives
and Special Collections). My appreciation, too, goes to Anita Schorsch and
Gary Buss at the Museum of Mourning Art, Elissa O'Loughlin at Balti-
more's Walters Gallery, Melinda Kennedy at the Princeton University Art
Museum, Peter Huestis at the National Gallery of Art, Martin Durant at
the Victoria and Albert Museum, and Christina Philips at the New York
State Museum.

I wish to thank the dedicated curators of the historic house museums
presented in this book: Laura Stutman and Margo Burnet at Stenton, Sandy
Lloyd and Patricia Mousely at Graeme Park, Meg Schaeffer at Wright's
Ferry, and Emily Kroll and Martha Leigh Wolf at Morven. I was also fortu-
nate to view the related collections of The National Society of The Colonial Dames of America in the Commonwealth of Pennsylvania. The society's collaborative commitment to historic preservation heartens me.

I am grateful to the English Department at Texas A&M University for
granting me a semester sabbatical and for the continued support of my department head, J. Lawrence Mitchell, and my colleagues and friends.
Thanks to Dennis Berthold, Margaret Ezell, Kate Kelly, Howard Mar-
chitello, David McWhirter, and Paul Parrish for their encouragement. I appreciate Marian Eide for letting me think out loud and Patricia Phillippy for
our rich exchanges. I am especially indebted to Mary Ann O'Farrell,
Pamela Matthews, and Larry Reynolds for thoughtfully reading the manuscript at various stages. And a singular thanks to my friend and mentor
Lynne Vallone.

Beyond the department, I would like to thank Stephanie Attia for reminding me of the nuances between the present and the past. I also want to
acknowledge my colleagues in early American studies. Thanks first to my
teacher J. A. Leo Lemay for setting high standards and for introducing me to
the pleasures of manuscripts. I am particularly grateful to David Shields: his
continued guidance, warm collegiality, and good humor inspire me. I also
thank David and the other, anonymous, reader for Cornell University Press
for their intelligent and helpful remarks.

Initiated as a graduate student fellow by the salon culture fostered at the
Philadelphia Center for Early American Studies (now the McNeil Center)
in 1994–95, I experienced the richness of interdisciplinary inquiry—a testament to Richard Dunn's hospitality and intellectual rigor, which keeps
students and scholars coming back for more. I now happily find myself
among the Society of Early Americanists, an unparalleled forum for conver-

sation across the humanities. I would also like to warmly acknowledge Karen Carlson and Richard DuVaul for their invaluable insights and encouragement.

My family deserves special recognition for its unconditional support and affection. I honor my parents, Eileen and Frank Stabile, who selflessly care for successive generations of our family, from their own parents to their grandchildren. I am blessed with the continuity they give myself and my siblings, marking our lives with their gracious rituals of commemoration. I am also thankful for my delightful nephews, Logan and Justin Worth, for the simple joys and generational promise they unknowingly bestow. And finally, I thank my family in Texas, Angela and Bob Baker, for providing me with a home away from home.

I save my best thanks for last. To K.B. for his boundless generosity, steady patience, quirky humor, and tireless confidence in me. I depend on them more than he knows. MLTY.

Susan M. Stabile

College Station, Texas

Memory's Daughters

The Genealogy of Memory

The analogy between memory and a repository, and between re-membering and retaining, is obvious and is to be found in all lan-guages; it being natural to express the operations of the mind by images taken from things material.

—Thomas Reid, *Essays on the Intellectual Powers of Man* (1815)

THE NOSTALGIA FOR HOME

Longing for her childhood home, which formerly stood at Fourth and Chestnut Streets in Philadelphia, Deborah Norris Logan writes in her diary in 1830: "Dreaming took its turn, not connected nor sensible, but very vivid, depicting clearly the old house, and the associations known in childhood, which though they have no longer a local habitation, my spirit still haunts. The cold and beautiful temple and the habitations of strangers usurp the place." Haunted by a nostalgic ache for her ancestral home, which was de-molished and replaced by the monolithic Second Bank of the United States, Logan revisits the old, familiar places through the "local habitation" of her memory (see figure I.1). The house, she laments, stood for almost sixty-eight years and "never was occupied by any other family." But regrettably usurped by what she called "that Great Temple of Mammon" as the "habitation of strangers," the house was soon forgotten.[1] Built by her father in 1755 and in-herited by her brothers, Charles, Isaac, and Joseph, the house was sold in 1818 to the directors of the Second Bank of the United States for $102,000. The bank opened its doors in 1824, only to close them following bankruptcy in 1836. Three years later Deborah Logan died, regretting the ensuing public

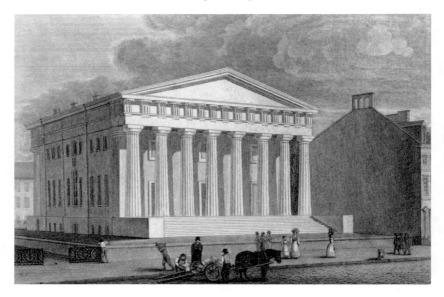

I.I. William Strickland, *Second Bank of the United States,* engraving published by Cephas G. Childs, 1829. Courtesy of the Print & Picture Collection, Free Library of Philadelphia.

amnesia that erased her family home from American cultural memory. Despite countless preservation efforts to sustain the bank building's historical appeal, no publicly accessible record of the house remains.

Once the secure repository for its patrons' valuables, the Second Bank of the United States became—and remains—a patriotic marker of the American revolutionary past. Like "symbolic bankers," as Kenneth Burke says, preservationists since the nineteenth century have "manipulated this medium of exchange to their special benefits," ensuring the bank's persistence as a valued historical site.[2] Constructed during the residual nationalism inspired by the War of 1812, the Second Bank conveyed the young nation's democratic promise. It was opulently decorated for the marquis de Lafayette's celebrated return to the United States in 1824, making a lasting impression on the French diplomat. The following decade it became the memorable site of the landmark battle between Andrew Jackson and Nicholas Biddle over the concept of a national bank. Serving as the Customs House from 1845 until its appropriation by the National Park Service in 1939, the building has been continuously renovated and preserved. In March 1960 it was slated as a portrait gallery for Charles Willson Peale's collection of Founding Fathers and revolutionary heroes, displayed at his museum on the second floor of Independence Hall from 1802 to 1828.[3] In order to adapt the bank vault to a gallery, the National Park Service initiated a round of renovations from 1972 to 1975, work that was resumed by the University of Pennsylvania in 1999 and continues today.[4] For over a century, the Second Bank has been restored and modified to suit our persistent need for a usable past.

In constructing public memory, national cultures have traditionally established "imagined communities," or narrative constructions, which could be reinvented over and over.[5] As the national capital from 1790 to 1800, Philadelphia remembered its revolutionary past while refashioning itself as a federal city. Its lingering patriotism resulted in a fantastic construction of public memory through ritual revelry, reconstituted symbols, and elaborate myth making immortalizing the city's short but heroic history.[6] Federalist parades, birthday celebrations, and endless memorabilia deified George Washington. Tapping into Washington's cult status while rejecting his "monarchical" style, Democratic-Republicans lauded Thomas Jefferson's assumption of the presidency on 4 March 1801, as a second American Revolution, a second Declaration of Independence marking a new republican era. Along with the growing list of national holidays, including the Fourth of July and Washington's birthday, Jefferson's inauguration day became a customary fete. Ten years later the widely contested War of 1812 was considered yet another reenactment of the American Revolution, ushering in "an era of good feelings" that confirmed the promise and progress of the Republic's democratic experiment.

Wanting to perpetuate the heroic myths of the revolutionary generation, republicans necessarily transformed their invented traditions into more lasting memories.[7] The construction of "national memory" demands consensus, imposing a "duty to remember" in a kind of fixed and reverential relationship to the past. At the same time, it requires material reminders for future veneration.[8] Both fixed and reverential, the monumental Second Bank of the United States boldly pronounced the rising glory of America. Though all the earlier American banks had adapted existing domestic residences for their purposes, the Second Bank was imagined on a much larger scale.[9] Its directors accordingly promoted an architectural competition for "a chaste imitation of Grecian Architecture, in its simplest and least expensive form." William Strickland won the contest and fashioned a Doric temple resembling the Parthenon. Typifying the Greek Revival style, which flourished from 1820 to 1860, the bank's architecture inaugurated what became known as the "National" style. Its simple facades and Ionic columns expressed the republican taste for classical symmetry, unity, and order, which in turn signified the economic, political, and symbolic power of the new nation. Like a Greek temple, the bank was an auspicious repository of cultural "valuables." While it literally kept the nation's coffers, it also reflected the republican values that fashioned national memory. Remembering Greece's golden age, the bank replicated the glorious myth for the new Republic.

The National Portrait Gallery, currently housed inside the Second Bank, perpetuates the heroic myth even today. In the barrel vault supported by two rows of Greek Ionic columns (where the bank clerks' desks once stood), the gallery remains a kind of temple, a historical sanctum. Its collection of one hundred eighty-five portraits of colonial and federal leaders continues the architectural motif of progress, as the bank vault runs in heliotropic fashion from east to west. Progress, however, is nostalgically frozen in these idealized portraits that once anticipated the nation's future and now arrest the modern viewer in their static moments. Aptly defined as "imaginative forgetfulness perfecting memory," nostalgia relies on our distance from and narrative improvement of the past.[10] Essential to national memory, nostalgia continues the romantic myth of the Republic's golden age by glossing over historical realities. Collective remembering, then, is based on forgetting. In order to remember what the Second Bank of the United States represents, we necessarily forget the Norris house, which once stood in its place. There is no image, no guide, no mention of the house or its inhabitants at the exhibit. Then and now, the bank marks a definitive tension between domestic and public memory.

Unlike their male contemporaries, who reinvented the past through communal fantasy, myth, and ritual, women in the early Republic participated in national memory building through genealogical associations. Locating the family—and the home—as the foundation of national memory, historical and heritage societies proliferated to house papers of prominent families; publications of formal genealogies abounded.[11] In contrast to the homogenizing tendency of national memory practices, women's preservation efforts focused on the local, the particular, the domestic. They aimed at accurately re-creating the historical record rather than invoking the past to fashion the future. Living and writing in "the eventful Period in which the present Generation have lived," Deborah Logan participated in the historic preservation movement at its inception by commemorating the forgotten Norris house (see figure I.2).[12] Three years after the Second Bank's completion and nine years before its demise, she composed a manuscript titled "The Bank of the United States: Formerly the Norris House and Garden" (1827), which provides a detailed account of the demolished house, its inhabitants, and their contributions to civic culture.[13] Despite the misleading title, the essay underscores the house's historical importance, reducing the mammoth bank to a single, passing reference.[14] Logan wrote the manuscript as an heirloom for her son, copying it into her commonplace book along with detailed genealogies of the Norris and Logan families. It was pub-

I.2. Norris House, from H. Ritchie, *Views in and near Philadelphia,* First Series (Philadelphia, 19–), Plate 1. Courtesy, American Philosophical Society.

lished posthumously, in 1867, again in the early twentieth century, and finally in 1951.

The essay's publication history, from privately written manuscript to publicly circulating book, underscores the same tension between genealogy and public memory now displayed by the bank and its portrait gallery. Just as the house was destroyed and then forgotten in order to monumentalize the bank, so Logan's personal recollections are missing from the published version of her essay.[15] The editor's erasures influenced the narrative's reception much as the gallery's choice and arrangement of portraits guides the visitor's experience of the exhibit. Both construct a version of public memory that dismisses domestic life and individual interpretation. By privileging Logan's manuscript in the discussion that follows, I resume her genealogical approach to memory making.[16] More than ancestral descent, genealogy is a rhetorical practice. It makes the familiar suddenly unfamiliar; what has unquestioningly been accepted as an American "tradition" looks strange and different to the genealogist.[17] Instead of looking at the "big picture" painted by consensus history, genealogy focuses on the particular, the anomalous, the other story. At odds with nationalistic narratives that emphasize shared origins, unbroken continuity, or universal memory, genealogy records what is without history.

Restoring the domestic world of memory, Logan substantiates her grandfather's conviction that "the female branches of our family are the best genealogists."[18] She begins the essay by presenting herself as the sole antiquarian responsible for reviving the memory of the Norris house: "I was born in the house that formerly occupied the site of this beautiful building, and I want to present it to those, who may come after me." Because the house itself is a vehicle for remembrance, she reconstructs it room by room—like an ancient memory palace.[19] A three-story mansion with numerous balconies and piazzas, the Norris house was architecturally unique, "its appearance altogether Singular, & different from any that I ever saw," according to Logan. With only two wooden buildings beyond it "on the same side of the street above the State House," it distinguished itself as a singular domestic dwelling.

The ground floor had four rooms divided by an entry hall, a staircase in the middle, and a hallway to the piazzas on either side. Behind the entry was a small room and adjoining kitchen with a door opening to the piazza. A pantry and greenhouse stood at the kitchen's back. The mansion also boasted a hothouse, "the first of its kind in our city," a detached wash house, and cellars renowned for their impressive hydraulic systems. During the Revolutionary War, Logan proudly recalls, the Norris house "furnished more lead than any house in town to make bullets to repel the enemy." The small room beyond the kitchen, "formerly of much comfort," was designated an intimate gathering place for the family's women and children. Here they would eat, read, converse, and tend to their needlework and other domestic crafts. Above the kitchen was an "excellent laundry" and an "airy apartment" with deep shelves to dry herbs cultivated in the garden. "The kind and charitable ladies of the household," writes Logan, distributed the herbs to Philadelphia residents, as it was the "only place at that time in the city" for natural remedies. Also upstairs were several chambers and a large drawing room. The drawing room, she remarks, had "strong, substantial furniture, brightly rubbed," and "Turkey carpets," which were "yet a luxury not every where to be seen." Admitting that "to this enumeration rooms of all descriptions may be added," Logan glosses over the other furnishings, describing them as "substantial and good, and well kept, though greatly differing from the display of modern magnificence." Probably a mixture of Queen Anne and Chippendale styles, the old furniture tangibly preserved the past in the present moment.

Rather than detail the beautiful furnishings, Logan interprets the rooms for the private, familial memories they embodied and evoked. Having descended from the powerful Lloyd and Norris families and married into the prominent Logan clan, Deborah Norris Logan recounts a political genealogy of Pennsylvania that traces her respected family lineage. She thus commemorates the many births, marriages, and deaths that occurred at the Norris house. Along with herself, her three brothers and her own eldest child were born at the ancestral estate. Here, too, she married George Logan, the grandson of William Penn's secretary, James Logan, on 6 September 1781. Balancing the happy occasions with sad ones, Deborah Logan also recounts the deaths and burials marked by the house. Her father, Charles Norris, died there on 14 January 1766 at the age of fifty-four. Later that year his eldest brother, Isaac Norris, "was interred from this house." In May 1767 her aunt Debby Norris, "who had always resided with him, and whose fondness for horticulture had created the garden," died at the age of sixty-eight.

In constructing her genealogy, Logan necessarily traces Philadelphia's illustrious revolutionary history. The Norris mansion, she recalls, frequently housed her uncle Isaac Norris, who, like his son, served as Speaker of the Provincial Assembly. For many years, during the sessions, he "made his home here." Eventually an invalid, Isaac Norris held assembly meetings in the mansion, as the representatives "came here to attend on him and many sittings of that body were held in the back parlour of this house." Similarly, the Continental Congress found a home at the Norris house, as the "justly celebrated papers that emanated from the first Congress were penned by the eloquent and no less excellent John Dickinson, who had married the only child and heiress of the Speaker, and who, with his wife, was frequent and intimate guest of the family."[20] The same man who celebrated his nuptials at the Norris mansion also may have written some of his famous political tracts there. Instead of enumerating their many civic contributions, Logan emphasizes the men's occupancy of the back parlor—the informal withdrawing room for family and other intimates. Though one might expect the congressional proceedings to take place in the formally appointed best parlor in the mansion's front, their tenure in the more intimate spaces significantly confounds the distinction between national and domestic memory. Further endorsing the house's importance to national memory, Logan underscores her relationship to these revered political figures, who were uncle and cousin (by marriage) to her, deliberately introducing them as family members rather than as the idealized public heroes currently found in the Second Bank's portrait gallery. In so doing, she replaces the paternalistic invention of the "Founding Fathers" with a more authentic political lineage.

In writing her essay on the Norris house, Logan records what is without history. Recognizing that her account is prompted by nostalgia, by a recurring memory of an unattainable place, she explains: "Much does the recollection of its lovely aspect furnish to my pen, that I am fearful, if I only faithfully pourtray my remembrances, that I shall be accused of substituting the Beau-ideal of my mind, for truth & reality." She realizes that nostalgia both restructures and distorts memory, however, and promises to create an accurate picture of the Norris house for posterity: "I will be careful not to exceed in description, what once existed in this sweet spot of elegance & floral beauty." Wishing for "a magic pencil" to replace her "clumsy pen," Logan attempts to "give permanency to the picture of what once was, but now is to be no longer found, except in my fond recollection." Unlike the proponents of the monumental bank, Logan looked to the past to authenticate her experience rather than to manufacture national memory.

Born before the American Revolution and living into the early years of the Republic, Deborah Logan was lauded by her contemporaries for her careful transcription, preservation, and publication of historical manuscripts. In addition to writing numerous biographical sketches of the Founding Fathers—largely from memory and personal experience—Logan compiled, edited, and annotated the voluminous correspondence of William Penn and James Logan.[21] As the first female member of the Historical Society of Pennsylvania and as the youngest member of a prolific literary coterie, she was a celebrated keeper of cultural memory. John Fanning Watson constantly sought her opinion when compiling his romantic *Annals of Philadelphia* (1830), which, Logan remarks, has "mistakes without number. But it has a rapid sale. Poulson took 5 copies."[22] Unlike Watson, whose error-ridden though widely read *Annals* perpetuated the heroic (and often inaccurate) myths of national memory, Logan preferred a domestic form of historical collection and preservation based on careful archival research. She wrote more than seventeen diaries and at least one commonplace book "to preserve fresh in [her] memory passing events" that would be otherwise "lost to Posterity for want of Record." Writing from time to time about "what shall appear to me worthy of preservation," she explains, "I have frequently thought that it would be both profitable and pleasant if some person in every family would make it their concern to keep a Book in which they would record" ancestral traditions.[23] Preserving the Norris home through her meticulously kept diaries and commonplace books, Logan created an "archive"—a public repository of documents and the manuscripts themselves—that rivals the unbalanced history presented by the bank's current portrait gallery.

DOMESTICATING THE ARCHIVE

An archive is both a physical place and a metaphor for memory. A secure repository for documents and relics from the past, its organization reflects the ways an institution situates itself in relation to its cultural history.[24] Unlike the Second Bank's portrait gallery, which provides a ready-made interpretation for the public, the archive presents primary materials in need of interpretation.[25] Though its acquisition policies inevitably reflect received opinions about history, politics, and literature, the collection's coherence is entirely artificial. That is, an archive is the residue of the past, inherently fragmented and incomplete. What is more, it is taken from its original context, where it once had a very particular meaning. As part of the genealogical project, the archive invites its patrons to make their own interpretations. Here the past seemingly lives untouched.

The word *archive* comes from the Greek *arkheion*: initially a house, a domicile, or an address of the superior magistrates, or *archons*. Given their publicly recognized authority, the archons kept the state's official documents in their homes.[26] Domesticating public knowledge, the archive marks an "institutional passage from the private to the public." Such a passage precedes the formation of the archive. But as critics have recently argued, "the original relationship seems inverted: details about private lives are found in what have become public spaces."[27] It is precisely this inversion that inspires this book. Relegated to the public sphere, the contemporary archive poignantly mimics Logan's nostalgic longing for her lost home. The modern adaptation of a memory palace, the archive, as a physical place, is a system of artificial memory. As fragments and pieces of history rent from their original contexts, the archived objects long to be put together, collected, collated, named.[28] Marked by nostalgia, an archive presents a kind of homesickness, a pain or longing to return home or to some lost past, where one remembers a sense of wholeness and belonging.[29]

Memory's Daughters follows the archive's nostalgic urge to return home. Returning the archive to its properly domestic origins, I recuperate the house—the place of feminine and familial experience—as a site of memory, history, and knowledge. Unlike the bank's portrait museum, which promotes an aesthetic of the untouchable, the house preserves rather than petrifies cultural memory.[30] More important, my focus on the house as a particular, intimate, and material form of remembrance places women at the center rather than the margins of early national history. Tracing a female genealogy of memory, this book introduces a prolific yet previously overlooked coterie of women writers from the Delaware Valley—Deborah Logan (1761–1839), Susanna Wright (1697–1784), Hannah Griffitts (1727–1817), Elizabeth Fergusson (1737–1801), and Annis Stockton (1736–1801)—who circulated their manuscript commonplace books of poetry from roughly 1760 through 1840.[31] Based on a rhetorical tradition that considered topoi, or places in the mind, as domestic spaces where one gathered, arranged, and displayed ideas, the commonplace book recuperates the house, and the female mind, as locales of knowledge and memory.[32]

Like Logan, the other coterie members descended from Philadelphia's circle of prominent and politically influential families. Until recently, they were known primarily for their genealogical connections to the "Founding Fathers" rather than for their literary and political contributions in the revolutionary and early republican era. A friend and correspondent of notable politicians Isaac Norris and James Logan, Susanna Wright was born in Warrington, England, and traveled to North America around 1714, settling first in Chester and eventually in Columbia, Pennsylvania, in the late 1720s.[33] Wright forwarded James Logan's cultural project of populating the uncultivated regions of the Lancaster frontier by extending Philadelphia's Quaker influence. She entertained several generations of the Norris and Wright families at her home, Wright's Ferry. She was a physician, herbalist, and apothecary to her neighbors. A scrivener for Lancaster magistrate Samuel Blunston, Wright also transcribed public and private documents. Sometimes she was more directly involved in politics. She outfitted Benjamin Franklin's militia with wagons during the Paxton Boys riots of 1763 and campaigned during the 1758 assembly elections in Lancaster. One disgruntled politician asked, "Could any one believe that Susy culd act so unbecoming and unfemale a part as to be employ'd in copying such infamous stuff and to take her stand as she did at Lancaster in an Upper Room in a publick House and to have a Ladder erected to the window and there distribute Lies and Tickets all the day of the election?"[34] Wright is best known for her silkworms, and tradition has it that Franklin presented her silk samples to the British monarchy.

Linked to Susanna Wright through her mother's lifelong friendship, Hannah Griffitts was a first cousin of Deborah Logan.[35] Born in 1727 to Thomas and Mary Norris Griffitts, Griffitts gradually joined the literary circle that had been begun two decades earlier by Isaac Norris, Charles Norris, and Susanna Wright. Composing hundreds of manuscript poems in her lifetime, Hannah Griffitts was one of the most prolific of her coterie. Better known for her pious Quaker elegies, she also wrote scathing satires during the American Revolution. In three different poems she excoriates Thomas Paine and his radical pamphlets, *Common Sense, Crisis,* and *Age of Reason,* for being insincere and insensible. She rails against the 1764 Revenue Acts, 1765 Stamp Act, 1767 Townshend Acts, and 1773 Tea Act in several poems and criticizes the postrevolutionary celebrations and mythic rituals of the Fourth of July in others. Finally, she satirizes the Meschianza, the courtly fete hosted by Major André in honor of General Howe's departure for England during the British occupation of Philadelphia in 1777–78.

Logan transcribed the poem from memory into John Watson's unpublished manuscript for his *Annals* "in the same Page on which he had pasted Major André's drawing of the Meschianza Lady." Though Watson destroyed the poem by first pasting paper over it and then scribbling over the paper "to perfect the obliteration" and to pacify one offended reader, he took "care however to preserve the verse elsewhere."[36]

Unrelated to the other coterie members by kinship or ancestry, Elizabeth Graeme Fergusson was born into Philadelphia's Anglican gentry.[37] The grandniece of provincial governor William Keith, Graeme was the daughter of Thomas Graeme and Anne Diggs. Popular folklore remembers her for her unfortunate romances: a failed relationship with Benjamin Franklin's son, William, and an unhappy marriage to the Tory sympathizer Hugh Henry Fergusson.[38] Inheriting the ancestral home, Graeme Park, in Horsham, Pennsylvania, she clandestinely married Fergusson and promptly forfeited the estate under the laws of coverture. Though unwavering in her patriotic sympathies, she was continuously questioned because of her husband's contrary loyalties. In October 1777 she unwittingly delivered a treasonous letter from Jacob Duche (via her husband) to George Washington, urging him to defect to the British. Her involvement became public knowledge after Washington submitted the letter to Congress. Her reputation further sullied, she unsuccessfully petitioned the assembly to return her property after the Revolutionary War. She called on her influential friends John Dickinson, Elias Boudinot, and Benjamin Rush to act in her behalf, but despite their best efforts she was eventually evicted from her home at Graeme Park. Before her financial and political hardships escalated, however, Graeme managed to create one of the first literary salons in North America.[39] After leaving Graeme Park at the century's end, she continued her literary career, writing new poems and copying old ones into her five commonplace books.

A member of Elizabeth Graeme's salon and host of her own salon in Princeton, Annis Boudinot Stockton was born to Catherine Williams and Elias Boudinot in Darby, Pennsylvania.[40] Sister to Elias Boudinot, president of the Continental Congress in 1783, she married Richard Stockton, signer of the Declaration of Independence and president of the College of New Jersey. (She would later become mother-in-law to philanthropist Benjamin Rush.) During the British invasion of Princeton in November 1776, Annis Stockton not only collected and buried her family's valuables in the garden before temporarily fleeing the estate, called Morven, but also went to the college and secured the papers of the Whig Society.[41] She put the patriot cause first, leaving her own manuscripts behind, which were destroyed by the British.[42] In her absence British general Cornwallis used Morven as his headquarters, damaging much of the house, the surrounding land, and her remaining manuscripts. After the war Stockton entertained politicians and diplomats at Morven, including George and Martha Washington, Rochambeau, and the marquis de La Luzerne. In addition to participating in local relief efforts for Continental Army soldiers and their families, Stockton carried on a lively correspondence with George Washington and wrote at least eight elegiac poems in his honor. Washington's appreciative response to one poem in August 1788 highlights Stockton's public contributions to the war, insisting he would not "rob the fairer sex of their share in the glory of a revolution so honorable to human nature, for, indeed, I think you Ladies are in the number of the best Patriots America can boast."[43] The American Whig Society made her an honorary member at the revolution's end.

Though these brief sketches, gleaned largely from public memory, highlight the coterie's historical experience through its members' relationships to prominent fathers, husbands, and brothers, *Memory's Daughters* reconstructs a poetics of female memory. Exemplified by their manuscript commonplace books, women's memory practices adapted the eighteenth century's new modes of learning based on accumulation, order, and classification into a feminine art of collecting. During the Enlightenment, collections—dictionaries, encyclopedias, and anthologies—were thought to promote useful knowledge. Small bits of memorizable and applicable ideas accordingly became the hallmarks of polite learning. Making learning more readily available to women, commonplacing was an invaluable method of reading and storing information in the early United States.[44] As useful knowledge was requisite for all republican citizens, commonplace books could be made for personal improvement by men and women, boys and girls, at school and at home. Unlike the original Latin commonplace books for schoolboys, the modern variant did not stress classical learning as much as the universality of ideas and the correctness of taste. Contrary to the exclusionary gender codes in colleges, commonplace books initiated a feminine genealogy of learning in which mothers and daughters taught successive generations of women by bequeathing their manuscripts.

The Philadelphia coterie domesticated the commonplace book by adapting its universal ideas to the members' own particular, historical circumstances. Creating a "local habitation" for their memories, they transformed the rhetorical art of artificial memory into works of the imagination. As the eighteenth-century essayist James Beattie explains: "By Memory, we acquire knowledge. By Imagination, we invent; that is, produce arrangements of ideas and objects that were never so arranged before."[45] Women projected their domestic authority as collectors of household topoi to their stockpile of literary and cultural miscellany. They copied and commented on passages from their favorite books, they composed original poetry, and they preserved one another's verse. As compilers and authors, they established what has been called a domestic or scribal form of "publication."[46] As Beattie further describes the process of commonplacing: "It is easy, and far more advantageous, to write correctly and legibly, with durable ink, and in note-books provided for the purpose, and carefully preserved. And when a volume is finished, it will be an amusement, and a profitable one too, to read it over; to make an index to it; and to write upon the cover such a title, or summary of contents, as may serve for a direction, when afterwards you want to revise any particular passage."[47] Such "publication" understood the commonplace book as an unfinished and unedited collection that could be constantly revised, supplemented, annotated, and indexed. Contrary to the consensus building constituted by print culture's creation of public memory, the manuscript commonplace book was neither "fixed" nor "corrected." It was an archive.

Extending the art of commonplacing to other modes of collecting, the Philadelphia coterie established distinctly material mnemonic practices through the analogous domestic arts of shellwork, penmanship, souvenir collecting, and mourning. These arts commemorate an artisanal culture in which an artifact bears the mark of its female maker. This imprint, I suggest, is the gift of memory. According to classical myth, memory was originally a block of susceptible wax given to us by Mnemosyne, the mother of the Muses and the goddess of memory. The wax receives the impression of our ideas, senses, and perceptions. An invaluable repository for cultural memory, the archive is also "a kind of gift" for future generations, future publics, according to the critic Thomas Osborn—"a kind of debt."[48] This gift depends on individual interpretation, personal associations, and alternative narratives. Imagining each of the women's mnemonic arts as a type of archive, *Memory's Daughters* reverses the archive's institutional passage from the private to the public sphere, relocating personal and collective memories in the domestic sphere through the genealogies of the women who produced them. Rivaling the Second Bank, the Philadelphia Georgian country house was—and remains—the true treasure house, sanctum, and keeper of women's memory. It is here, in the spaces prohibited to the general public, that the past survives.

Rather than a history, this book is more of an anatomy, one that maps the material world the women were trying to preserve. It resembles in its topographical arrangement the commonplace books that organized the coterie's memories. Under topic headings (sites, objects, practices, occasions), the book abandons chronology and mimics the way remembrance actually works. Unlike national memories unquestioningly absorbed into the public imagination, personal memory is associative, recursive, and utterly incomplete. The coterie accordingly composed a memorial literature documenting the mutable materials of everyday life. Its members sought to create an authentic record of the real circumstances of living, preserving their houses, gardens, furnishings, and the things they inhabited, revealing them in the fullness of their meaning, wrapped in skeins of association. Such an approach, I hope, offers the reader an impression of the coterie's world with a heightened sense of immediacy. At the same time, it has the curious effect of speeding up time. Things, people, manners have a way of becoming antique with breathtaking rapidity. Such are the ways of memory.

The book is divided into two parts: Memory (that is, preservation and evocation of impressions stored in one's own memory) and Collective Reminiscence (renewing forgotten or effaced impressions of an absent other). *Memory's Daughters* begins by carefully re-creating the domestic spaces where the Philadelphia coterie lived and wrote. Such attachments to beloved places, I argue in chapter 1, suggest a feminine mode of memory, which interpreted vernacular architecture as palaces of memory. Based on close readings of the coterie's commonplace books, household inventories, and architectural manuals, and on extant physical evidence of the Georgian houses themselves, I illustrate how these women materialized memory through their handcrafted shellwork houses—memory palaces in miniature. Since the women's sensual experiences of space determined the memories invoked and stored in each room, I take the reader on a detailed tour through their country houses, creating intimate biographies of the Philadelphia coterie.

I recover Deborah Logan's writing spaces in the dining room and library of her home at Stenton in chapter 2. By contrasting her unpublished diaries with a variety of eighteenth-century manuals of penmanship and architecture, I illustrate how these idealized prototypes held little relation to women's actual writing practices. The shared geometric principles underpinning handwriting and architecture, I further argue, comprise memory's reciprocal system of acquisition and recall. Whereas the women's houses inspired and stored memory images as "local habitations," their handwritten manuscripts translated those images into a more tangible and lasting form of remembrance.

The book goes on in part 2 to establish what critic Susan Stewart calls "a language of longing," which is embodied in personal souvenirs.[49] Unlike the collection, popularized in the eighteenth century by the published "miscellany," "cabinet," "portfolio," "museum," or "repository," the souvenir personalized memory and recuperated the past. Exchanged as gifts between female friends, portrait miniatures, mirrors, fans, and silhouettes, as chapter 3 illustrates, together represent the substitution of an object for a distant or absent person or an all-but-forgotten event. By reflecting the face, these particular souvenirs were constant reminders of aging and the inevitable amnesia that accompanies it. But as collaborative tokens of memory, they manifested the otherwise forgettable past.

The souvenir's materialization of longing—and finally of irrecoverable loss—culminates in the women's ritualization of death and mourning. Because embalming was not practiced in early America, women instead preserved the immediately decaying body through complex funeral rites and mourning tokens. Using eighteenth-century mourning manuals as well as funeral invitations, mourning jewelry, and mourning art, I recover the material culture of death in chapter 4. From the moment of death as witnessed by watchful intimates, the loving preparation and laying out of the corpse, and the more public funeral procession, to anniversary elegies, mourning gifts, and gravestone art, I illustrate the female mourner's transformation of souvenirs into lasting memorials.

The book ends with a sustained meditation on collective memory and British–American literary history. It returns to the old Norris house on Chestnut Street, taking the reader through a tour of the formerly acclaimed garden. The garden, Deborah Logan and Elizabeth Fergusson agreed, was a new symbol for the republic of letters, bringing their coterie into British–American literary history. Concluding Mnemosyne's genealogy of female memory with her own coterie, Fergusson celebrates the garden in her companion epics, "Odes to British and American Genius." These poems trace the women's cultural inheritance from England's famous Litchfield group (including Samuel Johnson, David Garrick, William Hogarth, and Anna Seward) to the College of Philadelphia's eminent "Schuylkill Swains" (including Thomas Godfrey, Nathaniel Evans, and Thomas Coombe) to the Philadelphia coterie itself. Filled with *translatio* images of transplantation, the odes actualize—and more important, feminize—George Berkeley's much-quoted prophecy of the westward movement of arts and learning to "the Athens of North America." Like the ruins in a country house garden, women's commonplace books of poetry created landscapes of memory.

Though scholars have begun to redress the gender imbalance in the early American literary canon with editions and anthologies of women's poetry, there is no critical study of either women's manuscript culture or their commonplace books.[50] By examining these books in the cultural context in which they were produced, *Memory's Daughters* presents their modes of scribal "publication" as part of the proliferating print culture of the early Republic. A vital resource for historical memory, the commonplace book mediates between the largely artificial boundaries separating public and private, print and manuscript, knowledge and memory.[51] The commonplace book, then, is an archive in both senses of the word: as a physical object, it represents rhetorical topoi, or places for memory storage; as a text, it is the very stuff of memory making.[52]

By adapting commonplacing and other domestic arts into a feminine art of artificial memory, these well-educated, privileged, literary women forwarded a unique way of knowing, which undercut, subverted, and reapplied what might be understood as a limited female intellectual capacity. In the eighteenth century a woman's knowledge and her memory were considered indistinguishable. Despite the Enlightenment's innovations, it preserved the well-established Elizabethan notions of sexual difference, equating men with the mind and reason and women with the body and the material world. This scheme not only associated men with knowledge and women with feeling but also distinctly separated knowledge from the female body.[53] Memory, on the other hand, depended exclusively on a woman's body and engaged all her senses. A kind of associational thinking, memory was a specifically feminine way of knowing. Though women were considered the irrational and "weaker sex," they were credited with having a superior memory and affinity for detail. Understanding the female body as a vital site of memory, *Memory's Daughters* revives the early modern theories that equated female knowledge and memory: as Marius D'Assigny theorizes in *The Art of Memory,* "It is Memory alone that inriches the Mind, that preserves what Labor and Industry collect. . . . In a word, there can be neither Knowledg, nor Arts and Sciences without Memory."[54]

This new, material understanding of women's intellectual work challenges us to reconsider what public "historical" memory means in the republican era. Approaching memory as a lived practice rather than as a reinvented tradition, *Memory's Daughters* continues Deborah Logan's genealogical project. It returns to the domestic origins of the archive, revisiting the moments before the Norris house was demolished, before the Second Bank was built in its place, and before the bank became a public museum. Unlike the museum, which offers a ready-made interpretation of cultural memory, the archive invites patrons to put the fragments together into meaningful and often divergent narratives.[55] Appreciating the Philadelphia coterie's historic houses and manuscript commonplace books as a rich archive—as at once a physical space and a material object—this book explores the expressly feminine arts of collection and recollection. Preserving the archive "received in tradition from [her] ancestors," Logan similarly justifies her antiquarian interest in reviving the old Norris House, "for want of such a written record what a store of helpful and entertaining knowledge has been lost."[56]

PART ONE *Memory*

1

The Architecture of Memory

Lull'd in the countless chambers of the brain,
Our thoughts are link'd by many a hidden chain.
Awake but one, and lo, what myriads rise!
Each stamps its image as the other flies!

—Samuel Rogers, *The Pleasures of Memory* (1796)

THE INHABITED SHELL

"Men are like those workers who work tediously on wholly unformed, rough-hewn stones," writes François Poulain de La Barre in *De l'égalité des deux sexes,* "and women are like Architects, or clever Lapidaries who polish and easily work at their own good speed what they have in hand." As lapidaries, who cut, polish, and engrave gems, early American women constructed shadowboxes of houses, grottoes, and classical landscapes in miniature. They would begin these projects by polishing the wide variety of shells in their collection, since according to Hannah Robertson's *Young Ladies School of Arts* (1777), a "great many ladies have a taste for curious shells." Shells, Robertson continues, "generally come from the sea in a rough state . . . so that they require to be polished up to let their beauties appear." Some shells were simply rubbed with a piece of chamois leather, a porous stone such as tripoli, or even with a bare hand. Others required briskly scraping the surface with a knife or emery, dipping it into aqua fortis or another corrosive acid, and brushing it with gum arabic or egg white to restore the glossy surface. The artisans then sorted the polished shells according to color and size, separating the porcelains, cassandras, and limpets from the cornets, cylinders, and rhombi. Imitating familiar architectural designs in their patterns, women arranged their shells to suit their individual taste. With a deliberate sense of vernacular design, they would "take care to augment or lessen every object, proportionably to its distance from the eye. . . . whether it be a temple, castle, house, or the like."[1] Women thus applied the architectural standards of symmetry and proportion to the analogous art of shellwork.[2]

In 1757 Anne Reckless Emlen fashioned a miniature Philadelphia country house, combining shells, wax, and paper (see figure 1.1). Currently displayed at Deborah Logan's house, Stenton, the shell house is enclosed in a shadow box of plain board sides (22½" h × 20⅞" w × 10⅞" d) and set with an ornate background mosaic of small, dark shell roses.[3] A picket fence made of sticks and shells frames the pedimented entrance to the three-story, Palladian villa. Small pink shells suggest a brick facade on the five-bay design, and delicate white shells form the parallel belt courses. Crowned by Emlen's initials, the impressive house sits atop a steep cliff of glittering shells and sparkling shards of glass. A paper stairway winds downward into the enclosed garden and grotto below. Animating the scene are one wooden and two wax dolls dressed in mid- and late-eighteenth-century costume. Standing in the doorway, descending the stairs, and leisurely reclining in the garden, the female figures watch several carrier, or "homing," pigeons. A material reminder of domesticity, shellwork also provided an intellectual outlet for women as the poet Samuel Rogers notes: "To give proportion'd Beauty to each Part, / To make the whole subservient to the Art."[4] More than illustrating architecture's classical principles of proportion, Emlen's shell house became a "local habitation" for her memories. A miniature memory palace, the house represents what the theorist Gaston Bachelard calls the "phenomenology of the inhabited shell": a habitation's private recesses, on the one hand, and the hidden niches within an inhabitant's mind, on the other.[5] Women's shellwork distinctively illustrates the neoclassical fascination with the spatiality of knowledge and association of knowledge with geographical place.[6]

Along with the shells, women collected historical memorabilia regarding their architectural craft. In 1868, for instance, the great-granddaughter of Sarah Morris Buckley writes: "In the Provincial Era of Philadelphia Society, a favorite pastime with young ladies, was the construction of *Shells & Wax Work,* in various shapes & forms, such as Houses, Grottoes, Images. . . . My mother has now in her possession, a beautiful representation of '*Calypso's Grotto,*' & in most excellent preservation, although at this date, April 4 1868 over 103 years old."[7] As the accompanying clipping from the 27 April 1767 *Pennsylvania Gazette* attests, female boarding schools advocated "wax and shellwork in the newest and most elegant Taste" as "one of the more polite

1.1. Anne Reckless Emlen, Shellwork House, c. 1757. Courtesy of The National Society of The Colonial Dames of America in the Commonwealth of Pennsylvania at STENTON, Philadelphia.

Parts of Education [that] may be obtained" in eighteenth-century Philadelphia. Discovering an itemized receipt for lessons from the schoolmistress Mary McAllester, Buckley reconstructs her great-grandmother's experience of building a shellwork grotto a century earlier. Expenses included instruction (seven pounds), two and one-half yards of flowered paper (one shilling, ninepence), and frost for the church, house, and rocks (four shillings, sixpence).

More important than its monetary value, Buckley learns, is the shell-work's material associations with female memory and intellect. Dedicated to Calypso ("the concealer"), Buckley's damp, moist, and mysterious grotto represents the feminine rococo style (from *rocaille,* or rockwork found in caves and grottoes), which diverged from the hierarchical classicism of Emlen's Palladian design. It celebrates the female body's serpentine S curve, which the British painter William Hogarth called the "line of beauty." A uterine image that conceals the "secrets of generation" in its cavernous folds, the grotto also signifies the dark recesses of the female mind. Women were repeatedly admonished to keep their knowledge hidden: "Let your knowledge be feminine, as well as your person. And let it glow within you, rather than sparkle upon others about you." "But if you happen to have any learning," they were reminded, "keep it a profound secret, especially from the men." A woman's knowledge, like her sexuality, was considered threatening. Typically consecrated to solitude, contemplation, or some other poetic ideal, the grotto safely externalized a woman's otherwise invisible creative capabilities, making a private, secluded place for women's intellectual work in a "Secure retreat! / Fit for the Muses."[8]

Made and preserved by early American women for more than two centuries, shellwork houses embody the mnemonic relationship between rhetoric and architecture. As the British architect William Chambers suggests in his 1759 *Treatise,* "Materials in Architecture are like words in Phraseology, which singly have little or no power; and may be so arranged as to excite contempt; yet when combined with Art, and expressed with energy, they actuate the mind with unbounded sway."[9] Architectural features, like rhetorical topoi, were considered material "commonplaces" that depended on and reinforced human memory.[10] A regional or localized, ethnic or folk creation based on the imitation and adaptation of existing forms, vernacular architecture was a nonliterary method of design that stored complex building traditions in the builder's mind rather than in printed treatises or blueprints. Using a mnemonic rather than textual method, builders transformed past precedents into new structures. Such imitation emphasized both unity (repetition of formal building types) and variety (small differences among similar building types). In the same way, rhetoricians imaginatively displayed common "heads" (universal and transferable ideas) and specific topics (peculiar to each class of things) in new contexts. Vernacular architecture and commonplacing, therefore, established, as Dell Upton suggests, "an entire epistemological structure gathered to replication and maintenance of a tradition."[11] And that tradition was specifically mnemonic.

Such a topographic configuration of knowledge lent itself to the art of artificial memory begun by classical oratory, continued by medieval florilegia, translated by Renaissance commonplace books, and punctuated by the eighteenth century's gradual transformation of rhetoric into belles lettres.[12] Mnemonic treatises from the classical period through the eighteenth century universally described human memory in architectural terms.[13] Because the mind was considered a clearinghouse for ideas, and because rhetorical topoi ("places in the mind" in Greek) were imagined as material objects housed in the mind, commonplaces were portrayed by ancients and moderns alike as *sedes,* "dwelling places" or "local habitations" in which "lives of argument wait to be discovered and from which they must be drawn out." "What we call places [should be] such as may easily be grasped and embraced by the natural memory; for example a house, an intercolumnar space, a recess, an arch, or the like," writes the unknown author of the influential classical text on mnemonics, *Ad herennium.* Following the ancients, Erasmus later argues that commonplacing required that one "investigate all the places in turn, knocking at their doors, so to speak, in order to see what can be drawn out from them."[14]

In his essay "On Memory and Imagination" (1783), popular in the early American Republic, the moral philosopher James Beattie similarly reconstructs a classical memory system: "For this purpose, they arranged in their Memory a number of contiguous places where with they were well acquainted, the apartments of a house, for example. . . . The orator then formed a kind of imaginary connection between these several places, and the several heads of the discourse which he intended to deliver. . . . And hence, the several heads of a discourse were called Places, or Topicks." Envisioning contiguous apartments as manifestations of rhetorical "places" that stimulate an orator's memory, Beattie adapts Quintillian's memory house to a palpable floor plan for a modern commonplace book. Placed side by side like itemized columns on a page, the rooms represent general topics (or heads) for public discourse. Under each head, specific examples (or "*copia*") would be gathered from authoritative texts. Beattie's memorable *copia* are decidedly domestic, including such "moveables" as furniture ("tables and couches") and decorations ("statues and pictures"). Such homely images would enhance female memory, for a methodical arrangement of familiar *copia* "is readily understood, and quickly remembered."[15]

These moveables—furniture, textiles, and other decorative arts—are just the kinds of dowered items women brought to their marriages.[16] The material images of commonplacing, therefore, granted women a place in both rhetorical and architectural discourse from which they were otherwise excluded. Given women's cultural relegation to the domestic sphere, the house was the perfect image in which to store female memory. Mimicking household design, shellwork and commonplacing thus popularized the modes of artificial memory for a wider audience—including British-American women—for the first time. Using the well-established architectural metaphors for memory, women understood their houses as protective shells for private lives. A material metonym for the mind, the house represents the eighteenth century's gendered distinctions of space that limited women to the home on the one hand while authorizing their superior memory through images of domestic interiors on the other. The association of the female mind with the Georgian interior may have perpetuated the rhetoric of "separate spheres." But it also established a distinctively feminine understanding of space, knowledge, and memory, for the "Domestick Nature" of women's employments was "not like those of the other Sex which are often inconsistent with Study and Contemplation," but rather a convenient topos for their intellectual work.[17]

The Philadelphia coterie applied these architectural metaphors to their Georgian country houses, creating personalized memory palaces. Translated to the Delaware Valley, the English Georgian house type was an adaptation of the Italian Renaissance revival of Roman architecture. Characterized by its two stories, symmetrical facade, hipped roof, and a central entry that ran two rooms deep on either side, the prototypical Philadelphia Georgian (or "detached") house changed the earlier medieval hall-parlor and later three-cell plan into the center-passage plan. As both vestibule and room, passageway and social space, the center passage or hall negotiated the boundaries between the domestic interior and the exterior facade.[18] Like the rooms of an artificial memory house that are designed as convenient receptacles, the center-passage plan revolutionized domestic architecture by creating private spaces through controlled access to previously public rooms. The social activities formerly relegated to the multipurpose hall were now dispersed through the front parlors and dining room of the ground floor and the family's private life removed to the house's upper and posterior recesses (see figure 1.2). Compartmentalizing private and social space, the Georgian plan mimicked the rooms of the modern memory palace.

The Georgian house also functioned as a mnemonic topos for its female inhabitants. Just as builders accommodated general architectural plans to local circumstances, so women revised household spaces into discrete places for memory.[19] The private "closets" or "inner chambers" for female reading, writing, and contemplation represented the compartmentalized "rooms" in the eighteenth-century woman's mind: reason, fancy, imagination, perception, judgment, taste, and memory. Whereas reason and imagination occupied "the greater [i.e., foremost] Closets of the Brain," the "Closet of Memory," where "the Soul treasures up the Ideas of things," re-

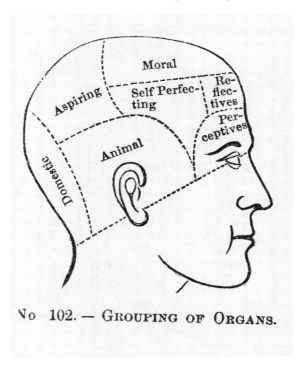

No 102. — GROUPING OF ORGANS.

1.2. From O. S. Fowler, *The Practical Phrenologist* (Boston, 1969), p. 9. Courtesy, Harry Ransom Humanities Research Center, The University of Texas at Austin.

ceded "to the less and hindermost" region (see figure 1.3). Resting in the cerebellum's posterior niches, interior memory places reflected the Georgian house's spatial arrangement of private, feminine rooms.[20] The secluded, indeed almost hidden, space of memory in the back of the female mind illustrates the feminine constructions of privacy in the eighteenth century. Just as the development of the novel generated an interest in psychological interiors by creating the female reader, so the convenient passage between rooms through the central hall encouraged the easy movement of a woman's memory, according to Marius D'Assigny, through "a Passage open and wide . . . by which the Spirits ascend up to it with ease, and without any obstruction."[21]

THE SEX OF ARCHITECTURE

Women's elaboration of the domestic memory palace required careful negotiation of architectural theory, which persistently gendered domestic

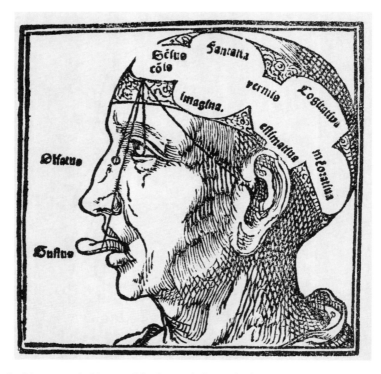

1.3. In this prototypical image of faculty psychology, which persisted through much of the Enlightenment, "Memory" is located in the posterior recesses of the brain. Johann Host von Romberch, *Congestorius artificiose memorie* (Impressum Venetijs, 1520), B1 verso. Courtesy, Harry Ransom Humanities Research Center, The University of Texas at Austin.

structures. "Architecture, indeed, has in a manner two sexes," writes Horace Walpole. "Its masculine dignity can only exert its muscles in public works. . . . its softer beauties come better within the compass of private residence and enjoyment."[22] As polar opposites, men and women represented the two spheres of architecture: exterior and interior, public and private. Whereas a building's "outward ornaments (ought) to be sollid, proporsionable according to the rulles, masculine and unaffected," according to the British architect Inigo Jones, its domestic interior displayed a woman's character.[23] The builder Richard Neve similarly describes the aesthetics of masculine exteriority in *The City and Country Purchaser* (1703): "Pass a running Examination over the whole Edifice, according to the Properties of a well shapen Man; as whether the Walls stand upright, upon a good Foundation; whether the Fabric be of a comely Stature." Like a man, whose "Province is without Doors," a building's facade presented the owner's public face.[24]

Domestic interiors, conversely, reflected private life, closely associated with the female body in the eighteenth century.

The architectural division of masculine exteriors and feminine interiors materializes the Enlightenment's cultural assumptions about sex and gender. Much like the gendered configuration of domestic architecture, modern biology understood interior spaces as expressly feminine.[25] Based on eighteenth-century "decorum" (i.e., the connection of a building's form and use with the owner or inhabitant's taste on the one hand and a female inhabitant's displays of etiquette and politeness on the other), rules for architectural design perpetuated the natural "order" of the sexes. Because a woman's body was considered naturally weak and her manner passive, she was conveniently confined within the house.[26] Given the conflation of female and architectural "interiors," women were persistently reminded: "The neatness and order of your house and furniture is part of oeconomy which will greatly affect your appearance and character, and to which you must yourself give attention." One moralist admonishes, "It is your own steadiness and example of regularity that alone can preserve uninterrupted order in your family," and another warns, "To go beyond your sphere, either in dress, or in the appearance of your table, indicates a greater fault in your character than to be too much within it." A woman's "sphere," then, extended from the circumference of her disciplined body to the strict organization of her house.[27]

To better illustrate the mnemonic significance of gendered decorum, I turn momentarily to a black-and-white print titled "KEEP WITHIN COMPASS AND YOU SHALL BE SURE TO AVOID MANY TROUBLES WHICH OTHERS ENDURE" (c. 1785–1800) (see figure 1.4). In the center is a compass and circle, which establish the print's moral parameters. Beneath the compass stands a well-dressed, upper-class woman holding a knotting shuttle that keeps her fingers (and her mind) from falling idle. The circumscribed image is framed further by a geometrically divided square composed of four rooms symbolizing the evils of drinking, card playing and gambling, prostitution, and prison. Such vices, critics cautioned, could ruin a woman's memory: "Drunkeness is offensive to the Brain," inducing forgetfulness. A forgetful and lethargic body further "begets and increases ill Humors, which have a bad influence on the Faculty of Memory."[28] As negative reminders that domestic order suffers by a woman's excessive pleasures, these rooms create a memory house of dictums for her to remember. "A Virtuous Woman is a Crown to her Husband," reads one maxim; "How blest the Maid whose bosom no headstrong passions knows, / Her days in Joy she Passes, her nights in soft repose," reads another. Beyond the compass of her domestic duties, then, a woman enters "into the way of the wicked . . . [and] the path of evil men." Organized by

1.4. "Keep within Compass," black-and-white print, c. 1785–1805, England. Courtesy, Winterthur Museum.

complementary virtues and vices, the memory house follows Erasmus's advice in *De copia,* where he considers virtues and vices as loci, or places: "These should be arranged [*digerere*] by similars and opposites," he writes, for "the memory is prompted in a similar way of opposites." A valued scheme for artificial memory, contraries are inherently mnemonic: "We may imprint in our Minds, and fix things in Memory," D'Assigny agrees, "by thinking upon their Contraries and Opposites."[29] The order of a woman's house, therefore, reflected her morality as well as her memory.

By the eighteenth century, architectural discourse had extended its influence over domestic and bodily decorum to equally corporeal theories of "proportion." Though the classical definition of proportion (i.e., the correspondence between the various parts and overall form) refers to an idealized male body, and by analogy to a building's exterior form, proportion also governed the feminine interior.[30] As the architect John Evelyn explains, "The irregularity of our humors and affections may be shrewdly discerned" from a building's order, proportion, and decorum. Since buildings reflected human proportion, and since men and women contained proportionately different humors, women were constantly reminded not to "excede the natural proportion, [as] both the Health and Memory also are impair'd in that Body."[31] The same tender organs that confined a woman to the house accordingly granted her a superior memory, allowing her to quickly see "an infinity of nuances, of items of detail, and relationships that escape the most enlightened man."[32] Controlling the female body, then, ensured household harmony.

Like decorum, the discourse of architectural proportion devolved into theories of gendered ornamentation. "We see this in nature," writes one critic, that "any woman who hopes to please must herself be suitably proportioned to look well in her dress." A well-dressed woman, it follows, exemplified architectural beauty, for "nothing is truly fine but what is fit, and that just so much as is proper for Circumstances of their several kinds, is much finer than all [she] can add to it," contends another. As the British architect Robert Morris similarly insists: "Rules well appropriate will ever please, / And proper Dress, is plac'd with Ease." Like Morris, William Kent literally imposed architectural order on female fashion, designing a "petticoat decorated with the columns of the five orders." Continuing the metaphor, Deborah Logan compares the single coat of paint on her dining room walls to an old woman's inappropriate dress: "Thee cannot think how odd it looks, like a modern dress on an antiquated person, but when another is on it will do better."[33] Proportion, like decorum, thus controlled outside surfaces, both human and architectural.

Though reinforcing modern notions of sex and gender difference, architectural decorum and proportion also opened up a space, within a predominantly masculine discourse, for female memory. Confounding the stereotypes that associated men with exterior surfaces and cerebral functions on the one hand and women with interior matter and bodily limits on the other, women synthesized these opposites through their domestic memory palaces. Like a memory house, the female body was the source of and receptacle for—rather than impediment to—empirical knowledge. Household spaces that conventionally emphasized a woman's inherent materiality now indicated the physical places in her mind. Women, therefore, transformed the rhetoric of separate spheres into a mnemonic art, following D'Assigny's precept: "For the better remembering of things, we ought to compare them with those things with which we are familiar."[34] What could be more familiar to a woman than her house?

TOPOPHILIC PLACES

Caring for the most intimate and minute details, the Philadelphia coterie experienced domestic architecture as lived rather than built space.[35] As inhabitants, these women accommodated interior spaces to their ongoing lives. Through what contemporary theorists call *proprioception* (the orientation of and perception by the body in space), women adapted architecture's gendered decorum into an artificial memory system entirely indebted to the female body. Women remembered the places they inhabited through their senses: sight, sound, smell, taste, and touch.[36] Thus, their bodies recorded a "local history" that was literally the "history of locales."[37] Though architecture and rhetoric alike considered locales universal and repeatable topoi, women developed unique "topophilic" attachments to their houses.[38] An affectionate affinity to beloved places, topophilia telescoped a house's vernacular loci to the female body itself. As Elizabeth Fergusson explains: "If one has been long accustomd to a certain Sett of Objects, which have made a strong Impressien on a man's Mind, such as a House, where he has passd many agreeable years, . . . they become objects of his affection. . . . I have also in my Life felt the Force of those Local attachments, to a Degree which has disturbd my Peace, and which to People not troubld, with an association of Ideas would Deem weakness"[39] (see figure 1.5). Treasured objects or spaces (i.e., a house) leave an indelible impression on one's mind (i.e., a memory), which together comprise a "local attachment" (i.e., the house and its memory image). Such associative thinking, Logan confirms in another context, is "something so congenial to what I have often felt, but I believe never saw described before that I took up my pen and thus endeavored to give my thoughts a local habitation."[40]

Women's appreciation of topophilic space reflects the eighteenth-century philosophy of associationism, which postulated a direct, physical link connecting domestic architecture, material objects, and memory.[41] Particular rooms or things contained traces of original experiences, triggering an endless train of related impressions. As one theorist contends, "The perception of an object naturally leads to the idea of another which was connected

1.5. This nineteenth-century drawing of the Graeme Park parlor fills the now empty room with intimate, historic objects of affection. Henry Collection, 40.17.2987. Courtesy of the New York State Museum, Albany, New York.

with it," directing our thoughts to the original. Logan similarly notes "that particular kinds of days and a particular aspect of things around us, should dispose our minds to receive pleasure. . . . I should suppose it proceeded from an association of ideas which reminded us of something past that was agreeable, and from the same Imagery, threw the same pleasureable sentiment over the mind." Linking memory with beauty and pleasure, associationism complemented women's innate sense of taste, according to aestheticians. They could see an object and by "a natural association . . . conceive its end." Looking at a building, a woman sensed "something of the character and expression" from the design, which in turn "owes all its power of exciting sentiments, either of the one kind, or the other, to the association of ideas." Women may not have built their own houses, but they understood architectural form through its practical (and mnemonic) functions. A woman's associations were consequently "either larger or narrower, greater or less, according to the good or ill Qualities of the Senses."[42]

Though associationists assumed women had vicarious knowledge of architecture, whereby the "little room lost in the stairs, anti-chambers and passages" delight us "by our sympathizing with the proprietor of the lodging," according to David Hume, women depended on their receptive nervous systems to directly incite their personal associations of domestic space. Translating sensation into memory through a complex system of vibrations, the sympathetic nervous system was believed to course throughout the body and terminate in the brain. As the clearinghouse for sensation, the brain, neurologists posited, relies on the nerves, which distribute "animal spirits" through the body. Such spirits, or impulses, according to Isaac Newton in *Principia,* were composed of ether, which "pervades and is hid in all gross bodies," and "all sensation is excited by the vibrations of this spirit mutually propagated along the solid filaments of the nerves."[43] Moving along the nerves in repetitious paths, the animal spirits permeated contiguous traces of sensation, stimulating other related ideas. These traces, in turn, formed the rudiments of memory. Thus the nervous system resembled the Georgian house's central-passage plan.[44] Like a hallway, memory was persistently described as "mazes and meanders" through the "medullary Labyrinth" and "inmost Recesses" of the brain's "dark Caverns of Oblivion." Memory, theorists concluded, is a place of passage, a system of entry (to memory rooms) or egress (moving between these rooms). It is a "hyphen, a connecting link" between people and the material world they inhabit.[45]

Memory results from human interaction with the physical world, but it also leaves its mark on that world. As Elizabeth Fergusson insists, local habitations "seem endowd with Life." Because humans share "a sort of assimilating Principle, From a Propensity To spread our selves over all things, almost every emotion, which in the least agitates the mind bestows upon its Object a momentary Idea of Life."[46] Through a kind of emotional transference, the same animal spirits that trigger the human nervous system and memory personify otherwise inert objects, making them unforgettable. Objects do not inherently provoke association; humans project meaning onto them. Breathing life into inanimate objects, women externalized and physically preserved their fleeting memories. "To live is to leave traces," writes theorist Walter Benjamin. "In the interior these are emphasized. An abundance of covers and protectors, liners and cases is devised, on which the traces of objects of everyday use are imprinted. The traces of the occupant also leave their impression on the interior."[47]

Inspired by the fond memories each of the Philadelphia coterie members had of her home, the remainder of this chapter is a walking tour through these historic country houses. Meandering from house to house and from room to room, the tour enacts the neurological train of associations experienced by the women as they inhabited these spaces. My descriptions of domestic interiors are primarily gathered from their extant objects and from unpublished manuscripts, which tenderly illuminate and animate these spaces.[48] But because of the fragmentary nature of archival preservation, my documentary tour, like memory itself, is often incomplete and uneven. In presenting the mnemonic traces of their houses, however, I invite readers into their most beloved places.

FAIRHILL

"Fairhill," writes Deborah Norris Logan, was built by Isaac Norris "upon the same plan as Dolobran (a seat from long antiquity possessed by the Lloyd family in Montgomeryshire, North Wales)."[49] Constructed between 1712 and 1717 at the crest of a rolling hill overlooking the Delaware Valley and the city of Philadelphia, it was considered one of the most beautiful country seats (see figure 1.6). A variant of the square, double-pile form, Fairhill's original H-shape plan made it unique among mid–Atlantic rural residences of the early eighteenth century. Rising into steep gables on either side of the recessed center, the legs of the H visually balanced the tripartite structure, which culminated in a balcony and cross-gable roof. Over the center stair hall a cupola punctuated the vertical ascent, and a door from the garret led out to a small balcony above the entrance. Below the fully lit garret of four chambers and above the cellar was the first story, composed of an unheated center hall with two rooms sharing a chimney block on either side. Unlike the typical H plan, structured around a center hall with two parlors and the main stairs on one side and a kitchen, service rooms, and back stair on the other, Fairhill had a detached kitchen from its inception. Burned by the British in November 1777, rebuilt in 1787, and finally demolished in the nineteenth century, "Fairhill" is no longer extant.

Though recent archaeological work has recovered the original floor plan and building materials, along with eighteenth-century drawings of the plantation,[50] Fairhill is most vividly revived through the collective memories of Susanna Wright, Deborah Logan, and Hannah Griffitts. Together they remembered Fairhill as an exclusively female retreat under Elizabeth Norris's tutelage. Though she never owned Fairhill, Norris cared for her aging parents; managed the house for her brother, Isaac, Jr., after their death; and mentored her young nieces when they inherited the property at his death.[51] Here she lived with nieces Hannah and Mary Griffitts, Mary and Sarah Norris, and cousin Mary Lloyd. Housing the Norris spinsters for several decades, Fairhill was a wonderful anomaly in the masculine country house tradition. A matriarchal estate, it authorized a distinctively female genealogy of memory.

In an undated poem, "To Eliza Norris at Fairhill," Susanna Wright re-

1.6. Pen-and-ink drawing of Fairhill, seat of Isaac Norris. Norris Family Scrapbook. Courtesy, The Winterthur Library: Joseph Downs Collection of Manuscripts and Printed Ephemera, no. 62x33. A watercolor drawing from a similar vantage point hangs in "Papa's Parlour" at Stenton.

constructs this feminized memory palace, crowning spinster Elizabeth Norris as queen.[52] Refusing "to yield Obedience,—or wear the Chain" of marriage, Norris was "set a Queen" over the plantation. More than having domestic dominion, Wright explains, Norris would reign "o'er her own thoughts, of her own heart Secure." Setting an example for the other women, she would "shake the ancient law" that trafficked women and their property rights through marriage. With their domestic situation secure, women could tend to the mental pleasures afforded by rural leisure: "Best found, when Leisure & Retirement reign / . . . Where Rural views,—soft gentle Joys impart, / Enlarge the thought, & Elevate the heart."[53]

Like Wright, Deborah Logan fondly brings the forsaken estate to life from her girlhood memories: "The entrance was into a hall, paved with black and white marble, two large parlors on each side, and an excellent staircase, well lighted. The courts and gardens were in the taste of those times, with gravel walks and parterres. Many lofty trees were preserved round the house, which added greatly to its beauty, and, at the time of my remembrance, the outbuildings were covered with festoons of ivy and scarlet bigonia."[54] Although wild vines have replaced the manicured walks,

Logan is transported by memory to "places that now are not." Wandering among "the Old Sites and buildings," she laments the changes made by its latest owner, John Dickinson, preferring the original landscape planned by her grandfather:

> The south aspect is exceedingly different from what it used formerly to be owing to its being now thickly planted with trees instead of open area of Grass-plot down to the Old Wall, which had a kind of Porch or arch with sides inside, opposite the South door, entirely covered without by Ivy as was the wall which still exists with its little buttresses, an out house, stood on the west of this plot with a brick wall joining it to the courtyard, the Gable of the house covered with a Creeper, as also the wall—there was another old building used as a wood house near the S.E. corner, which cousin Dickinson removed and built a milk house in its place. And a range of Kitchens and wash houses and out buildings on the north East.—It was a beautiful seat formerly. But I wonder now at the effect on my mind of the Ideal giving so much more space than I find it could have occupied.[55]

Existing only in memory, Fairhill's impressive architecture and gardens are amplified by Logan's nostalgia. Though she sees Fairhill again through childhood eyes, she is disappointed to find it reduced to Lilliputian proportions in adulthood.

Walking through the garden, Logan comes across the old library. Placed in what she describes as a low building, consisting of several rooms, the library was a "most delightful retreat for contemplative study": "The windows curtained with ivy; the sound of 'bees industrious murmur' from a glass hive which had communication from without, and where their wonderful instinct could be viewed. Beautiful specimens of fine arts and many curiosities were also collected there and the shelves were filled with the best authors, and materials for writing and drawing at hand."[56] Echoing the famous commonplace book of the Germantown resident and horticulturist Francis Daniel Pastorius, "The Beehive," Logan sees the library as a naturalistic memory place that "Extracts the Quint-essence" from nature's book.[57]

A cabinet of curiosities, Fairhill's library conserved specimens of natural history, fine art, and literature. Much like a commonplace book, the garden spot invited inhabitants to "imitate bees," keeping "in separate compartments whatever we have collected from our diverse reading, for things conserved separately keep better." Logan extended the textual analogy to the mind itself, which assigns and redirects us to particular mental places that store formerly collected knowledge. Collecting memories of Fairhill, Logan referenced Francis Bacon's work "Of Empire," where he submits that "the mind of man is more cheered and refreshed by profiting in small things."[58] In her poetic response to Bacon's mnemonic metaphors, she imagines the "Empire of the mind" as a microcosm for the country house, where "each prototype of Earth we find." Though women typically did not own their houses, "wisdom, knowledge, are thy own." "Rich in lore" and "the treasures science can bestow," a woman's mind was a well-stocked library. Logan concludes: "this Library / Is thine, and memory keeps the key."[59]

Creating new memories after the house's destruction, Hannah Griffitts composed a poem, "On the Burning of Fairhill by the British troops the 22nd of Novr 1777." Writing as "a branch of the much injur'd family," which is "Much affected with the circumstance," Griffitts offers her version of Fairhill's history. She recuperates the house and familial memories from the burned ruins, as she explains to Wright: "I sh'd be oblig'd to thee not to let these lines be seen, they were wrote just for our own family, and by one much affected with the circumstance—I thot they wd not be unpleasing to thee." Griffitts reconstructs the former house through memory, writing a private, emotional, and retrospective tribute to the once grand mansion and its inhabitants:[60]

> Beloved retreat forever now adieu
> Ne-er may thy ruins meet my trembling view,
> But oh—may future years and happier days
> from this sad work thy blooming structure raise
> And by the name thy pious founder bore
> Be thou possessd, nor feel a ruin more.

Though Griffitts resists looking at the scattered ruins and experiencing their melancholy associations, the poem materializes her feelings of loss. According to the eighteenth-century aesthetician Thomas Whately, architectural ruins help recover otherwise lost memories. A monument not only revives former times but also records "many more coeval circumstances, which we see, not perhaps as they were, but as they are come down to us, venerable with age and magnified by fame."[61] Tinged by nostalgia, Griffitts's memories idealize the former Norris estate.

The "once favord spot, of happiness the seat," Fairhill ameliorated the tensions of the Revolutionary War: it was a "Shelter of woe and Hardships soft retreat / Where mutual union did with virtue join." At Fairhill, "Heaven pronouncd each human blessing thine." Using the country house poem's standard comparison of the sanctified house and the worldly ravages beyond its gates, Griffitts imagined the house as more than a peaceful retreat. It was a testament to Quaker charity and hospitality, where "plenty crownd thy board." With an abundant dining-room sideboard (both an emblem of class privilege and taste and a commonplace topos for memory), Fairhill nourished its residents' bodies and minds. An intellectual sanctuary, "Here friend met friend and social converse joind / To cheer improve and Harmonize the mind." Here, too, "love sincere did easy freedom meet / Of Youth the Joy, of age the calm retreat." Though the British "one wide ruin oer its structure spread / Enwrapd in flames the Hospitable dome," the Norris women preserved the house in memory.

Thinking of Fairhill as home, Griffitts lived there intermittently from her parents' deaths in the late 1740s until her own death in 1817. Remembering when "the loss of my best earthly Blessing Drew the most Gloomy Prospects to my view," Griffitts gratefully acknowledges her "Dear Uncle & Aunt, [who] endeavor'd to alleviate this Bitter Stroke by many Tender Instances of Love & Care."[62] She returned to Fairhill again during the Seven Years' War, and when Elizabeth Norris died the following decade, in 1775, Griffitts acted as the executor and primary legatee of the will. Despite her sentimental recollections, Griffitts was intimately aware of the financial and social responsibilities of maintaining the beautiful country seat. Her later nostalgia for the ruined house, therefore, was not only influenced by but also shaped her knowledge of the house's physical details.

Designed to uphold the geometric standards of square design and to maximize movement and light within the house, Fairhill's H shape additionally formed "visual alphabets" for the memory. Like rooms in an artificial memory house, alphabetic characters provided lasting images for otherwise fleeting events and emotions erased by time. The H plan, then, may have signified what Griffitts called Fairhill's "*H*ospitable dome," crowned by a weather vane used by horticulturist Isaac Norris to predict meteorological conditions. It may have represented the gathering family's excitement in the "*H*all" at a coach's arrival, bringing guests for an evening's "*H*ospitality." It may have reminded the young women of a quiet evening reading aloud at a fireside "*H*earth." Or it may have preserved Fairhill as Griffitts remembered it: as that "Once favor'd spot of *H*appiness," "Shelter of woe and *H*ardships soft retreat" that "cheered improved and *H*armonized the mind." As the ordering framework at Fairhill, the Roman capital *H* preserved Norris family memories through a century of successive renovations and its eventual demise.[63]

Linking architecture to the original Roman alphabet, the builder Richard Neve writes in *The City and Country Purchaser*: "This way, like a Roman capital H, is much applauded by some; for say they this form maketh stand better, and firmer against the winds, and light, and air comes every way to it, and every room is near the one to the other."[64] The H shape, argues Neve, provides easy passage between spaces inside the house.

The Roman quadrata, or system of block print in capital letters, resembled images of the classical memory palace: individualized letters were formed and framed in perfect squares, much like figurative rooms. With its serif, or short cross-lines at the extremities, the Roman majuscule is a remnant of ancient monumental and epigraphic inscription on stone, wood, or metal. As Beattie maintained, with Roman letters one "will more clearly perceive what is written: and Memory will be assisted by the vivacity of the sensation it conveys to the eye, as well as by the distinct ideas it imparts to the understanding."[65] Fairhill's original H shape would be easily remembered long after the structure fell.

Just as Fairhill once materially embodied Norris family memories, so its architectural ruins, no longer extant, have been replaced and continued by women's documentary histories. Writing entirely from memory, Logan, Wright, and Griffitts together reconstructed Fairhill according to what they could feel but no longer see. A monument to former times, which future generations of Norrises would inherit, their manuscripts have restored Fairhill and its ruins. Especially colored by nostalgia, family memories tend to recede further from the event they narrate with each retelling. But like ruins that have "come down to us, venerable with age and magnified by Fame," as Whately suggests, they are the most intimate form of historic preservation.

STENTON

Two miles north of the Norris seat at Fairhill, Stenton was built in Germantown by James Logan from 1723 to 1730. Resembling Fairhill in its symmetrical, double-pile arrangement, Stenton also follows a classical central-passage plan. An adaptation of the English Georgian, Stenton boasts a symmetrically arranged southwest brick facade laid in Flemish bond, which is ornamented with four large, rudimentary pilasters, a water table of molded brick, and brick belt course. Above the cornice of simple rectangular modillions rises a steep hipped roof with three dormer windows, crowned by a pair of chimneys. The roof once had a balustraded gallery, cupola, and copper weather vane (see figure 1.7). The ground floor is centered on a double door with a transom and sidelights, and the second story is marked by six evenly spaced windows. The front of the house, Logan remembers, was "shaded by evergreens as with a verdant lattice, and the sun beams fall thro' on the windows with every varying form of beauty." Unlike the well-appointed, vine-covered front entrance that would greet and impress visitors, the sides of Stenton depart from the Georgian symmetry. Laid in the ordinary English bond, the southeast facade follows the front

1.7. Fully furnished and beautifully landscaped, Stenton is one of the properties preserved by The National Society of The Colonial Dames of America in the Commonwealth of Pennsylvania. Photograph by author.

arrangement in its central side door and transom with corresponding dormer windows on either side of the chimney. The northwest and northeast walls, on the other hand, relinquish the regularity of the house's exterior to provide for interior harmony and convenience.[66]

Deborah Logan lived more than half her life at Stenton—from her marriage to George Logan in 1779 to her death in 1839—not only making it her home but also appreciating it as a historic house worthy of preservation. Although she lived well into the nineteenth century, Logan thought of herself and her house as emblems of a former age. "My Old Establishment," she writes, "so unlike modern things, the furniture, the China, the [silver] plate, the Library, all were objects of curiosity." Walking from room to room, she noticed that "everywhere momentos meet my eye. My house and my heart are full of them." Replicating the predominantly symmetrical order of Stenton's plan, Logan diligently kept a commonplace book (1808) and diaries (1808 to 1839). Each entry, like a room in the house, harbored a different association. Meticulously arranged and dated, these manuscripts provide a topophilic map of Stenton's interior. Wishing her female ancestors had "written Diaries and left them as Heirlooms," Logan corrected their oversight, ensuring the ancestral home's literal and figurative preservation.[67] "I always leave [Stenton] with regret," she writes, "as it has been the scene of much of my happiness and endeared by many associations, and my residence now for above 40 years. Above all it contains the Remains of my honoured and beloved Husband, and was the birth place of two of my children and the Seat of their ancestors."[68]

Walking in the front door of Stenton, one enters the beautiful reception hall with its notable brick floor, gold-colored woodwork, and a fireplace set off to the right. For decades, Logan's guests were welcomed with vibrant, seasonal displays from her garden. Like a medieval florilegium, which gathered and arranged topoi into rhetorical bouquets, Logan's flowers were sentimental and mnemonic prompts. "Double Balsams, nasturtions, and Queen Margarets" for "Flora's Altar" decked the corner table in autumn. These flowers, along with the chestnuts she gathered, never failed "to bring my beloved Gustavus back to my mind, indeed his Image is associated with such a multitude of things." Springtime flowers, in contrast, inspired memories of her own childhood: whereas "the tender blossoms of the Sassafrass remind me of my dear Isaac, and of our walks in the Spring to gather them for tea," the "Cowslips, Hyacinths, violets, and blossoms" recall other youthful companions.[69]

Logan also filled the entrance halls with more mundane objects. During annual housecleaning, for example, the "disjointed contents [of the parlors] were crammed into the Hall where with smoky pictures, china, glass, towles, Buckets, Brushes, and whitewash, none but the most determined could force their way." The detritus of collected objects and dust alike undoubtedly brought back memories. Ordering the chaos, Logan "brought a low chair into the Hall with [her] work basket and was seated." Reflecting on former times, she "walked up and down [her] empty Hall, after having sat in [her] lonely chair at the door watching the declining sun gilding with his parting beams the glowing West 'till gave place to night."[70] A liminal space between indoors and out, Stenton's hall represents the present's convergence with the past.

Externalizing the brain's mazy course of memory passages, the hall branches off into subsequent loci, which store as well as encourage reminiscence. Framed by both full and broken Doric columns, the hall's three Palladian-arched doorways open into the "best parlour" on the left, what Logan fondly called "Papa's Parlour" on the right, and the stair hall to the back. Wandering into the best parlour, one immediately sees a fully paneled room with chair rails along its sides and recessed window seats beneath the interior shutters. The impressive fireplace across the room with its Valley Forge marble surround formerly framed the portrait that hung above it: "How often I contemplate the Portrait of my beloved Husband, which hangs in the Parlour, and which is a striking likeness to him, do I apply those lines of Cowpers, 'Life has past / But poorly with me since I saw thee last.'" The adjacent closet, topped with an ornately carved sunburst shell, displayed the most valuable china and silver for the guests' admiring eyes. But behind it Logan had discovered hidden literary treasures for her private perusal: "in a vacant place between the back of the best parlour closet and the closet in my room, stuffed with Newspapers a Century old and a Book partly eaten by the mice, without the title Page, but which appears to be a very old translation of Marcellinus." Like the memory images hidden within the posterior walls of the cerebellum, the interconnecting closet held similarly mnemonic treasures. A nostalgic tribute to another age, the old papers reinforced her appreciation of manuscripts as heirlooms: "when we remembered many that are gone, it seemed like a revival."[71]

Across the hall is Papa's Parlour, once used as George Logan's office and later as a workspace for Deborah and her domestics. Less formal than the best parlor, it has only one fully paneled wall over the fireplace mantel and a paneled dado around the rest of the room. Still filled with a gentleman farmer's paraphernalia (a compass, a barometer, and an early-eighteenth-century map of Philadelphia County marking both Norris's "Fairhill" and Logan's "Stenton"), the parlor brings back memories of their marriage, which wed the two prominent Quaker families. As a widow, Deborah Logan would look sadly at George's vacant chair and her own solitary teacup and saucer, reminiscing that in "happier days, when we had our tea, my beloved husband used often to take his Flute, or set down to the Piano, and this was the time for me to recollect, sometimes audibly, some of the 'immortal verse' with which my memory hath been stored." Overwhelmed by painful memories, Logan would invite the young women of the household to join her, comparing herself "with the Dames of Antiquity, surrounded by their maidens, and some of them . . . would equal the lovely nymphs and roseate bloom and auburn tresses. They set with me when I am alone and work round my Table."[72]

Through the double doors beyond Papa's Parlour stands the grand stairway in the back passage. The stair winds evenly around, like its carefully turned balusters, carrying the paneled dado from the stair hall to the attic. At the stair's foot are the "Blue Lodging Room" on the left and the dining room on the right. The dining room opens to the piazza, overlooking the garden and leading to a detached kitchen. Comprising two large rooms with fireplaces and a common chimney, the kitchen included a cooking area and a greenhouse. Commenting on the unusual light provided by the collapsed piazza, Logan mentions that it "would both be more pleasant in winter without the Piazza, but the irregularity without doors would be too perceptible and the heat in summer too intollerable—besides the inconvenience of having no covered way between the house and kitchen but I like this light and cheerful aspect much."[73] Providing access to the kitchen in the house's back, the piazza, like the hallway, replicates the memory's movement from the nervous system's labyrinthine course to the posterior recesses of the brain.

In the left corner of the stair hall is the blue lodging room, which became Deborah Logan's bedchamber sometime after her husband's death. The fireplace is flanked by built-in press closets (for storing clothing, manuscripts, and books) as well as a door leading to the best parlor. Sitting in the parlor "with the Doors opened thro the Hall and the moonlight sweetly entered thru the vine covered window," Logan "fell into a reverie of the Past. It was the room where in the wise and virtuous James Logan and his excellent wife had lived & where he died. Here also my tender beloved and regretted Algernon drew his last breath." Here, too, she would invite Algernon's friends after his death on 19 December 1835 to view his posthumous portrait: "Took my beloved son's likeness as he lay a beautiful Corpse . . . drawn from the face as first seen in death." The room harbored happy memories, too: "My beloved Gustavus was fond of being here, and has been the frequent companion of my mind in this visit. the Desk made for him is in my Chamber, with his name wrote, as Boy's are won't—the Books the Children used at School, and many mementos."[74] After his untimely death at age fourteen on 20 August 1800 Gustavus's carved scribblings permanently inscribed him in his mother's memory. Each time her fingers traced his pen's indentations, she repeated his infantile movements and recalled his small hands, which she once held gently in her own. Spanning three generations from childhood to death, the blue lodging room was particularly precious to Logan.

Across the hall from the blue lodging room is the dining room, or what she called her "winter writing establishment." Guests would notice just beside the door a framed watercolor painted by her son Algernon. The largest room on the first floor, the dining room also has chair rails and window seats but is distinguished by its elaborate mantel shelf and fully paneled fireplace wall. Logan spent her early winter mornings writing in the dining room, as chapter 2 more fully illustrates: "I am now seated in the dining room," she writes, "and no noise but the ticking of the Clock, the wav'ring of the fire and the scratching of my bad Pen on the paper. I am as contented and easy as is necessary."[75] Keeping her small maple desk in the corner, she created a secluded place for study and contemplation.

More than a writing space, the dining room signified ritualized hospitality. With its elaborate sideboard, mahogany breakfast and dining tables, and twelve mahogany open-back chairs, it warmly welcomed company: "We had our dinner and before the cloth, etc. was quite removed, in were ushered two old Ladies. . . . they were seated on the Sofa and I before them on a low chair, the stove was warm, and I was mindful of the household rites, had a Glass of wine and some preserved Ginger brought to them, and then the chat began." The dining room, therefore, preserved several generations of family cordiality. Breaking an old punch bowl, Logan laments: "It had long survived all its first patrons and friends, and almost, these of the beverage it had been designed to contain and the house and closet in which it used to be kept in its second stage of existence, and has led a life of retirement with a cracked and mended constitution, with me, for many years." A remnant of the eighteenth century, the retired punch bowl, with its cracks and repairs, could no longer contain its traditional drink, as Logan's footnote suggests: "Punch, more oftener called for in the Olden time than now; We used in warm weather to have a large bowl made at noon every day." But saving "a fragment with an enameld Camelia upon it, which will tell of . . . the old house, and their accompanying ideas," she is reminded of the "old-fashioned" decorum now regrettably forgotten. Like an architectural ruin, the fragmented porcelain remembered the "Olden times."[76]

Leaving the dining room and ascending the stairs to the second floor, one finds the "white lodging room" on the immediate right, two small nursery rooms off to the far left, and a pair of large adjoining bedchambers divided by folding doors straight ahead. Logan describes the panoramic view from the hall: "One of the north windows is opposite to a very fine Holly tree which has an appearance of opening into a Greenhouse. The South window is curtained with Glycene, Jasmine, and wild Ivy, and often decorated with Pots of Myrtle and Geraniums and Roses." Another window held a small aeolian harp, whose "sweet breathings of Zephyrus over the strings" sounded like " 'a Stream of Rich distilled perfume,' as Milton has it." Beyond the large double doors sprawls the "yellow lodging room," the largest and most opulently decorated room in the house.[77] To the right of the entrance is the grand fireplace wall, fully paneled and finished with a blue and white Dutch tile surround, another "curiosity" to her early federal visitors. Here Logan entertained her intimate friends as they sat around her tea table. Here, too, she watched her niece Debby Logan "lay and beguile the hours of pain and languor with heavenly Patience" before death, "in the hopes of immortality."[78]

The adjoining room—with its characteristic blue-checked bed hangings, mahogany high chest, dressing table, and mahogany stools made by

Philadelphia cabinetmaker John Elliott—was Logan's "summer apartment." Once the site of James Logan's famous library (as the carved niches in the bedroom's left-corner chair rail suggest), this room served as the seasonal bedchamber during her marriage and early widowhood. Later it became her library: "I spent this day very much as I like, alone, and chiefly in the library; according to my ideas, the Recluse, if he has a mind and is able to embody his thoughts, to reflect, compare and command Ideas; has much more the means of entertainment within his grasp, than those who are accustomed to seek it in the variety of objects in the world." With its four windows "festooned by the twisted drapery of Jasmines, Glycenes, and sweet briar," the library offered a cool, bright place for reading and contemplation. Picking up a book, Logan would settle into "the easy and low seat of an Old Sopha, brought by my grandmother from England, when she returned from her visit there in 1708." Finally, when the library's bookshelves were full to bursting, Logan filled the press closet, "that old mine of pamphlets," with literature: "There are but few modern Compositions but what have their Prototype: I found to day, in the Press Closet in the Library, an Old Latin Poem." Like the downstairs closet that materializes her mind's memory places, the library closet—filled with original and transcribed manuscripts—signifies the collection of " 'immortal verse' with which [her] memory hath been stored."[79]

Following Logan as she "passed from room to room in the glimmering twilight, [and] thought of their former inhabitants who have long since passed away," one is struck with the relative invisibility of female history. She enumerates the countless hours spent in "the turmoil of whitewashing, scrubbing the paint and floors, with dirt and litter like a retreating army, driven from one position to another." Marking the passage of time through the seemingly endless domestic monotony, she remarks: "It was an odd coincidence that I should be employed in the same work that I was on this day 50 years ago—Clearstarching." Despite the successive generations of Logan women who maintained Stenton, little evidence of their presence remains. "I wish," writes Logan, "the former inhabitants had left more momentos of themselves I mean my Lady Predecessors in the family. Amiable and pleasing while they lived their short existence has passed and like the track of an arrow thro the air has left no path behind it."[80]

In one bedchamber, however, she finds the handwritten marks of "the lovely daughters of the venerated James Logan, on a Pane of Glass," who "inscribed their names with that of their friend Sarah Norris." Though it is not clear from Logan's diary what the young women scratched into the pane, their cousin Charles Read apparently wrote on an adjoining window: "O Woman! lovely Woman! Nature made you / To temper man. We

had been Brutes without you!" Reiterating the ornamental and complementary roles of women to improve and adorn a man's life, Read unknowingly explains their visible absence among the house's relics. As
Logan sadly concludes, the glass, "fragile as it is, has outlasted their fragile
existences."[81]

As her literary tour through Stenton illustrates, Logan remedied the
flaws of her house's gendered history, leaving her indelible marks in each
room she described. Her commonplace book and diaries—the very heirlooms her female ancestors denied her—were the "means to preserve fresh
in [her] memory passing events. . . . the habit of noting down as they
occur, the incidents of the times . . . [or anything] that shall appear worthy
of preservation."[82] As the anonymous author of Logan's obituary later
wrote in *The Friend*: "She was herself a relic of the past! and the young
hung with delighted attention, on her glowing and beautiful recitals of a
by-gone age."[83]

GRAEME PARK

Returning from England in August 1766, Elizabeth Graeme composed a
nostalgic poem about her homecoming, "Some Lines upon my first being
at Graeme Park; after my return from England." Dedicated to "Memory,"
the poem begins with an invocation to Mnemosyne to awaken Graeme's
dormant memory as she walks through her family's mansion:

> Come Memory come; and with Time's Pencil show
> Each former Pleasure; and each poignant Woe;
> Those past Ideas place in strong review.

Scanning each room for its familiar associations, Graeme constructs a memory palace that endures in her mind long after she leaves the estate thirty
years later (see figure 1.8). Having been abroad for more than a year, and
having returned to mourn her mother's death, she longed for the distinct
comforts of home. "Bright Memory range them in my Mental Eye," she
writes, "And Recollection never let them die." Struck by life's temporality,
Graeme characterizes memory as immortal: it outlasts as it preserves human
life.[84]

Memory's permanence, she realized, depends on its written transmis-
sion. Copying the poem into her first commonplace book, "Poemata Juvenilia," Graeme ranks memory among the "imitative Arts": "Produce each
Page, your ample Book unfold, / Form'd in the Frame of lively *Fancys*
Mold." As part of the *ars memorativa* tradition, the commonplace book em-

1.8. Etching, Elizabeth Graeme Fergusson. Courtesy of the Historical Society of Pennsylvania (Gratz C14B16).

ployed the same architectural principles as the classical memory palace. Using Vitruvius's *Ten Books of Architecture* as her model, she writes:

> When loft *Domes,* and *Pallaces* I saw
> (Vitruvius Pencil did their Limits draw)!
> Gave the proportions to the Massive Stone
> And Made the Charms of *Architect* his own.

The poem moves quickly from Vitruvius to the British Palladians, presenting England's "Earl of Burlington" as the "Modern Vitruvius" and imagining Graeme Park's Palladian translation into a characteristic Delaware Valley country house. Personalizing her memory palace, Graeme could finally "call Memory home / Nor let the Nymph far from my Bosom roam."

Seventeen miles north of Philadelphia in Horsham, Montgomery County, Pennsylvania, Graeme Park sits idyllically behind two large sycamore trees and a stream called Park Creek. It was built by Sir William Keith, provincial governor of Pennsylvania, between 1726 and 1728 and

1.9. Set in the idyllic countryside of Horsham in Montgomery County, Pennsylvania, Graeme Park is one of the finest examples of Georgian interior design of the mid–eighteenth century. Photograph by author.

renovated into a polite retreat with allees, gardens, and a deer park by Thomas Graeme between 1737 and 1772 (see figure 1.9). Made of finished fieldstone, the mansion's front, or north, facade welcomes visitors through its formal garden enclosed by a stone wall. Here Elizabeth (Graeme) Fergusson sat "at the Door of Graeme Park, strolling on the Terrass or watching the Moon that friend to Contemplation," remembering "how happy we have been there."[85] Here, too, she awaited the arrival of the post, bringing letters that had traveled "O'er western Seas and raise[d] the starting Tear."[86] No longer extant, a detached kitchen, servants' quarters, converted malthouse, and milkhouse were sheltered by the back and side walls, made of unfinished rubble. Despite its Georgian adaptations, the house's exterior is notably asymmetrical. Though four twelve-light dormer windows and two chimneys balance the attic beneath the hip roof, six unevenly spaced, eighteen-light windows characterize the second floor, and five windows and an off-centered door make up the first. Boarded up to simulate the other windows, moreover, the far east window on the north side (once serving as a second door into the best parlor) and another window on the west side of the second story give the building an even more unbalanced appearance.[87]

The asymmetry also characterized the mansion's original three-cell plan with its three very dissimilar rooms in a line: a parlor (with a cellar below), a hall with a main stair, and a kitchen with a service stair to the garret.[88] By 1772 Elizabeth Graeme Fergusson witnessed her father's alterations to the house and experienced the rearrangement of interior space. The original hall was separated from the stair passage, and the parlor's exterior door was closed and covered by symmetrical paneling. Four unequally sized rooms resulted: a large parlor, a small stair hall ("entry"), a center room ("office"), and "the dining room." The center room was not only the smallest but perhaps the busiest space, with its one window and three doors leading to the front entry hall, the west parlor, and the south-side exterior. Formerly the kitchen, the back or west room served as the Graeme family's dining room. It is lined by a chair rail on three walls and has two interior doors and one exterior door on either side of the fully paneled chimney wall with its off-center fireplace (which still retains the original cooking hearth) and left-side closet. Above these rooms were three impressive bedchambers and a stair hall on the second floor, and two heated bedchambers and two small storage rooms beyond the garret stair hall.

The asymmetrical design and gradual renovations underscore Elizabeth Fergusson's disjointed experience of her house. Living at Graeme Park for fifty-six years, she became progressively estranged from the ancestral estate. Inheriting the property at her father's death, she spent most of her life fighting to retain it: coverture laws, Tory affiliations, and poverty eventually removed her from her beloved home. From inhabitant to owner to inhabitant again, Fergusson constantly negotiated her place in and relationship to Graeme Park. "In-habitation" suggests a woman's physical and emotional familiarity with the places in which she is located as well as the way she remembers those places. Fergusson's recollections undoubtedly reflect these disruptions. As a result, most of the primary documents that remain about Graeme Park record legal and proprietary actions rather than Fergusson's emotional responses to her progressively inaccessible home. "And if the painful Picture back you bring," she writes, "Thy *Memory* fly! And let *Oblivion* take! / With dull *Obscurity* (her gloomy Mate)."[89] What follows, then, is my attempt to return the poet to the intimate spaces of her forlorn mansion.

The house remains famous for the east parlor's impressive wooden panels extending from ceiling to floor and the deep cornice molding that surrounds the room. With a broken pediment over the fireplace and projecting mantel echoing the full pediments over the doors on either side, the chimney wall has an imposed symmetry. Only one of the doors is a legitimate entry; the other hides a plaster wall, visually balancing the room's geometry. The paneled walls were further decorated with a collection of family portraits as well as two old maps, twelve avian pictures, and three looking glasses with twelve small medal plaster-of-Paris heads of famous poets. Setting the stage for the famous Graeme Park literary salon, the poets' busts overlooked the beautiful parlor furniture: a dining room table and six cushioned Windsor chairs in the center; a smaller dining table, round breakfast table, and two card tables along the chair rail, which were set up for food and games; a marble slab sideboard set with a glass bowl, two decanters, two tumblers, and eleven wine glasses; and a small mahogany tea table furnished with a set of enameled tea china.

Mapping her memory from childhood to adulthood, Fergusson noted two parlor furnishings that were particularly precious: an eight-day clock and a harpsichord. Made by the London clockmaker William Tomlinson in 1722, the clock was "the announcer of *fleeting* Time," whose hourly knell "ha[d] producd in [her] Spirits almost Commensurate with any [clearer] Recollection of past Time." Determined to preserve the old family clock that has outlived all but herself, Fergusson writes a prose essay, "An Old Woman's Meditations On an old Family Piece of Furniture."[90] She appraises her own sixty years against the clock's appreciating age as it "measurd Time Seventy five years! You move tho your maker is no more." Fergusson affectionately personifies the clock as holding a "Station between things Animal and Inanimate" and promises, "Never whilst I posess a Dollar will I consign thee to the Garett [or] the Cellar as an old remembrance, nor will I resign thee into the Hands of an unfeeling Bawling *Auctoneer* to hawk your werth on a Depreciatd Scale." A topophilic measure of time, the clock revived happy memories of the past and confounded the alienation that marked her later life.

The youngest child and sole survivor of her family in 1797, Fergusson nostalgically welcomed the clock's familiar sounds. More than evoking tender, domestic memories, the clock marked the beginning of her literary aspirations:

Ah what various Sensations the Sound of that *Clocks Hammer* has raised in the Bosoms of my Parents, Brothers, Sisters, and my own in a course of years three fourths of a Century since it first movd in our House! . . . I See in Idea this moment the little Round Walnut Table placd close by a clean Hearth, and clear Hickroy fire; My Mother and Sisters in Rotations reading some moral Pathetic interesting story, or dramatic Piece, while my good Father sat on the other side with his own small Mahogony stand reading the Paper of the Day or some treatise writ peculiarly in his own Medical-Profession.

When the clock struck eight, Fergusson remembers, she was sent to bed, often in the middle of her favorite stories. She recalls listening to her mother's dramatic recitation of Nicholas Rowe's play, *The Fair Penitent*, "*Calista* contemplating on the Love and mingled Remorse the remains of the once Galant Gay *Lothario.*" She revisits the voyeuristic pleasure of opening Samuel Richardson's epistolary novel *Clarissa* or the "unfinishd journal wise letter of the artless *Pamela.*" And she recollects the mixed pleasures of Elizabeth Rowe's pious *Hymns* and Lawrence Sterne's *Sentimental Journey*, "where Humer and Sentiment are so happily Blended and Contrasted." But at the stroke of eight she was forced to prolong the story's ending until the following night, for "shut was the Book and shut the Scene unless caried on in youthful Dreams."

Whereas the clock's knell recalled familial memories, the tinkling notes of the harpsichord recorded the parlor's transformation into a heterosocial literary salon, which filled the room with music, improvisational performances, and witty repartee. Brought back from England in 1766 by Francis Hopkinson at Fergusson's request, the harpsichord would have been played by Hopkinson, Jacob Duche, or Fergusson herself, perhaps putting her lyric poetry—such as "Content in a Cottage" and "A Song"—to the old Scottish melodies of "The Lass of Peatty's Mill" and "Tweed Side." Among her habitués were Provost William Smith's "Schuylkill Swains" from the College of Philadelphia: Francis Hopkinson, Jacob Duche, Nathaniel Evans, and Thomas Godfrey. Also participating were John and Mary (Hopkinson) Morgan, Reverend William and Rebecca (Moore) Smith, Elizabeth (Hopkinson) Duche, John Dickinson, Ann (Borden) Hopkinson, the musician James Bremmer, the physician Benjamin Rush, and the poet Annis Stockton. As the host of these "attic" evenings, as Rush called them, Fergusson set the aesthetic standards: "The genius of Miss Graeme," writes Rush, "evolved the heat and light that animated" the salon gatherings: "Once while she instructed by the stores of knowledge contained in the historians, philosophers, and poets of ancient and modern nations, which she called forth at her pleasure; and again she charmed by a profusion of original ideas, collected by her vivid and widely expanded imagination, and combined with exquisite taste and judgment into an endless variety of elegant and delightful forms." Rush presents her mind as a commonplace book that accumulated and stored information from her four-hundred-volume library. Her guests accordingly came into her elegant east parlor to "court the thought-inspiring Muse." As her nephew John Young romanticizes about her famous salon: "Graeme Park may vie with Arcadia; for poetry may easily convert Neshaminy into Helicon, the meadows into Tempe, and the park into Parnassus."[91] The parlor, therefore, exemplifies the country house aesthetic of leisure, intellectual pleasure, and recollection.

As the parlor became a more public space in the late 1760s, the Graeme family receded into the back dining room and upstairs chambers.[92] With two windows draped in blue worsted curtains and interior shutters on each side wall, the best chamber above replicates the parlor's grandeur below in its floor-to-ceiling paneling and arched doorways flanking the chimney wall. Originally her parents' bedchamber, the east room saw the deaths of both Thomas and Ann Graeme as well as two of their daughters. Fergusson thus likens it to a tomb, "within whose walls bounded melancholy Room / Are laid the ashes and the dear remains" of her "sweet associates on these earthly plains."[93] Reminded of death's ravages by a five-by-six-inch cherubic image of a "Death's Head" on the chamber wall, Fergusson periodically revisits her grief. Though she attended her sister's death, as "these hands clos'd the dear Myrtila's Eyes; / These Ears were pierced with her departing Crys," Graeme regrets being in England when her mother died:

> Could I have thought her Dissolution nigh
> With trembling Hand I would have closd her Eye
> And snatcht the mournful last departing Sigh.

Never experiencing "the rapture of a Fond Embrace" or "viewing her Maternal Face," Fergusson envisions her mother on the downy bedstead, "wrapt among the dead!"[94]

Filled with sad memories, the best chamber soon became Elizabeth's room, which she shared with her husband, Hugh Henry Fergusson, for a brief two and one-half years before he fled permanently to England in 1775. Considering herself a unique kind of widow, Elizabeth Fergusson modified the room once again, fitting it with "one bed, one bedstead, without Curtains, four Blankets, two pairs of sheets one Quilt & Counterpain, a bolster & two pillows with cases for the Servant Maid." In addition to holding the requisite dressing furniture (including a small cabinet, an old trunk, two small pine tables with the "old dressing Glass," and a washstand), the best chamber was a place for contemplation and writing (with its two desks, a fringe loom and stand, and her mother's needlework pieces). Her husband's absence and their childless marriage, along with painful rumors of his infidelity, undoubtedly haunted the bedchamber, however:

> No tender Husband soothd her Cares
> None her Domestic trouble shares
> No lisping children prattled near
> To Charm a partial mother ear.[95]

The canopied and curtained bed, along with the necessary warming pan beneath the cotton-ticked down covering, gave Fergusson privacy and comfort in her loneliness.

The other bedchambers are similarly furnished, but the west room is distinguished by the addition of what one inventory describes as a "covert table," which may actually be a secret "writing closet" built into the room. With a transom inviting light from the adjacent window, the room's closet has an interior wall of shelves, the bottom one making a convenient writing space.[96] Such a closet beautifully represents the discretely private places in a woman's memory. Perhaps this was also a bedroom for Anna Young when she lived under her aunt's tutelage from the time of the death of her mother, Jane Graeme Young, in 1759 until the age of sixteen in 1772, when her father took her back to Philadelphia. "Since Providence has placed it in my Lot I shall try to Educate Anny . . . as Well as I can," writes Fergusson. "Her length of time at Graeme Park in the Summer is a very great Draw Back on her writing, and Sewing. Her reading a Proper Choice of Books with Explanations on them is my Branch, and I keep her close to it."[97] Responsible for her niece's education, Fergusson taught Anna to write and circulated her manuscript poetry throughout their coterie.

In her commonplace book kept for the five Willing sisters, for instance, Fergusson copied Young's poem "An Epistle from Damon to Sylvia With a Present of a Small Writing Desk with a Mirror and Letter-Case in it which when a Child She had given her on learning to write." Composed in 1777 for Young's fiancé, William Smith, the poem reconstructs the small writing desk at which she sat in her upstairs chamber at Graeme Park. Though the desk is no longer extant, Young's description animates it for the modern reader. Sitting at the escritoire as she composes the verse, Young runs her hands over the desk's hinged tablet, or writing surface, containing "Marks which it has gained by serving" her. She repeatedly mentions a "a Mirror too it ownd which is no more." Looking at the empty wooden cavity that once held a mirror, Young remarks on the glass's temporality: "Lest thy Image as its Form Removd," she writes, the "Spotless Paper shall its loss Supply," gaining a modicum of immortality through the written word. And opening the letter case, or secret compartment, that held her correspondence, she would remember how writing letters—a "commerce of the heart"—was dictated by "Duty, Friendship, Liberty, and Love." The desk, therefore, materializes Young's childhood memories of penmanship instruction. She recalls learning to write round hand and later Italian script with "Infant Strokes" that expressed "each Effusion of [heart]." She laments her mother's untimely death, retreating for solace to her desk "when a Parents abscence [she] deplord; / [Her] Childish Mind its early sorrows pour." She thanks her aunt, Elizabeth Fergusson, who "rear'd [her] infant years." A sentimental relic from her past, the desk will likewise please her fiancé, Young hopes.

Unlike the formalized room arrangements on the floors below, the attic chambers served as a general storehouse for furniture, decorative objects, and family memories. The garret symbolized the intimate memory places in Fergusson's mind. What critic Jonathan Swift satirically dubbed the disorganized and trifling "furniture of a woman's mind" served as a fitting domestic metaphor for female memory.[98] Fergusson's material possessions, like moveable *topoi*, were personally accumulated, arranged, and reused at different moments of her life. Just as "a housewife goes to her garret, only at certain times," according to essayist Beattie, so Fergusson familiarly visited her own attic, for there were few "corners of it which she is unacquainted with, or neglects to look into."[99] The east room stored bedchamber furniture (four beds, two tables, a trunk, a fire screen, a chest of drawers) and an array of chairs (three Windsor chairs, six leather-bottomed chairs, three or four rush-bottom chairs, and an easy chair), and the northwest room housed an even greater variety of objects. It held furniture (four Windsor chairs; tables for dining, tea, and cards; and a trunk full of valuable linens); work materials (a table of flowered work, bags of feathers, fifty-one candle molds, and a weaving loom); a library (bookholder, bookstand, and bookshelves; and more than four hundred volumes, including essays from the *Tatler, Spectator, Guardian,* and *Rambler*; David Hume's two-volume *History of the Stuarts*; six volumes of Spenser; three volumes of Shakespeare; and four volumes each of poet Edward Young and philosopher Adam Smith); decorative arts (several looking glasses with carved, walnut, and gilt frames; pictures; maps; the eight-day clock, and the harpsichord); and kitchenware (copper oven, kettles, and coffeepot; brass skillet and iron tea kettle; "Queensware, delf plates, and knife box"; and several sets of andirons, small scales, and weights).[100]

A collection of practical and sentimental objects, the attic assemblage also records the harsh material realities of Fergusson's life. As she explains in her 1769 poem, "The Easy Chair," a poet's "Bliss [is] high describd, but often lost, / In Life's real troden Dale."[101] Inspired by memory and fancy, poetry could offer only a temporary, fanciful reprieve from daily misery. After her father's death in 1772, Fergusson's property, and its embodied memories, were continuously threatened by the laws of coverture, the demands of poverty, and the domestic theater of the American Revolution. Though cherished as mnemonic objects, her "moveables" now literally defined her tenuous socioeconomic status. Whereas "real property" (or real estate) continued the male prerogatives of primogeniture, moveables encompassed all the furniture, textiles, silver, and other valuables carried by a woman from a father's to a husband's home as part of her dowry.[102] The colonial marriage market trafficked women as moveable commodities, upholding Pennsylvania coverture laws that prohibited a wife from buying, selling, or managing property (even inherited property) without her husband's permission.

Inheriting the Graeme Park property fee simple (an estate in land of which the inheritor has unqualified ownership and power or disposition) as well as more than fourteen hundred pounds of debt at her father's death, Fergusson struggled to make ends meet for the next two decades. Unprepared to manage a farm at her former summer retreat, Fergusson was ambivalent at best about her inheritance: "I love the Country: and Retirement but it is a Philosophical Repose Not the Bustle of an Extensive Farm which Suites my taste."[103] With her father's debts looming and her own slowly mounting since her Tory husband's surreptitious flight to England, Fergusson worried about the security of her home. The Pennsylvania Supreme Executive Council was confiscating the property of traitors to the patriot cause. Fergusson formally petitioned the council several times throughout the 1770s, successfully maintaining ownership of Graeme Park but relinquishing many of her moveables: "What Moveable Estate which was but Small was Seized and Sold, tho' it consisted of things that were all purchased by my Father, before I saw Mr. Fergusson."[104] She was able to buy back some of the confiscated items at a government estate sale on 15 October 1778, however, including four rush-bottom chairs, an easy chair, four bedsteads, a chest of drawers, four flour casks, a candlestick, a pair of kitchen scales and weights, and four pigs.[105] The conspicuous absence of luxury or sentimental items among the redeemed property suggests her purchases were based on practicality and a limited budget rather than nostalgia.

By the 1780s Fergusson was more than three thousand pounds in debt and in danger of foreclosure. In addition to the confiscation of "Tory" property, she endured several military encampments at Graeme Park. At one time approximately two thousand patriot soldiers bivouacked in her yard. Meanwhile, the best parlor was converted into a guard room (the furniture being moved to the northwest garret room). With the disruption of her private life within the house and the cumulative destruction of the landscape (by tents and log huts, the slaughtering of virtually all her livestock for food, and the accidental explosion of six or seven thousand cartridges), Fergusson watched her property fall into ruins. She subsequently made several attempts to sell the estate, advertising in local newspapers in 1773, 1776, and 1782. Unlike the preceding sketch of Graeme Park drawn from documentary evidence in Fergusson's private correspondence and commonplace books, the advertisements offer little more than a topographical description of the property. Fond memories gave way to bitter realism. Receiving several bids for Graeme Park in January 1791, she writes to Rebecca Smith: "I am looking now like the Bewildered Dove for place of Rest but where my tent will be fixd is as little known to me as to your self."[106] Substituting the temporal metaphor of a tent for her ancestral dwelling, Fergusson exemplifies her forced dissociation from her home.

On 30 April 1791 Fergusson sold Graeme Park to the widower of her niece Anna Young, William Smith. Though she retained property rights through her various petitions and struggled to maintain the estate on her own, she nonetheless considered her absent husband in this final transaction, writing to Smith: "Should Mr. Fergusson and I ever live together or Should he ever See these Letters, let him See if he chuses to read them, that I did not rashly sell my Farm . . . tho Mr. Fergusson has no legal Right to Graeme Park yet I would Submit my Conduct to Him in an afair of this Importance as much as tho he had never forfeited these Rights. . . . had Land got lower I must [have] gone on this Parish for Support."[107] Understanding Fergusson's predicament and still enjoying life in the city, Smith does not rush Fergusson out of her home: "Dr. Smith and his Wife both used every argument to engage me to Spend the remainder of my Days There," writes Fergusson. "And as to remaining at G Park after it became the property of another I thought I Seemd as a kind of Interloper or hanger-on that made me far from easy. nor have I the least Idea of returning there But only for a Day or so in the Summer Season." An interloper in her own home, Fergusson became increasingly estranged from her once familiar and intimately mnemonic places. Although the deed was signed in 1791, Fergusson remained at Graeme Park until December 1793, when Philadelphia's raging yellow fever epidemic forced Smith to move his family to the country.

At one o'clock in the morning on 24 December before leaving Graeme Park forever, Fergusson writes to her long-time friend and correspondent, Annis Stockton: "A few lines, and but a few for the last time, from this Spot can I write my dear Mrs Stocken; I leave it as my home in a few hours; and Sleep seems at present to have lost its power over my faculties. I therefore wish to devote the last night to one or two dear Freinds. . . . with a peculiar Force my mind is intended and by the present Scene it seems as tho' the Images of all those . . . that have made their abode at this place for half a Century glided in procession before my Eyes. . . . adieu as to Graeme Park."[108] Looking around one last time, Fergusson commits the house to memory.

The following day she moved just four miles from Graeme Park to a small village called Crooket Billet. Here she lived with the Todd family until sometime in 1797 or early 1798. Her first day at the Todd residence, Fergusson continued her nocturnal epistle to Stockton: "My dear Mrs Stocton the other side as you See was dated from G[raeme] Park. . . . At 12 on that Day, I left that Spot for this place." Rushed for time, she glosses over her feelings, confining them to a few stanzas in her "Willow Ode" as her final "adieu to Dear G Park." The poem records her tearful departure:

> There flows no Brook there Stands no Seat,
> Which daily she goes Bye;
> But thoughts are linked with each Retreat
> That fills the moistened Eye.

Retreating from the estate, Fergusson memorizes each favorite spot, for Graeme Park will soon be only an imaginary memory palace:

> Twas here we walked or there we Sat,
> Twas there we workd or Read;
> In Serious Books, or prattled Chat,
> While Hours unheeded fled.

Just as she marked the passing time by the old family clock, so Fergusson watches her favorite places fade into memory. The "local habitations" she formerly personified as intimate friends now "Convey / . . . Anguish to the Mind." At the same time, "Each local spot" embodies memories she could bring with her. Unlike the moveables that would have to be sold, her recollections could not be confiscated, bought, or devalued at a public auction. The nostalgia that tinges her poem on returning to Graeme Park in 1766 returns as she longs for her irrecoverable home.

After the death of Mrs. Todd in 1787 or 1788, Fergusson was homeless once again. But her final residence at the house of the clockmaker Seneca Lukens brought her two miles closer to Graeme Park: "The farm house I now Board at, is two miles from Graeme Park. . . . The master of the house bought 9 acres of G. Park from Mr. Smith. And I now Sit by the Fire of the wood of that Estate." Nearer Graeme Park but restricted by the farm's inconvenient topography, she laments, "My new Lodgings are unfortunate for me. I am on a Hill . . . and I must walk down the Hill to go twrds the Billet or town." By this time, moreover, Fergusson had sold the lion's share of her possessions, returned the borrowed books that contributed to her four-hundred-volume library, and saved just enough furniture and keepsakes to fill a single room at the Lukens house. After maintaining a 555-acre plantation and grand Georgian country house that was once the boast of the Philadelphia literati, she was now reduced to a modest, single-room dwelling. Realizing her domestic confinement, she confesses that her limited social circle has become even smaller: "now contracted my Self into so narrow a Circle that I think the next narrower must be that House which no man breaks the Comandments for in Coveting of his neighbor."[109]

Confined to one room and estranged from society, Fergusson spent the remainder of her life writing. Though she no longer had many tangible mementos of Graeme Park, she tapped into her memory and recopied her old poems into commonplace books for her friends. The textual expression of artificial memory, her commonplace books collectively served as a memory palace, which replaced and preserved her lost home. From her longtime companion Eliza Stedman, one gets a sense of Fergusson's final days at the Lukens farm: "Her confined income, not her inclination, caused her for years to live a retir'd life. Her active mind must have employment. Writing became her constant pursuit; her unremitted application to this mode of filling up her hours often astonished me; all her faculties continued in full power till she had no longer use for them; what a blessing to be thus favored with sight, memory, & the use of her limbs to the last, except three days."[110] Elizabeth Fergusson died at the Lukens house on 23 February 1801.

WRIGHT'S FERRY

Describing her 1714 voyage from Warrington, England, to Pennsylvania, Susanna Wright situates herself in space like a cartographer, mapping the longitude and latitude of remarkable sites. Between Liverpool and Cork she "saw the Island of St. Michaels Latitude 38 & the next day saw St. Georges Lat 39 Truaria 39–20 & Pico Latitude 39. . . . The wind SW our Course WNW the wind being brisk drove it to the northward before it reached us."[111] Wright keeps her bearings, though, marking her passage from home by unfamiliar places. Moving from the ship's navigational orientation on the Atlantic to its interior accommodations, she later remembers the hazards she endured: "The cabin swims with water several times & our close cabin broke down. The ship would rowl & tumble us all to one End of the cabin & tumble us out of bed but all the hardship we Endured I hope will be maid up with the pleasures of this Land." Such a tempestuous journey must have amplified her emotional disorientation as she watched her ancestral home fade into the distance. In the letter's postscript she notes with finality: "I often think of all my relations and frds left in England but cant think of seing England any more[.] the pleasantries of this Country & the toyle of the Sea will hinder me. I must once more bid thee farewell but hope not forever. My truly loving Cousin tho at this distance thee in one quarter of the world & I in anot[he]r." Charting their hearts in remote hemispheres, Susanna Wright arrives in North America.

Living in Chester before moving to Columbia's unfamiliar and unsettled frontier, Wright would have longed for her native home in Lancashire. Fifty-eight years later, after building her own home at Wright's Ferry, she reconstructs the Warrington house from memory. She begins with its paternal lineage: "the House in which my Father was born 105 years ago, & where his Parents lived & died:—after my grand Fathers death, the House was purchased by my grand-Mothers Bro[the]r who was Father to S. Fothergill's Wife." Overcome by nostalgia, she remembers, "I had past many of the happiest Days of my Life in it; those Days, unclouded by Care or Sorrow, which are quickly over, & can never return, & was intimately acquainted with every Part & cranny of it." Most precious was "a large old Clock that had been my G[o]d Fathers, when my Father was a Child, & which stood in my Uncles Parlour when we left Engld," which "continued to go excellently well, after having measured Time to its several Owners for a 100 Years—& alas!"[112] Though she is self-conscious about her sentimentalism in relating "uninteresting Anecdotes of a House, & a Piece of its Furniture," rather than offering a philosophical reflection on time, Wright sustained a lasting connection to the house through her memory.

Longing for the childhood home to which she "can never return," Wright established a family seat in the New World. Unmarried, childless, and living primarily in the neighboring house she inherited from Samuel Blunston, Wright regarded Wright's Ferry as her ancestral home. Her attachment to the house is most evident in her will, in which she bequeaths one hundred acres of "Land and Plantation in Hempfield Township" along the Susquehanna River to her nephew Samuel Wright, providing he divide the land and "Ferry house" with his three brothers. Most telling among her provisions, however, is her concern for the women and children. As long as Rhoda Wright remains her brother's widow (which, she says, "I hope and believe will be to the end of her Natural life"), the main house and garden ("now occupied by Susanna Bethel") will continue as the family dwelling. Finally, she stipulates that Wright's Ferry mansion "shall continue to be a home for all the Children as long as they or any of them are destitute of other Convenient home[s]."[113] Reiterating her former attachments to the Warrington house, she ensures Wright's Ferry's familial legacy.

Situated near Second and Cherry Streets and parallel to the Susquehanna River, Wright's Ferry mansion was begun in the spring of 1732 as an emblem of regional English design that extended the Quaker conservatism embodied in James Logan's Stenton to the uncultivated borders of western Pennsylvania, "then a most remote frontier settlement in the midst of the Indians subject to all the inconveniences, labours, privations & dangers of an infant establishment."[114] Broadening his Quaker ties beyond Philadelphia, Logan encouraged Wright's westward emigration. As one unpublished account of Lancaster County's settlement indicates, "the first proprieters being all connected or related to each other there was an harmony and friendship among them beautiful to behold and pleasing to recollect."[115] The geographical distance between settlements made these connections all the more vital. As Benjamin Rush remarks in 1784, Wright "told me that she had lived 62 years at this place and that when she first came here there were no inhabitants in York County and none on this side of Lancaster 10 miles from the ferry."[116] Describing her initial estrangement in a poem, Wright laments:

> From all the social world estrang'd
>   In desert wilds in woods
> Books and engaging friends exchangd
>   For pendant rocks and floods.[117]

Missing her social life in Chester County, Wright would cultivate the well-established Quaker connections in Columbia while maintaining Wright's Ferry as a pastoral respite for Philadelphia travelers (see figure 1.10).

Travel accounts throughout the eighteenth century underscore the rural pleasures and hospitality at Wright's Susquehanna home. "How happily situated are our friends at Hempfield!" writes Benjamin Franklin in a letter of 11 July 1752. "I languish for the Country, for Air and Shade and Leisure, but Fate has doom'd me to be stifled and roasted and teased to death in the City. You would not regret the want of City conversation if you considered that 9/10 of it is Impertinence." Enjoying the refined conversation at Wright's Ferry, Franklin writes in another letter: "Your guests all got well home to their Families highly pleased with their Journey and with the hospitality of Hempfield." Like Franklin, Sally Barton remembers her visits with Wright, remarking: "Great reading and taste for several branches of Literature makes her company much coveted by all the great and Learned who travel this way. . . . she spends most of her time in her library which is large & well chosen." Finally, Elizabeth Fergusson fondly reminisces about her time spent at Wright's Ferry in August 1762: "The limestone water so affected me that I was detained at Mrs. Susan Wrights on the Susquehanna and could not proceed further on my tour. It seems like a fairy dream, like some of Susquehanna's islands, when the majic wand of memory wakes up those days."[118] In the end, Wright lost neither books nor engaging friends, as her earlier poem anticipates.

More noteworthy than Wright's celebrated hospitality is her lesser-known participation in planning and building her Wright's Ferry home. Unlike the other women in her coterie, Wright not only owned her house but also oversaw its construction. Remembering Samuel Fothergill's description of "all the alterations he had made, as he had in a manner rebuilt" the Warrington house, and observing the tentative plan and successive ren-

1.10. Formerly part of the Lancaster frontier, Wright's Ferry Mansion stands at Second and Cherry Streets in what is now Columbia, Pennsylvania. Courtesy, The von Hess Foundation, Wright's Ferry Mansion.

ovations of the house of her neighbor and companion, Samuel Blunston, Wright helped create a cohesive building plan for Wright's Ferry reminiscent of her family home in England. As the architectural historian Bernard Herman explains, "Operating within a tradition where building agreements contained little more than specifications for material, building dimensions and height, construction schedule, payment, and the catchall phrase 'in a workmanlike manner,' Susanna Wright, her father, and brother were as much participants in the building process as the craftsmen in their employ."[119]

Despite James Logan's influence (and Susanna Wright's nostalgic memories of Lancashire), the Wright's Ferry mansion more closely resembles Graeme Park's original three-cell plan.[120] With an unfinished attic above and stone cellar below, the west, or original, front fenestration displays a three-bay second floor over a five-bay ground floor with the continuous bay service wing visually centered between the chimney piles. Although the first floor appears somewhat asymmetrical with the central entry window slightly smaller than the two flanking it, the second floor compensates with its balanced tripartite composition. The west elevation's masonry is dressed with evenly set limestone, and the remaining walls are laid with roughly coursed rubble. Besides the front and back doorways into the entry, there were doorways in each gable, providing outside access to the parlor and kitchen.[121] A gable roof with pent eaves on the east and west elevations extends the full length of the building (see figure 1.10).

Walking into Wright's Ferry from the front door, one enters the unheated entry, which runs the full depth of the house. Lit by a sash window, the entry hall is finished with a paved (probably brick) floor, facing exterior doors, and doors leading to the parlor and dining room. Two paneled and battened Dutch doors composed of upper and lower elements hang prominently on the front wall and more discreetly beneath the stair for rear access. Based on a transitional design that incorporates characteristics of the open Georgian stair and the older winder form, the staircase has baroque baluster turnings, rare among the eighteenth-century vernacular styles of the Delaware Valley. Foregrounding the best rooms (the elaborately paneled parlor and parlor chamber) and obscuring the service wing (the roughly finished kitchen, pantry, and kitchen chamber) in the back, the floor plan continues the house's interior hierarchy by containing the service rooms (including the kitchen, servant chambers, and guest chambers upstairs) in a continuous gable and extension of the building. Unlike other regional houses with a detached kitchen and service buildings or with the service wing on another floor, Wright's Ferry blends these spaces into the original house plan. The house thus reinforced the conventional social segregation of the family's, servants', and guests' spaces.

Although architectural historians have reconstructed the house's original exterior structure and internal floor plan, scholars have found it difficult if not impossible to place Susanna Wright intimately in her home. With little documentary evidence and even fewer material objects to authenticate her daily life at Wright's Ferry, preservationists have relied on educated guesswork. The von Hess Foundation has done a splendid job approximating the house's original furnishings with a rich display of regional and historical decorative arts.[122] The beautiful parlor furniture, along with the original wall paneling, helps visitors imagine Wright as she entertained her Philadelphia guests during their frequent visits. One can almost see her exchanging books with James Logan and Isaac Norris or brokering a deal for Benjamin

1.11. Silver cup with Wright family coat of arms and Susanna Wright's name engraved on the side. Courtesy, The von Hess Foundation, Wright's Ferry Mansion.

Franklin's militia during the frontier wars.[123] Also displayed is Wright's cherished silver cup, which is engraved with the Wright family coat of arms. Made in and carried from England, the cup signifies her wish for genealogical continuity through her ancestral homes (see figure 1.11).

Similarly, the upstairs chambers recall Wright's creative talents. Whereas the writing desk in one room evokes images of her escritoire (bequeathed to her nephew Samuel Wright), where she likely wrote her poems and letters, the comparatively unadorned work room equipped with a spinning wheel (and the requisite southern exposure) reminds visitors of her reputed silkworm manufacture. Unfortunately, only a few extant silk samples, a well-rehearsed canon of anecdotes, and Wright's posthumously published essay on silk production survive.[124] Each spring, after feeding the silkworms with mulberry leaves, Wright covered them with a dry-ironed linen tucked into a drawer so they could spin their cocoons. The finished cocoons were then placed in boiling water, from which she skimmed the floating silk filaments. Winding them onto a spindle, she washed the silk yarn in soap and water until it became "soft as cotton" and ready for spinning. A telling metaphor for Wright's place in cultural memory, the silk reminds us of her mute namesake and literary pseudonym, "Philomela." Like Philomela and her sister, Procne, who narrate Philomela's story through a collaborative tapestry, two centuries of scholars have pieced together disparate recorded moments into what remains an incomplete biography.

Without adequate material artifacts or Wright's own topophilic memories to guide their interpretations, historians have turned to oral legend and collective memory. Attempting to reconstruct Wright's life in the early nineteenth century, Deborah Logan notes: "As it appears to me to be like a duty which the living owe to each other, as well as to the dead to rescue merit from descending into immediate oblivion I have endeavoured to trace the following notices of a Lady who tho well known & generally esteemd by the most eminent characters in this state whilst she lived, yet nothing I beleive respecting her has ever yet appeared in Print. What I now mean to offer is from recollection alone but my oppertunities for information were such as to enable me to give those recollections with certainty." Given the lack of printed materials about and by Susanna Wright, Logan depends on her own recollections. She not only records visits to Wright's Ferry but also transcribes from memory some of Wright's poetry: "I spent in copying out some verses from memory of Susanna Wright." Except for the collection of Wright's poetry collated in Milcah Martha Moore's recently published commonplace book, her prolific poetry remains scant. In addition to sketching and other "little works of fancy," writes Logan, Wright wrote poetry that was "greatly & deservedly admired whilst she lived. and would abundantly satisfy the world of her merit could they be produced, but as she wrote not for fame, she never kept copies and it is to be feared, but little can now be recovered."[125]

Logan continues her reminiscences with Wright's public contributions as a legal arbiter, scribe, and herbalist: "So great was the esteem in which [Wright] was held by her neighbors for integrity and judgement, that disputes of considerable interest were frequently left to her sole arbitration by the parties concerned. her advice was often desired on occasions of importance respecting the settlement of estates and she was also resorted to as a Physician by her neighbors. . . . & having considerable knowledge in Physics, dispenses medicines gratis to all the sick around her who are unable to employ a Physician."[126] Other historians have continued the mythmaking: "She sat for hours each day by a little square window put together by wooden pegs and guarded by a hand-wrought iron bar, interviewing the Indians, listening to their complaints and giving advice."[127]

The difficulty of recovering the material life at Wright's Ferry could be in part a legacy of the Quaker disregard for the material world in preference for a spiritual one. As Logan explains, Wright's "situation on the banks of the Susquehanna is delightful but being educated a Quaker (tho her good sense will not suffer her to retain the stiffness and formalities of one) she is remarkably plain in her dress & manner of living." The supposed stiffness and formality contradicts the more prevalent anecdotes about Wright's gracious hospitality. But since many of Logan's recollections are from childhood, it could be that she misunderstood the older Wright. On the other hand, some of Wright's poetry suggests a healthy skepticism toward material objects. Objects are "too fading to be lov'd," she writes. In "My Own Birthday—August 4th 1761," for instance, Wright portrays memory as an elusive bubble, seeing it in metaphysical rather than material terms:

> And what are they?—a Vision of all the past,
> A Bubble on the Water's shining Face,
> What yet remain, till the first transient Blast,
> Shall leave no more Remembrance of their Place.[128]

A transparent prism that catches light and color, a bubble provides both a momentary window through which to see the world and a mirror that reflects objects in its circular frame. As window and mirror, the bubble illustrates how memory requires both the accumulation of impressions as memory images and the retrieval of those images through recollection. As fleeting as the memories it represents, the bubble demonstrates the importance of writing down remembrances in commonplace books.

Wright's undated poem "On Time" similarly records the passage of time in spatial terms:

> Since Moments past are as a Dream,
>   A fleeting Evening Shade,
> Which close like a divided Stream
>   Like dying Tapers fade.—[129]

Like bursting bubbles and other fading objects of memory, candle tapers dwindle. Candle wax recalls the classical memory image of Mnemosyne's block of wax impressions, but the human heart, Wright concludes, is the most reliable repository for preserving memory. Wright questions the physical traces of memory in domestic spaces and objects, locating remembrance in her own body instead. Thus, when her father, John Wright, died at home in 1749, she writes: "Your memories from my breast shall never stray, / . . . Though to these eyes, you never must return."[130]

Despite her incomplete history, Wright remains a luminous figure in our cultural memory. "This excellent woman, straightened forth, attain a high degree of intellectual and literary eminence," writes Logan, "and it is only to be regretted that so few of her letters and writings are now to be found, as they were deservedly valued in her time and she had so many correspondences." She goes on to say that Wright "had an excellent Memory as well as a most clear and comprehensive judgment." Benjamin Rush similarly extols Wright's intellectual gifts. In a journal entry for 7 April 1784 he recalls:

> Saw the famous Suzey Wright, a lady who has been celebrated above half a century for her wit, good sense and valuable improvement of the mind. She has been for many years the friend and correspondent of Dr. Franklin. She is now in her 88th year and has declined a good deal in strength and in her mental faculties. . . . She told me further that her appetite was good, that she still retained her relish for books "that she could not live without them"—and that, to use her own words "the pleasure of reading was to her a most tremendous blessing." She said she could remember the events of childhood better than she did the middle of her life.[131]

At eighty-eight, Wright showed signs of dementia as her short-term memory degenerated. But her ability to remember her childhood may also suggest memory's power when images are empirically and sentimentally absorbed. Lacking any account of Wright's experiences in her home on the Pennsylvania frontier, however, we can only surmise what she felt. Because Wright lived most of her life at the Blunston house, she did not, like the other women of her coterie, experience the visceral pleasures of inhabitation. All that exists in the historical record is her nostalgia for her Lancashire home, suggesting that lived rather than built space makes individual memory precious.

MORVEN

Named for the mythical kingdom in Scottish poet James McPherson's *Poems of Ossian*, Annis Stockton's New Jersey home, Morven, remains somewhat of a historiographical mystery. Like the textual lacunae that shroud Ossian's translated poems, legends abound about Morven's original construction, subsequent demolition during the American Revolution, and

1.12. Morven. Photograph by Dan Dragan for Historic Morven, Inc. Reproduced with permission.

eventual renovation in the nineteenth century (see figure 1.12). During the Revolution the Stocktons fled Princeton, leaving Morven on 29 November 1776 and returning in early 1777. The house was used in their absence as British headquarters under Cornwallis until Washington's forces recovered most of New Jersey. But despite the British plunder, and despite Benjamin Rush's report (echoing Oliver Goldsmith's popular poem *The Deserted Village*) that "Princeton is indeed a deserted village. . . . the whole of Mr. Stockton's furniture, apparel, and even valuable writings have been burnt," there is no architectural evidence that the house (along with the college and church) was destroyed at that time.[132] It is more likely that a fire in the building's main block in 1821 is the source of these stories.

Although the current restoration of the mansion raises questions about the original eighteenth-century architecture, the remaining brickwork, typical of period New Jersey houses, gives a sketch of the exterior shell. Morven was built by Richard Stockton in the late 1760s and renovated by his namesake, Richard "the Duke," who completely rebuilt the central portion in 1790 and added a portico in the 1810s. Because the house sits on a high basement instead of rising abruptly from the ground, the first- and second-floor windows on either side of the central doorway are set evenly above the basement windows. Composed of two full stories and capped by splayed flat arches made of brick, the house's central block as well as the single, lower western wing was laid in Flemish bond up to the brickwork just above the splayed (probably stone) lintels to the second-story windows. Also made of stone, the horizontal belt course accentuated the visual movement between the first and second stories. Unlike the later federal entrance flanked with Tuscan columns, the original center, suggests the architectural historian Constance Greiff, probably had more dramatic proportions: a pedimented doorway with arched fanlight, without pilasters, but with an eared or crosseted architrave. Cutting through the central keystones of the second-story windows, the cornice, made of simple moldings crowned by a row of modillions, or curved brackets, gave the roof a somewhat steeper slope than its present angle. Imitating Greek Doric entablature in its triglyphs and metopes, the cornice marks Morven as an example of the later Georgian style, modified by the lighter classical influences of the architect Robert Adam.[133]

The current east wing and piazza were later additions. As Annis Stockton writes to her daughter Julia Stockton Rush in 1788: "The carpenters and masons surrounding me . . . as soon as I get this room done, which I hope will be soon now to go to Graeme Park." Although the addition mimicked the house's west wing, being on the same plane and two stories high, its three front bays, central door, and interior chimney noticeably diverged from the four-bay west entry. Describing the piazza to her daughter Mary Stockton Hunter in 1791, Annis Stockton writes: "I have got into one of my pensive moods, that yields what I call the luxury of feeling resembling sorrow, yet of that kind, which we love to indulge in, as tho it was a perfect enjoyment. in one of those moments—the enclosed Ill penserosa ode flowed impromptu and I repeated it almost as wrote [i.e., rote] and when I retired to my chamber I wrote it with scarce an alteration."[134] The meandering view afforded by the piazza, much like the animal spirits rushing between her heart and brain through the nerves, literally and figuratively prompted Stockton's memory. Her visceral response to the landscape (highlighted by the rose clasped to her bosom in figure 1.13) thus inspired a spontaneous poem, which she committed first to memory and then to paper.

The interior footprint repeats the formal balance and symmetry of the facade. Though the first floor is currently organized around a T-shaped hall that runs the full depth of the house with a stairway on one side and a passage to the west wing on the other, architectural evidence suggests that it was originally L-shaped.[135] Two contemporaneous accounts differ as to whether the entry hall was a legitimate room. On the one hand, Morven

1.13. *Stockton, Annis Boudinot (Mrs. Richard) (1736–1801).* Oil on canvas; 77.0 × 64.7 cm; 39 × 34 ¼ in. (frame), PP226, American, Painting, Princeton University. Bequest of Mrs. Alexander T. McGill. © 1970 Trustees of Princeton University. Reproduced with permission.

was described in 1783 as "large for a country house, it has four rooms on a floor commodious but not grand."[136] On the other hand, Annis Stockton's 1781 inventory noted a hierarchical layout arranged in a conventional L plan, from first chamber, second bedchamber, front parlor, dining room, back parlor, to kitchen. Stockton's inventory intimates that the south front of the first floor opened into a spacious entry, from which one could enter a larger room (the front parlor) or a smaller one (the dining room) on either side of the entrance hall. Though the inventory does not mention a third smaller room on the second floor, two rooms in the first floor of the wing, or one or more rooms over the kitchen, there may very well have been additional bedrooms to house Stockton's five children. In addition, Morven was renowned for its hospitality to family, friends, and diplomats: "We had all our friends at once with us last night. . . . We have not been clear of fresh recruits for near three weeks every night a new set of travelers . . . and in the midst of harvest so that with harvest shifting beds and lodging five or six people every night but with one spare bed, I am almost strung out."[137] Protecting the Stockton family's privacy while accommodating its generous hospitality, Morven provided separate, private familial spaces rather than the medieval version of the multifunctional hall.

Despite the ambiguity regarding Morven's original footprint, both the T and L plans (based on the same Roman block print as Fairhill's H plan) have mnemonic resonance. Essentially the same shape with an additional arm on the T, these perpendicular characters embody what mnemonic theorists describe as contiguity. The adjacent, touching lines of these figures prescribe an orderly pathway for organizing and retrieving memories. As Beattie explains, "The thoughts of [the] mind are apt to follow each other in a train; and . . . between those which are contiguous there is for the most part some connection, either natural, or established by custom."[138] Since architectural associationism similarly inspires a train of memorable impressions, the contiguous contours of the L- or T-shaped design imitated, and perhaps even invoked, a chain of associations in Stockton's mind. For the rooms in Stockton's house, running from the most public to the most private, follow the mind's organization from the rational (front) to the mnemonic (rear) recesses.

Though none of the decorative details remains, one could assume that Morven's rooms followed the Princeton vernacular style. Although the best rooms were wainscoted from floor to chair rail, other rooms were limited to embellishments around the fireplaces, cornices, chair rails, windows, and door frames. The front parlor was furnished with mahogany plain-back chairs with crimson damask bottoms, and two mahogany card tables lined the periphery. One wall was decorated with a large gilt-frame looking glass, which visually framed an arrangement of ten copperplate prints throughout the room. The formal portraits of Richard and Annis Stockton may also have been displayed, presenting their family's status and good taste to visitors.[139] Here Stockton would have welcomed her many guests, including George and Martha Washington, Rochambeau, and the marquis de La Luzerne. This entry, too, greeted the members of the Continental Congress, who frequented Morven during their temporary relocation to Princeton in 1783. And here her delighted company would walk out into the yard on 4 July 1783 to see the "quality of Princeton . . . and lamps . . . hung up on Mrs. Stockton's cherry trees."[140]

Across the hall was the elegantly appointed dining room; the southwest room, or stair hall, led to a small parlor, which seems to have served as the family's informal dining space with its small walnut dining table, larger mahogany one, sizable mahogany tea table, eight pictures, and set of iron andirons, tongs, and shovel. The formal dining room was furnished exclusively with mahogany, including a sideboard, dining table, round tea table, and eight chairs. It had one large mirror and ten pictures on the walls as well as the typical fireplace accoutrements. One can imagine the elegant sideboard glittering with decanters of wine, fine glasses, a knife box, and silver engraved with the family arms and motto, "Omnia deo pendent." Though Stockton considered the formal dining room to be the masculine analogue to the feminine kitchen, pantry, and dairy, as one poem suggests, she superintended many elaborate public dinners at Morven.[141] Rehearsing her latest repast with George and Martha Washington, for instance, she writes: "The president and Mrs. Washington visited the College . . . after which Mrs. Washington sat with us till one o'clock and partook of a collation of fruit and cake, and wine and sweet meats, which I had in readiness for I had heard the etiquette of the journey was settled that they were not to lodge or dine at a private house, the whole journey."[142] The dining room thus held patriotic memories of the American Revolution, Continental Congress, and first president for Stockton.

Whereas the parlor and dining room staged early national memories, the bedchambers upstairs hosted more familial moments. With a fully dressed bedstead of chintz curtains, holland sheets, rose blankets, and a cotton counterpane or coverlet, the best chamber was probably where Stockton gave birth to her six children: Julia (b. 1759), twins Mary and Susan (b. 1761), John Richard (b. 1764), Lucius Horatio (b. 1768), and Abigail (b. 1773). Here, too, she would have tended to her husband, Richard, in his lingering illness and death in 1781. After reading Edward Young's popular poem *Night Thoughts*, she poignantly writes to Elizabeth Fergusson in 1780: "If you could for a moment witness my situation, you would not wonder at my silence, totaly confin'd to the chamber of a dear and dying husband, whose nerves have become so iritable as not to be able to bear the scraping of a pen on paper in his room, or even the folding up of a letter, which deprives me of one of the greatest reliefs I could have in my present sittuation."[143] The bedchamber that witnessed her children's births also reminded Stockton of her greatest loss throughout her twenty years of widowhood.

After Richard Stockton's death the chamber was transformed into a writing space. Along with a mahogany dressing table and glass, nine pictures, and six mahogany chairs, the chamber had a mahogany bureau with glass doors (i.e., a secretary, or desk, and bookcase). Annis Stockton picks up her pen and writes again to Fergusson. Though painful memories initially made writing difficult, she returns to the comforts of pen and ink: "A few Evenings ago my mind was engagd in thinking how Short a time it appeared Since I began my Career of Life, And how fast every thing that delighted and adornd me then was fleeting." Correspondence guarantees remembrance through its reciprocal gestures, collapsing the past and present into a single moment. Finding her childhood memories reduced to mere ephemera, she commits her mature thoughts more permanently to memory. "My pen, inke, and Paper lay on the Table," Stockton remarks, "and I diverted my self with arranging the idea of the moment with what I now enclose with this Letter."[144]

Sitting in the chamber on another occasion and listening to the birds outside the window "singing all together and it happens to be very still about the house," Stockton writes to Fergusson: "There was for some time the most delightful consort ever I heard in my Life. I am sure you would have enjoy'd it."[145] Since rural settings, according to eighteenth-century aestheticians, improved and encouraged female recollection, Stockton may have followed the avian chorus beyond the house and wandered along Morven's verdant grounds.[146] As she apologizes to Fergusson: "My dear Friend would not have had such a respite from the clack of my pen but for the employment that my garden has for some time added to my other cares—for it begins to grow so pleasant out of doors that I can scarce keep myself from rambling constantly."[147] Drawn to the lush and colorful garden, she experienced a stream of involuntary associations. The traditional English flowers (anemones, ranunculus, and tulips, to name a few) provoked both her memory and imagination: "The art of gardening aspires to more than imitation," theorists explained; "it can create original characters."[148] Supposedly copying Pope's neoclassical landscape at Twickenham, Stockton's garden reminded her of favorite passages from Pope's poetry, which she imitated in her own neoclassical verse.[149] Gardens summon the memory; poetry preserves it.

Writing a detailed letter to his wife from England in 1767, Richard Stockton describes his itinerary for a trip to Twickenham's famous gardens and grotto. He arranged for an artistic companion to sketch an "exact plan of the whole" to delight his wife and provide a model. Scholars have critiqued the letter as anachronistic, however, since Pope's garden was altered beyond recognition within a year of his death in 1744. In addition, Morven's garden was well established by the time Richard Stockton was in England.[150] Despite its historical inaccuracy, the Twickenham allusion reveals the garden's importance to Annis Stockton. Unlike history, memory relies on resonance with rather than a literal record of the past. Houses, objects, gardens—and the ways they are remembered—ultimately create cultural memory. With an antiquarian interest in Twickenham, Stockton desired a souvenir that would carry the famous English garden, or at least of piece of it, into her own.

Unsuccessfully searching for curious shells, Richard Stockton visited other notable sites, promising to collect ancient curiosities to adorn Morven's grotto: "I shall bring you a piece of Roman brick, which I knocked off the top of Dover Castle. . . . I have also got for your collection a piece of wood, which I cut off the effigy of Archbishop Peckham, buried in the Cathedral of Canterbury more than five hundred years ago; likewise a piece from the king's coronation chair, and several other things, which, merely as antiquities, may deserve a place in *your* grotto."[151] As antiquities, the brick, wood, and king's relics literally bring remnants of the past into the present moment. Though each object's value lies in its history, its meaning to Stockton would be determined by its new context. The actual past is erased in order to create an imagined one that has contemporary significance.[152]

Though it unclear whether Annis Stockton ever received these relics, the current state of Morven's garden highlights the mnemonic significance of collected antiquities. Now being reconstructed by archaeologists and landscape historians, the eighteenth-century garden is in ruins, covered by nineteenth- and twentieth-century landscape designs applied by subsequent owners.[153] As fragments and artifacts are uncovered, they become valued relics—surviving remnants—of Stockton's beloved garden. Inherently incomplete, the relics are merely memory traces of the original prospect. But left behind by the past, they revive Stockton's interest in historic gardens, cultural curiosities, and their cumulative contributions to our collective memory.

Stockton lived at Morven until about 1795. A family dispute presumably prompted her to move in with Julia and Benjamin Rush on 19 May 1797. Her son ensured her financial security and insisted that she spend the summer with him and his family at Morven. Before moving, she visited another daughter, Abigail Stockton Field, at White Hill, seeing it as "a fairy land" that brought back long-forgotten childhood memories.[154] Four years later Stockton returned to White Hill, where she died on 6 February 1801.

Walking through the Philadelphia coterie's country houses, one recalls the shell house with which this chapter opens. Just as Anne Emlen collected, arranged, and transformed the disparate shells into a miniature Palladian mansion, so Hannah Griffitts, Deborah Logan, Elizabeth Fergusson, Susanna Wright, and Annis Stockton fashioned their homes as distinctive memory palaces. Their intimate attachment to these places, as their manuscripts attest, persisted despite financial entanglements, unsuccessful marriages, widowhood, spinsterhood, and war. Though such disappointments forestalled the promised retirement of country house life, they also provoked endless streams of association and reminiscence. Memory improves with familiarity to its objects, eighteenth-century aestheticians contended, particularly when those objects elicit pleasure or pain. Recounting their cumulative losses, these women mapped their lives through intimate domestic spaces and objects, forming links to the past and ensuring connections with posterity. Wandering from room to room, they noticed that "memory wakes the past." "Still Memory gives th' enchanting sound," as Logan explains, "But never from my mind be torn."[155]

Pen, Ink, and Memory

Our thoughts are fleeting, and the greater part of our words are forgotten as soon as uttered: but, by writing, we may give permanency to both. . . . and the Memory is prepared for receiving a deep impression.

—James Beattie, *Essays Moral and Critical* (1783)

THE WRITING CLOSET

"Books are faithful repositories, which may be a while neglected or forgotten," writes Deborah Logan, "but when they are opened again, will again impart their instruction: memory once interrupted is not to be recalled."[1] Convinced that the art of memory depended on writing, Logan kept daily diaries (which she called her "everyday writing") as well as manuscript commonplace books, negotiating the endless domestic interruptions at Stenton by writing early in the morning "before the busy hum of day / The joys of quiet chase away."[2] She followed the advice of the moralist Lady Pennington to "conduct her house in a regular method," setting aside "many vacant hours" for "improvements of the mind, as are most suitable to her genius and inclination." Logan would rise before dawn—"the sweetest [hour] on the face of time"—ritualistically beginning her winter mornings by lighting a fire in the dining room stove (see figure 2.1).[3]

As the room slowly warms, she retreats into her bedchamber to dress. Standing in her shift before the washbasin and mirror on the dressing table, she bathes her face, ears, and neck in cold water, holding her eyes open "for a considerable time," finding "it very beneficial to [her] sight." Drying her

2.1. In this contemporary view of Stenton's dining room, one glimpses the details cataloged in Deborah Logan's account of her "winter writing establishment." In addition to the characteristic tables and chairs are what she calls a "Turkey carpet" and a small writing desk in the far right corner. Courtesy of The National Society of The Colonial Dames of America in the Commonwealth of Pennsylvania at STENTON, Philadelphia.

face, she slips into the soft layers of what she calls her "home costume," or "Costume of Comfort," of "a nice black petticoat, a dark calico short gown, a lace handkerchief, clear starched cap with a clean white ribband, a clean fine checked apron just out of the drawer," and comfortable, old shoes. She then picks up her broken spectacles, harboring "the forlorn hope of pinning them to [her] Cap ribband to keep them to [her] eyes."[4] Suitably dressed, she returns to the dining room and drowsily surveys the cozy scene:

> I should like a picture of my morning & evening hours to be preserved, as spent in the old dining room with the great improvement of my Coal stove and Lehigh Coal. My low Green, cushioned chair, one I found in this house 50 years ago, but repairs and new covers, still make it respectable, and my beloved Dr. Logan always use to set in it—then there is a table under the south window the board of which is rubbed bright and here a few cherished Plants are daily put get nourished by the sun beams, our ordinary dinner table stands under the window, which table occasionally has on it a small green bench with more Plants, then there is my little maple desk containing my

ever and anon wanted, Books, and writing materials, the drawer of which is mostly open, whilst I set near it and before a mahogany Stool, covered with a very white square board which serves me as a table, and before which I usually set to write. then there is a nondescript place on the hearth between the stove and the chimney, wholly unknown to architectural embellishment which kept clean and duly whitewashed, affords room for a little green bench for plants of a frosty night, and other etceteras wanted for the fire—just at my side and between me and the Stove, Lodge [the dog] usually lies, with often the company of a Black Buck Cat—Reddy hangs above the desk in his nice new cage, and poor blind Mocky hard by, attended to as well as I can, from rememberance of his former value and Beauty. and this, with my workbasket and Books, is a pretty true description of my winter establishment.

Having made a memorable sketch of her winter writing "establishment," Logan sits down to breakfast at the dining table under the south window. She then repairs to the stove, which is "keeping water hot where with [she] washe[s] the breakfast apparatus."[5]

After putting the dining table to rights, she moves the easy chair and one of the four mahogany stools between the stove and the south window, whose sill is filled with crape myrtles, geraniums, a beautiful *Daphne indicum*, and a China rose.[6] She drags "her little white deal Board" to the window to complete her makeshift writing table (figure 2.2).[7] Among the scattered writing paraphernalia on her desk sits a delicate glass of violets gathered from her garden. Logan fills her arms with the necessary supplies: a leather-bound album of paper and a portable inkstand with a quill, penknife, ink bottle, and casters holding ink powder and pounce. As the penman George Fisher suggests in *The American Instructor* (1753), a writer should have a "Pen-knife Razir Metal, Quills in good Store; / Gum Sandrick Powder, to pounce Paper o'er," and "Ink, shining black; Paper more white than Snow," as well as "Round and flat Rulers."[8] Arranging these supplies on her deal board, Logan lights a candle and sinks into her husband's stuffed wing chair, awaiting the sunrise.

Opening the copybook, Logan prepares the paper to receive and absorb the ink. She reaches for the inkstand, lifting the caster of pounce. She sprinkles its contents (probably gum sandarac) onto the paper's surface, gently rubbing and evenly smoothing the particles with a small piece of cotton.[9] When using better-quality (or "sized" paper roughened by erasure), she skips the prefatory pounce and, careful not to smudge the wet ink, dusts the finished manuscript with chalk powder, biotite (powdered magnesium),

2.2. Although Deborah Logan's "little white deal Board" is no longer extant, the footstool from which she built her makeshift desk is housed at Stenton. Courtesy of The National Society of The Colonial Dames of America in the Commonwealth of Pennsylvania at STEN-TON, Philadelphia. The Winterthur Museum owns another stool from the set of four commissioned by Charles Norris and made by John Elliott, Jr., in 1755–56.

or sand.[10] Whatever the method, the writing paper is soon ready for her inscription. Logan takes one of the goose quills from her inkstand, only to find that she has "not even the pleasure of a Pen and Ink worth a button." She regrets that her writing master, Anthony Benezet, had not taught her the skill of making her own pen. So she makes do with what she has, cobbling together a rudimentary quill. Removing the cover from her glass inkwell, Logan inspects the ink's color, preferring the permanence of a solid black to the troublesome red, brown, or yellowish tint, which quickly fades. Mixing in some ink powder to attain the desired color and texture, Logan is ready to write. She slants the paper to the left, dips the quill into the inkwell, scrapes off the excess at the well's mouth, and places the finely nibbed point sideways on the awaiting page. Pleased with the grace and legibility of her script, Logan concludes: "I think of all his scholars my Good Master Benezet succeeded in making me write 'Plain and easily to be Read' as he always recommended."[11]

During the summer months Logan keeps her writing rituals virtually unchanged except that she moves from the downstairs dining room to the li-

2.3. A view of Deborah Logan's upstairs "summer apartment" at Stenton. The window seats would easily accommodate a small table for writing. Courtesy of The National Society of The Colonial Dames of America in the Commonwealth of Pennsylvania at STENTON, Philadelphia.

brary upstairs (see figure 2.3).[12] "This morning I rose at the first dawn to obtain a few minutes," she writes, "but notwithstanding, this has been written thro many interruptions." As "Seclusion and quiet" were "an indespensable condition" for writing, she longs for solitude. But sharing the library with her husband, George Logan, she complains: "Usual sort of occupation—only I can scarce find a moments time to write," for "Dr. L. almost continually inhabits the Library, and I hate to be asked what I am writing—if I shut myself up in my room—pop—some one is at the door every moment, so that I hardly can collect my implements and set down before I am interrupted." After her husband's death in 1821 Logan has more time and space to devote to her intellectual work, spending the mornings as well as afternoons in the library. Despite her grief, she achieves the seclusion she desires, and writing is suddenly made easy: "When I am entirely alone I can write but never can compose any thing at all cleaver when others are setting by, and I suppose observant of what I am doing."[13]

Formerly the famous library of her father-in-law, James Logan, the room was framed by copious bookshelves hugging the walls. Like her predecessor, Deborah Logan was known for her archival interests and often entertained local antiquarians in the library, who "expatiated on old Books and papers and praised [her] industry in transcribing so much from them." They discussed "Characters and times by-past and raked up from oblivion old anecdotes and things. 'Grey with the Rust of Years.'" Surrounded by the textual artifacts of memory, Logan nostalgically muses: "We were Grey enough then for we were deep in antiquities, but we were not Blue nor any approach of it." Though she welcomed her guests' curiosity, Logan typically inhabited the library alone. "And surrounded by Books," she writes, "most of them indeed in union with every thing else, and savouring more of the past than the present. here, and alone, I like best to be." Shaded by the "fine Old Trees," the library was a delightful summer apartment. Sometimes Logan reclined on "the easy and low seat of an old Sopha, brought by [her] Grandmother from England in 1708" with "many another wreck and remembrance of olden time." Other times she sat at her little oval writing table in the south window with her cat lying on a nearby chair and her bird sitting atop the workbasket on the table's corner. Perhaps she even pulled the small table over to the cushioned window seat that would afford at one glance a pleasant view of the library and the garden beneath it.[14]

Comparing the intimate scene in the library to "a Perfume, [which] may be named, but cant be comprehended only by its actual presence," Logan invokes all her senses at once, creating a synesthetic landscape of smells, sights, and sounds that together preserve and stir her memories. Using the rhetorical device of *ekphrasis*, she "paints a Picture" with words. She imagines, for instance, a more naturalistic window treatment than the blue-checked curtains, remarking that "the Glycene, [jasmine], and wild Ivy form the most beautiful festoons and drapery around the southern window," which emits a softened green light over her writing table. Between the purple clusters of glycene that "'gently Creeps luxuriant'—between the lattice," she sees the garden: "the Broom with its strings of Golden Blossoms, the beautiful Horse Chestnut with its thick covering of leaves," an old buttonwood tree, and "a very flourishing pyramid of small scarlet Ipomora," which "the humming birds delight to visit." Logan enjoys the breeze that "has played among the Glycene's 'till it has stolen their fragrance," and she listens to "the fine tones of [her] Eolian harp in one of the yellow room windows, and the Door opened to admit the Sound." Like the perfumed scene so difficult to describe, the harp's sound is similarly "untranslatable": "The low murmur of the wind as it passes over the strings of my harp . . . speaks to me of the Past."[15]

Listening to the harp and thinking of the past, Logan walks across the room to the press closet—"that old mine of pamphlets"—adjacent to the fireplace. She opens the doors and peruses the shelves. Among the old boxes of books and manuscripts, she discovers some old family papers: "I attempted to put a closet in the library to rights and the papers that fell into my hands detained me.—they were not of the oldest time but many from my beloved husband, notes from my hon'd mother, from the children, from dear and revered friends." As material relics that suspend both time and place by holding the writers' imprints, these letters "awakened much tenderness" and "a renewed acknowledgment" of the deceased epistlers. Unearthing other intimate archives, she stops to read, "and instantly [her] mind recurs to the period when it was written, and then 'bussy meddling memory!' calls up associations of contemporaries." Among the old papers are the "many Books and fragments of Books of letters of James Logan," which, she writes, "I was glad to recover and which will afford me much entertaining in looking over."

In addition to her transcription of James Logan and William Penn's correspondence, Deborah Logan kept drafts and fair copies of her *Memoirs of the Life of George Logan* and of her many contributions to John Fanning Watson's *Annals of Philadelphia* in the press closet. Finally, she cataloged her own manuscript volumes: "The New Book in which I now begin to write does not please me half so well as did the Old one which I have just filled and consigned to a shelf in the closet, besides my other 'Works.'" Like a private commonplace book that stored and displayed her impressions, the press closet was an archive for family memories. And manuscripts afforded the privacy breached by published texts, as Logan remarks: " 'Right Splendid Quarto's and handsome Octavo's' if they had been consigned in manuscript to the Shelves of Authors, instead of being sent abroad thro' the Medium of the Press, to proclaim their own imbecility."[16]

My reconstruction of Deborah Logan's writing spaces at Stenton highlights the material connection among early American architecture, handwriting, and memory. Taken together, the dining room and library extend the mnemonic analogy of domestic topoi discussed in chapter 1 to the corresponding art of penmanship. As the spaces where Logan wrote and stored her manuscripts, these rooms resemble the recessed spaces in the back of the female mind, which collected and retrieved memories. Routinely imagined as "repositories" or "storerooms" for "accumulating knowledge and profiting by our study," the dining room and library likewise emulate the commonplace book, where "we divide up and copy out [memory images] in particular order."[17] Using a common metaphor for commonplacing, Logan complains, "I am famished as to Intellectual food." "Amidst interruptions of every kind," it is impossible "to produce volumes of clear narration or well-digested thoughts." "The recipe I suppose, for such a state, is to Read—Good Books of Course," she quips, "chewing the cud of sweet and bitter thoughts." A physical process much like digestion, gathering and internaliz-ing commonplaces present a kind of intellectual buffet, where the diner creates a feast of mingled textures and flavors according to her literary palate. Memory, theorists suggested, is the "Soul's Belly or Storehouse, or the Receptacle of the Mind." And commonplaces are food for thought.[18]

Trading gastronomic for textual *copia*, Logan similarly believed "the aim of collecting commonplaces is to make available a large library in a small volume" and to maintain "a copious and well-stocked portable library" in her mind. Since the classical period, memory has been imagined as "a ready library in miniature," where "some carry with them whole Libraries in their Memory."[19] Describing mental places as pages in a book, Logan ac-cordingly explains: "The mind, after turning over the nearest leaves . . . in the Book of the Past—Oh how she flies to the Ages long gone by! how she lives in the Present to contemplate what remains of them." She follows John Locke's popular notion that Memory "is as it were the Storehouse of our Ideas," confessing, "Perhaps to a fault, I love to ponder upon the things that are not, or give them a new existence in the storehouse of memory."[20] The upstairs library was thus a fitting storehouse for Logan's written memories.

As memory places, the dining room and library at Stenton represent the reciprocal relationship between commonplacing (reposition) and handwrit-ing (deposition).[21] Whereas reposition entailed committing perceptions to memory, deposition involved translating those memories into writing, for "discharging things committed to memory, is not unlike expunging writing out of Table-Books," according to John Willis. Just as memory repeats our sensory impressions, so writing repeats or copies these sensations on paper. As reciprocal processes, the penman John Jenkins suggests, memory and writing both require that "the mind should be wholly undisturbed, and thus free to attend critically to the copy, intent to imitate it." The "faithfullest Guardian of Memorandums," manuscripts were thought to copy and pre-serve memories in the order in which they were originally formed. Under-stood as the craft of penmanship rather than the composition of ideas, "writing" was the art of "copying" during the eighteenth century.[22] Hand-written characters, therefore, were imagined as rhetorical topoi that could be memorized, arranged, and elegantly displayed: "For the places are very much like wax tablets or papyrus, the images like the letters, the arrange-ment and disposition of the images are like the script, and the oral delivery is like the reading."[23] Since penmanship was likened to arranging and im-pressing memory images (alphabetic characters) onto places (writing tablets), it required the same standards for imitation as commonplacing.

Organized with an index and table of contents for quick retrieval, the manuscript commonplace book was a repository of memory images as well as a collection of alphabetic figures.[24] "All by the help of twenty four letters," script retained memories "by various forming and combining of which, and by the transposing and moving of them to and fro, all words, utterable or imaginable, may be framed." Jenkins promoted a method of penmanship in *The Art of Writing* (1791), which innovatively taught the popular round hand as a system of six principal strokes (direct *l*, inverted *l*, curved *l*, *j*, *o*, / or stem) that are skillfully combined, arranged, and connected. Rather than learn a cohesive system of script by imitating individual characters, writers would memorize and join these basic strokes into readable letters: "The component parts of each letter being placed separately, not only for the help of the memory," writes Jenkins, "but that the mind may be impressed with clear and distinct ideas of the letters, which is absolutely necessary in order soon to write an easy and legible hand."[25] Script required memorizing basic forms and then combining and arranging those images into alphabetic characters.

Mnemonic theorists, faculty psychologists, and writing masters through the eighteenth century agreed that penmanship was integral to memory.[26] In a reciprocal relationship, memory (the mental accumulation of images) and handwriting (the material manifestation of thought) were interdependent. "Memory may be both susceptible and tenacious, and the understanding greatly improved, by writing," explains the essayist James Beattie. "Thus attention is fixed; judgment is exercised; clear ideas are conveyed to the understanding; and the Memory is prepared for receiving a deep impression." Such an impression on the mind, like inked characters on paper, would have "the distinctness and durability of print." "What is written is permanent, and may be reviewed at leisure," Beattie continues. In other words, memory is an accessible, legible text that fixes impressions for later perusal. A manuscript, in turn, assists memory by "the vivacity of the sensation it conveys to the eye, as well as by the distinct ideas it imparts to the understanding." A visual catalyst, a fine and legible script, it was thought, imprints images on the mind, making them "more legible, and . . . not so soon defac'd."[27] A mnemonic image for memory itself, script both stimulates and preserves associations. Handwriting's indelible imprint thus translates the classical image of Mnemosyne's block of wax into a more tangible medium.

Rather than treat writing as a natural antecedent to memory, faculty psychologists conversely saw script as a necessary addendum to mnemonics. Locke, like Beattie, characterized the memory as "very tenacious." But emphasizing the "constant decay of all our Ideas, even of those which are struck deepest, and in the Mind the most retentive," he prescribed writing as the antidote to forgetfulness. As "deposition," writing not only preserves ideas for reperusal, Locke contended, but also provides a "repeated Exercise of the Senses, or Reflection on those kinds of Objects, which at first occasioned them." Otherwise, "the Print wears out, and at last there remains nothing to be seen." Like the animal spirits repeatedly coursing through the nerves' passages to the mind's memory places, transcription revisits the original sensations that produced them. Fearing that memory will leave "no more footsteps or remaining Characters of themselves . . . as if they had never been there," and comparing amnesia to faded print, Locke suggested impressing characters in durable ink. Similarly, René Descartes proposed writing as the panacea to an often unstable memory, as "we trace on paper whatever ought to be preserved, employing the most abbreviated symbols."[28] Because the memory is unstable, he argued, writing was invented, to keep previous thoughts from vanishing, on the one hand, and from distracting us from new ideas, on the other. Tracing memories on paper, handwriting transparently reflects thought. Script creates continuous, visual images much like the chain of associations traced by the memory.

Although their main concern was teaching a variety of legible scripts, eighteenth-century writing masters also included advice for memory improvement in their published copybooks. George Fisher, for example, indulged in a three-page reverie on Memory, the mother of the Muses, in *The American Instructor* (1753): the Muses, he says, "were called the Daughters of Jupiter and Mnemosyne, to shew that Learning cannot be had without the Intellect and Memory." In other words, "God is the Author of Learning, and Memory the Mother and Nurse thereof." In some inexplicable marriage of God and Memory, "Learning" is born and sustained by the milk of Memory. Tracing the maternal genealogy of memory back to Mnemosyne, Fisher gendered memory not only as feminine but also as an especially female form of knowledge. Like Fisher, the writing masters George Bickham, John Jenkins, and William Massey reiterated the connection of penmanship, knowledge, and memory. In *The Universal Penman* (1743), for instance, Bickham claims that "the Memory of past Things is preserved, and the Foreknowledge of some Things to come is Revealed" through writing. Jenkins likewise asserts in *The Art of Writing* (1799) that script will "assist [writers] in properly arranging their own ideas;—strengthen their memories and improve their minds," and William Massey characterizes penmanship as a historical register in *The Origin and Progress of Letters* (1763):

Writing, the muses register,
Time's doctrine downwards do's convey,
. . . .
The memory's chief storehouse do's assist her.[29]

Arranging ideas, registering history, and storing memory, writing makes the art of commonplacing possible. The material counterpart to memory's storehouse in the mind, handwriting embodies the past and ensures future knowledge.

Animate memory—from Mnemosyne's gift of impressionable wax to its visible manifestation through writing—underscores the importance of the body to mnemonics and penmanship. Just as the art of memory depended on the susceptible, impressionable (female) body, as chapter 1 illustrates, so its expression through handwriting is written from and through the body. Crafted by moving, breathing persons, script then and now is a type of living writing (see figure 2.4). Unlike the static nature of printed texts arrested by typeface, script is immediate, unmediated, and dynamic, "where the bold Figures seem to live." Also called "cursive" or the "joining hand," script (self-reflexively called a "hand" when ascribed to an individual writer) implies a literal extension and movement of the mind and body onto paper. As if part of the autonomic nervous system, script directly translates physical sensation from the nerves to the extremities, the extremities to the pen, and through the pen to the paper. "For as the pen must follow the mind of a writer," postulates one eighteenth-century writing master, "a just idea of the best formed characters ought to be well impressed on the mind, that they may be instantly ready to drop from the pen when called for." Such an involuntary impulse, modern critics agree, awakens the graphic qualities of script: "the moment the pen touches the paper and leaves even a slight trace of ink, the paper becomes a space, and the boundaries of the area are awakened and respond across the space to the touch of ink."[30] The hand thus animates and displays the memories otherwise hidden in the mind. As Logan similarly explains: "I covet the faculty of writing quick. . . . Sarah fills a page directly, and glances along the lines right speedily, whilst I with a snails pace . . . relate the dull and vapid subjects which present themselves to my dull mind."[31] Associating her hand and mind, Logan concludes that script—as written memory—requires both tactile agility and mental swiftness.

As rhetoricians of the period emphasized, writing is a progressive manifestation of thought. It is a multilayered "repository" that explicitly depends on the human body for its visible translation into readable text: script is the repository of the body, the body of the mind, the mind of the soul, the soul of the memory, the memory of the sensations, the sensations of the nervous system, and so on. As one writing master posits: "There is a natural and easy movement of the fingers and pen, necessary to draw the letter with freedom." The "position of the body is of considerable consequence," he explains, "in order to write with facility and grace."[32] These

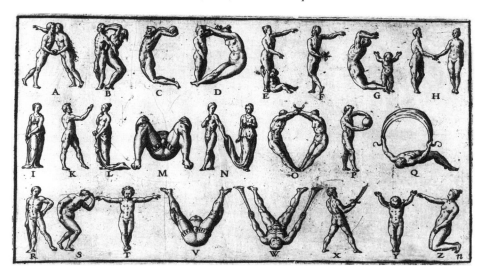

2.4. As Theodore DeBry's popular engraving *Alphabeta et charactères* shows, letters can be made by "joining" various combinations of the human form. Courtesy Edward E. Ayer Collection, The Newberry Library, Chicago.

views anticipate those of the theorist Elaine Scarry, who declares that a handmade object is a projection of the human body that contains "within its interior a material record of the nature of human sentience" out of which is made.[33]

Appreciating the value of pen, ink, and paper, Logan also viewed manuscripts as a material record of both her thoughts and feelings: "I sometime write I believe, to give vent to my feelings, to preserve an incident an expression of a thought from immediate oblivion—so transitory are things below." A more permanent form of memory, writing is a natural, physical outlet for emotions. Since the emotions, or "affections," were moved by the same animal spirits that controlled memory, and since those spirits (along with the natural and vital spirits) made up the soul, handwriting captured the movements of the soul. "If it is ever that I feel inclined to envy any thing it is the happy talent of describing naturally and vividly emotions of the Soul," writes Logan.[34] Since the classical period, when Plato noticed that "the conjunction of memory with sensations, together with the feelings consequent upon memory and sensation, may be said as it were to write words in our souls,"[35] mnemonic theorists have imagined memory as a kind of "inner writing," or "writing in the soul," which can be transcribed on paper.

The material embodiment of life on the page, the "joining hand" involved a synesthetic experience of all the senses.[36] Letters (anatomized by writing masters into the head, hairline, jaw, ears, neck, shoulders, arms, and feet) visually imitate the human form, and their formation likewise encompasses the movements of the entire body. Script, writing masters contended, envelops the senses and manifests thought:

> Tell me what genius did the art invent,
> The lively image of a voice to paint?
> Who first the secret how to colour Sound,
>
> . . . .
>
> With bodies how to cloath ideas taught,
> And how to draw the picture of a thought?
> Who taught the hand to speak, the eye to hear?[37]

Though many penmen underscored handwriting's legibility by noting its visual beauty, all agreed that script requires an accumulation and amalgamation of all the senses.[38] Painted voices, listening eyes, speaking hands, and colored sound characterized the command of an elegant script.

Blending the senses, handwriting not only thoroughly engaged the body but also reversed its boundaries, making "what is originally interior and private into something exterior and sharable."[39] An accumulation of sensations, script manifested the movements of the nervous system that pulsed just beneath the skin. By the eighteenth century nerves were held to be solely responsible for sensory impressions and consequently for knowledge, memory, and manuscripts. The material basis for consciousness, the nervous system responded to signals from outside and inside the human body. The same animal spirits that moved ideas into the memory and understanding, therefore, were likewise responsible for the memory's translation into script. The sympathetic nerves, according to the seventeenth-century neurologist Thomas Willis, caused involuntary commerce between "Actions and Passions almost of all the Parts of the whole Body."[40] Since women's nervous systems were more susceptible to sensation than men's, and since script embodied all the senses, a woman's handwriting was an art that both received and engraved impressions.[41] As writing masters further explained, the "joining hand" allowed a woman to "communicate her Mind without Speaking"—"and all by the Contrivance of twenty four Letters." A physical "Image of the Voice," manuscripts made visible "each private purpose, and intent."[42]

The depiction of script as the complete embodiment of memory implicates the material scene of writing itself. Because memory is a synesthetic conflation of impressions, and because those impressions are transmitted through the artifacts of penmanship, I re-create in what follows the ergonomics of handwriting in the early Republic. In order to amplify the corporeal and mnemonic qualities of writing, I organize the remainder of the chapter like a commonplace book under the respective "heads" of "The Escritoire," "Paper Memories," "The Animate Quill," "Visible Ink," and "Legible Hands." Mimicking the symmetrical shape of the memory places in the Georgian house, the desk's hidden drawers, locked doors, and tiny pigeonholes are material repositories for manuscripts. The manuscript, in turn, serves as a depository of recorded memories. As such, paper represents the modern analogue to Mnemosyne's block of wax. An extension of the hand, the quill translates the memory's imaginary wax impressions to the paper's surface. The ink's complex chemical composition of gall nuts, gum arabic, and tannic acid makes penned impressions readable, for as the poet Samuel Rogers says, memory's "pencil dipt in Nature's living hues, / . . . trace[s] its airy precincts in the soul."[43] As inner or "soul writing" script, finally, makes memories legible. In recuperating these scriptive artifacts, I hope to evoke the reader's imagination and appreciation of handwriting practices from which we are so far removed; as Lord Kames suggests, "Real objects make strong impression, and are faithfully remembered: ideas, on the contrary, however entertaining at the time, are apt to escape a subsequent recollection."[44]

THE ESCRITOIRE

"I am seated on my own easy chair beside my desk with a stool before me covered by a white square board instead of a table, which serves me as such," writes Logan. The makeshift desk stands "between the Stove and my little maple desk in the dining room, my favourite seat, where I have Books, work basket, and Pens and Ink at hand."[45] *Beside, before,* and *between* her writing desk (where she stores her manuscripts) and the little deal board (at which she actually writes), Logan literally and figuratively creates the domestic "sphere" of the female writer. Because penmanship manuals fostered an idealized representation of the "Writing Woman," they necessarily offered general, ergonomic guidelines, which taught writing as a corporeal discipline, controlling everything from posture and hand movements to facial expression. Ideological rather than practical in nature, the rules do not characterize Logan's writing space at Stenton. Like movable and adaptable commonplaces that can be reworked in new rhetorical contexts, her writing furniture was similarly versatile, adjusted for her own comfort and convenience. Logan, therefore, challenged penmanship's rigid regime by creating a movable feast. More significantly, she confounded the desk's usual association with deposition; a storage rather than writing space, the desk was a repository for memory. Logan's writing furniture thus suggests the connection among a woman's body, her memory, and the material world.

As part of a series of images accompanying the entry "Art d'Écrire" in Denis Diderot and Jean le Rond d'Alembert's *Encylopédie,* the image in figure 2.5 noticeably depicts the metonymic connections between the female body and her writing furniture.[46] Impeccably dressed, the woman sits formally at her writing table. Perfectly aligned with the desk and its accompanying chairs, she follows the inflexible seating directions common to eighteenth-century penmanship manuals:[47]

> I. Let the Height of the Flat of your Desk, whereon you lay your Book or Paper, be about two Foot three Quarters from the Ground; the Height of your Seat one Foot three Quarters; let your Seat's Edge be distanc'd from the Edge of the Desk (which comes next to your Body) half a Foot.
> II. Let the Room for your Knees and Legs to come under your Desk, be one Foot.
> III. Lay your Book or Paper, on which you write, streight before you.
> IV. Let the Elbow of your right Arm be distanc'd from your Side about four Inches.
> V. Let your Body be nearly upright, and right against your Book or Paper; and if you suffer any Part of it to touch the Edge of your Desk, which it is best to avoid if you can, let it be but slightly.
> VI. Let the Weight of your Body rest on your Seat and your left Arm; and hold your Paper or Book fast down, on which you write, with the Thumb and four Fingers of your left Hand.[48]

The writer modestly averts her eyes from the viewer, looking downward as her hand moves the quill across the paper. A common painterly symbol of femininity in the eighteenth century, her soft, white arms mirror the smooth whiteness of her face and chest, which together reflect the paper's shape and texture.[49] The slope of her shoulders and the flowing curves of her gown imitate the cabriole legs of the writing table and the two accompanying Queen Anne–style armchairs in the picture's background. Her headdress and the bonnet-top crest rail on the chairs' backs seem almost identical ornaments.

Looking at the picture from left to right, one notices that the woman is the first figure in a metonymic series of three identical chairs. Her body not only perfectly simulates the chair's design but also appears to substitute for the concealed chair. Like the chair, the writing table imitates and anticipates the writer's feminine form. Following the popular S curve of the Queen

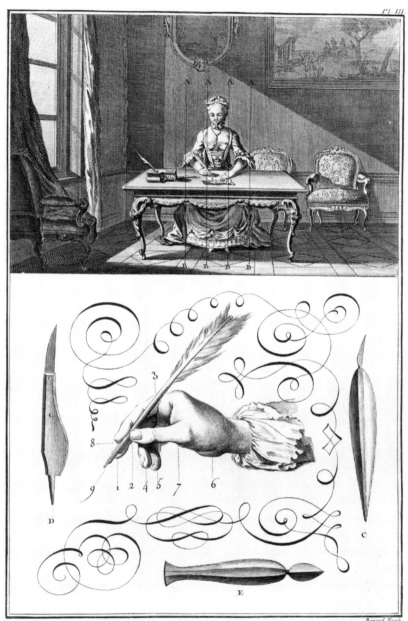

2.5. Charles Paillasson, *L'art d'écrire* (s.l, s.n., 1760), plate 3. Courtesy, The Winterthur Library: Printed Book and Periodical Collection.

Anne style, which the English painter William Hogarth called "the line of beauty," the table displays human characteristics: its "carcass" is composed of "feet," "legs," "knees," and "hips," which ideally form a continuous curve from top to bottom.[50] Just as her dress's folds maintain the table's outline, so the idealized writer forms a continuous curve from head to toe, from hand to paper. "Leaning against the table, sitting awry, and holding the pen awkwardly," writing masters admonished, are ungraceful habits that not only jeopardize a woman's health but also "when once acquired, [are] with great difficulty removed. Neatness and elegance should likewise characterize whatever is the offspring of female industry." The unbroken movement and contours of the furniture and the writer's body finally extend to the script itself. Following the vertical AB axis superimposed from the woman's head to her feet, the viewer notices that the writer's posture and the slant of the script before her are perfectly aligned: "Even at Head and Feet keep Letters all," writes one writing master:

> To have your Letters all the one Way inclin'd.
> Grace every Letter with perfect, full and small,
> And keep a due Proportion in them all.[51]

But unlike the flowing slant that characterized the italic hand, the woman's vertical letters, like her body, are poised and static.

Although the image has vertical continuity, its horizontal axis cuts the picture in half at the woman's waist. Drawing the viewer's eyes above the writing table, the desktop's horizontal line emphasizes her face, chest, and paper, sublimating her lower body. It effectively divides the body into "appropriate" spheres, highlighting a woman's countenance while disciplining her body into a comely posture. The writing table, Gerald Ward suggests, "divides the world in a planar fashion: it creates spheres above board (all that is moral and good) and below the table (all the immoral and bad). Faces, arms, chests, and breasts are above the table; buttocks, genitals, legs, and feet are below. Most sounds made above the table are socially correct; many sounds made below the table are not."[52] Forwarding the etiquette propounded by professional penmen, such a design authorized a woman's ability to pen manuscripts at a time when writing was still considered a masculine pursuit.

Originally a portable box that could be placed on a table or simply arranged on her lap, the writing desk formerly drew attention to a woman's thighs. In other words, it was a material reminder of the dangerous "exhibition" of female handwriting. As Joseph Addison satirically admonishes in

Spectator no. 16: "I have a whole Bundle of Letters in Womens Hands that are full of Blots and Calumnies, insomuch that when I see the Name *Celia, Phillis, Pastora,* or the like, at the Bottom of the Scrawl, I conclude on course that it brings some Account of a *fallen Virgin,* a *faithless Wife,* or an *amorous Widow.*"[53] By likening penmanship errors to sexual transgressions, Addison presents writing as action that belies feminine passivity.

But the gradual displacement of the lap desk by the escritoire and other free-standing structures by the eighteenth century downplayed the female body (and all its libidinous associations) by drawing attention toward the polished tabletop. The tabletop, in turn, reflected the woman's face and the text before her. The paper's reflection of her countenance might emphasize femininity's association with the passive, blank page—the natural recipient for the masculine pen's ink. But it also authorized women's writing, for "all shou'd be fair that Beauteous Woman frames." Limited to the smaller, diminutive italic or round hands, women could become "blushing Scriblers" instead of lascivious virgins, wives, or widows. Their "pretty Lines and Charms" thus appeased the threat of their manuscript productions. If that fairness, according to the physiognomy of script, reflected an unblemished soul as well as the body's sublimated desires, women could transfer to penmanship their facility for "all that's curious, innocent, and fine!"[54]

Given the strictures against female writing on the one hand and the physiognomic nature of penmanship on the other, writing masters encouraged women to consider their countenance in the formation of script.[55] More than good posture, facial composure was essential to legibility. Writing "should not be too long applied to at a time; since the body, and even the countenance, may thus get a certain tendency to one attitude," writes one colonial writing master. "A proper manner of holding the pen, or pencil, or needle, with an easy but graceful attitude of the person, and an agreeable moderate attention of the countenance, should first be taught." Women "are distinguished by their handwriting as well as by their faces," theorizes another, "for it is very seldom that the shape of their letters agree any more than the shape of their bodies." Offering alphabetic instructions that ensured women's physiognomic virtue in *Instructions for Young Women* (1754), Madame Johnson guided the female pupil from the formation of individual letters to the transcription of single phrases in their copybooks: "*A*ffectation ruins the fairest Face"; "*B*eauties very seldom hear the Truth"; "*H*umility adds Charms to Beauty"; "*M*odesty charms more than Beauty;" "*T*ruth needs no Disguise or Ornament"; and "*V*anity makes Beauty contemptible." Such an emphasis on the face underscored the mnemonic value of handwriting, for as the physiognomist John Caspar Lavater argued, "the motions, habits, and inclinations" of the mind were "clearly and distinctly written in characters so visible and manifest" on the face.[56] Formed in part by a pleasant countenance, script, then, transformed memory's "inner writing" into legible signs.[57]

Although Logan did not write at a conventional writing desk and ignored the strict bodily comportment promoted by writing manuals, she considered "the little desk that contains my papers" a literal repository of memory.[58] Probably a desk-on-frame secretary, a kneehole desk, or perhaps even a desk-and-bookcase in typical Queen Anne or Chippendale fashion, Logan's desk represents the hidden memory places in her mind.[59] Much like the Georgian house plan, the desk's design would have emphasized memory's private, domestic recesses.[60] One can easily imagine, for instance, the removable wooden box inside the hinged, slant top, which would occupy the entire width and much of the depth of the desk's interior. Like Stenton's geometric facade, as chapter 1 illustrates, the box would have a "prospect door" balanced on either side by a two-tiered arrangement of symmetrical doors, drawers, or pigeonholes. A single, hinged portal fashioned with a keyhole, the prospect door promised a hidden alcove for private or secret documents, as figure 2.6 illustrates. Common to kneehole desks, the door often had a second lock on its other side leading to additional hiding spaces. Separated by thin columns and crowned by decorative fascia resembling an entablature, the desk's pigeonholes framed the prospect door. As practical storage spaces, pigeonholes were also apt metaphors for memory reposition: "You will have as it were a well organized set of pigeonholes, from which you may extract what you want," according to one early modern theorist. All one needed to do was "knock at their doors, so to speak, in order to see what can be drawn out from them."[61] As a repository, a house, a desk, a drawer, or even a pigeonhole could endlessly store and restore memories.

Though once signifying both the writing closet and the writing furniture at which one wrote, the "escritoire" was also a memory palace in miniature. With neither a room of her own nor a proper writing desk for composing manuscripts, Logan transformed the dining room and library into writing closets for solitary, though frequently interrupted, moments of writing. She challenged the anthropomorphic rules of writing based on an idealized female body and avoided the hazardous postures of being corseted behind a desk, whereby the "freedom of respiration or breathing, and of the circulation of the blood, are interrupted, and the health and life hazarded."[62] Instead, she wrote comfortably in her ungirdled "home costume."

2.6. This Pennsylvania walnut desk (c. 1765–90) is similar to the one in figure 2.1. The symmetrically arranged drawers and pigeonholes around the central prospect door not only resemble Stenton's Georgian exterior but also serve as mnemonic metaphors for interior places in the mind. Courtesy, Winterthur Museum.

Periodically opening her little maple desk, she read the old manuscripts, which touched "many a chord that has long slept in silence."[63]

PAPER MEMORIES

Opening a new commonplace book or diary was a ceremonious event for Logan. Staring at the pristine sheets, she hesitates before reaching for her quill: "I wish the ceremony of opening the new book was over, and I had fairly gotten over my reluctance of spoiling its purity with ugly scrawls." "Yesterday afternoon," she writes, "Dickinson brought me home an Album splendidly bound in Morroco Leather of very fine paper, handsomely ruled, in Quarto size, Diary—too pretty by far to be spoiled and be made free with by my scrawl for which this Book at present seems quite good enough—Besides it was my dear Dr. Logan's book." Aware of the permanence of putting pen and ink to paper on the one hand, and nostalgic about writing in her deceased husband's copybook on the other, Logan envisions the paper as a blank slate that would receive her impressions. Picking up her quill, she accordingly notes: "I want to fill this vacancy."[64]

Connecting Locke's well-known concept of the tabula rasa to the synesthetic art of memory, moreover, Logan recognized the dangers of a mind going blank and appreciated the tactile possibilities of paper to capture fleeting impressions: "I might as well avail myself of this old Blank Book to write in even if only continued for the present; for my memory of yesterday grows bad. They are easily obliterated whilst the events of my childhood . . . [are] vividly recollected." Conversely, other memories were best left to oblivion: "The rest of this day must remain in this Book a Blank," writes Logan. "For some things occured which I would wish it were possible to obliterate for ever from my memory. And I hope they are not recorded any where."[65] Losing her short-term memory as she aged, Logan delighted in the pleasant associations still so vivid in her mind and blotted out unpleasant recollections. By selectively committing memories to paper, she carefully framed how she would have the past remembered.

In order to relive and preserve these associations, Logan suggested daily writing as the best remedy for dementia: "Call in memory to your aid, let her paint anew the scenes which have delighted you . . . and then try to perpetuate the impression by committing something of it to writing."[66] Her description of memory repeats early mnemonic theorists almost verbatim: "This *laying up* of our *Ideas* in the Repository of the Memory," explains Locke, "signifies no more but this, that the Mind has a Power, in many cases, to revive Perceptions, which it has once had . . . [and] as it were paint them anew on it self."[67] Memory is not simply a representation of perception; it is the facility to recuperate original experience, as Lord Kames later illustrates: "Objects once perceived may be recalled to the mind by the power of memory. . . . having seen yesterday a spreading oak growing on the brink of the river, I endeavor to recall these objects to my mind. . . . I transport myself to the place where I saw the tree and river. . . . And in this recollection, I am not conscious of a picture or representative image, more than in the original survey: the perception is of the tree and river themselves, at first."[68] More than the externalization of ideas, memory is a way to awaken the senses and recapture original experience. Since memory depended on "feeling," (as both physical sensation and emotional impression), and since feeling was understood as "nothing but the impulse, Motion, or Action of Bodies, gently or violently impressing the Extremities or Sides of the Nerves," according to the neurologist George Cheyne, the nervous system could revive the sensations, emotions, and impressions that precede and form memory.[69]

The notion of translating sensations into memory and memory into writing has both classical and early modern precedents, which persisted through the eighteenth century. The ancients described memory as the permanent impress of a stylus on a wax tablet or of a signet ring on a wax seal. A gift from Mnemosyne, wax is the viscous stuff of memory, according to Plato: "Whatever is so imprinted we remember and know so long as the image remains; whatever is rubbed out or has not succeeded in leaving an impression we have forgotten and do not know."[70] The perceptions and sensations are not ephemeral but rather corporeal movements, according to Plato; they assume and then stamp a palpable shape on the susceptible wax. The point of a stylus or the carved insignia on a ring transferred physical sensations (via the extremity of the hands) into mental impressions. And the durability of those impressions determined the fine line(s) between remembrance and forgetfulness. An unforeseen prelude to modern penmanship, memory was what the ancients called "inner writing" or "writing in the soul."

Early modern philosophers imagined this soul writing as a tabula rasa, switching metaphors from wax to paper. Underscoring memory's corporeal nature, theorists located its origin in the nervous system, the primary sensory receptor. "Perception," concludes Locke, "is only when the mind receives the impression, transmitted by the conduits of the nerves until it reached the blank sheet." Figuring memory's internal processes as the translation of nerve impulses into readable characters, Locke devised a new method of teaching writing, which parallels his mnemonic imagery: "Get a Plate graved, with the Characters of such an Hand as you like best . . . [and] let several Sheets of good Writing-Paper be printed off with Red Ink . . . go over with a good Pen fill'd with Black Ink, which quickly bring his Hand to the formation of those Characters, being at first shewed where to begin, and how to form every Letter."[71] Placing the quill tip into the grooved figures for practice, a beginning writer would merely retrace the alphabetic forms until they were memorized and written independently of the template. Handwritten memory, therefore, required repeated impressions.

By the eighteenth century such templates for imitation were compiled in copybooks and widely published: "Last rose the Engraver's imitating Skill,— / That trac'd them off, and multiply'd at will."[72] The mass reproduction of sample scripts through copperplate engravings thus linked the persistent notion of memory as a "copy" of sensations with both handwritten manuscripts and the printed page. Created by special tools that deeply carved an image into metal, a copperplate engraving was first rubbed with ink. Wet paper was then placed on it and pushed between two heavy rollers, which impressed the image onto the paper. Finally, the paper was hung up to dry. Sometimes tracing over the engraving with a pencil or dry pen before setting ink to paper, the unskilled writer unwittingly materialized her mind's "blank sheet." Like memory, handwriting by this method was a doubled impression.

The act of writing enacts the reciprocal functions of memory's "inner writing" as reposition and deposition: physical sensations are internalized as mental impressions that form memory images; moved by the animal spirits, these images are stimulated and revived by the nervous system; the nervous system carries the revived impressions to the extremities of the fingers; the fingers externalize the memory images as written characters. The end of a physical process that ensures lasting memory, writing offers a type of permanence, remarks Marius D'Assigny, for "if the Characters . . . be fairly written and remarkable to the Eye and Fancy; for as they give a deeper Impression into the mind, they become more legible, and are not so soon defac'd."[73] Just as a writer accomplished a legible hand through repeated exercise, so memory's legibility is improved, as Locke suggests, by reflection.

Similarly imagining a kind of inner writing that controls memory through the nervous system, Descartes uncharacteristically merged the body and mind in what he called "corporeal memory."[74] He imagined memory not only as paper but more specifically as the folds in the paper's surface. The brain's vestiges move the soul in redundant patterns, he writes, "thus causing it to remember something; in altogether the same way that the folds in a piece of paper or linen cause them to be more readily folded the way they were folded earlier than if they never had been folded thus."[75] These habitual folds, much like the grooved template in Locke's writing method, prompt repetition—a key exercise for an agile memory. A persistent metaphor for memory, folded paper could be marked, indexed, and collected, as Francis Bacon had asserted, "to help us shake out the folds of the intellect within us, and to draw forth the knowledge stored therein."[76] Such embedded folds, like the creases in the brain's surface, illustrate memory's complex system of movement and storage. Thomas Willis explains, "In what form [the animal spirits] unfold themselves . . . produce the acts of the Memory."[77] The margins of a piece of paper, like the invaginated folds in cloth, provide the somatic space necessary for reviving past moments.

Like the empirical theories of perception that would dominate the eighteenth and early nineteenth centuries, Descartes's "corporeal memory" depended on the autonomic nervous system. According to his theory, blood from the heart flows into the brain, dividing into the brain's convolutions through nerve fibers, arteries, and veins. Among these convolutions, blood particles produce the animal spirits. Such spirits gather in the pineal gland, disperse throughout the brain, and radiate into all the organs, limbs, and muscles of the body. Like the ancients' block of wax, the pineal gland was believed to be soft and malleable. Descartes explains:

> When the soul wants to remember something, the will causes the gland . . . to thrust the spirits toward different parts of the brain, until they come across that part where it finds the traces left there by the object it wants to remember. . . . The pores of the brain, by which the spirits have formerly followed their course because of the presence of this object . . . [are] opened once more in the same way. . . . Thus the spirits, coming in contact with these pores, enter into them more easily than into the others, by which means they excite a particular movement in the gland, which represents the same objects to the soul and causes it to know that this is what it wanted to remember.[78]

Like the successive folds in a piece of paper, the brain's porous fabric changes its shape to accommodate the traces of sensory impressions and memory images once stored there. Like a writer tracing over an engraved template until the fingers remember the shapes, the mind recalls memories through the porous pathway of spirits circulating from the pineal gland throughout the brain. Because the original sensations leave traces in the pores' passages, they can be easily reopened and closed—like pleats in a re-peatedly folded fabric—by the animal spirits.[79]

This textual image for memory flourishes in the context of paper pro-duction in the early modern period. Made from macerated cotton and linen rags since the fifteenth century, paper was a textile that gradually unfolded its meaning. As the *Boston Newsletter* of 1769 explains:

> Rags are beauties, which concealed lie,
> But when in paper how it charms the eye:
> . . . .
> By pen and press such knowledge is displayed,
> As wouldn't exist, if paper was not made.

Hidden in the rags' folds, knowledge, beauty, and memory become visible on the paper's surface. Using the same rhetoric as mnemonics, the poem suggests that the transformation of rags into paper resembles the transmis-sion of memory to written forms. Rags were first sorted by quality: pure, white linens made the finest paper; colored linens, canvas, old rope, and woolens created lesser-quality sheets. Once sorted, the rags were washed and left in a damp heap to rot for several days. The "sweated" rags were cut into small pieces, placed in a wooden mortar, and pounded to a pulp. Transferred to a vat, the pulp was next diluted with tepid water.[80]

The papermaker would then take one of two identical molds (wire sieves mounted on wooden frames) and a deckle (a removable wooden rim creating a sieve and preventing the paper stock from overflowing the mold's borders) and dip them into the vat. Lifting the mold out of the stock, the artisan would gently shake the fibers along the plaited wires until it formed a mesh. With the pulp evenly distributed across the frame, the maker lifted the deckle, turning the mold over and depositing the "paper" onto a piece of felt. Alternating layers of felt and paper ("post") were then relieved of any remaining water by the standing press. Strong enough to be separated from the felts, the paper, called *waterleaf,* was pressed again and hung to dry. The waterleaf was dipped in "size" (a solution of starch or hot gelatin) to reduce ink absorbency. The sized paper, finally, was pressed, dried, and pressed again.

Until the mid-eighteenth century paper was made in "laid" rather than "woven" patterns. That is, molds were made of parallel crossbars (or wire "ribs") and widely spaced "chain" wires overlying them. This rectangular grid of chains and wires crossing at right angles left small indentations in the paper. In addition, "watermarks"—pictures or letters fashioned in wire and sewn with knots of fine wire to the mold—made distinctive impressions on the paper's surface. Much like the wax impressions in Plato's story or the starched folds in Descartes's materialist theory of memory, the process of papermaking followed the same techniques of absorption and impression. Each sheet (a memory place) required a frame (a signet ring or paper mold), a viscous pulp pressed into shape (wax or macerated rags), and a distinguishing wire or mark (memory image). As paper was made sheet by sheet, the repetitive process and the mingling of fibers among the mazy course of plaited wires thus resemble the habitual course of fluid spirits running through pores leading to and from the pineal gland in Descartes's theory of memory.

Properly prepared to receive pen and ink, paper was an invaluable proxy for memory; according to Kant, a "pocket notebook" will "substitute for the most extensive and reliable memory, and can compensate for the lack of it."[81] Writing not only preserved memory but also completed it, filling in forgetful gaps with textual *copia.* Memory, therefore, was understood as a repository that both stores and restores original perceptions—as if by some perpetual tabula rasa. As Logan suggests, thick quartos "made of the best Paper, Rule and Bound" made memory possible. Repeating the impressions left by the papermaker's hand and instruments, paper, like memory, is like living life over again.

THE ANIMATE QUILL

"Oh for a good Pen," wishes Logan, "for mine are so rascally bad that they make me deface my book sadly."[82] Conveying what Descartes called corporeal memories from her mind to the blank page, the "good pen" facilitated the internal movements of the animal spirits from the heart to the fingers. The pen, as Elizabeth Fergusson explains in her 1775 poem "Lines to a Gentleman Whom Made Laura a Good Pen," mimics the nervous system in its mechanistic transmission of spirits:

> How can we term a feather light
> And trifling as air,
> When it conveys such high delight
> . . . .
> Fashions the feather for the heart
> And finely points the quill?[83]

Communicating heartbeats to paper, pens were typically made from a bird's flight feathers (see figure 2.7). The strength and grace of the bird, as one copyist explains in onomatopoetic detail, determined the graceful movement of the quill in a writer's hand:

> To write very fair, your pen let be new,
> Dish, dash, long-taile flie; false writing eschew;
> Neatly and cleanly your hand for to frame,
> Strong stalked pen use, best of a raven;
> And comely to write, and give a good grace.[84]

With such metaphoric potential for gliding movements, a quill ostensibly comes to life in the writer's hand, continuing the reciprocal rise and fall of a bird's flight: "Use a swift flying motion of your hand, / Sweet strokes, choice Letters, you may thus command." The upward and downward strokes of script thus proportionately move the fingers, hand, and arm in vertical and horizontal strokes across a slanted page. A kinetic art, handwriting transferred the physical sensations of bodily position, presence, and movement stimulated by sensory nerve endings to the "flying motion" and "light Pulse" of the pen.[85]

Like a bird's wings, the pen and the hand together created synchronized movements.[86] As complementary writing instruments, they "performed with but one Tool and at one Motion." Such a motion was valued not only for its practicality but also for its "Freedom and Beauty." A mechanical art, penmanship required the "natural and easy movement of the fingers and pen, necessary to draw the letter with freedom."[87] Emphasizing the singu-

2.7. Quill and inkstand at Stenton. Photograph by author.

lar, natural, and easy movement in script, writing masters thus described the quill as a physical extension of the human hand. How one cut and held her quill, therefore, largely determined the rhythm and beauty of the corresponding script. Fisher explains the process of pen cutting in *The American Instructor:*

> After you have Scraped the Quill as above, cut the Quill at the End, half through, on the back; and then turning up the Belly, cut the other half. . . . Then enter the Pen-knife a little in the back Notch, . . . holding your hand pretty hard on the Back of the Quill, as high as you intend the Slit. . . . Then by several Cuts of Side, bring the Quill into equal Shape, or Form, on Sides, and having brought it to a fine Point, place the [knife] at the Extremity of the Nib; and then by other proper Cuts, finish the Pen. . . . Note: That the Breadth of the Nib must be proportioned to the . . . down-right black Strokes of the Letters, in whatever Hand you write, whether Small or Text.[88]

The pen's nib, or mouth, determined the stroke's width. Written with a lighter touch, hair strokes were made by the pen's edge; in contrast, full strokes drawn by a heavier pulse required the nib's flat incline. As the merging point of pen, paper, and ink, the quill's nib is the site of confluence between the interior and exterior, between oral memory and written discourse. As the human hand animated the silent pen, the pen's "mouth" became the nexus of memory, voice, and script.[89]

Despite the obvious importance of quill cutting to fine, legible writing, women were not systematically taught how to cut a pen. As Madame Johnson explains, "As the fair Sex can with Ease procure good Pens, I shall not trouble them with any unnecessary Directions on how to make them."[90] The procurement of pens apparently was not always so easy, as Logan contends, lamenting that she never learned to make her own. Attending Anthony Benezet's school for girls in Philadelphia, she learned the art of penmanship without the corresponding skill of cutting: "These wretched pens—I never could contrive to make an instrument so important to me. I wish Master Benezet (of kind and pious memory) had insisted on my acquiring the art—he made delightful ones himself." As "a Scribe, or Scribler," who "should not be able to make them for herself," Logan depended on family, friends, and even local writing masters to cut pens for her. "I sent some quills to Beckys schoolmaster to ask the favour of making a few pens," she writes; "they looked nice but I cannot make use of them so that I have to cobble together ones myself—and spoil my Book."[91]

Even when Logan found someone to make her pens, there was no guarantee that her quills would not be modified by other writers. "My pens are all rendered almost useless to me," she frequently complains, "by these fine writers clipping them to suit their delicate writing." Adapting her pens to suit their own hands, Logan's domestics compromised her characteristically beautiful script: "I find alterations which do not at all accord with my liking. The Pens have been scribbled with."[92] Since other writers tampered with her pens, the quills no longer fit Logan's hand. Logan thus highlights the symbiotic relationship between the pen and hand as the analogous instruments of memory.

A writer depended on what contemporary phenomenologists call *body memory* to execute the swift, graceful movements of the pen. She first "get[s] a perfect idea of each principal stroke well impressed on the mind" and then "acquire[s] the right motion of the fingers, or pressure of the pen, in order to draw the strokes upon paper." Memory, writing masters asserted, moves from the mind (which stores the letter images) to the hand (which learns the motions for shaping letters) to the pen (which imitates the hand in drawing the strokes). Relying on muscle memory, the hand, penmen explained, no longer required conscious thought. Learning "clear and distinct ideas of the proper position of the fingers, the hand, the arms, and the body," the writer was not "divided between two objects; viz.—holding the pen right—and secondly, the movement of the pen or shaping the letters."[93] An extension of the autonomic nervous system that controlled respiration, hand movements in writing were as natural and involuntary as breathing. A writer could think about what (rather than how) she wrote.

Like rote memorization, a writer's body memory required repetition of the prescribed hand movements until they became automatic. As one writing master dictates, "First . . . get an exact Idea of a Letter, which is done by a frequent and nice Observation of a correct Copy." With an accomplished command of the hand, one can express ideas on paper, "which is attained by constant and careful Practice after good Examples."[94] Such repetition not only guarantees a legible hand but also suggests the value of physical and mental repetition for the memory: "As long as their action is robust and long-lasting, or is reiterated several times," writes Descartes, "that prevents these figures from being readily erased." Ideas consequently "take shape there once again long afterwards, without requiring the presence of the corresponding objects. And in this memory consists."[95] Just as the pineal gland could retrace ideas without the original objects that stimulated them, so the hand, through muscle memory gained by repeated motions—left to right, up and down—could transmit memories as thoughts dropping softly from the pen.[96]

Given the emphasis on the hand's repetitive and automatic motions, published copybooks were filled with directions for properly holding and "exercising" a pen. In *The Art of Writing,* for example, John Jenkins includes an image of a young woman holding a quill in her right hand while securing the paper with her left. Though she learns the moral rigors of writing well by filling her page with such commonplace maxims as "Love God, Obey your Parents, and Improve your Time for Eternity," the writing master circumscribes her picture with a particularly materialist lesson: "If you would win a Pen of Gold learn first of all your Pen to hold." Emphasizing her hand's conduct, he creates a tedious ergonomics of quill holding:

1. Let the pen be held between the balls of the thumb and middle finger, near the corner of the nail of each.
2. Let the fore-finger lie directly on the outward side or back part of the pen.
3. Let the thumb be bent outward, and the end raised about as high as the first joint of the forefinger.
4. Let the third and fourth fingers be naturally bent under, towards

the hollow of the hand, that the middle finger may move free and easy, without crowding upon the third.

5. Let the hand be turned well over to the left that the pen may range against . . . and the nib strike the paper in a square and proper direction with the slope of the letter.

6. Let the paper be placed exactly square with the writing table, before the right shoulder.

7. Let the left arm form a square upon the table, with the two forefingers following the pen within half an inch to keep the paper firm and smooth.

8. Sitting in this position, the body will naturally lean upon the left arm or elbow; . . . the right arm and hand will be at perfect liberty to command the pen with freedom and ease.[97]

Like the directions for sitting at the writing desk, rules for pen holding focused on the body from the waist up: the way the fingers touch the pen, the way the left arm touches the table while the two forefingers gently follow the pen across the page, the way the entire body leans into the left arm to give freedom to the right hand. Set in motion by either an internal mechanism (the nerves) or an external stimulus (the pen), writing primarily involved the tactile sense.

Though writing manuals emphasized the synesthetic qualities of handwriting, they particularly accentuated the sense of touch. "Bear your Pen lightly, keep a steady Hand, / And that's the Way, fair Writing to command," suggests one penman. "With a light touch and steady hand," rehearses another, one can reveal otherwise hidden memory traces: "And then the Letters by soft Touches try; / The Mind will thus th' Ideas fully trace."[98] Fully tracing the mind's impressions, the sense of touch received the position of a master sense. Though a lower-order sense, "the feeling of touch" (as it was called) was considered the "the foundation of all the other sensations; it is the genus of which they are more perfect species."[99] As the antecedent to touch, the nerves extend throughout the body, insinuating themselves "into the Organs of the other Senses." Despite its ubiquitous presence throughout the body, however, the sense of touch was considered particularly acute in the hands and arms, or "the wandering pair." As Thomas Willis later theorized, this neural pair is perfectly synchronized at the nerve's extremities to receive the "private mark of the involuntary function" of touch.[100] The nerves accordingly carry memory images from the medulla (rather than the cerebellum) to what Willis calls the "Common Sensory" of touch. Carrying the mark of memory, then, writing was automatic.

The neurological emphasis on involuntary movement, moreover, not only reinforced the primacy of touch in writing but also specifically associated touch with the motion of the pen. Touch, eighteenth-century theorists contended, was a reciprocal sense: one does not touch without being touched. Feeling the pen in one's hand, a writer experiences the reciprocity of touch, or "the act of pressing one body upon another," by putting the pen into motion. "Thus all the Senses may be considered as so many kinds of Feeling," and all sensation is the "impressing of motion." The place where pen and hand meet in motion, touch necessarily positions the body in the material world. It allows one to distinguish both a physical sense of oneself and the external influences of the world on the body. As the eighteenth-century philosopher George Berkeley deduced, touch is synonymous with what he terms "bodily situation," conveying ideas of both distance and spatial arrangement. Suppose, he hypothesized, there is an unbodied spirit with perfect sight but no sense of touch. Such a spirit would have "no idea of distance, outness, or profundity, nor consequently of space or body, either immediately or by suggestion."[101] All sensory experience could be translated into a form of touch or feeling, and touch was measured through bodily contact and motion. How to sit at a desk, how to hold a pen, and how to move it with "Freedom with Command! / With Softness strong" depended on this sense.[102]

As the culmination of a woman's bodily sensations and memory traces, the hand and quill suggest a wonderfully feminine poetics of the pen. A "channel" that both holds and carries ink, the pen is an animate receptacle much like memory.[103] Its hollow, cavernous body, though tubelike, makes mnemonic vestiges visible through metaphors of transmission, conveyance, and birth. Since body memory required repetition and imitation (i.e., copying), and since handwriting in turn relied on body memory rather than detached reason, the pen traced the nerves' passage from the cerebellum or medulla, the alternately feminine seats of muscle movement and memory. The physical act of writing with a quill, therefore, ironically suited the well-disciplined female body and her receptive memory, as Jenkins illustrates: "For as the pen must follow the mind of the writer, a just idea of the best formed characters ought to be well impressed on the mind, that they may be instantly ready to drop from the pen when called for."[104] Dropping thoughts on paper, the pen, like the pores and nerves in Descartes's neurophysiological theory, was a direct conduit from the brain's memory folds to the blank page. Awaiting the movements of the fingers—the final receptors of the mnemonic animal spirits conveyed through the nervous system—the pen guaranteed the permanence of written memory, for through the "knowledge of letters," Jenkins says, "mankind is enabled to preserve the memory of things done in their own times, and to lay up a rich treasure of knowledge for all succeeding ages."[105]

VISIBLE INK

Though Logan could not adequately cut or mend her own pens, she made her own ink. Created from gall nuts or oak apples (which provided the necessary gallic or tannic acid), ink was treated with iron sulfate (copperas or vitriol) to make it black. Gum arabic was added for viscosity. And a liquid (water, wine, vinegar, or even urine) was blended in the final stage to ensure proper consistency. The result was a slightly corrosive acidic ink that bit durably into the paper's surface. Sometimes women tried the more old-fashioned method of quenching a burnt cork in aqua vitae and dissolving it in water with melted gum arabic. And sometimes they relied on published guides on ink making such as those found in Hannah Robertson's *Young Ladies School of Arts* (1777), the same book that offered directions for making the shellwork houses discussed in chapter 1. Making ink, according to Robertson, was simple: "Take five ounces of galls, six ounces of vitriol, four ounces of gum and a fresh egg; a little powder of walnuts, four pints of beer, and put them into an earthen pot; add a little sal-ammoniac to keep the mixture from moulding."[106] Most of these ingredients would be conveniently found in the kitchen or pantry. Ink making, like food preparation, then, was just another domestic task. Once the ink was mixed, its color and consistency could be adapted to suit a writer's particular taste, as another recipe illustrates:

> To make common ink, of wine take a quart,
> Two ounces of gumme, let that be part;
> Five ounces of galls, of cop'res [copperas] take three,
> Long standing doth make it the better to be;
> If wine ye do want, raine water is best,
> And then as much stuffe as above at the least,
> If ink be too thick, put vinegar in,
> For water doth make the colour more dimme.[107]

With a sprinkle of this and a dash of that, ink could be made frequently to keep it fresh, avoiding mold, dust, and other household contaminants.[108] Though Logan would have followed such commonplace recipes in her youth, she eventually eschewed these troublesome directions in adulthood. Beginning instead with store-bought ink powder (probably a mixture of gall nuts, iron salt, and gum arabic sold in small packets), she simply mixed in the final liquid and then stored the ink in a glass container.[109]

The neurophysiology of memory illustrated in the processes of paper and quill making also resonates with the methods of ink making and storage. Given the kinetic movements of the nervous system that control the hand's speed and fluency in writing, and given the pen's dependence on ink to turn those motions into visible characters, ink was similarly valued for its flow and visibility. Although the pen's nib and corresponding pressure and angles of the hand ultimately determined ink flow, visibility was more closely linked to the autonomic nervous system, which controls breathing, pulse, and respiration. Iron-gall ink was, in fact, visible only when it was exposed to the air. Though repeated oxidation over time caused the color to fade from black to brown, it was essential to making manuscripts readable. Thus, like oxygenated blood, which carries the animal spirits throughout the body, ink has the chemical potential to bring memory to life. An iconic iteration of the heart's activity, ink, as the poet Anna Young Smith expresses it, would "thy Tinctured heart Retain." A pigment, color, or stain (i.e., ink) as well as a vestige or trace (i.e., script), a "tincture" made heartfelt memories perceptible. Receiving the ink, paper was said to "*Breath[e]* nothing Piety, Resignation, and a cordial good will to mankind." As automatic as breathing, writing was impossible to stop "where the heart is Engag'd," according to Smith's aunt, Elizabeth Fergusson: "And if I do not soon stop," she warns her correspondent, "I shall send you a Volume."[110] Through the medium of ink, words flowed like volumes of oxygenated blood from the heart to the page.

The externalized movement of memories from the woman's body to the pen and ink follows what early modern anatomist William Harvey called the "circle of perfection." Drawn by the arteries and veins, the circle traces the blood's pathway from the heart to the organs. Following the Platonic concept of "anima" (i.e., the spirit that moves in a circle and communicates life, function, and consistency in animated objects), Harvey theorized that the blood moves by systematic pulsations in the heart. Like the heart muscle's pumping of blood through the body by synchronic and rhythmical contractions (systoles) and dilations (diastoles), the light "pulses" of the writer's hand controlled the ink's flow, preventing it from clotting at the pen's nib or bleeding too quickly onto the paper. Applying more pressure on downward strokes and a lighter touch on ascending lines, the writer controls the tinctured traces of ink. As the penman Edward Cocker suggests:

Hair strokes, with light poize, the pens edge desire,
Full Strokes, with heavier pulse, the flat require.

. . . .

Strokes which descend from right to left make small,

From left to right express with Fulness all.

. . . .

Your head and heart, your hand and eye must bend,
To make the motions of your Pen transcend.[111]

Up and down, left and right, soft and heavy, the pen's rhythmic cadence imitates a heartbeat. When the ventricles contract, the valves between the aorta
and the ventricles close as the result of increasing pressure, while the valves to
the pulmonary artery and the aorta open. Flowing through the heart, the
animal spirits would propel the pulse as the nerves, "being filled to a fulness,
shake off and as it were explode, a Systole for the whole Heart," according to
Thomas Willis. As a result, "the blood, from either side of the bosom, is cast
out as it were by the impulse of a Spring or Bolt."[112] Flowing and pulsing
from the head to the heart (and eventually to the hand and eye, as Cocker
suggests), the animal spirits in the blood resemble the corresponding circulation of ink from the pen's body to its tip. Through a type of respiration on
paper, the oxidized ink seemingly breathes.

Just as ink flow indirectly depends on the reciprocity of the heart and
other internal organs in the autonomic or sympathetic nervous system, so
does ink's visibility on the page rely on the "sympathy" of respiration and
handwriting. Iron-gall ink's pigment required oxidation to ensure its visibility. Only then was it a memory aid. "But it is vain to attempt to describe
difficulties which however tormenting, are all wrote with lemon juice when
they are committed to paper, and disappear," complains Logan. Dark, thick,
black ink was infinitely more reliable. "I find alterations which do not at all
accord with my liking," she grumbles on another occasion: "The Ink emptied out and the little Glass washed, all of which was not only unnecessary
but mischievous. I hate pale thin Ink." "Vexed at this Pale Ink—watered by
one of my officious maidens," Logan chastises the same domestics who
clipped her quills for continuing to disturb her "regular habits": "They have
taken away my Ink-stand out of the Library, and has for a substitute a tin
box which turns the liquid the present color. I don't like it [lighter and
brouwner than the usual clear, solid black]." Conceding that the fault lies
also in the complex chemistry of the ink itself, she adds a footnote: "The
[ink] was red when first written. It was, I suppose some chemical effect of
the tin. . . . This vile ink—The Ink was very nearly red when I wrote with
it yesterday, but I see it nor partly of its own color."[113] Determined by
chemistry, an ink's variability reflects the tenaciousness of the memory it
tries to capture. Iron-gall ink, with its dependence on oxidation and its erasure by lemon or vitriolic juices, sometimes resisted memory's immediate
imprint. But with proper consistency and color, it made memory visible.

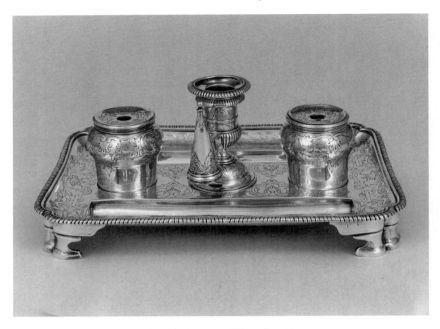

2.8. Inkstand. Courtesy, Winterthur Museum.

Given its potential to materialize memory, ink required proper receptacles for storage. Usually having a heavy bottom for balance and a small neck
and mouth for easy pouring, an ink bottle could prevent the inevitable spills
that plagued the early American writer. "An accident with spilling the Ink
has just now occurred," writes Logan, "and my poor writing Board that
covers the Stool that serves me for a table, and near which, I constantly sit,
has been deluged by it. . . . I must try what can be done to restore [the
table] to its usual color."[114] Ruining furniture and clothes as well as marring
a beautiful manuscript, spilled ink was a common nuisance. But carefully
kept in an inkstand, along with casters of pounce or sand, ink could be conveniently moved out of harm's way. Inkwells that were once concave indentations in a desk's surface were by the eighteenth century separate,
portable trays that could be carried from one writing space to another (see
figure 2.8). Logan undoubtedly appreciated such a convenience in her seasonal relocations to the dining room and library.

As an earlier scene of this chapter illustrates, Logan would ensure and
control the paper's natural absorbency of the ink by rubbing sandarac into
its unsized surface or, with sized paper, sprinkling sand or dabbing blotting
paper onto the wet page. Whatever the method, the result palpably imitated

the ways in which the memory receives the imprint of sensations. Although the grains of sand are actually nonabsorbent, the ink is dispersed upward through the spaces in the sand's coating, effectively coagulating. Exposing the surface area of the ink to air—showing again ink's respiratory characteristics—the sand enables it to dry more quickly.[115] Superimposing blotting paper over the handwritten page, a writer not only sponged the excess ink but also copied the memory's absorption of sensory impressions. "From Blots keep clean your Book," writers were admonished. A pristine manuscript would prevent blots on future memories. Tracing the "airy precincts in the soul" with her pen's variable ink, Logan externalized the animal spirits moving through her blood by circulating ink in ascending and descending pulses on paper.[116]

LEGIBLE HANDS

The culmination of the writer's sensations, script records her distinctive mark or imprint. It not only reflects the coordinated qualities of the paper, pen, and ink but also translates the body's movements into readable characters. Although the pen and hand were considered complementary instruments, the hand and script (tellingly called *hand*) were presumably indistinguishable. A writer's hand should be transparent, legibly revealing her thoughts and memories for herself and others. As a writer, Logan always "endeavoured to write plain and legible. who would read my book if written in such a character?" As a reader, she expected the same readability: "I could not derive all the knowledge and pleasure from [a manuscript's] perusal which I might have done had it been written in a clear plain hand, for its small, obscure and running, the letters in some places scarce discernable." Made of the careful combination of individual characters, the joining hand is clear only when each component is well crafted: "They are penned too in a fine and uncommon character," complains Logan, "and this circumstance makes it almost impossible for me to read them—the kernel ought to be very good when the Shell is so hard to open." Deciphering countless old manuscripts written in cramped and unintelligible hands, Logan preferred "lines and characters [that] are neat and beautiful."[117]

Her emphasis on legibility distinguishes the particularly private nature of women's manuscripts from the public script of more worldly business. Unlike the rapidly scrawled running hand marking professional communiqués by men, women's script was fashioned more leisurely. Written slowly, their deliberate script ensured intelligibility. Women differentiated their writing from that of their male counterparts, whose illegibility displayed socioeconomic status. A mark of gentility among British-American men through the early nineteenth century, illegible scripts flowed "with a kind of Artificial Negligence." As the writing master Jenkins remarked in 1813: "It is much to be regretted that it has become of late years in a degree fashionable to write a scrawling and almost unintelligible hand."[118] The fashionable mark of exclusive society, unintelligibility was also achieved through the use of secret hands.[119] Valuing privacy over secrecy, and preservation over concealment, the Philadelphia coterie made legibility—indeed, even transparency—requisite to its mnemonic arts.

This transparent aesthetic of a woman's handwritten and personal "character" reflects the architectural principles of decorum and proportion discussed in the previous chapter. The rhetoric describing penmanship was virtually identical to the architectural discourse for building design. "As in Building, so in Writing," suggests one writing master, "we must at the beginning, lay a firme foundation; otherwise the Superstructure will never answer our expectation." Applying "certain first and fixed principles," advises another, provides "the foundation upon which the whole is built." Employing the same rules of design to script, women agreed that the "Design of Writing is to convey your Ideas." Stripped of ornament, a plain script should "strike the Eye" and "make a proper Impression."[120] As both the unspoken intention and physical arrangement of characters, as figure 2.9 suggests, a writer's "design" upheld the classical architectural standards of *utilitas* (use) and *venustas* (beauty). Like a well-designed building, which was never "more grand than it is useful; nor its dignity a greater praise than its convenience," critics observed, fine handwriting was "esteemed not only for its Use, but for its Beauty, excelling all other Arts when rightly performed."[121]

"Which is one of the most useful of all arts?" asked the penman Jenkins in 1791. Answer: "The art of writing."[122] As *utilitas* encompassed the ways a structure fits its particular situation and function, so script—with its array of "hands"—indicated a writer's social position and character. For example, the secretary hand, superseded by the round hand by the eighteenth century, was used for business, and the italic hand was still widely used for private correspondence.[123] The italic hand, moreover, became feminized, for it "better fit" the "fair sex," according to writing masters, "in the slenderness of its characters [and] the delicacy which appears in the formation of them."[124] Whereas men learned several professional hands, women specifically learned the italic and round hands. The italic hand is shown in figure 2.10. A script's usefulness, then, was determined by the gendered body that wrote it. Like architectural decorum, which highlighted the affinity between an inhabitant and her habitation, handwriting naturalized a woman's domestic circumstance. As Logan complains, "Devoted to those cares which

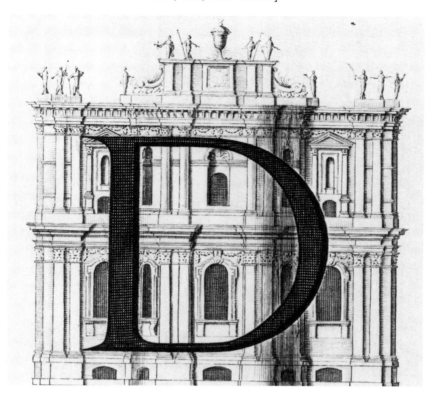

2.9. John Ayres, *A Tutor to Penmanship* (London, 1698), p. 93 (shelfmark 59.d.3). Copyright the British Library. Reproduced by permission of the British Library.

women usually have to perform . . . with daily repetition," "I am often deterred (from writing about something) from a sense of the time it will take to write the necessary circumlocutions, and introduce the thought with propriety."[125] Composed in the house between domestic duties and in discrete spaces, a script's careful proportions on the page imitated women's restricted space in the house. Such writing, theorists contended, is "durable and distinct," "[does] not occupy too much room, and may be performed with expedition."[126]

Visually pleasing, handwriting, like architecture, was also an animate art of proportions. For "the well adjusting of their Parts" and "placing them to the best advantage," penmen agreed, letters required a "due Proportion" and a "regular Slope." When "the Tops and Bottoms or Heighth and Length. . . . be wide or narrow, upright or slope," then "the Equality of such Writing will Strike the Eye." Much like architectural standards of

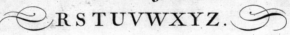

2.10. Various eighteenth-century hands, from George Bickham, "The Alphabet in All Hands," in *The Universal Penman* (London, 1743). Courtesy of Dartmouth College Library.

beauty based on proportion, a symmetrical script caught the viewer's eye. Since beauty was apprehended through the same senses that stir the memory, an elegant script that would strike the eye would also captivate the memory places in the mind, for "flowing Strokes in true Proportion rise; / They charm the Sense, and captivate the Eyes." An expression of taste, writing masters professed, beauty was "peculiar to that Sex which is therefore called Fair." "Soft, bold, and free," their "manuscripts will please; / Where all is masterly, and wrote with ease."[127] A feminine art of pleasing much like politeness, the ability to copy and appreciate beautiful script was simply a matter of taste.[128]

The eighteenth-century aesthetic standards of use and beauty in both architecture and handwriting are based in Euclidean geometry. Derived from natural and universal principles that are copied, combined, and arranged, geometry is a mnemonic art of mathematical topoi. As Thomas Sheraton points out in the frontispiece to the *Cabinetmaker and Upholsterer's Drawing Book* (1802): "Time alters fashions and frequently obliterates the works of art and ingenuity; but that which is founded on Geometry and real Science, will remain unalterable."[129] Such fixed geometric forms illustrate architecture's convenient adaptation to penmanship, for "writing is a fine art, and is to be acquired only by imitation."[130] And each letter, like a geometric memory place, would be formed in an actual or imaginary square, which determined its size and proportion.

Though virtually all British and American writing manuals of the eighteenth century acknowledge an indebtedness to geometry, none so clearly illustrates this lineage as Thomas Hawkes's *Art of Writing Geometrically Demonstrated* (1747). In order to correct the popular pedagogy of teaching the round hand through geometric forms, promoted by the British penmen Charles Snell and Joseph Clarke, Hawkes turned to the works of the architect William Halfpenny for his revisionary model. Widely published in the American colonies, Halfpenny's *Art of Sound Building* provides the abstruse geometrical formulas and graphs for Hawkes's imitation. As a result, Hawkes's text reads more like a builder's guide than a penmanship manual: "To turn an *Arch* over such that may look *beautiful* to the *Eye*," he points out, "Let the following *Ellipsis* be *observed*, which was the *Invention of the ingenious* William Halfpenny. *To him and his Works I am obliged for the Discovery of this New Geometrical Method of Forming Letters.*[131] The prefatory poem "To the Ingenious Author," by Joseph Dimsdale, nicely summarizes Hawkes's method:

SEE from Proportion how just Letters rise!
And Beauties regular delight the Eyes;

'Tis Symmetry and nice perfective Art,
That to each Work full Value must impart:
For if you take this Secret Charm away,
Nature's disfigur'd, Beauty will decay.

Inviting the reader to view the visual and tactile movement of handwritten letters, Hawkes goes on to argue that writing "proceeds from the *Eye* and the *Hand*." Whereas the eye determines size and proportion, the hand sets the "Design for *Use* and *Beauty*."[132] Symmetry, as the poem intimates, mediates between the eye's judgment and the hand's soft touches. The cornerstone of architectural classicism, symmetry was the basis of beauty and, therefore, naturally appealed to the refined eye.

Though these texts imagined the construction of symmetrical space (and letters within that space) rather than actual architectural forms, they provide a useful theoretical model that exemplifies the mnemonic and ergonomic links between handwriting and physical space. In order to determine the width, height, slope, and thickness of a given letter, Hawkes used basic geometry, as figure 2.11 presents, beginning with either a parallelogram or a perpendicular intersecting two horizontal lines: "First make a *Parallelogram,* as *abcd,* Fig. 6, whose Length *ab,* is equal to the Length of the intended *Elliptical Arch* and *ad,* the Breadth, divide the Line *ab* into any Number of Parts . . . for a small *Arch,* as this Method of Writing consists of no other."[133] Based on a diagonal drawn from a fixed point on the lower to the upper line, the height was fixed at twice the width. And the diagonal's length marked the slope of the intended letter. Hawkes then drew a parallel diagonal, extending a line from the perpendicular's right angle to this second diagonal. This line, in turn, determined the thickness of the impending stroke. Finally, subdividing the original parallel lines into points forming an arch, Hawkes established the curve and turns of the top of each letter.

Here follow the virtually identical directions for geometric figures and angles which Halfpenny provided his audience in *The Art of Sound Building:* "First draw the Base Line A, B, and raise the Lines AC and BD, Perpendicular to the Same, and each equal to your designed Heighth, and draw the line CD, which is halve in the Point E. This being done, divide the Lines AC and EC, and ED and DB, each unto the same Number of equal Parts, and draw intersecting Lines according to the Directions above given, and you will have the Arch required AEB" (figure 2.12).[134] Crediting Halfpenny with the invention of the ellipsis, or "the elliptical arch," Hawkes sees this indispensable geometric form as "being of great Use to Carpenters, Masons, Bricklayers," and writers alike. Using a proportional arch over a gateway or window as his primary example, Hawkes essentially leads the reader

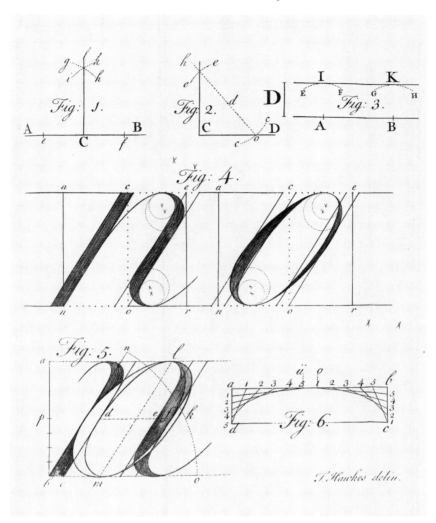

2.11. Thomas Hawkes, *The Art of Writing Geometrically Demonstrated* (London, 1747), plate 1, figures 1–6. Courtesy, The Winterthur Library: Printed Book and Periodical Collection.

through an imaginary threshold to view his new method of writing. Like a door or window that opens into a house's private spaces, geometric script was a transparent window to the memory. As the prefatory poem suggests, without the symmetrical arch's "Secret Charm," "Nature's disfigur'd, Beauty will decay." Since memory depends in part on the apprehension of beauty in writing, an elegantly turned script would "strike the eye," and as a result, "the Mind will thus th' Ideas fully trace."[135] Both architecture and

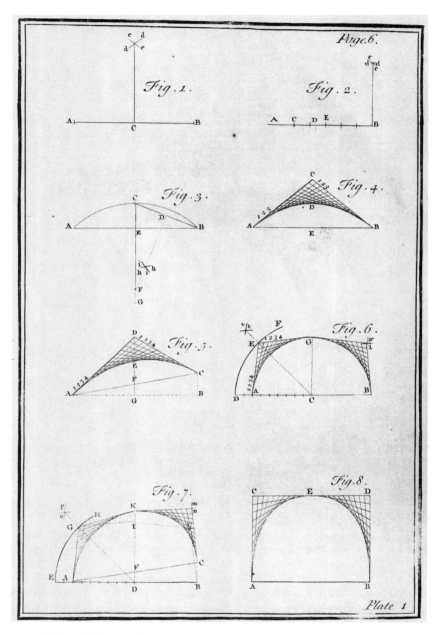

2.12. William Halfpenny, *The Art of Sound Building* (London, 1725), p. 6, plate 1. Courtesy, The Winterthur Library: Printed Book and Periodical Collection.

handwriting, Hawkes concludes, derive their memorable forms from geometry.

With its geometric proportions, handwriting specifically located its foundation in the five orders of architecture: the Tuscan, Doric, Ionic, Corinthian, and Composite. Essentially structural topoi in "their combination, multiplied, varied, and arranged, in a thousand different ways," the orders determine the proportion, shape, and character of alphabetic figures.[136] Imitating the figure of the human body, moreover, the orders are noticeably anthropomorphized. "The general proportions of Architecture have a striking analogy to those of the human body and seem to be taken from its principal characteristics," writes one architectural theorist. In other words, the combination of architectural orders, like the patterns of the "joining hand," imitate the perfect proportions of the human body, each part of which beautifully contributes to the effect of the whole. "It is in this light that we shall consider the five Orders of Architecture," he continues. "In the progression of these five Orders we thus see strength, grace, majesty, and magnificence."[137]

The "strength and solidity" of the "robust and well-sinewed" Tuscan resemble the Roman block print carved into Trajan's Column. The "man of noble and well-favored build" of the Doric, "the most ancient of all the orders," typifies the simple, geometric Greek capitals, which formed the basis of the Latin alphabet. The Ionic's "general proportions of a beautiful woman, with a little more bulk than a slender girl," correspond to the gently slanting secretary hand (see figure 2.13). The "simple, natural sweetness" of the Corinthian forms the flourishes of the delicate italic hand. And the Composite order's "Medlie, or an Amasse of all the precedent Ornaments," of the Ionic and Corinthian suggests the round hand, or *lettre anglaise,* which combined the secretary and italic hands. Reflecting the analogous proportions of the architectural orders and the human body, script was similarly gendered. The progression of architectural orders from masculine to feminine characters thus set the standards for eighteenth-century penmanship, in which "some bodies are stout and robust; others are delicate and elegant."[138]

A closer look at the early modern descriptions of the italic and round hands taught to women during the eighteenth century better illustrates my point.[139] Though the penman Cocker attributes the elliptical shape of the italic hand to geometry, and though he transforms the ellipses into circles, as in the English round hand, he ultimately credits the female body with the definitive shape of italic script: "This Hand in its best Dress, is no less charmingly Beautifull, than those Illustrious Dames inhabiting in the Place of its Nativity; And like them too it is as much beholding to Art as to Nature for the Gallantry of its Beauty." Comparing the Italian and English

2.13. "Ionica," from John Shute, *First and Chief Groundes of Architecture* (1563). Courtesy, Harry Ransom Humanities Research Center, The University of Texas at Austin.

forms of the italic hand, along with the contrasting beauty of their women, Cocker describes its English adaptation: "It is more pleasing to the Eye, for there is not a Letter in this Hand, no, not a part or Particle of any Letter therein, but is obliged to the Oval for something of its form. . . . The Letters in our Hands are generally more substantially bodied, and therefore of more duration. To make the Italian Hand correspond with ours, we abate much of its Eliptical form, it being more round and solid . . . and lay them more slanting."[140] Its visible charm, he contends, emerges from the roundness of the female body that forms it. The rounded shape, delicate strokes, and energetic slant, Cocker suggests, imitate an Englishwoman's ample proportions, celebrated by such baroque portrait painters as Sir Anthony Van Dyke and Sir Peter Lely.[141]

Considered the most beautiful and ornate script, the italic draws its signature flair from the ornamental capital of the Corinthian column, as figure 2.14 illustrates. Like the young Greek virgin for which it was named, the Corinthian order's outlines were described as gentle and well rounded; they were governed by a simple, natural grace in every part. Many writing and architectural manuals that describe the origin of the orders repeat some version of Corinthia's tragic story. As the architect Asher Benjamin narrates it:

> A young woman of Corinth being dead, her nurse placed on her tomb a basket containing certain trinkets, in which she delighted, when alive; covering it with a tile to shelter them from the weather. The basket happened accidentally to be set on a root of the acanthus, which pushing forth its leaves and sprigs in the spring, covered the sides of it; and some of them, longer than the rest, being obstructed by the angles of the tile, were forced downward, and by degrees, curled into the form of volutes. Callimachus, a celebrated sculptor, passing near the tomb, observed the basket . . . the form pleased him exceedingly.[142]

Like the entablature resting atop the Corinthian capital, a tile was placed over the basket of sentimental girlhood trinkets. And like the leaves pushing forth their blooms in downward curling branches, the italic hand was celebrated for both its celerity and ornamental flourishes.

Resisting Cocker's gendered description of the italic hand, however, Madame Johnson admonishes women to avoid unnecessary ornamentation in "A New and Easy Introduction to the Art of Writing" (1754): "There is but one Hand absolutely requisite for young Women to improve themselves in, and that is the *Round Hand,* which is much preferable to the *Italian,* tho' formerly, indeed, the later was in high Repute amongst the Ladies. . . . to practice any ornamental Flourishes whatsoever . . . in regard to Penman-

2.14. "Corinthia," from John Shute, *First and Chief Groundes of Architecture* (1563). Courtesy, Harry Ransom Humanities Research Center, The University of Texas at Austin.

ship, lies in a very narrow Compass; for if they can but once attain to make their Writing look fair and legible, 'tis as much as is required as their Hands."[143] Bemoaning the "ornamental Flourishes" of the italic hand, Johnson illustrates the limits placed on women's writing. In an unusual attempt to free women from the decorative fetters of the italic hand, Johnson prefers the round hand—a fusion of the italic and secretary hands—for its fairness and legibility. Whereas the quickly written and oval-shaped letters of the italic hand typically culminated in pointed arches in the minims (or letter shapes such as *m* and *n*), the round hand was considered solid and uniform in shape. Acknowledging that women are unfairly characterized by ornamental flourishes, and perhaps downplaying the misogynist criticism leveled against writing women, Johnson warns, "in regard to Penmanship," a woman (and her ornaments) "lies in a very narrow Compass."

The evolution of the italic into the round hand recalls the italic hand's influence over typeface. Considered a transitional stage in typeface, the eighteenth century gave round characters a newly perpendicular axis, diverging from the old style's incline. According to the handwriting expert Laetitia Yeandle, what was basically the Italian hand, which we use today, came to assume different forms. The upright form, which is more akin to printing, became known as the roman hand, and the sloping cursive form as the italic.[144] The equivalent of our contemporary "Times Roman" font, roman script was used in handwriting as well as printing; the difference between roman and *italic*—then and now—is distinctly typographical. The running hand's upstroke and thick downstroke continued in the contrast of thick and thin elements in the new, "modern" typefaces. Serifs, too, became both flatter and sharper. Most influenced by the calligraphic forms of William Caslon's "Old Face" and John Baskerville's "Improved Style," colonial typeface illustrates its indebtedness to script.[145] Like script, these typefaces were derived from architectural models.[146] Based on earlier Dutch forms, Caslon's typeface was considered exceptional in its beauty and utility. Improving on Caslon's type, Baskerville focused on alphabetic proportions: "Having been an early admirer of the beauty of Letters," he writes, "I became insensibly desirous of contributing to the perfection of them. I formed to myself ideas of greater accuracy than had yet appeared, and have endeavored to produce a Set of Types according to what I conceived to be their true proportion."[147] The connection between script and typeface, like the affinity between script and architecture, lies in their anthropomorphic replication of the human body's ideal dimensions. By the early nineteenth century, however, print and script diverged, as typesetters replaced somatic models with a rational, mathematical one. Dissociated from the body (or more specifically, the writer's hand), print signified concealment or anonymity whereas script underscored its corporeal expression.

Much like rhetorical topoi, the variety, combination, and invention of new scripts and typefaces underscore the written word's indebtedness to architectural models and metaphors. Appreciated as "a Medlie, or an Amasse of all the precedent Ornaments, making a new kinde, by stealth . . . a borrower of all [her] Beautie," the Composite order (as figure 2.15 indicates) was decidedly innovative in its synthesis of the Corinthian order's proportions and the Ionic's angular volute and dentils.[148] Such a combination, critics worried, threatened the unique architectural "caractère" of each order: "The Ionic and Corinthian Orders remain models of beauty; they have fixed and decided characters; they are undisputed originals." But when the two are blended into the Composite, "the nature of this Order remains mixed and resists definition. It inspires sensations that, if not equivocal, are wanting in delicacy," claims one theorist.[149] "It appears to have been picked and culled from all the other orders," asserts another, "and is sometimes badly arranged."[150] Like rhetorical topoi and alphabetic characters, which are arranged proportionately to ensure their clarity, the architectural orders require careful arrangement. Whereas the Corinthian order signifies eternal virginity, the Ionic depicts chaste matrons, for Ionic architecture "is like a beautiful woman: she should please in herself; she needs few ornaments."[151] But taken together as the Composite, they become a dangerous, indefinable mixture.[152]

Given the persistent cultural anxieties associated with the female body, architectural design (like the design of writing furniture discussed earlier) underscores the value of a building's physiognomy—downplaying the body while accentuating the face.[153] Made of arches, perpendicular lines, and angles, the face's profile, or contour, set the standards for a building's *caractère*.[154] The exteriorized display of both architectural and human character, the *face* was defined as any member that has a great breadth and small projection in the front of a building. The *pediment* is the triangular or arched "forehead" that crowns the gates, windows, or niches of a building's front facade. The *fillet,* or *lift,* is called the "eyebrow," and the rose-shaped carving in the middle of an Ionic volute is called the "eye." And the *calvetto,* or round concave molding, is called the "mouth" when in its natural situation and the "throat" when turned upside-down. Architecture, like handwriting, thus offered women a physiognomic outlet, tracing the same individual character stamped on the face and soul to the corresponding building or script: "And is it possible," physiognomists asked, "that this incontestable diversity of writing should not be founded on the real difference of moral character?" Switching from the italic to the round hand, then, women

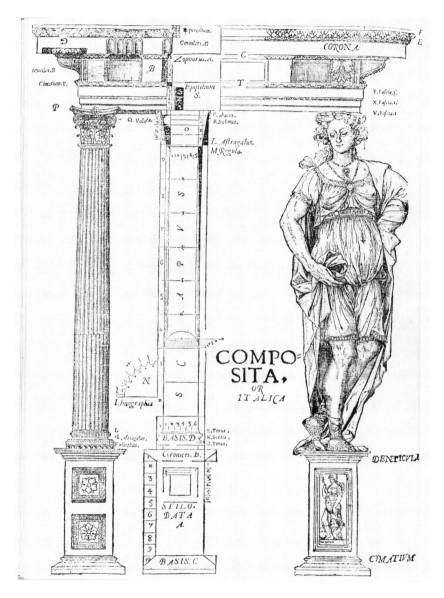

2.15. "Composita," from John Shute, *First and Chief Groundes of Architecture* (1563). Courtesy, Harry Ransom Humanities Research Center, The University of Texas at Austin.

could justify their preferences by imitating the appropriate architectural orders. "And no wonder that those who so much delight in the Change of Faces," writes one penman, "should affect the same in Hands too."[155]

With their mutual emphasis on the human face, along with the face's exteriorization of memory, architecture and handwriting together constituted a mnemonic art. Whereas an architectural order was divided into the pedestal (plinth, dado, and cornice), column (base, shaft, capital), and entablature (architrave, frieze, and cornice), an alphabetic figure was anatomized into a head, neck, shoulder, body, hip, legs, and feet. Both represented a human form from head to toe, and both privileged the head over the body through theories of physiognomic *caractère*. As the top of the column (a figure for the human body), the capital signifies the head. The capital not only marks the difference between architectural orders in its varying ornamentation but also sets the standard for script size and shape. Architectural and written capitals, then, continue the physiognomy of memory, for one need only "draw up a number of common heads (*capita*) or containers (*receptacula*) for words, which afterwards, with the application of a little more effort, can be subdivided more narrowly."[156]

Linked by their mutual reliance on human sensation, architecture, penmanship, and memory experienced geometric beauty both through the idealized proportions of the human body and through the actual lived bodies that created those movements. Comparing architectural proportions with human sensation, the eighteenth-century theorist Le Camus de Mézières claims, "Harmony is the prime mover of all great effects; it has the most natural ascendancy over our sensations." Harmony of proportions, he continues, "alone forms the enchantment that delights our souls." As the seat of sensation and memory, the soul apprehends the beauty of built form. Like the upward and downward strokes of the pen, and like the sense of dynamic movement expressed by a script's continuous slope, a building was as animate as a page of script, for "movement is the means to express, the rise and fall, the advance and recess, with other diversity of form, in the different parts of the building," according to the architect Robert Adam. Rising and falling, advancing and receding, every built form expresses its unique rhythm.[157] Such architectural vocabulary further aligned this rhythm with a heartbeat, as *systole* referred both to the human pulse and the "manner of spacing Columns." What architects called *intercolumnation,* or the space between two columns, penmen termed *interlineation:* "A little room may be left for interlineation, if that should be necessary. Let the lines be perfectly straight, and of an uniform breadth; let the points be accurately marked, and the words properly separated."[158] The natural and easy slope of perpendicular lines, the beauty and uniformity of the turns, and the evenly proportioned space thus determined the visual sense of movement and distance that characterized both a well-made building and an elegantly written hand.

In this chapter I used a detailed analysis of Deborah Logan's writing spaces and materials to explore the many ways in which the architectural images of female writing and memory overlap. Based on the geometric principles of use and beauty, handwriting, like architecture, translates the body's intimate experience of domestic space into memorable images. An extension and expression of the phenomenological body, written memory authorized a woman's body as the site of knowledge. No longer separated from her mind, her body transferred otherwise purely cerebral memory places into more tangible forms. Re-creating the intimate scene of writing, I wished to present the complex material—and distinctly mnemonic—aesthetics of early American women's writing practices. And Logan, I am sure, would have approved: "Oh dear Reader! When an hundred years shall have flown what would thee not give to see things as I behold them now! . . . I am in the Library, and it is the loveliest of afternoons, a brisk air stirs my harp—I only regret that the sun hastens so fast."[159]

PART TWO *Collective Reminiscence*

3

Among Her Souvenirs

A triffle may become a Pledge of price
If Friendship mark it with her sacred Name.

—Deborah Norris Logan, commonplace book (1808)

THE FACE OF MEMORY

"Today I paid CW Peale one hundred dollars for my Portrait," writes Deborah Logan in July 1822. "To say truth, tho' like me, it is so ugly, that I feel no inclination to let Posterity think me quite so disagreeable, as they unquestionably will from this picture. But the artist wanted to make up a sum of money, and I very gladly paid it to him, because I thought I had not done entirely well in delaying to give him an opportunity to finish his work." Concerned that she is "one year older, nearer to Eternity, uglier and more infirm," Logan delays the portrait's completion for three more years. She brings the portrait home to Stenton and hangs it over the clock in the library but is haunted by her own visage "looking at me." A material reminder of time's passage, the portrait is "a very churlish thing—my kind friend and neighbor has caractured me sadly. . . . I believe I shall be tempted to put it out of my way altogether." Encouraging the portrait's destruction, her cousin Sally Norris Dickinson "advised me to burn it," remembers Logan. "It don't vex me much, but to be sure it is inexpressibly ugly . . . [and] everyone present condemned it."[1]

Despite the handsome sum pocketed by the portraitist Charles Willson

3.1. A copy of Deborah Logan's portrait by Charles Willson Peale is preserved at Stenton, where the original was burned by a relative in 1934. Courtesy of The National Society of The Colonial Dames of America in the Commonwealth of Pennsylvania at STENTON, Philadelphia.

Peale, Logan's original likeness no longer exists, as figure 3.1 suggests. In 1934 Maria Dickinson Logan ensured that posterity would never remember her relative as ugly, disagreeable, or infirm, taking Sarah Dickinson's suggestion all too seriously, as her marginal note in Deborah Logan's diary explains:

> On reading her account of how Charles Willson Peale as she says caricatured her portrait so that she wanted to put it out of the way altogether. I took down her Portrait lent out the Face put it in an envelope. did the same to the background took it over to Stenton where the Colonial Dames were giving an entertainment, It was cool and there was a roaring wood fire in the Dining Room. . . . I dropt the Face in & then the Background & both went up in Smoke. Then

turned toward the Stenton Grave Yard and said "Deborah Logan Pax vobiscum."[2]

Ironically staging her fiery drama at the Preservation Society's commemoration of Stenton, Maria Logan misreads her mother-in-laws's diary, taking the older Quaker's self-conscious complaint about portraiture out of the larger context of her celebrated life as an antiquarian.[3] The ritual destruction of the portrait—cutting the face from its background like a frameless silhouette, slicing Peale's careful brushstrokes into unrecognizable pieces, and enclosing the scattered fragments in an envelope to be delivered to the dining room fireplace—occurs in the very place where Deborah Logan wrote and preserved historical archives and personal memories for almost sixty years.

The significance of the lost portrait goes beyond its historical or even its sentimental value. Painted when Logan was a "Dame of 64" by the eighty-two-year-old Peale "(without Spectacles!)," the portrait suggests the accumulation, indeed the culmination, of an aging woman's memories. Extending the physiognomic importance of written memory discussed in chapter 2 to the mnemonic value of the face itself, the painting signifies the lost cultural reverence for elderly women as living repositories of knowledge and cultural memory. Responsible for the transmitting of memory from one generation to another, old women in the early Republic responded to personal and social change by devoting themselves to the traditions and values of the past. "My Old Establishment, so unlike modern things," muses Logan, "the furniture, the China, the plate, the Library, all were objects of curiosity." "She was herself," notes a contemporary, "a relic of the past!"[4] As cultural curiosities, aged women linked the past and future. A series of events, moments, impressions, and memories, aging was more than progressive biological decay.[5] It was a process of proportions: as the body physically declined, the mind—no longer subject to youth's whimsical passions—steadily improved. "Age is the time in which the Mind is most discerning, and furnisht with the best Materials for Wisdom," writes one early modern theorist.[6] With "deep Gratitude that the Mind, the Eye and the Hand are not impaired, as yet, by infirmities of age," Logan hopes never to be "deprived of her intellectual furniture."[7] Like a memory palace, her mind was furnished with mnemonic images. And like a commonplace book, her face externalized those memories into interpretable signs. Thus, at the moment of Logan's physical dénouement, her portrait palpably captured the calibrations of an active memory.

As the physiognomist John Caspar Lavater explains the face of memory, "the various thoughts which arise in the mind, the different passions which agitate the soul" of woman, share an intimate correspondence with her countenance. "More rapid than speech," her face "betrays her sentiments and emotions."[8] A container of memory, the countenance invites a diagnostic mode of reading. Interpreting her own likeness, Logan remarks that Peale "left the chin as prominent and the mouth as indented as ever, and only added a few wrinkles."[9] One might infer much about Logan's memory, then, by applying Lavater's physiognomic principles to her portrait in figure 3.1. Like rhetorical topoi, each feature—from the forehead, eyebrows, and eyes to the nose, mouth, and chin—manifests a particular "place" in her mind. Despite her advancing age, few wrinkles line Logan's placid forehead to betray the "stormy passions" and "perturbation of mind" that typically mark old age. The wide space between her eyebrows "designates a quick apprehension, a calm and tranquil soul," and their symmetrical arch indicates "solidity of judgment, and of clear sound sense." Beneath her eyebrows is "the province of the eyes."[10] Looking directly at the viewer, Logan's eyes are not only the "faithful interpreter of the mind" but also "the window of the soul, the index which we read each varied emotion of the heart."[11] Her long, prominent nose, "the ridge of which is large, denotes a mind endowd with qualities of a high order." Similarly, her subtly pursed mouth provides the "index" to her character, representing both her "nature and disposition." Finally, her angular chin "betokens a sensible mind, and a benevolent heart."[12] Framed by a matronly, starched cap and neckerchief, Logan's face reflects the virtues of her agile mind.

Lavater's physiognomic guidelines offer a feminized reading of Logan's face that subverts the eighteenth century's domestication of memory. Through a kind of double inversion—turning the mind inside out and reversing it from back to front—he relocates memory from the hidden and posterior recesses of the cerebellum to the place of reason in the forehead's visible surface. Mingling reason and memory, Lavater downplays the Cartesian scheme that typically genders these faculties as masculine and feminine. Since aging proportionately increases the mind's vitality as the body declines, it deemphasizes women's overdetermined corporeality. Old age, critics would explain, "delivers us also from the tyranny of the passions" so that "reason is restored to us."[13] No longer limited by her body, the elderly woman, like the Cartesian man, enjoyed an unwavering stability of mind.

With the restored reason of old age, women could retreat from the mundane constraints of everyday life into an almost purely mental existence, reflecting on the past and preparing for eternity. "What a gradual weaning from the concerns of Life Old Age forces on us," writes Logan.[14] Despite her reservations, retirement promised improved mental capacity for the aged, as the theorist J. G. Zimmerman argues in his treatise, *Solitude* (1797):

it "accustoms the mind to think: the imagination becomes more vivid, and the memory more faithful, while the senses remain undisturbed, and no external object agitates the soul." With an improved memory, one might "compare what we were formerly with what we are at present" and "reflect on the various events we have experienced or observed." Solitude helps integrate one's evolving self-image. Painted when Logan was old and at a stage of relative retirement, the portrait accordingly reflects a calm and reflective mind focused on memories of a fleeting past. "The flight of time, the everlasting progressiveness of all around us, our own advance to maturity and decay," remarks Logan, "are themes that are constantly present to my mind." But lingering over days long past, she happily loses "sight of the present time in recollection."[15]

Logan's desire for continuity between the past and the present is called a "life review" by contemporary gerontologists.[16] A form of purposeful and directed remembering either for oneself or for telling to others, the life review revives treasured memories and objects through the lens of old age.[17] It is a time for women to gather, sort, and integrate the moments of their lives, for the role of "a modest compiler," according to historian Hannah Adams, "befits a true woman."[18] As Elizabeth Fergusson describes the process: "And now my dear Madam on a Review of Life after a few years are fled. . . . How strip'd of Pleasure does the world appear; But the Skeleton of former Pleasures and Beauty . . . all are deeply impressed on my Memory. . . . all seem to pass in Review before me."[19] Though past moments are mere skeletons of former sensations, reminiscence retains original memory traces.[20] Seemingly repetitious, old memories appear new when revisited at later periods in our lives. The new forms, and more important, the new significance the elderly compiler attaches to them, make reminiscence meaningful.

Putting old forms in new contexts, the life review shares the cumulative and reflective nature of the manuscript commonplace book. A material means of collecting the past, commonplacing allowed women to commemorate, "to always (almost) observe the anniversaries of Births and Deaths of those I love," as Logan comments. "They seem like watch words to awaken long trains of ideas and call up tender feelings and affections."[21] Similarly marking anniversaries on her calendar, Fergusson remembers her ill-fated wedding twenty years earlier: "Of taking a Retrospect of my past Life, I have this day felt myself unusualy serious, and affected. It has ever been one of many peculiar weaknesses belonging to me, to have the Springs of past Sorrow fresh opend on the anual return of the Day . . . I have Retrod every hour of this *Day twenty years* with the most lively emotions."[22] Initiating a stream of associations, commonplace books reproduce memories, compensating for the cumulative losses that accompany aging.

Whereas the commonplace book figuratively employs domestic objects as memory images, the life review returns these images to their literal, material contexts. Connecting commonplace fragments, the life review marks a distinct shift from memory to reminiscence. Memory, as the preceding chapters illustrate, requires the body's internal processes to create and preserve sense impressions through architectural and handwritten images; reminiscence, which Marius D'Assigny defines as the "recovery of the same ideas which were formerly lost, or renewing those impressions in the memory that were blotted out," enlists the external world of material objects. Located in the present moment and dictated by contemporary desires, reminiscence reframes the past by creating a resemblance between mnemonic objects and their literal referents. Objects embody memories that might otherwise remain dormant or forgotten. They provide an immediate, and seemingly unmediated, link to the past, as the critic Susan Pearce remarks, telling "the stories of our lives in ways which would be impossible otherwise."[23]

Maintaining their mnemonic connections to the house and its objects, women in the early Republic accordingly attached a type of interiority to objects. "Giving Life to Dead objects," reminiscence entails an "assimilating Principle" or "Propensity to spread our selves over all things," according to Fergusson, so that "almost every Emotion, which in the least agitates the mind bestows upon its Object a momentary Idea of Life."[24] Using these objects to stir the internal processes that create and control the memory, women not only subverted the physical effects of aging but also translated these debilities into mental acuity. Though "dryness, stiffness, and rigidity of the fibres" defined old age since the classical period, holding memorabilia in one's hand would restore the heat emanating from the heart and animal spirits to the extremities. Mnemonic objects provided what Johann Cohausen describes as "a constant, equal and effectual supply of smooth balsamic and lubricating particles from the circulating fluids." Though humoral theories continued to diagnose the elderly as dry and cold, there was not, according to Cohausen, a corresponding "chilling of affections" or lack of sensitivity as one aged.[25]

Instead, the sense of touch, as a form of embodied reminiscence, establishes a "threshold activity": animating the inanimate, touch "traverses the boundary between interiority and externality and reciprocally returns to the agent of touching."[26] Touch encompasses both the body's sensations and the object's contact with the body. As the phenomenologist Maurice Merleau-Ponty explains, "I am able to touch effectively only if the phenomenon finds an echo within me, if it accords with a certain nature of my consciousness, and if the organ which goes out to meet it is synchronized with it."[27] Virtually indistinguishable, the self and object merge to renew a unified identity and a continuous narrative of the past in old age. But as experience is increasingly mediated and abstracted through objects, the lived relation of the body to the material world is substituted with "a nostalgic myth of contact and presence." At once "sadness without an object" and "the desire for desire," nostalgia is the bittersweet sense of separation from an irrecoverable past. With the characteristic touch of utopianism coloring nostalgic reminiscence, Logan treasured those objects that brought back happier moments. In her persistent desire to recover the past, nostalgia was the most potent form of reminiscence.

The nostalgic myth of contact and presence returns us to Logan's mutilated portrait and our impossible desire for the original. Doubly removed from its sitter and its nascent context, the existing copy can never adequately embody the memory traces of Peale's work or its proximity to Logan herself. It can only invite our reminiscence at a remove. Looking at the portrait, we experience a kind of nostalgic distance from an object that requires what I call "collective reminiscence" to bridge the gap. "If we go outside the self, this is not to become fused with the objects but rather to look at them from the point of view of others," writes the theorist Maurice Halbwachs; "there are no recollections which can be said to be prior interior, that is, which can be preserved only within individual memory."[28] The requisite introspection and retirement of the old thus ironically bring them in contact with others. Painted for posterity, Logan's portrait anticipated and implicated future viewers in her memory's preservation.

The historical framework of collective reminiscence not only pacifies nostalgic longing but also requires an ethical relationship between the object and its respective viewers: we must imagine ourselves in the position of others, approximating their response had they been in our position.[29] Because reminiscence can only resonate rather than entirely recover a now-distant past, it is always incomplete. But using an ethic of collective presence and contact, people can synthesize their intimate remembrances of a memory object or its all-but-forgotten referent into a more complete narrative. Though Maria Dickinson Logan attempted such an ethical stance by putting herself in her relative's place before destroying the portrait, she tragically replaced the shared, perhaps even transcendent, aesthetics of nostalgia with unsympathetic literalism. Had she read Logan's words and image in their appropriate context, she would have treasured the portrait as we do.

Given the destruction of Deborah Logan's portrait and our nostalgia aroused by its copy, this chapter focuses on the ultimate failure of physiognomy to permanently preserve either the face or the memories reflected in the countenance. Arguing instead for the necessity of mnemonic objects and collective reminiscence to arrest the progressive dementia that accompanies aging, I show how Logan and her coterie adopt preservation methods that go beneath the skin's surface to the seat of memory itself. Despite the Cartesian accentuation of the face at the expense of the aging body, and despite the preponderance of late-eighteenth-century literature promoting retirement in old age, I demonstrate how the skin—as the organ of touch—invokes a specifically "embodied reminiscence." The objects intended to beautify the face and forestall the effects of aging, moreover, are the very artifacts of collective memory, or *reminiscentia*. Looking specifically at the hand mirror, folding fan, portrait miniature, and silhouette (as well as the poetic epistles that characteristically accompany them), I contend that these objects not only represent, reflect, or protect the face but ultimately preserve what the face cannot. Much like Freud's metonymic fetish, whereby a part of the body is substituted for the whole (i.e., face for the body) or an object is substituted for the part (i.e., mirror, fan, miniature, or silhouette for the face), until finally the whole body can become an object substituting for the whole, such *reminiscentia* were external metonyms for the face and mind. "There is a great convenience in having something of the kind to refer to," admits Logan, for in "the association of ideas one thing recovers another, and so I go on."[30]

THE TOILETTE: PRESERVING HER FACE

Made in 1783 by the Philadelphia cabinetmaker Thomas Tufft, Deborah Logan's dressing table has five lipped drawers, three in a row above two on either side of the curved skirt, which provided storage spaces for treasured *reminiscentia* (see figure 3.2).[31] Like the rooms of a Georgian house or the hidden compartments in a writing desk, the toilette table was a cabinet for memory, ritualistically prompting a life review. Logan would take out the mnemonic tokens from time to time, sharing them with her intimates and musing: "I love to look upon objects that have met their eyes who are gone, the characters endeared to me by reading their integrity and value in the unintentional Records of themselves which they leave behind."[32] Then, looking in the mirror for an illusory record of herself, she would appreciate the sentimental rather than the practical value of her toilette in old age, "for I have long ago given up the fruitless task of endeavouring by its act to make an old woman look like a young one."[33] Preserving her memory along with her face, the toilette signified the past.

On the dressing table's surface, Logan displayed the requisite dressing box, looking glass, perfume bottles, and cosmetic boxes.[34] She may have acquired a decorative patchbox filled with silk, velvet, cloth, or paper patches

3.2. Deborah Logan's dressing table. Courtesy of the Historical Society of Pennsylvania (X-59).

to apply over blemishes.[35] Snuffboxes were also popular collectibles, as her diary records: "a gold snuff box with exquisite painted portraits of Maria Louisa, the king of Rome, and Napoleon himself, the first two removed with a spring to discover the latter. The owner revers that it was the original box made by Napoleans directions and the miniatures painted by Isabey." Beside the snuffbox lay a beautiful fan with an elaborately ornamented leaf. "I had myself a fan belonging to one of my Aunts which had on it the first division of Poland figured by a Large Plum Cake," writes Logan: "The monarchs of Europe sat at the table among whom was Catherine of Russia, and the Empress-Queen Maria Theresa, and Frederic of Prussia, dividing it with his sword." Finally, Logan kept these relics in special boxes, which she covered with calico and scraps of engravings, "more to preserve them, than as appropriate ornaments (they are quite décolleté)."[36] Together these items present both the decorative and mnemonic arts of a woman's toilette.[37]

Perhaps she inherited the lovely, japanned dressing box descended

3.3. On display at Stenton is a japanned dressing box (c. 1710–30) that probably resembles the one that James Logan mentioned in his records for 1712. Courtesy of The National Society of The Colonial Dames of America in the Commonwealth of Pennsylvania at STENTON, Philadelphia.

through the Logan family, ordered by her father-in-law in 1712 (see figure 3.3). Such an ornamental box materializes the peculiar link connecting dressing furniture, cosmetics, and the preserving art of japanning. An occidental imitation of Asian lacquer work, japanning was a type of varnish and surface decoration.[38] More notably, japanning was both the craft of professional cabinetmakers and the polite art of young women. Furniture-building manuals explained the relatively simple process in detail: the practitioner first coats the surface of wood with varnish; after it sufficiently dries, he applies animal, figural, or floral motifs, which are built up on the wood with gesso (a mixture of chalk, whiting, glue, and water that acts as a primer); finally, gilding or silvering provides the finishing touch. Explicitly coupling varnishing with cosmetics, handbooks for the female arts included almost identical directions for furniture and facial "varnishes."[39] A woman could learn from one small book the analogous arts of preservation; one might compare, for example, the following recipes in *The Young Ladies School of Arts* and *The Toilet of Flora*:

To Make Varnish for Oil Paintings

   According to the number of your pictures, take the whites of the same number of eggs; and to each picture take the bigness of a hazel-nut of white sugar candy dissolved, and mix it with a tea-spoonful of brandy; beat the whites of your eggs to a froth; then let it settle; take the clear, put to your brandy and sugar, and varnish over your pictures with it: this is much better than any other varnish.[40]

An Admirable Varnish for the Skin

   Take equal parts of Lemon Juice, and Whites of new Laid Eggs, beat them well together in a glazed earthen pan, which put on a slow fire, and keep the mixture constantly stirring with a wooden spatula, till it has acquired the consistence of soft butter. Keep it for use, and at the time of applying it, add a few drops of any Essence you like best. Before the face is rubbed with this varnish, it will be proper to wash with the distilled Water of rice.[41]

These typical and age-old combinations of eggs, brandy, and lemon juice created a translucent, resinous glaze that preserves the surface of the face and decorative objects alike, providing a lasting shine and impenetrable seal.

   Though many considered the eighteenth century "*par excellence* the age of powder and paint," face varnish—particularly white cerulean paint—had its critics by the century's end, as figure 3.4 illustrates. One detractor in 1777 writes, "From each new acquaintance, she still exacts garnish; / Like iv'ry her teeth, and her cheeks are like—varnish," and another complains in 1811: "Nothing but selfish vanity, and falsehood of mind, could prevail on a woman to enamel her skin with white paints, to lacker her lips with vermil-lion." Mental falsehood, in turn, expresses fictional beauty, for "*The skin's power of expression,* would be entirely lost, were I to tolerate that fictitious, that dead beauty which is composed of white paints and enamelling."[42] Dis-tinguished from "cosmetics" by the nineteenth century, lead- and mercury-based "paint," like varnish, had its industrial uses and personal dangers. As James Stewart explains in *Plocacosmos* (1782): "Ceruse is white calk of lead, used in painting and cosmetics, made by calcining that metal in the vapor of vinegar. . . . Ceruse makes a beautiful white colour and is much used by the painters both in oil and water colours. It makes the principal ingredient in the fucuses used by ladies for the complexion. Taken inwardly it is a dan-

3.4. Thomas Rowlandson, *Six Stages of Mending a Face,* 1791–1792. Rosenwald Collection. Photograph © 2002 Board of Trustees, National Gallery of Art, Washington. Reproduced with permission.

gerous poison and soon shews its malignity on the outside, spoiling the breath and teeth and hastening wrinkles and the symptoms of old age."[43] Despite its known toxicity, white face paint was easily applied and widely used. Covering rather than assisting the skin's natural glow, however, it fatally seeped into the pores, causing palsy, convulsions, nervous weakness, colics, fainting, catarrhs, intestinal disorders, and pulmonary failure:

> The secret venom, circling in her veins,
> Works through her skin, and bursts in bloating stains;
> Her cheeks their freshness lose, and wonted grace,
> And an unusual paleness spreads her face.[44]

The destruction, therefore, was reciprocal: painting the face poisoned the body; the contaminated body, in turn, ruined the countenance.

The indiscriminate destruction of the body and face reasserts the physiognomic principles, however flawed, that diagnose internal maladies by fluctuations in the complexion. Published two years before Logan's death, *The Toilette of Rank and Fashion* (1837) maintains that "there exists so intimate a relation between our interior and exterior vessels, that almost every error or irregularity in the organ within, shows itself first on the surface of the body, particularly on the face." A vestige of early modern humoral medicine, this text propounds that the "just proportion of the fluids, and the circulation of the blood [are] determined in no small degree by the skin." Each organ, each humor, had its correlative function and location in the skin. "If these fluids become thick and languid," the author cautions, "the whole momentum of the blood is propelled towards the interior parts: a continual plethora or fulness of the blood, is thus occasioned; the head and breast are greatly oppressed."[45] Unlike varnish, which hermetically sealed the face, unhealthy skin—averse to perspiration and signaling an obstruction of the humors—apparently blocked the blood's circulating blushes from reaching the face. The pointed regression to humoral and solidistic medicine poignantly reinforces the eighteenth century's understanding of the memory's indebtedness to the nervous system, which culminated in nineteenth-century sentimentalism. Humoral, sensate, and breathing, the skin enclosed, animated, and revealed the memory.

The boundary between inside and out, surface and depth, a healthy complexion was a transparent medium for the mind. Women tried countless remedies to preserve the skin, believing, "In all cases the mind shines through the body; and, according as the medium is dense or transparent, so the light within seems dull or clear."[46] Justifying face painting with an analogy to portraiture, proponents contended that just as "complexion lends animation to a picture," so it "gives spirit to the human countenance." Spirited and eloquent, the complexion (from the Latin *complexus,* "combine" or "entwine") infused the countenance with color and energy: "Even the language of the eyes loses half its eloquence, if they speak from the obscurity of an inexpressive skin. The life-blood mantling the cheek . . . [is] the ensign of beauty and the herald of the mind."[47] Reflecting the oscillations of thought and memory, suggests Elizabeth Fergusson, the face is the varnish for the mind: "For our feelings varnish outward things / . . . Like Opticks various; various Objects show!"[48] The countenance contains and animates memory; the complexion combines, reorders, and revives mnemonic impressions through reminiscence.

Unlike varnishes and paints, which marred the skin's legibility, homeopathic remedies offered natural alternatives to accent rather than blur the natural blush. Most enduring from the seventeenth through the nineteenth centuries were the various recipes for "Virgin Milk":

The tincture of Benjoin [benzoin] is obtained by taking a certain quantity of that gum, pouring spirits of wine upon it, and boiling it till it becomes a rich tincture. If you pour a few drops of this tincture into a glass of water, it will produce a mixture which will assume all the appearance of milk, and retain a very agreeable perfume. If the face is washed with this mixture, it will, by calling the purple stream of the blood to the external fibres of the epidermis, produce on the cheeks a beautiful rosy colour; and, if left on the face to dry, it will render it clear and brilliant.[49]

An ablution rather than a cosmetic, virgin milk restored facial chastity, seducing the blood to the skin's surface and raising a temporary blush. Sweet-smelling and soothing, virgin milk provided a healthy "varnish" and effective rouge.

In addition to restoring the natural flush of youth, some cleansers offered the extra benefit of combating wrinkles. *The Queen's Closet Opened* (1713), for example, proposes a simple method:

A Water of Flowers good for the Complexion of Ladies
   Take the Flowers of Elder, a Flower-de-luce, Mallows, and Beans, with the Pulp of Melon, Honey, and the white of Eggs; and let all be distilled. . . . This water is very effectual to take away wrinkles in the Face, and gives a Vermillion-Tincture to the Skin.[50]

Raising a blush or effacing wrinkles, these recipes promised to revive youthfulness; effectively stopping the clock, they erased the ravages of time. Concocted in early modern and Victorian stillrooms alike, "Aura and Cephalus" was another long-standing favorite anti-wrinkle combination, a cosmetic heirloom passed from one aging generation to the next:

Recipe for Aura and Cephalus
   Put some powder of the best myrrh upon an iron plate, sufficiently heated to melt the gum gently, and when it liquefies, hold your face over it, at a proper distance to receive the fumes without inconvenience; and, that you may reap the whole benefit of the fumigation, cover your head with a napkin.[51]

More than opening the pores to expel impurities, this method suggests a type of reciprocal respiration. *Aura,* the recipe's author briefly waxes, means "gentle breeze" or "invisible breath" in Greek, and *Cephalus* means "head." Implicating the face, the head, and the breath, this anti-aging remedy celebrated the living countenance.

Though Logan and her coterie may have used similar recipes to ward off wrinkles or maintain the skin's healthy luster, they would have been careful not to mask their age altogether. Elderly women in the early Republic were admonished to always look and act their age.[52] As the popular etiquette writer the marchioness de Lambert complains: "Nothing is more ridiculous than making it appear, by studied ornaments, that you wish to recall the departing graces. An avowed old-age is least old."[53] "But, when the wrinkled fair, the hoary-headed matron, attempts to equip herself for conquest," condemns another critic, "her rouge can never arouse."[54] Comparing a sallow complexion with its accompanying frosty hair, an additional detractor carps: "To behold one whose countenance, whose figure, whose every gesture proclaims that the last sands of life are running out, clinging to the levities of the world," is not only one of "the most disgusting, but one of the most melancholy spectacles which can be surveyed."[55] Such unseemly women, critics universally conclude, are anachronisms, stepping out of their natural time and place.

Women's ages, like the annually recurring seasons, are fixed—and irreversible. Old women cannot arrest youth by carrying it "to an age in which they ought not appear," critics warned.[56] Logan agrees, naturalistically separating the stages of life. As the "sober season," autumn represents the review of the past and the prelude to death: "Like my own time of life, [it] has gentle and reflective pleasures, and its own peculiar beauties." In the "autumn of Life" the elderly steadily "keep in view the point at which we shall soon arrive."[57] The ephemeral season of exuberant color and sudden decay, autumn thus typifies the aged woman's liminal position in the life cycle: she is necessarily Janus-faced, looking toward the past while preparing for her impending death.[58] As such, she appears anachronistic, located between rather than within discernible moments of time.

Looking one's age was more than an issue of vanity or politeness for Logan and her circle. Daily reminded of the attendant decay of the face and mind, and haunted by Montaigne's maxim "*Old-age impresses more wrinkles on the mind than on the face,*" they feared the onset of dementia, the tragic dissolution of the mind and memory.[59] The progressive experience of anachronism, dementia begins with a disorientation in time, in which one's short- and long-term memories fuse, privileging the past over the present. Loss of time leads to confusion of place: immediate surroundings become unfamiliar and divested of the mnemonic significance they once held. Without an ensured sense of time and place, people eventually become unrecognizable. Intimates become strangers, and the self is suddenly alien. An increasing process of literalism, dementia halts the figurative replacements of reminiscence.

The memory's gradual cessation, like wrinkled skin, results from hardened arteries and blocked circulation, according to Elizabeth Fergusson. Gradually infantilized, the mind returns to childhood:

> The Blood no longer thro the heart shall flow
> No true pulsation beating Arteries show!
>
> . . . .
>
> No Circulation swift revolves around,
> But dead Stagnation in each vein is found.[60]

Since the Aristotelian notion that the aged body dries up and becomes cold persists well into the nineteenth century, people fashioned cosmetic remedies for internal maladies. They tried to jump-start the heart by applying pastes and poultices, not only to restore the circulation's "internal juices" but also to return elasticity to withered skin and strength to brittle bones.[61] Concerned more with preserving their memories than with temporarily restoring their wrinkled faces, however, Logan and her circle sought more lasting solutions. They preferred nostalgic to cosmetic antidotes, reviving the faltering juices and consequent onslaught of forgetfulness by holding *reminiscentia* in their newly warmed hands.

Their awakened touch, in turn, commenced a life review that integrates the past, neither denying it on the one hand nor protracting it on the other. As Logan illustrates in her poem "Lines Written in Old Age," she would welcome the skin's destruction in exchange for her mind's preservation through reminiscence. She imagines time's passage as a "ruthless wing" and "sweeping Scythe" that "level thought—and Fancy bind." She worries: "I cannot bear to see Decay / Usurp the place where Reason lay." But bargaining with Time, she allows him "to stamp his ruin on the face," if only, as the mnemonic refrain implores, "he would leave my Mind to Me." Her mind unspoiled, she ends the poem with relief:

> Leave me in the Dream of other years,
> Leave me the free expansive thought,
>
> . . . .
>
> Then could I bear Time's spoils to see,
> So he would leave my Mind to Me.[62]

With memory ("the Dream of other years") and reason ("the free expansive thought") restored, then and only then could she bear the physical ravages of aging.

In a similar poem, "An Ode on the Advances of Old Age" (1792), inscribed to Elizabeth Fergusson, Annis Stockton laments the gradual decay of the aging body and withering mind. The poem begins by enumerating the compounded loss of physical charms. Her posture bends ungracefully, a "hoary dew" tinges her auburn hair, the sparkle fades from her eyes, the bloom disappears from her cheek, her waistline spreads, and her alabaster neck folds into unseemly creases. But these alterations are trivial, the poem's speaker contends, if "each mental Blossom spare / And grant that they may never die!" What matters is the preservation of her mind:

> The mild affections in my Breast
> Abstracted, Delicate, Refind,
> Each sweet Idea there imprest
> . . . .
> And *time* that does each grace distroy
> Is quite disarmd of all its power.

The heart transfers former feelings into memory images that are abstracted, refined, and stamped on the mind. As the accompanying note explains, the act of writing the poem itself affected Stockton's memory: "A few Evenings ago my mind was engagd in thinking how short a time it appeared Since I began my Life, And how fast every thing that delighted and adornd me then was fleeting. My *pen, inke,* and *Paper* lay on the Table, and I diverted my self with arranging the idea of the moment."[63] Arranging the idea of the moment, Stockton merges the past and present, keeping the perils of dementia at bay.

Like Logan and Stockton, Susanna Wright and Hannah Griffitts endure time's unfeeling passage by maintaining, even improving, their mental powers as they age. Though Wright worries that "Fancy's drooping Wing / Unplum'd by Time no more can rise," she engages "each lenient Art" that might "temper Nature's rugged Cares, / And Smooth the Path of Age." Unable to combat the dangers of dementia alone, Wright seeks the consoling effects of collective reminiscence offered by her shared genealogy with Hannah Griffitts:

> Thy Mothers social Hour was mine,
>   As kindred Minds allied.
> Such would thou be, cou'd youth to Age,
>   The engaging Hand extend.[64]

An endless chain of entwined hands, her metaphor exemplifies the mnemonic power of touch in linking successive generations.

Griffitts reassures her sixty-four-year-old friend in a poetic response, "To Susanna Wright: On Some Lines wrote by herself on her Birthday":

> Distinguish'd view in this superior Mind,
>   The Fire of Wit matur'd by ripening Age.
> And striking Sense with soft Submission join'd,
>   Inspires Venera's animated Page.

Bestowing the pseudonym Venera (from the Latin *venerari,* "to venerate") on Wright, Griffitts illustrates the traditional veneration of elderly women. She judges Wright's mental dexterity by the impressive quality of her poetry, noting a distinct improvement with age. Wit and sense—the cornerstone of belles lettres and the secret of a lively countenance—noticeably animate Wright's verse.

Sally Barton similarly praises Wright's astute mind six years later in a letter to Louisa DeNormandie: "the celebrated Susy Wright a maiden Lady above 70 years of age remarkably sensible . . . at this advanced age she has all the vivacity of a woman of 40 the compleat exercise of all her faculties— converses freely & is an excellent companion."[65] With all the mental perspicacity of a woman thirty years younger, the seventy-year-old Wright defies the incorrect aspersions cast on the aged, in which the accumulation of "years—no Taste for blessings given," as Griffitts explains: "No relish to enjoy, / Is all their Portion ceaseless Toil."[66]

Grateful that "The Powers of Reason,—I retain" and "The Powers of memory,—to retrace," Griffitts also was lauded by her younger contemporaries as particularly sharp in her later years.[67] Logan notes in her diary in 1816 and 1817: "Visited my Cousin Hannah Griffitts now in the ninetieth year of her age. She has been blind for many years, but retains her other senses and her fine intellectual faculties to admiration." Though she miscalculates Griffitts's age the following year, Logan commemorates the birthday in much the same fashion: "Full of consolation this day she entered her ninetieth year. How few reach that period: and with a mind still strong and vigorous and unimpaired by age."[68] In "A Glance of Character" Griffitts accordingly praises the superior wisdom of the aged:

> How different, glows a wise & virtuous age,
>   The wreath of Honor—Glory, and renown,
> Beams, with fresh Lustre Thro' th' escampled page,
>   Embalm their Memory, & Their Labors Crown,—
> Judicious age,—will shelter in the shade
>   of Calm Retirement, walk of wisdom's vale.[69]

Though supposedly retired from worldly cares, an old woman, according to Griffitts, is "th' escampled page." Like a commonplace book, or what Logan similarly calls "a pictured leaf in memory's page," an elderly woman's mind is an invaluable collection of memories, wisdom, judgment, and taste.[70] An animate archive, her mind is a cultural treasure.

Logan's dressing table thus integrated the choreography of her toilette with her daily writing practices. Because paper and ink, rather than cosmetics, ultimately preserved the face's physiognomy, the toilette "accommodates a lady with the conveniences for writing, reading, and holding her trinkets, and other articles of that kind," according to cabinetmaker Thomas Sheraton.[71] As such, it housed the shared ingredients used in cosmetics and handwriting. Lemon juice, sandarac, gum, eggs, beer, brandy, and even urine created a reliable face varnish and legible ink. A woman applied the white lead foundation to her cheek by "dipping the finger, or a piece of paper, or what is preferable to either, a hare's foot prepared for the purpose"—much as she spread sandarac or pounce by hand or a soft hare's foot across the freshly inked page, bringing a receptive "finish" to face and paper alike. Ultimately safeguarding her memory, Logan prefers "the sombre tint from the Pencil of Reflection" to be "drawn across [her] mind."[72]

THE BREATH OF MEMORY

Holding cherished items from her toilette table, a woman could initiate a contemplative life review through her sense of touch. Just as the memory depended on sensory stimulation of the autonomic nervous system, as chapters 1 and 2 illustrate, so reminiscence relied on those same internal movements during old age. Given the hand's indebtedness to the heart's warmth, and given the heart's influence over female recollection, women breathed life into inanimate objects that embodied their fleeting memories. Though metonyms for the face and mind, the mirror, portrait miniature, fan, and silhouette also signified the heart, for the "language of the heart," mnemonic and cosmetic theorists agreed, was "expressed by the general complexion." The heart, in turn, would stimulate and impress the mind: the heart's warmth "removes asperities," "polishes the rough surface," and "animates the dormant faculties of the mind." Because the mind improves as the body decays, it was reasoned, the heart strengthens its symbolic potential in old age. "At a certain height, the faculties of the mind expand, and the fibres of the heart dilate," explains one theorist. The heart awakens dormant memories, which are otherwise "insupportable when unanimated by the soft affections of the heart." The process of animation, moreover, is reciprocal: the heart activates the memory; the memory, through "the charms of the imagination, instantly converted into sensations of the heart."[73] A life review required more than the constancy of nostalgic objects. It demanded reciprocity between the heart and mind.

A form of resuscitation, reminiscence was imagined through respiratory images until the nineteenth century. Joining youth's vitality with the elderly's hindsight, a life review could revive the ailing body as it restored the mind. As one critic explained the circulatory process, there is "a very brisk and lively motion of the blood of young people," which, "according to the laws of animal oeconomy," guarantees health, vigor, and growth. This "lively motion" decays as one ages, resulting in "a sluggish circulation, which by degrees ceases altogether in the finest and smallest vessels," causing stiffened muscles.[74] Despite the inevitable dissolution of any one body, respiration halts the degeneration of aging when experienced as a kind of collective breath: "Warm, active, and balsamic particles thrown off by the lungs of young people in the air, which they respire, may give such a quality, as when sucked in again by a person in years, shall communicate an extraordinary force to the circulation humours in his body, and so quicken and enliven them, as to bestow a kind of reflective youthfulness, which, by constant repetition, may for many years keep off and delay those infirmities, to which people of the same age are generally subject."[75] Like mouth-to-mouth resuscitation, respiration requires two mouths, two hearts, two pairs of lungs, and a single breath. Breathing, in other words, is communicable. Repeatedly inhaling youthful exhalations, the aged could reinvigorate the circulation and restore the mind. Seeking such an infusion as she aged, Logan thus admits, "I think a mixture of old and young makes the most pleasing society."[76]

Resuscitation underscores the collective nature of reminiscence. Like the absent or aged body they represent, *reminiscentia* are inherently incomplete and require a narrative supplement to restore the past to the present moment.[77] Epitomized by the handwritten letter, such narratives breathe life into otherwise dead objects.[78] The mirrors, miniatures, fans, and silhouettes collected and exchanged by the Philadelphia coterie were accompanied by and sometimes even wrapped in a familiar letter. Such "Lilliputian Packets," as Elizabeth Fergusson called them, could be held in the hand or kept close to the heart.[79] Unable to speak entirely for themselves, *reminiscentia* thus relied on letters to infuse life into the memories they embodied. According to Fergusson, correspondence "Brought distant ages to our present Views / And former Actions to our eyes renews."[80] Mimicking respiration, letters revealed "Every Movement of the Soul." Further, it "Breath'd Love, delight, the sympathizing Tear," so that "Paper may be almost said to live." Describing her ailing heart as like a letter enveloping a souvenir, Fergusson charts her blood's swift circulation, "which by motion rushes more fast into the vessels than can be discharged and when to creep produces instant death by bursting the *Pericardium,* that is the Bag that encloses the Heart."[81] Enclosing her heart, a letter was a natural vent through which emotions uncontrollably gushed: "Things rise out of one another so that every fresh thought seems but a prelude to the former; at this Rate I shall Scribble infinitum."[82]

Like collective respiration, the circulation of letters was reciprocal. As "conversation carried upon paper, between two friends at a distance," according to rhetorician Hugh Blair, letters provided the "ever agreeable and innocent pleasures that flow from social love, from hearts united by the same laudable ties."[83] Controlling the flow of blood within the pericardium through mutual love and sympathy, letters mingled hearts. "Those letters are only good, which contain the natural effusion of the heart, expressed in unaffected language," writes one critic. They must "shew with singular clearness the delicate features and shades which distinguish the mind of the writer."[84] Replicating the blood's circulation—moving away from and back to the heart—letters were considered "the commerce of the heart." Like shared breath, sympathy swelled correspondents' hearts.

Circulating from hand to hand and from heart to heart, letters collapsed the Philadelphia coterie into a single, unified body sharing one heart. Like the blood's circular path from the arteries to the heart, emotions flowed between correspondents. As Annis Stockton explains: "How often when I am reading Mr. Pope's Letters, do I envy the day the knot of friends that seem'd to have but one heart by which they were united and their greatest pleasure was giving each other pleasure."[85] Like the concentric layers of boxes on Logan's dressing table, or a precious locket housing a coveted lock of hair, letters contained the heart, for "within the body is both the heart and the heart's content—the other."[86]

Sent between affectionate correspondents as a supplemental narrative to the mnemonic objects they accompanied, letters diminished spatial boundaries between individuals and erased the marks of time. Boasting an aesthetic of immediacy, epistles were euphemistically described as "writing to the moment" during the eighteenth century. They initiated the life review, bringing past scenes into immediate focus. As Sarah Barton writes to Elizabeth Fergusson, the "Dear, and only Surviving friend of my Youth," on 15 February 1794: "Your Immediate address, has brought to my mind a retrospect of past scenes & a review of the many Diversities of fortune we have both Experienced, which naturally Excited pleasing painful reflections."[87] As mnemonic devices, letters provided tangible evidence of remembrance. Sending an epistle to Deborah Logan "as proof that I had not forgot thee," Sally Norris Dickinson appreciates the value of friendship to reminiscence: "But strangers are not like those whom we remember as long as we can remember any thing."[88] Because letters functioned as material surrogates for an absent beloved, they stalled the amnesia of aging. As such, they were exchanged as tokens of affection between generations of women: "Well knowing that affection is Hereditary in your Family," writes Fergusson: "I

Say A thought Struck me, That your Dear Children might like to be in Possession of Epistles that Breathd nothing but Piety, Resignation, and a cordial good will to mankind . . . under this Idea I send you a Packet."[89] Sent between the old and the young, letters exemplified collective respiration. Young women inherited epistolary heirlooms and responded in kind, as Griffitts fondly remembers: "Thy Pretty Companion (Sally) gave me a specimen of her writing, neatly done indeed, & her little piece of drawing, I have sent to be framed, & will keep it to remember her."[90] Locked in boxes, copied into commonplace books, or enclosed in shadow boxes, letters provided the essential narrative to telling *reminiscentia*.

THE MIRROR STAGE

"Passing by a looking Glass in one of the Chambers just now," remarks Logan, "I was perfectly shocked to see myself—So Old and so Ugly. But what else can be expected at Seventy Seven?"[91] Similarly shocked at her own reflection in the mirror, Fergusson contemplates concealing her age, only to concede, "But let that little Error pass / I cant forget I keep a Glass!"[92] Standing before the mirror as if confronting an unexpected stranger, these women experienced what contemporary psychologists call the "looking-glass self." Dominating the literary representations of aging, the looking glass suggests a mode of alienation from one's body in old age and the consequent dependence on others to provide a recognizable image of one's self.[93] There is a split between who we see in the mirror and who we imagine ourselves to be: as we age, we consider our youthful selves to be hidden somewhere in our decaying bodies.

This painful sense of fragmentation and the alienating effects of identification with an image is, according to gerontologists, the inverse of the mirror stage of infancy. The mirror stage is the first separation by which we conceive our individuality. Assuming a form that mixes elements of the other, we identify with a reflection of ourselves through the mother's intimate care. Through this identification the infant sees the self as a harmonious and ideal unity while experiencing her own body as uncoordinated. The virtually simultaneous impression of visual unity and fragmentation gives rise to the ego and ushers the infant into the imaginary—the imagistic state before language. The mirror stage of old age, on the other hand, perpetuates the loss of the imaginary. Old age is triangulated through three disparate images of the self: the first likeness is incorporated into the other; the second figure is a memory of a past self; and the last semblance is the present and unrecognizable reflection one sees in the mirror. Contrasting the social and biological representations of selfhood, the "looking-glass self" leaves an elderly viewer in a state of denial or utter repudiation of her reflection.

Confounding the mirror stages of infancy and old age in her poem "The Four Stages of Life," Fergusson exemplifies the recursive construction of identity throughout the life cycle:

> While every Scene of Life appears more vain,
> Than Childhoods Folly when we Manhood gain.
> The Wisest Mortals are but Infants here
> When scand by Beings of the Nobler Sphere.[94]

Writing the poem on 7 July 1753 at the age of sixteen, Fergusson clearly understands the cultural representation of life stages that dominated early modern thought.[95] Staged as discernible steps on a rising and falling staircase, the ages-of-life motif offered an orderly model of behavior over the life cycle. Though distinct stages, these steps are ironically reflexive, as figure 3.5 suggests: entering and exiting the world in a similarly helpless fashion, a person experiences the cradle and grave as mirror images of each other.[96]

Maturity, or middle age, was the province of middle-class men, but economically dependent women were persistently thrust back to the "transitory and precarious duration of personal attractions" of youth, as *The Female Aegis; or, The Duties of Women from Childhood to Old Age* (1798) reminds its female readers: "Elegance of form and brilliancy of complection are acident gifts of Nature." "Everyone loses in advancing in life," admonishes the marchioness de Lambert, "and the women more than the men." Encouraging old women to assume the "politeness," "dignity," and "repose" befitting them, Lambert substitutes social graces for "exterior graces, as time destroys them."[97] Controlled by rules of etiquette, women were infantilized throughout their lives.

Struck by the mirror's significance, Annis Stockton considers her own mortality on giving two small mirrors to her granddaughter and another young acquaintance in 1793. The gifts and accompanying poems suggest the parallel identity crises that females experience in adolescence and old age. In the first poem, "To a little Miss, with a toy looking glass," Stockton illustrates the mirror's moral physiognomy:

> Enclos'd My Dears the promised glass
> Which will reflect your lovely face
> And when you'r good, will show most fair
> But if you'r naughty, come not there.

3.5. "The Life and Age of Woman: Stages of Woman's Life from Infancy to the Brink of the Grave," by A. Alden (1836). Courtesy, Library of Congress, Prints and Photographs Division, LC-USZ62-42435.

In the companion poem, "To a little Miss a year older than the one to whom the Glass was promised, with a toy looking Glass," Stockton repeats the instructive admonition:

> May you grow up a pattern to your sex
> And when a bigger glass your face reflects
> May it still shew you good as well as fair
> Your parents joy and providence care.[98]

In both cases Stockton suggests a predictable reflection of moral character in the girls' faces and mirror images. More important, she illustrates the punitive and vapid socialization of girls to be pretty, nice, and above all, good. When girls resist or fail to "mind what those who love [them] say," they no longer resemble themselves or at least the social representations imposed on them. Thus, Stockton bestows a weighty object lesson along with her small gifts:

> For when angry passions rise
> They quite becloud your pretty eyes
> And make mamma think nancys flown
> And papa does not know his own.

Defying their parents' rules as well as repudiating the natural oedipal identification of childhood, adolescent girls necessarily reject the images of infancy to forge new identities different from and alien to their parents. Seeking that lost image in old age but finding only the fractured face of the "looking-glass self," women look once again to other women for a unified identity.

Paired with Stockton's previously discussed poem, "An Ode on the Advances of Old Age," with its encyclopedic catalog of fading beauty, the toy looking glasses tell another story. Stockton gave these small tokens when she was fifty-seven years old, undoubtedly remembering the ode she had sent Elizabeth Fergusson just one year earlier. Considering the fragmented self-image presented in her own mirror, Stockton, like other aging women, would rely on her friends to reintegrate the pieces of her splintered psyche. Shared reminiscences between lifelong friends bridged memory gaps, tempered the disorienting looking glass, and ultimately forged a collective identity between women. Friendship "forces us to resemble" one another, writes Lambert; it is "reciprocal assistance" that "requires conformity, equality of age, or what approaches to it, and a similarity of inclinations and pursuits."[99] Familiarity provided images by which aging women could define themselves. Leveling the difference between life stages, critics agreed that the elderly were "all of a consanguinity, formed of the same materials, and designed for the same end; this obliges us to a mutual tenderness."[100] Though a woman may no longer have recognized herself in the mirror, she maintained a natural identification with other women. Based on the moral philosophical notion of sympathy, friendship was a social mirror for women: as Hume says, they "reflected each other's emotions" because "those rays of passion, sentiments and opinions may be often reverberated."[101]

Exchanged between peers, then, a mirror assists reminiscence and mends the shattered image of the "looking-glass self" in old age. It offers a continuous reflection throughout the life stages and incorporates the alienating mirror image with an interior sense of selfhood. Such a collective sense of identity compensates for the unfamiliarity of one's own face by projecting it onto a stable relationship,[102] as the anonymous poem, "To a Lady on her making a Present of a Looking-Glass," intimates: "Thy gift, dear *Chloe,* when thy gift I see, / Presents an image of myself to me." Though the mirror directly reflects the recipient's image, it also suggests a physiognomic link to her heart:

> My heart's as faithful as the glass is clear,
> For on my heart that beauteous form of thine,
> Has more life than in the mirror mine.[103]

Permanently impressed on her heart, the image of the beloved, the poem's speaker insists, outshines yet at the same time animates her own reflection. This reflection, moreover, proceeds directly from the heart. As the painter Charles Le Brun theorizes, the blood continually passes through the heart, which accordingly sends spirits to the brain. The brain, finally, transforms the blood's spirits into passions that naturally animate the countenance.[104] Thus the mirror encloses the heart and reflects its content.

The simultaneous emphasis on the face and heart, on the self and other as the composite mirror for identity, underscores the definitive irony of old age. Whereas some theorists recommended solitude for the mind to review and arrange "all the ideas and impressions it has gained in its observations in the world," others believed that the elderly look toward others to supplement their reminiscences.[105] The "secret ties, these sympathies, this sweet inclination" of friendship, the latter contended, blossom in retirement. The calibrations of a decaying body and improving mind as one ages cause a consequent rise in sociability: as Lambert explains, "In proportion as reason improves, as the imagination encreases in brilliancy, and as the heart becomes pure and refined, the more the sentiment of friendship appears requisite to our happiness."[106] Reconciling the "looking-glass self" with the internalized versions of herself, an aged woman balances solitude with society. Alone, her mind "links one proposition to another, joins experience with observation, and from the discovery of one truth proceeds in search of others," Zimmerman states.[107] But only when experience and observation are verified by a sympathetic friend are these reminiscences viable. The triangulated self-images of old age, therefore, require social reflection, for to reflect means to throw back from a surface, to form an image of an object, and to contemplate ideas. Prompting physical and subjective reflections, the mirror is an apt metaphor for collective memory.

Preserving past and present selves, the looking glass represents the mind's lasting powers over one's mirror image. As Logan writes in her "Sonnet on Retirement": "This is my pleasure—that with active mind / The present, past, and future can survey."[108] Inspired by William Cowper's "Sonnet to George Romney," Logan applauds Romney's physiognomic art, the artist's skillful showing of the "mind's impression too on every face, / With strokes that time ought never to erase."[109] Thus memory traces are not only recoverable; they are infallible and permanent. Like Logan, Fergusson stresses the mind's synthesizing mnemonics. Reversing the early modern theories of perception and memory reposition, whereby a subject absorbs sensory impressions, Fergusson imagines an internal mirror that stamps memory images on both the mind and its external objects:

When one fond Object occupys the mind

. . . .

We make them Mirrors by Ingenious Skill,
They all reflect the object of our thought
Strong with that Image is each substance frought.[110]

Objects become mirrors of thought, and thoughts become objectified. Externalizing her thoughts, Fergusson thus transforms the memory places in her mind into objective correlatives embodied by collected *reminiscentia*.

Such a transformation accentuates the importance of the mirror to the life review of old age. As mnemonic object and metaphor, the mirror represents the ways the mind arranges, stores, rearranges, and then variably displays memories over time. Like filling a commonplace book with retrievable topoi, the mind holds both the original memory and its trace or copy, to "arrest the fleeting images that fill / The mirror of the mind, and hold them fast," as Zimmerman explains. Holding up memories as if to a mirror, a woman ideally integrates what she sees in the looking glass with images of her past self. Objects initiate recollection, promising "new information by every reflection." Contemplating the past, the aged woman "blends all the ideas of past and future in the actual enjoyment of the present moment."[111] A mirror of the mind, reminiscence fuses time and its fractured images, creating new and meaningful narratives by which to live.

THE LANGUAGE OF THE FAN

On 25 January 1765 Elizabeth Fergusson sent a beautiful folding fan to her friend Juliana Ritchie, inscribing a poetic epistle on the fan leaf. Though the fan is no longer extant, the poem, along with Ritchie's response, is copied in Fergusson's commonplace book, "Poemata Juvenilia."[112] Taken together, the poems illustrate the mnemonic value of letters—as inscriptions of the mind, heart, and hand—between friends. Like a mirror, the fan reflected a woman's emotions and continued the epistolary "conversation on paper" on its handmade paper leaves. Fergusson's poem, "Wrote to a Lady on the Back of a Fan," establishes the fan's living language:

To Mrs. R——e
Accept this Triffle from a Female Friend,
Selfish the Motive for to gain an End;
When *Western* Seas divides us far apart;
Regard this Bauble of Esteem a Mark!
When cooling Breezes are denyd by Heaven;
Nor gentle Gales by fanning Zephers given:
This small *Machine* shall makes amends by Art
And guard your Face from wounding many a Heart;
No light coquetish airs Shall flirt it round;
Nor shall it flutter with an angry sound:
Serene and Graceful shall its motion prove,
And tho' attractive, yet forbidding Love!
All Love that rises not from Friendships Flame
Must *Juliana* from her Breast disclaim.

Sent to an absent friend, the epistolary fan translates motion into emotion. The winnowing fan was an indispensable accessory of a woman's toilette, protecting the face, repelling insects, and dispersing unpleasant odors. More important, it preserved and encouraged collective reminiscence.[113]

Given reminiscence's reliance on touch, the fan's fluttering hand motions shared a physiognomic link with the heart. As Joseph Addison's *Spectator* (1711) explains: "There is scarce any Motion in the Mind which does not produce a suitable Agitation in the Fan; insomuch, that if I only see the Fan of a disciplin'd Lady, I know very well whether she laughs, frowns, or blushes." Laughing, frowning, and blushing through expressive hand movements, a woman's fan, like her face, spoke volumes. There was, according to Addison, the angry flutter, the modest flutter, the timorous flutter, the confused flutter, the merry flutter, and the amorous flutter.[114] Fergusson, however, appreciates the fan's movements as distinguishing marks of female friendship: "All Love that rises not from Friendships Flame / Must *Juliana* from her Breast disclaim." As an epistolary "Bauble of Esteem," the fan awaits a reply, bearing a "Selfish" "Motive for to gain an End."

Ritchie's response two days later sends "Millians of thanks for the fan, I receive it as a pledge." With a letter inscribed on its surface, the fan not only frames her own face but also impresses Fergusson's image on her heart. Elaborated by the fan's fluttering motions, this pledge inspires collective reminiscence:

This little fluttering gay Machine,
With pleasure I now review
For it inspires a grateful Sense
And makes me think of you.

2

As various Forms the *Printers* Hand;
Has here displayd with Art;
Friendship in distant Realms shall [draw]
Your Image on my Heart.

3

All vain attempts to be admired
I totaly decline
And to my best Accomplishd Friend
The dying Swains Resign.
      London, Norfolk Street, 27 January 1765

The epistolary fan's perpetual motions inspire warm recollections. Written by Fergusson and held in Ritchie's receptive palm, the fan transferred mnemonic images from one heart to another. Facing outward, the painted fan leaf signaled Ritchie's emotions to the world. Conversely, the epistolary side held toward her face "makes me think of you," for "Friendship in distant Realms shall [draw] / Your Image on my Heart."[115]

The epistolary nature of Ritchie's fan highlights what early practitioners called "the language of the fan." Though contemporary critics question the validity of such a discourse, it held great significance during the fan's heyday in the eighteenth century. Developed by Charles Francis Bandini and alternately published by the fanmaker Robert Clarke and William Cock in 1797, fan language, or "Fanology," was all the rage.[116] Typified by the directions on the "Conversation Fan" in figure 3.6, fanology promised to "Improve the Friendship and set forth a Plan for Ladies to Chit Chat & hold the tongue." It comprised five basic positions or signals: (1) move fan with left hand to right arm; (2) move fan with right hand to left arm; (3) place fan against the bosom or heart; (4) raise fan to mouth; and (5) raise fan to forehead or brow. Emphasizing the hand, face, and heart, these fan positions are manifestly mnemonic. As the forehead physiognomically portrayed both reason and memory, so the mouth expressed the heart: "The mouth," according to Charles Le Brun, "has no other use than to follow the Emotions of the Heart": "when the Heart complains, the Mouth falls in the corners; when it is at ease, the corners of the Mouth are elevated; and when it has an Aversion, the mouth shoots forward and rises in the middle."[117] A kind of speaking motion, fan positions signified the letters of the alphabet, conveniently divided into five groups of five letters each by omitting the letter "J": A–E, F–K, L–P, Q–U, V–Z. Using the five positions, one could sign any letter by a two-number combination: the first indicates the group, and the second tells the position of the letter in that group (i.e., 2:1 stands for *f*,

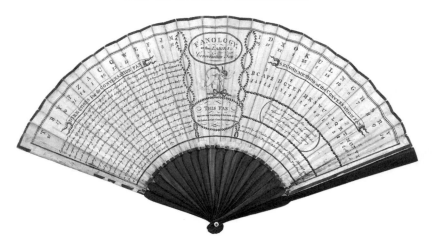

3.6. "Fanology or the Ladies Conversation Fan," published by Robert Clark, London, 1797. Oldham Collection, 1976.311. Courtesy, Museum of Fine Arts, Boston. © 2002 Museum of Fine Arts, Boston. All rights reserved. Reproduced with permission.

the first letter in second group). To spell *friendship,* then, a woman would choreograph the following gestures: F (2:1), R (4:2), I (2:4), E (1:5), N (3:3), D (1:4), S (4:3), H (2:3), I (2:4), P (3:5). Though tedious and time-consuming, fan language—performed face to face—was quickly memorized. Approximating the intimacy of handwritten letters, fans spoke the heart's desires.

In addition to elaborately instructive fan leaves, etiquette books translated fan language into a usable art, as in figure 3.7. In *The Young Gentleman and Lady's Private Tutor* (1770), for example, Matthew Towle agreed with fanmakers that "the Fan is genteel and useful," and he created six "genteel and very becoming" fan positions. Obscuring the mnemonic juxtapositions of the hand, face, and heart, however, Towle changed the standard five movements to six relatively static positions, trading mnemonics for a systematic discipline over the female body.

1. Observe the Curt'sie, the Fan between the tip of the Thumb and first Finger, the head of the Mount easily leaning towards the Right Elbow.

2. Represents a young Lady sitting in the second Position of the Fan, the mount of the Fan in the palm of her right Hand, and the handle in the palm of her left, the Fan erect and the left Elbow easily bending towards her left Side, and her right a proper Distance from her right Side.

3.7. Matthew Towle, *The Young Gentleman and Lady's Private Tutor* (London, 1770) (shelf-mark 8404bb.23). Copyright the British Library. Reproduced by permission of the British Library.

3. Represents a young Lady sitting in the third Position of the Fan, the mount of the Fan in the palm of her left Hand resting in her Lap, and the handle in the palm of her right Hand, the right Elbow bending easily towards her right Side, her left Elbow at proper Distance from her left.

4. Represents a young Lady sitting in the fourth Position of the

Fan, the mount easily bearing in her Lap, with her left Hand upon the handle and her right Hand upon that, both bending genteelly towards the Body.

5. Represents a young Lady standing in the fifth Position of the Fan, the Fan extended; the handle to the Fan in the palm of her right Hand, the end of her Thumb touching the great Stick towards her right side, and her little Finger touching the Stick towards the left Arm; thus you see the Fan extended and fit for Service, and the Fingers thus placed render the Hand genteel and agreeable, and the Elbows being at a proper Distance from the Side, render the whole Body agreeably genteel.

6. (See Figure the Third in Walking) The Fan in the right Hand, bearing easily on the Point of the First Finger, the Head of the Mount pointing over the left Arm, the Elbows at a proper Distance from the Body.[118]

Such stoic positions emphasize the body's rigid posture rather than variable facial expressions.[119] A convenient way to display the well-turned hand, fan comportment closely resembles the writing postures described in chapter 2.

Such a strict corporeal regimen, I would suggest, underscores the fan's conventional use in courtship practices.[120] Responding to the fan's seductive motions, anxious suitors were threatened by the erotic possibilities and potential rejection. Playfully indulging her critics in an undated epistolary poem, "The Restoration of a stolen fan," Annis Stockton rehearses their anti-fanology rhetoric. It opens with a suggestive flutter that insinuates "meaningful looks": "The fan surrender'd to a meaning look / Which spoke your heart in earnest to regain it." She then boasts a litany of romantic conquests, aggravating her critics' insecurities. So skilled is she with her fan that

> Vanquish'd generals drop their honours down
> And at the victors feet their ensigns lay
> Fidelias wit has gain'd the civic crown
> And now I send the tributary bay—

Her martial barbs parody Joseph Addison's Spectator, who establishes a female fan academy where "women are armed with fans as men with swords." Like Towles's six genteel positions, the Spectator licenses the fan's weaponry: "Handle your fans, unfurl your fans, discharge your fans, ground your fans, recover your fans, flutter your fans." By the poem's end, Stockton abandons her militaristic maneuvers for "friendships fascinating ties."[121] Like the speakers in Elizabeth Fergusson's and Juliana Ritchie's poems, she wins the prize of female friendship.

As marks of friendship exchanged among the Philadelphia coterie, fans were tokens for collective reminiscence. Embodying the heart and accenting the face, the fan spoke the language of memory. Though upper-class women were taught the art of fan making, most women purchased hand-painted or printed fan leaves and inserted sticks of wood, ivory, tortoise-shell, or mother-of-pearl into the mounts.[122] Outlived by their more durable sticks, fan leaves, as Logan explains, were often replaced: "The new mountings of Fans (putting new Paper upon Old Sticks) was an article of millinery business, and upon taking them to be done, your taste was consulted as to what mount you would fancy, by having all the Shop spread before you—the usual price of such a reparation was half a Crown. In the old times you seldom bought an Ivory fan under two dollars."[123] But as the plates from Diderot's 1765 *Encyclopédie* in figure 3.8 illustrate, more than replacing old leaves, fan making was a highly technical and distinctly collaborative art, employing more than twenty types of artisans, including leaf designers, printers, stick carvers, inlayers, gilders, ribbon weavers, and assemblers. The process was made easier by the invention of the pleating mold in 1760: the pleated leaf (or two glued leaves) was adhered to slips, or ribs (the narrow upper portion of the sticks), which were supported by a set of sticks gathered at the base by a rivet and folded up between the two outer guards.

Although images were haphazardly painted on early fan leaves without any forethought about its mounted or folded outcome, by the mid-eighteenth century artists accommodated the decoration of the fan to its utility. They revamped the mount's design, maintaining images on either side of the leaf, but replaced the singular, panoramic scene of the principal side with a tripartite scheme of cartouches. Like the mounts, the sticks of pleated fans changed over the course of the century. Called *monture se-quelette* by 1760, fan sticks narrowed and radiated from the rivetlike spokes, creating spaces between the sticks and interrupting the previously continuous surface decoration. Such careful spacing between images on the fan mounts and sticks signaled that fan styles had moved from the baroque and rococo to the neoclassical. Revived by the architectural and interior designs of the Adam brothers, neoclassicism required order, regularity, and symmetry—the same aesthetic and organizing criteria as for the manuscript commonplace book.

The individually framed images of both hand-painted and printed fans resemble the collected, arranged, and copied topoi in commonplace books.[124] Each cartouche contained an evocative memory image. Reminiscent of Descartes's memory folds, resembling "folds in a piece of paper or linen caus[ing] them to be more readily folded the way they were folded

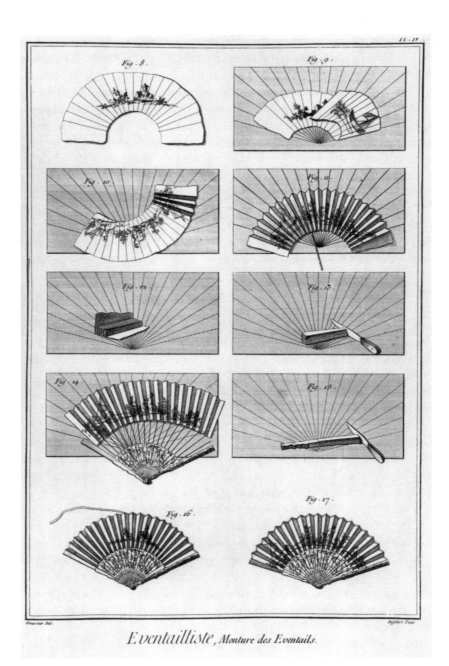

Fig. 8. Fig. 9. Fig. 10. Fig. 11. Fig. 12. Fig. 13. Fig. 14. Fig. 15. Fig. 16. Fig. 17.

Eventailliste, Monture des Eventails.

3.8. "Evantailliste," in Diderot and D'Alembert's *Encyclopédie,* 1756, Plate IV, shows the method of folding a fan leaf. Courtesy, Harry Ransom Humanities Research Center, The University of Texas at Austin.

earlier," the pleated fan manifested the places in a woman's mind.[125] With its carefully folded leaves mounted on decorative sticks, the fan's opening and closing movements, like the mind's reciprocal reposition and deposition of images, suggest a unique form of textuality. Made of antique laid paper, fan mounts retain the chain lines of the deckle and mold. When held to the light, fan leaves preserve the subtle marks of their maker, much like a telltale watermark.[126] Just as a folio sheet was folded in the middle to create two leaves (or four pages) of a manuscript or book, so a fan leaf was creased to display its balanced decoration on recto and verso sides.

The physical resemblance of the folding fan and manuscript commonplace book highlights their shared mnemonic functions. An equally textual form of knowledge, the fan imitated the commonplace book's circulation of personal and cultural memory. Fans commemorated the ritualized milestones of birthdays, courtship, weddings, and funerals, cogently reflecting a woman's life stages during reminiscence.[127] As *aide memoire,* fans also displayed historical, cartographic, or botanical information on their mounts—the same practical and universal knowledge compiled in commonplace books. As John Gay intimates in his poem *The Fan* (1714), "The Fan shall flutter in all female hands" so that "their minds improve." As the "polished sticks the waving engine spread" and "round the rivet pearly circles shine," women coordinated the fan's movements to express their emotions. Creating a semiotics of female friendship rather than courtship, the fan prompted collective reminiscence by "Signals that are seldom misinterpreted / By the eye that is in the know."[128]

FACES IN MINIATURE

When Elizabeth Fergusson's name incorrectly appeared on a list of Philadelphians killed by the yellow fever epidemic two years earlier, Juliana Ritchie asked a mutual acquaintance to return the portrait miniature she had lovingly given her childhood friend. Fergusson corrected the mistake and "immediately returnd the Picture wrapt in a Paper with the following Lines."[129] Enclosing the delicate portrait in a poem, "Lines on Returning a Miniature Picture to the Lady that Desired It," Fergusson maps the miniature's circular journey. Like the epistolary fan mailed thirty years earlier, this poetic epistle was an act of reminiscence. It nostalgically remembers the passing years since the portrait was first painted and given as a token of friendship. At the same time, the miniature signifies the devastating advances of old age. Anatomizing her love for Ritchie as "Heart[s] congenial" stronger than "kindred Blood," the poem depicts the social body of remembrance and the usefulness of material *reminiscentia:*

Judge not my Friend I carelessly Resign;
These Features once which represented Thine;
But years advancing fast to Deaths cold Shade;
Whisper I Soon may in the Grave be laid:
Perhaps no Heart congenial may be nigh,
With Pious care to close my Sightless Eye;
Perhaps no Friend attentive may be near
To write my *julia* that I held her Dear
But sure on whom this Semblance you bestow
Tho Kindred Blood may throu their Chanells flow
Will never Love you with a Brighter Flame
Than her you once esteemed as Betsy Graeme.
Philadelphia, 1795.

The poem moves in two directions simultaneously, preserving "Features once which represented Thine" and remembering Betsy Graeme before she married the disreputable Hugh Fergusson while looking forward to the inevitable "years advancing fast to Deaths cold Shade." Though she does not die until 1801, Fergusson is haunted by Ritchie's mistake. Imagining the miniature's posthumous return, she morbidly foresees her own deathbed. Forlorn and friendless, she worries that she will die alone; no friend will close her eyes or transcribe her final wishes. Resuscitated by love's "brighter flame," however, Fergusson is inspired to "write my *julia* that I held her Dear." Friendship, she concludes, is stronger than genealogy, for the rejuvenating transfusion of reminiscence, like blood and breath, "throu their Chanells flow."

Worn on a person as jewelry, displayed in specially designed rooms called *cabinets,* set in the top of snuffboxes and memorandum cases, or secreted in a woman's dressing table, the miniature was the most personal form of portraiture. It was what one critic calls "the notation of the moment and the moment's consequences."[130] The miniature transcended place and time, it made absence presence, and it granted immortality. A descendant of the reliquary boxes that housed sacred bones and memorabilia, the portrait miniature extended female friendship beyond death. "Such striking resemblances," the American miniaturist Charles Fraser promises, "will never fail to perpetuate the tenderness of friendship, to divert the cares of absence, and to aid the affection in dwelling on those features and that image which death has forever wrested from it."[131] Linked to nostalgic versions of childhood, the miniature thus presents a diminutive, manipulable, and domesticated version of experience.[132] With no natural precedent, the miniature is purely a social creation that arrests the biological process of aging and immutably etches itself into the folds of memory.

The portrait miniature also grew out of a particularly textual tradition: the illuminated manuscript. Like carefully folded fan mounts with their decorative cartouches on both recto and verso leaves, the miniature had a folio heritage.[133] Coming into general usage during the eighteenth century, the term *miniature* derives from the Latin *miniare,* meaning "to color with red lead."[134] Red ink, which was made at home by women throughout the century, was used to decorate the initials and borders of a manuscript book before the invention of printing. Linked to the book miniature and later to the detached portrait miniature, limning (painting on a transparent, white surface with watercolors) and illumination (the art of decorating manuscript texts) animate seemingly transparent surfaces.[135] Wrapping Juliana Ritchie's miniature in an epistolary poem, Fergusson rehearses the miniature's gradual evolution from the handwritten page. She then transcribes the poem in a commonplace book, extending the miniature's textual genealogy to the mnemonic arts.

A literary commonplace, the miniature portrait shares the visual and narrative qualities of mnemonic topoi during collective reminiscence. On and off the manuscript page, portrait miniatures typically contain a memorable inscription or impresa, a word or motto that "propounds some general instruction to all," according to the Renaissance antiquarian William Camden. The impresa mimics the symbiotic relationship between the body's memory impressions and the mind's corresponding images. A kind of imaginative embodiment, the miniature contains "a correspondency of the picture, which is as the body; and the Motto, which as the soul giveth it life."[136] Much like the illuminated book's impresa, the detached miniature exchanged by intimates carries a private inscription on its verso side or in the decorative case that enclosed it. Sometimes reiterated by a lock of the sitter's hair, the impresa ultimately represents the social body of reminiscence: it embodies the beloved's image, which finds its way into the recipient's heart. A reciprocal gesture, the impresa preserves and reveals the shared "secretes of the minde."[137]

As part of the neoclassical aesthetic of imitation, miniature painting, like commonplacing, was inherently derivative.[138] Interpreting the copy (i.e., the painting or memory image) required intimate knowledge of the original (i.e., the sitter or sensory impression). As William Byrd explains: "I coud discern so many good things in the portrait, when I knew them so well in the original, just like those who pick out the meaning of the Bible . . . because they were acquainted with the subject before."[139] Painting, then, was a kind of quotation. Theorists and practitioners alike promoted the Augustan defense of imitation by describing painting in writerly terms. "Painting is a sort of Writing," suggests one theorist. "It ought to be Legible" but "no more an

Exact Copy of the Face than a Literal Translation will be of the Original Book."[140] Imitation is "a perpetual exercise of the mind, a continual invention," contends another, and can "hardly be charged with plagiarism."[141] Arguing that "poets practice this kind of borrowing without reserve," Sir Joshua Reynolds borrowed liberally from John Dryden's essay "A Parallel of Poetry and Painting" (1695).[142] As sister arts, they shared a kind of rhetorical *ekphrasis:* poetry is a speaking picture; painting is mute poetry.

Additionally, poetry and portraiture followed the neoclassical distinction between the general and the particular. Artists provided a familiar but generalized form against which viewers could project their own more detailed conceptions of the subject. As Samuel Johnson illustrates in *Rasselas:* "The business of the poet . . . is to examine not the individual but the species; to remark general properties and large appearances." Focusing on prominent features, the poet would "recall the original to every mind" by neglecting "the minuter discriminations."[143] Similarly, painting depended "more upon the general effect produced by the painter, than on the exact expression of the peculiarities, or minute discrimination of the parts," according to Reynolds.[144] Only then, said the critic William Gilpin, is the viewer's imagination excited "with a thousand beautiful ideas."[145] The interpretive possibilities latent in the finite text or canvas, therefore, became fully realized in the viewer's mind. Linked to theories of imitation, poetry and portraiture finally required familiarity with the original. Otherwise, interpretation would be completely subjective, leaving viewers, as Reynolds notes, "disappointed at not finding the original correspond with their own conceptions."[146] The portrait miniature, like its accompanying verse epistle, therefore, demanded intimacy between painter and subject, subject and viewer, who necessarily viewed them "in hand near unto the eye."[147]

As *The School of Miniature* (1733) explains, five traits characterized the detached miniature's inherent intimacy:

1. It is in its Nature more delicate than any other sorts of painting.
2. It requires to be beheld near at Hand.
3. It cannot well be executed but in small.
4. It is perform'd on Vellum or Ivory.
5. The Colours are moisten'd with Gum-water only.[148]

Usually measuring only one inch by one inch, the miniature not only depicts the face and encloses the heart of its sitter but also creates an intimate form of reminiscence through its gentle tactility. "It is a kind of gentle painting," wrote the Renaissance miniaturist Nicholas Hilliard. "It is secret."[149] Just as the sense of touch stirs an aged woman's circulation, animating hidden memories, so her hand guarantees the proximity between her face and its semblance. Much like the epistolary moment that collapses time and distance between loved ones, the portrait miniature negotiates the aesthetic boundaries between the general and the particular: as Susan Stewart observes, it is "particularized in that the miniature concentrates upon the single instance and not upon the abstract rule, but generalized in that that instance comes to transcend, to stand for, a spectrum of other instances."[150] The miniature is a mnemonic object that indelibly captures a moment in time. But held at different moments over a life span, it betokens time's progress, forgotten sentiments, and one's own advancing age. Returning Juliana Ritchie's image in old age, Fergusson regards the miniature as a memory trace that reunites a copy with its original.

Miniatures in their purest form were painted in watercolor and opaque body color on very fine parchment, or vellum. The vellum, in turn, was attached with starch paste to pasteboard sheets cut from playing cards, called *tablets.* The tablet was then placed under pressure between a book's leaves until it was nearly dry. Removed and placed face-down on a smooth grinding stone, the tablet was burnished on the back to ensure the vellum's adhesion.[151] By the eighteenth century miniaturists preferred the hard surface of ivory to the delicate texture of vellum. As John Payne explains in *The Art of Painting in Miniature* (1820), one should choose a piece of ivory for its general transparency, "holding it grainways to the light, then holding it up and looking through it, still turning it from side to side, and very narrowly observing whether there be any streaks in it."[152] Since a transparent rather than opaque white guaranteed the clear semblance of "face-painting in miniature," the ivory's oily and unabsorbent surface was carefully prepared to achieve its physiognomic potential.

Because it repelled watercolor, the ivory was first sanded—much as writing paper was treated with pounce or sandarac before receiving the pen's ink. Payne describes the laborious process of sanding the ivory in minute detail: "You must pound some pumice stone in a mortar, as clear and fine as you can. . . . scrape the leaves of ivory with a sharp pen knife, until the scratches of the cutting saw be entirely obliterated; then take . . . a piece of Dutch polishing rush . . . and carefully polish your ivory with it, not by passing your hands backwards and forwards, but in a circular manner, until you have it pretty level."[153] With pumice and penknife, along with the requisite amount of gum arabic to ensure the desired texture and hue, miniature painting simulated script's telling physiognomy. Repeating the back-and-forth pattern of letter circulation, polishing ivory further remembers the mnemonic techniques of handwriting and shellwork discussed in previous chapters. The ivory's transparent whiteness thus accepts and preserves the memory images evoked during reminiscence.

Once the ivory was ready, paint was applied, first in thin washes to block out the general shapes and then by layers of cross-hatching or stippling to delineate the contours and details. Working from the outside in, the miniaturist began by drawing the face's outline. "You must endeavour to fix in your mind a clear idea of the whole which you intend to draw," suggests the miniaturist Emma Kendrick, "being very mindful not to particularize too much in your first sitting, but to try to obtain the general effect of the head and face."[154] Just as the penman memorized shapes and strokes, so the artist memorized basic forms. Claude Boutet illustrates such alphabetic standards in *The Art of Painting in Miniature* (1752): "Let them first well be Master of every Particular, for it is the A,B,C, or Alphabet, which when well learned, is easily joined together into Words; and he who can delineate well, the Eyes, Nose, Mouth, Ears, etc. will readily form a well proportioned Face."[155] The painter filled in the details after sketching the outline. Following the general rule "that it is much easier to warm the tints of your face, than to cool it, by working proper colours over it," as Payne says, the artisan lent interiority to the visage in broad, faint washes: muted colors for the eyes, grayish shadows beneath the eyebrows, and a warm purple under the nose.[156] That done, hatching commenced.

Using interlacing lines that crossed in various directions, a painter hatched color as in a cross-hatched manuscript, leaving a space equal to the width of the line to produce an evenly lined surface. As *The Compleat Drawing Book* (1740) delineates the process, hatching is closely related to the miniature's precursor in book illumination: "First slightly making them all of a Thickness, and after by various Retouchings strengthen them to the Tone of Colour in your Original whether you use *black* or *red Chalk,* or *black Lead;*—Which may be used singly or thus compounded, working the fainter Parts with *black lead,* and give Strength with black Chalk. Or finishing your *Drapery, Hair* and *Eye-Brows* in this Manner, and the *Flesh* or naked with *red Chalk.*"[157] Just as an illuminator decorated initials and borders of a manuscript page, so the miniaturist framed the face.

Hatching was usually followed by stippling, or placing dots in the lines' interstices until the whole had the appearance of being exclusively stippled.[158] "There are several Ways of Stippling or Shading," explains one practitioner. "Some do it with round Points, others make them longish, others again hatch with fine Strokes crossing each other in all Directions, till the whole appears as if stippled or wrought with Points; this last Method is the best, boldest, and soonest perfected."[159] Supplementing the hatched lines, stippling guaranteed a perfectly blended image with lines "equally blended with and confounded into each."[160] Stippling not only completed the face's outline but also animated the complexion, as *The*

School of Miniature demonstrates: "You must Stipple upon the Lights with a little Vermillion or Carmine, mixed with a good deal of White and very little Oaker, to lose them well into the Shades, and make the Tints imperceptibly die away into each other, taking heed while you are stippling or hatching that your strokes follow the out-line of the Flesh; for altho' your hatching must cross in all Directions, that ought to appear a little more, because it rounds off the parts."[161] Completing hatching's intimate analogy to book illumination, stippling likewise required red ink. More than calligraphic pigments, however, vermilion and carmine created the human blush, emphasizing the portrait miniature's individuation from the printed page. Optimizing the ivory's natural translucency, stippling thus added a warm skin tone, allowing the face to glow through the watercolor back to the ivory's surface.

The miniature's gradual animation not only suggests intimacy between hand and face, artist and subject, object and viewer, but also signals memory's participation in the process. A gradual transfer of memory from artist to viewer, the portrait miniature materializes and invites collective reminiscence. Like handwriting and commonplacing, painting begins with the "remembered line"—tracing a sitter's silhouette and filling in the blanks by remembering characteristic features.[162] A good painter, remarks the Renaissance artist Albrecht Dürer during the portrait miniature's early heyday, is "inwardly full of figures." Invention requires that an artisan has "well stocked his mind by study," for "all he need do is pour forth that which he has for a long time gathered into him from without."[163] Like memory's deposition of well-stocked images onto the handwritten page, painting externalizes an artist's thoughts on canvas. Though working from outline to feature (i.e., from the outside in), a miniaturist also employs the inverse process, expressing remembered beauty (i.e., from the inside out).

As the British painter William Hogarth later suggests, the painter must read the language of objects "and if possible find a grammar to it" in order to "collect and retain a remembrance of what [he] saw by repeated observations."[164] The American miniaturist John Singleton Copley followed an equally mnemonic model: "All our Ideas of things is no more than a remembrance of what we have seen," he writes, "so when the Artist has a model in his Appartment and Views it, [then] turns to his picture and marks whatever he wishes to express on his Picture, what is it but remembrance of what he has seen?"[165] Carefully observing a subject's "Passions and Physiognomy," a skilled artist will "retain the same in [his] Mind, and understand it with a well grounded Knowledge."[166] Since neoclassicists believed that art imitated nature, they relied on their memories to transfer a living countenance onto canvas.[167] The subject projects her interior world through her face; an observant artist internalizes this projection and stores it in memory; and the memory surfaces through the hand's touch.

The portrait miniature's complex subjectivity, therefore, exemplifies the collaboration of collective reminiscence. Sometimes hidden in or selectively displayed at a woman's dressing table, the miniature conjured an aging woman's daydreams. Through nostalgic recollections, women could safely preserve their complexions, trading the life-threatening dangers of cerulean white face paint for opaque watercolors on ivory.[168] The miniature thus captured a static moment and integrated the aging face with its remembered physiognomy. Saving (and returning) images of others rather than of themselves, women relied not only on collective narratives during their bittersweet daydreams but also on the familiar rendition of another woman's face. Like the epistolary resuscitation between the young and old, a miniature forestalls the pain of aging as it revives memories.[169]

SILHOUETTE SHADOWS

"Ellen desired me to cut for her a Profile likeness of my Grandmother from one in the possession of my Mother," writes Deborah Logan. "As it was but little more trouble I have cut a half a dozen for the different members of the Family—if the enclosed pleases you as bringing to mind the features of one whom all that knew her respected and loved—please accept it as a small token of affection from your cousin."[170] Taking out her scissors and cutting six copies of her grandmother's "profile," Logan rehearses the silhouette's dual significance. It was a physiognomic replica of an old woman's mind and an inherited token of affection, passed down from her grandmother to her mother and eventually to Logan herself. Pasted into Maria Dickinson Logan's 1886 transcription of Deborah Logan's 1808 commonplace book, moreover, are additional hand-cut silhouettes of the younger Logan's granddaughters.[171] Together these profiles narrate an intimate, female genealogy of five generations.

As both creator and collector of silhouettes, Deborah Logan continued what began—at least apocryphally—as a female art form. Though *silhouette* is an eighteenth-century term derived from Etienne de Silhouette (the French controller-general of finances in 1759 and amateur profile cutter), this craft actually began in ancient Greece when Korinthea, daughter of the Greek potter Dibutades, traced the outline of her beloved's shadowed profile before he left on what she feared would be an endless journey (see figure 3.9). Arrested in time and space, the "shadow portrait," or "shade," as it was also called, offered a permanent and static model of the beloved in his absence. A simple outline, "the profile readily fixes itself in memory," as David Rosand notes.[172] Logan's collection of female profiles, therefore, pre-

3.9. Joseph Wright of Derby, *The Corinthian Maid,* 1782–1786, oil on canvas. Paul Mellon Collection. Photograph © 2002 Board of Trustees, National Gallery of Art, Washington.

served a pictorial album of family history and shared affections for future reminiscences.[173]

Logan's multiple copies of her grandmother's profile—which were cut, collected, and arranged in her commonplace book—illustrate another mode of commonplace collecting. Though it is not clear whether Logan traced her grandmother's extant image and separately cut the imitations or whether she folded the paper to make duplicates, her silhouettes have a distinct affinity with the folio page and folded fan leaf.[174] Two folds in the paper furnished four silhouettes. Such "copies" represent a timelessness akin to universal topoi by providing memory traces of absent or dead relatives. Eighteenth- and nineteenth-century Philadelphians (namely, upper-class Quakers) accordingly compiled "shadow portraits" into "albums," which invited collective viewing and reminiscence.[175] Like commonplace books, these albums were ready-made blank books into which silhouettes were pasted or pinned. Hand-coated black (or sometimes blue) pages were sewn into covers ranging from simple paper to leather bindings; most were marbled paper over paperboard.[176] And just as commonplace books were organ-

ized under rhetorical "heads," silhouette albums contained profile duplicates in order to divide their "subjects" into categories. Acknowledging the
silhouette's innate textuality, physiognomist Lavater defines the silhouette's
distinctive "language," "reading" the countenance as "an open book."[177]
Facial features provide the lexicon; their characteristic arrangement on a
given face forms a readable, if not transparent, text.

As the profilist Charles Willson Peale described his silhouette albums, "to
contemplate the immense variety of characters in a collection of profiles . . .
is a feast to the physiognomist and philosopher" alike.[178] Flippantly calling his
cutouts "block heads," Peale intimates a type of interiority that supplements
the silhouette's inherent lack. This lack not only remembers Korinthea's
original artistic impulse, which emerged from feelings of loss, but also emphasizes the silhouette's reliance on immaterial shadows. To create his block
heads, Peale used the cut-and-paste method of creating shadow portraits.
Whereas the hollow-cut profile entailed cutting from a paper's center and
mounting the holed sheet against a contrasting background so that the image
showed through the resulting space, the cut-and-paste method reversed the
process. The profilist cut and saved the central image and adhered it to a card
of contrasting color.[179] Though both techniques highlight the shadow's outline, Peale's block heads, one might say, signify the substance of a face's
ephemeral shadow. Physiognomists downplayed the silhouette as "the
faintest and emptiest" form of a human visage, but they conversely admitted
that it is "also the truest and most faithful image of the human being that one
can give."[180] The silhouette ignores the living countenance's variability and
statically captures a person's essential form. Embodying the interior black
space rather than highlighting the exterior line held in relief by its background, Peale's cutouts thus provide a tangible memento of the absent person, for a "shadow outline, avoiding all detail, assists remembrance."[181]

Accurately detailed, rapidly completed, and relatively inexpensive, silhouettes were the most accessible form of American portraiture by the turn
of the nineteenth century. Unlike the portrait miniature, which took more
than ten hours in at least three sittings to complete, the silhouette was like
"writing to the moment." Silhouettes, or "speaking expressions," not only
arrested the moment but took just moments to make: "time of sitting, one
minute." As the profilist Auguste Edouart narrates the virtually instanta-
neous process: "I looked at him five minutes only, and my mind was so
much struck with the expression of his features, and the *tout ensemble* of his
figure; that I returned home, and at once made the Likeness. Upon several
occasions, I have seen him since, and I found it very correct." In order to
quickly impress the countenance on his memory, Edouart applied the neoclassical ideals of simplicity and imitation, extracting general characteristics

from the inessential particulars. A good profilist, therefore, distinguished "the Parts as appear dark . . . from those which are faint or smaller," "strong Touches being what gives Spirit to the Outline."[182] A silhouette's faithful outline avoided other inward additions, which produced "a contrary effect of the appearance of a shade."[183] Erasing the contradictory emotions displayed by the sitter's living complexion, the pasteboard or "Paper Skull" offered a new and improved semblance.

Logan cut her own silhouettes by hand, and she carefully observed the profile work of one of her tenants, who "takes miniature effigies in Wax, Profiles, the likenesses striking, coloured like life, exquisitely done, the drapery, the Hair, the appearance of cloth, of Lace, of Ornaments inimitable," but she certainly knew as well about the various mechanical methods of making silhouettes.[184] Given the widespread popularity of Lavater's *Physiognomic Fragments* in the early Republic, Logan would have at least seen an image of his specialized chair for steadying a person's pose, along with the paper screen that kept the shadows of an artist's hand off the finished silhouette (see figure 3.10). As Lavater explains his method: "The shade should be taken on post paper, or rather oiled paper, well-dried. Let the [sitter's] head and back be supported by the chair, and the shade fall on the oiled paper behind a clear flat polished glass. Let the drawer sit behind the glass, holding the frame with his left hand, and having a sharp black-lead pencil, draw with the right."[185] Like the mirror, which reflects an aging woman's visage, this method used light's reflection. But rather than show a direct image, it projected the face's shadow onto the canvas. The profilist thus materialized the mnemonic process by which the memory first impresses and then traces an image in its receptive folds.

In addition to Lavater's device, Logan would have been familiar with the physiognotrace. Created by Gilles Louis Chretien 1786, patented by the English inventor John Hawkins in 1803, and added to Charles Willson Peale's Philadelphia Museum the same year, the physiognotrace was used by male and female patrons alike. John Jay Smith describes his visit to Peale's museum as a child:

> A cousin of the husband of my great aunt, Milcah Martha Moore, was the second wife of Charles Willson Peale. . . . My aunt paid them an annual visit to tea, and occasionally (it could have been twice or thrice) my mother and I accompanied her. After tea we all went—delightful thought to a boy!—without paying, to the great Museum, saw the sights, listened to the organ, . . . got our profiles cut by the yellow man [profilist Moses Williams], and came away, at least I did, with unbounded admiration for the genius that could so accomplish much.[186]

A Sure and convenient Machine for drawing Silhouettes.

3.10. Johann Caspar Lavater, "A Sure and Convenient Machine for Drawing Silhouettes," frontispiece to John Caspar Lavater, *Essays in Physiognomy,* vol. 3 (London, 1797). Courtesy, Harry Ransom Humanities Research Center, The University of Texas at Austin.

A member of Logan's circle and a compiler of commonplace books herself, Milcah Martha Moore may have circulated silhouettes along with her collected poetry.[187] Her grandnephew, moreover, was hardly alone in his fascination with the physiognotrace. Judging by the exponential number of machine-made silhouettes (eight thousand four-inch-by-three-inch profiles were cut in 1803 alone), Peale's museum made this quick and inexpensive art form available to the general public. Clearly pleased with his success, Peale writes: "Much company continue to visit the Museum to get their profiles taken— In fact, it has been the best article to draw company, that I ever had, the Idea of getting a likeness at the cost of only *one Cent,* has a happy effect; such is the love we have of our pretty faces."[188]

Given women's preoccupation with their "pretty faces" in the early Republic, as the proliferation of cosmetic manuals and anti-beauty satires attests, Peale made the physiognotrace particularly appealing to his museum's female patrons. Whereas he encouraged the men to view the extensive natural history specimens, Peale recommended that the women get their silhouettes cut.[189] Using the physiognotrace themselves, moreover, American women reclaimed Korinthea's profiling art as their own. As Peale's advertisement in the December 1802 *Aurora* proclaims: "A physiognotrace, of so simple a construction, that any person without the aid of another, can in less than a minute take their own likeness in profile. This curious machine, perhaps, gives the truest outlines of any heretofore invented, and is placed in the Museum for the visitors who may desire to take the likeness of themselves or friends."[190] Kindly ignoring the marks of age by capturing only the essential features, the silhouette collapsed the face's evolution—from youth to age—into a single moment. As such, it prompted collective reminiscence. Drawing one another's profiles at Peale's Museum, women remembered the past and restored friendships in old age: as the advertisement promises, "friendship esteems as valuable even the most distant likeness of a friend."

Just as the mirror, fan, and portrait miniature evoke reminiscences during an old woman's life review, so the silhouette captures the permanent outline of her face. With little or no background scenery or stylized props, her countenance stands in stark relief. Without the marks of historical time or place, the silhouette is a kind of anachronism. But unlike the progressive anachronisms prompted by dementia, the dark profile arrests a woman's face in atemporal stasis. The shadow portrait surpasses the fragmentation of the looking-glass self and defies the attendant marks of aging. It offers instead an unchanging outline onto which women can transfer collected memories during reminiscence. Though the profilist Edouart advises that "the Likeness to be taken according to the Seven Ages of Shakespeare, and the effect would be interesting to those, who are reasonable enough to admit the change brought by age," the silhouette, I contend, actually combines these ages into a single, retrospective moment.[191] Finally, it fuses the shared experiences of generations of women, as Logan illustrates in circulating copies of her grandmother's hand-cut profile.

With James Logan's translation of Cicero's famous essay *Cato Major, or His Discourse on Old Age* (1744), early Americans were given a self-help manual for aging. "Old age need not be a time of lustreless ennui," writes Cicero; "on the contrary, it may well be very busy indeed, always in the middle of some activity, or projecting some plan—in continuation, of course, of the interest of earlier years."[192] Admittedly a treatise for men, Cicero's advice was not so easily translated to the lives of elderly women.[193] Given the call for retirement and solitude in old age, women became even further ensconced in the domestic world of the country house, retreating into what they called "local attachments," as Fergusson beautifully explains:

A kind of Relic which the Heart retains
A pensive languour all my Senses Seals;
. . . .
This local weakness chains me to these Bowers
. . . .
While I alone am mournful left behind.[194]

Hermetically sealed, women's hearts, like their houses, replay successive life stages, stuck, as it were, in an endless repetition of memories with little promise of change or escape. Unlike men, whose "continuation" of interests keeps their minds "green and vigorous . . . in Old Age," as Sir Richard Bulstrode notes, women are bereft of useful instructions to keep their minds active. The marchioness de Lambert complains: "Attention is directed to the improvement of men alone; but as to the women, at all seasons of life they are left to themselves: their education is neglected in their youth; in the sequel they are deprived of consolation and support for their old-age."[195] Repeatedly told that beauty rather than intellect was the most charming female attribute, women were left mentally destitute in their supposedly golden years.

Like Lambert, Logan lamented Cicero's (and her father-in-law's) gendered oversight. But equally committed to preserving women's mental faculties during old age, she creates her own method for women to follow: "(But I am going on, as if I were beginning a Treatise of Old Age for the benefit of my own sex, who were not thought worthy by Cicero of the least mention in his)—they say I have a young mind, and if it is so, and it has preserved some of the embellishments of youth without sacrificing the title to respect due to advancing years, it has achieved something desirable indeed."[196] Continuing the interests of earlier years, as Cicero prescribed, Logan forestalled the ennui of aging, marrying a young mind's vigor with an old one's accumulated wisdom. Reiterating Cicero's warning that "in order to keep my memory trim, I recall everything I have said, heard, or done on that day. These are the exercises of the intellect, this is the training-field of the mind," Logan writes: "It is not good policy in Age to quit employment, especially any of a mental cast, for the mind is then thrown back upon itself, and instead of striking out some new direction of its energies as it is wont in youth, it is too apt to fold up its wings and remain inactive and discontented."[197] In order to keep her memory trim, then, Logan promotes the advantages of diary keeping and commonplacing in old age: "Having been at a stand to consider whether there is any use to myself or other in the Record of so unimportant and insignificant a life.—yet as people of my age miss a stated employment much more than a person in the busy entrance of life can imagine, I shall offer no other apology for reassuming my occupation."[198] Beginning her diaries and commonplace books in 1808 at the age of forty-eight and continuing them until her death thirty years later, Logan keeps her mind limber and memories permanent as she ages.

Though Maria Dickinson Logan's merciless literalism misread her mother-in-law's diary and ultimately destroyed a valuable portrait, a copy remains on the walls of Stenton. A mere trace of the original painting, which itself traced Deborah Logan's aging countenance, the copy leaves the modern viewer with a nostalgic feeling of loss. The unsatisfying fissure dividing the painted copy, the original, and the human face, moreover, recalls the similar disjunction of recovered reminiscence, memory image, and initial sensory impression experienced by the elderly. Looking at her portrait just before her death, Logan "did not know her own representation."[199] Such disorientation, this chapter has argued, finds coherence in the face's mnemonic potential. Combining the mnemonic (and cosmetic) arts of preservation through collecting *reminiscentia,* women became artists, as the *Gentleman's and London Magazine* for 1792 illustrates:

> Transcendent artist! matchless skill is thine,
> To do thee justice mocks my weak design;
> Since to thy skill, the faint attempt must fail,
> Who'rt copy, painter, and original.[200]

Though it overlooks face painting's inevitable failure to preserve the face, the poem highlights women's superlative gifts of memory. As copy, painter, and original at once, an aging woman exemplified the act of reminiscence in her face's narrated lines. Displacing their skin's inevitable wrinkles onto miniature objects that better reflect the face, women enact what Susanna Wright called "an extensive View" of the face's artistry. "With the same Fire, & the same Judgement," that animated "all that Raphael or that Titian drew," women created an art of remembrance, nostalgically transforming the subtle arts of the female toilette into the collaborative acts of reminiscence.[201]

4

In Memoriam

The Balsamic Art is not only the best way of reviving Mens Memories and bringing their Merits fresh in our minds; but is also the most durable.

—Thomas Greenhill, *Nekrokedeia, or The Art of Embalming* (1705)

INTIMATES WITH GRIEF

"Attention and repetition help much to fixing any ideas in the memory," explains Locke in his *Essay Concerning Human Understanding,* "but those which naturally at first make the deepest and most lasting impression, are those which are accompanied with pleasure or pain."[1] Commemorating the anniversary of her mother's death in 1750 with an annual elegy for more than half a century, Hannah Griffitts describes the lasting impression left by her iterative feelings of loss:

> I think, it is 53 years, this day—since the first sorrow peirced my heart—by the Death of a Beloved Mother, my earthly all, & This deep wounding, (all ended with Succeeding Afflictions) drew an early and heavy Cloud over the Morning of my Day. . . . if I may be favor'd, at Last to meet my lost beloved, in "the Joy of her Lord,"—I trust, every visible attachment—or Concern, will more & more lose its Importance with me. . . . Life has lost its Balm,—& the world has Nothing to Bestow. . . . if favord, thus, at last, A healing Balm, for all the past.[2]

Sustained and revived by these ritual elegies, her grief resists consolation: it is both a deep wound that pierces her bleeding heart and a temporary blindness that veils her mother's absent body. An act of perpetual mourning, Griffitts's elegy cycle supplies the missing balm to ameliorate her pain. This metaphorical balm signifies the neoclassical elegy's characteristic expression of consolation, but it also suggests a more literal allusion to the art of embalming corpses with fragrant resin or aromatic oil. Though embalming was not routinely practiced in the United States until the Civil War, women were nonetheless familiar with balsamic practices as they washed and laid out the dead.[3] They were, as Griffitts phrased it, "Strangers to Joy—and Intimates with greif."[4] Given their intimacy with the corpse, on the one hand, and the cultural expectation to mourn, on the other, women transformed their knowledge of embalming into an art of memory. Following moralist William Kenrick's advice in *The Whole Duty of Woman* (1694), women laid the dead to rest, "embalm[ing] their memory and perfum[ing] it with the fragrance of [their] virtues."[5]

The figurative transference of grief from Mary Norris Griffitts's dead body to her daughter's seasonal recollections of that body suggests another mode of collective memory used by the Philadelphia coterie. Buried in the female mourner's memory, the deceased becomes an internalized image, or topos, which occupies a place in her mind. Memory is not only an intellectual commonplace for the bereaved but also a palpable metonym for the deceased body that has long since decomposed. To "preserve her memory" essentially means "to preserve her." Incorporated into and embalmed by the mourner's memory, then, the beloved's remains are physically preserved until the mourner's death, when, as Griffitts says, "I again shall see thee face to face,/And Clasp thy Soul, within my fond Embrace."[6] Unlike the Puritans' dour memento mori tradition, which focused on the putrid and sinful corpse, or the Victorian sentimentalization of death through elaborate funerary art, eighteenth- and early-nineteenth-century Christians negotiated their ambivalent feelings about death through their hope for resurrection.[7] More than an immortal reunion of body and soul, resurrection suggests a symbiosis between the corpse and the mourner, who together comprise the "remains" (see figure 4.1).

The term *remains* signifies this singular body of death. As a noun, it represents not just the putrefying corpse but also what the corpse leaves behind: a surviving physical fragment or the lasting trace of a feeling, on the one hand, and the mourners who succeed the dead, on the other. As a verb, *remains* performs the act of mourning itself, as the abandoned mourner abides, continues, or stays in the same place. Such an act connotes neither stasis nor immobility but rather continuity between the living and the dead.

4.1. Robert Dighton, "Life and Death Contrasted, or, An Essay on Woman," 1792. Courtesy, Museum of Mourning Art, Arlington Cemetery, Drexel, Pennsylvania.

Finally, it carries the now obsolete echoes of an ethical stance in which *remains* means waiting for an event (i.e., resurrection) or inheriting a responsibility (i.e., to mourn).[8]

Though women have traditionally inherited the work of mourning, they have also been criticized for their supposedly excessive grief. As William Alexander asserts in *The History of Women* (1796), mourning "in all ages and countries, [has] been more particularly allotted to women, as the best fitted for them, not only by the sympathetic feelings, but also by their greater readiness in calling forth these feelings almost at pleasure."[9] By the last quarter of the eighteenth century, consolation manuals and elegies typically gender grief as the feminine other, to be overcome by the rational, male mourner.[10] The female mourner, it follows, is merely a redundant third term: she is the remains, the excess. Seeking continuity with rather than detachment from the dead, women too often have been misunderstood as inconsolable. Contrary to the masculine model, which "marks a rite of separation that culminates in ascension to stature [and] rehearses an act of identity that depends upon rupture," female mourners "seem unwilling to render up their dead."[11] Maintaining filial ties, Griffitts's elegy cycle to her mother is an unending "poem of connectedness" that celebrates death's two bodies through its mortal remains.[12]

Taken together, the fifty-three elegies constitute a narrative that traces Griffitts's protracted experience of mourning. Grief, her elegies show, is an increasing process of abstraction, weaning one's desires from death's material body by preserving it exclusively in the memory. Each elegy not only revives the moment of death but also absorbs her mother's body into her own through a complex series of metonymic substitutions. These substitutions do not replace the deceased but rather provide the desired continuity until they can be permanently reunited in the afterlife:

> Thou ne're shall pass my Anscious soul, unsung,
> Till grief be Dumb, & every nerve unstrung
> Till, the frail Tenure, life, shall be resign'd
> Entomb'd the Body, & enlarg'd the mind
> Till I again embrace the Parent lost.[13]

Entombed with grief, Griffitts's body shares her mother's grave, "when every grief lyes shrouded in the Tomb" and "where death shall ne're Dissolve the union more."[14]

Reinforcing the duality of the "remains" as both corpse and mourner, Griffitts imagines a single, unified body: she is the body; her mother is the soul. She enacts the reunion of her mother's soul and perfected body in heaven by envisioning herself as her mother's mortal body awaiting the final embrace. Remembering the dead, then, is a reciprocal process between the dead and the living. As "a child of Earth . . . left below," Griffitts preserves her mother's memory by "weep[ing] my loss, & drink[ing] the Tears of woe." But swallowing her tears like a fragrant balm, she is figuratively embalmed by grief. As consolation writer Richard Cecil explains: "Though seemingly swallowed up of this grief, like Jonah, you shall find a resource 'in' it, and finally be preserved 'by' it."[15] The mourner, like the remembered dead, is preserved, for "Love divine, embalm'd the bleeding wound."[16]

Such preservation highlights the female mourner's liminality. Told to "forbear my tongue & stream mine eyes / Let not a doubtfull mourning Tho't arise" on the one hand, she is reminded of her elegiac duty to inscribe "This Page with monumental woe long as my pulse shall beat, shall everflow" on the other.[17] Refusing comfort, the mourner disregards the cultural admonitions against immoderate grief. "While united to the weakness of mortality," writes Griffitts, "I think it my Duty [to mourn] the memory of my beloved Parent as often as This painfull day shall (more deeply revive her to my remembrance)."[18] Foregoing masculine detachment or repression in order to "achieve" consolation, Griffitts's elegy cycle resists conclusion. She persistently wavers between grief and consolation. Unlike the neoclassical elegy, which strictly manages its lamentation with codified images and conventional rhyme schemes, Griffitts's elegies, though repetitive, vary among free verse, alternating quatrains, and heroic couplets from one year to another. The shifting poetic form, like the grief it expresses, defies the expected rules of moderation.

This resistance underscores what Griffitts sees as consolation's prescribed artificiality, the suppression of genuine feelings with muted gestures. Though the consolationist Benjamin Grosvenor claims that "the natural postures of grief have no offence in them; but there are unnatural distortions of rage and despair,"[19] John Weaver traces the history of feminine excess, describing the unruly and potentially fraudulent mourner in his book *Ancient Funerall Monuments* (1631): "They had, at these burials, suborned counterfeit hired mourners, which were women of the loudest voices, who did meete at appointed places, and then cried out mainly, beating of their breasts, tearing their haire, their faces, their garments, . . . keeping time with the melancholick musicke."[20] Read by early American women well into the nineteenth century, Weaver's book would have influenced Griffitts's understanding of her gendered role as an elegist. In response to the long-standing tradition of disorderly women, postrevolutionary mourning manuals necessarily propounded "the heavenly science of gaining by losses and rising by depressions," which would "prepare the heart for the reception of this treasure . . . [through] this system of means."[21] Although she resists performing the all-too-familiar and staged histrionics of counterfeit mourners, Griffitts also rejects the heavenly ratio as patently false. She prefers instead what the contemporary feminist philosopher Margaret Urban Walker calls the "moral remainder."[22] Dismissing the proportion of means, Griffitts enacts a kind of mystical division in which she is the "remainder"—"a child of Earth left below." Unlike the hired female mourners whose excess comes from their unnatural affiliation with the dead, the moral remainder intimates both an ethical obligation to mourn the other and an intimate bond between the mourner and the mourned. Griffitts expresses "the Real mourner's Tear and "Consecrates thy hours to Grief Unfeign'd."[23]

With few exceptions, her elegies begin by rehearsing the painful separation experienced at the moment of death. Because the mourner internalizes the "deadly wound," dying connotes the absence of pain for the deceased. While the mourner dies, the dead lives. "There is nothing after Death, and therefore Death is nothing," writes Richard Allestree in *The Whole Duty of Mourning* (1695): "It is without Essence, or Substance."[24] Griffitts thus envisions the "full-perfected" soul as "Enrapt in Bliss": it is "Untouch'd by Mortal Cares—Unfelt its Griefs," and "Unstain'd by Sin."[25] But the mourner, she explains, endlessly repeats the moment of death through memory:

> Feel it I must in my Remembrance feel it,
> In my Remembrance Pass the Scene Again.
> For Oh—This dark Unhappy Day—Revives
> My load of Sorrow—and Recalls my Pain.[26]

With each recurring memory, Griffitts relives the physical anguish of loss. Recalled, revived, and remembered, grief's wound becomes more deeply impressed in her flesh. Each loss recapitulates previous ones, making cumulative wounds deeper. An engrafted memento mori, her injured flesh is a reminder of her own mortality and her duty to remember the dead: "The deadly blow is found / And must be felt, while memory shall endure."[27] While she embalms her mother's memory, Griffitts, too, is embalmed by grief, for death's "awful Stroke depriv'd my Soul of more, / Than Life."[28] Unlike consolation's ascetic discipline of self-denial, her spiritual mortification, in its distinctive corporeality, resembles her mother's decaying corpse.

Though the mourner's heart perpetually bleeds, the departed soul is resuscitated in death. Death both reverses and complements life: "It is but a departed Breath from dead Clay, enlivened at first by Breath cast upon it," claims one consolation writer.[29] Mimicking God's Creation in her hope for immortality, Griffitts repeats the respiratory imagery of death:

> Till the freed Spirit breathes its native air,
> And meets its Bosem friend in Calm repose,
> . . . And escil'd spirits—breathe pure liberty.[30]

Fulfilling the painful task of living, the effectually dead mourner gasps for eternal breath while the beloved's liberated spirit freely exhales new and lasting life. Describing faith in the resurrection as respiration, consolation writers imagine the mortal heart and immortal soul as synonymous: "As all the pulses in the most distant veins of the body depend upon that of the heart, so it is with the movements of the soul: 'as a [wo]man's heart is, so is [s]he.' "[31] Just as a woman's heart envelops the beloved's memory, her soul mirrors the one she mourns. Once reunited, their breath seems reciprocal, much like the mutual pain of separation: "peirc'd, with agony my bleeding-heart; / Thou from my Soul—The dearest-comfort tore." Much like women's epistolary resuscitation, which invokes and revives the absent body, the bereaved shares a solitary heart with her "Bosem friend," where "Death, Insures me, Thine." With this vow the mourner dies again but this time feels no pain. She lives in death. And "all [her] Soul dissolv'd in melting tears."[32]

An act of the imagination, Griffitts's faith in immortality foretells an empirically unknowable future "(far beyond our finite span) / . . . A Depth; above our reach to comprehend." With such uncertainty about the afterlife, Griffitts looks backward to a more familiar past. Unable to "trace [death's] origin; or grasp its end," she seeks an original memory "trace" of her absent mother.[33] Because reminiscence, as chapter 3 argues, depends on a nostalgic rift between the past and the present, it exemplifies the temporal, spatial, and emotional remove from which one mourns. An insatiable longing for the absent beloved, mourning shares with reminiscence a discernible desire for return. It is this desire that sustains grief: "No matter what fills the gap, even if it be filled completely, it nevertheless remains something else. And, actually, this is how it should be. It is the only way of perpetuating that love which we do not want to relinquish."[34] The slippage between desire and object, between substitute and original, illustrates the complex process of memory deposition, which the mourner necessarily reverses in her attempt to reunite with her beloved: sensory experience (origin) < memory of origin (trace) < reminiscence (reconstituted trace).

Seeking a palpable connection to the past, mourning invokes memory and preserves the dead: "Their manner of existence is changed, but the existence itself is not lost. They are not blotted out of being, nor out of life," Grosvenor remarks.[35] Textualizing her loss, Griffitts imagines grief as an "Iron Pen" that writes across her heart as if it were a receptive and immutable manuscript:

On Evry Passion—Every Faculty;
It Prints my Loss, and Stamps it deeply There,
In never fadeing Characters—(in my heart).[36]

Grief leaves its signature mark on the mourner's mental faculties: reason and memory receive the indelible stamp; fancy and imagination inscribe the loss; affection and sensibility transform blood and tears into ink. Ostensibly writing from her body, Griffitts creates a fluid poetics that eloquently speaks her heart: "My heart doth bleed my tears do flow / . . . far beyond the Power of tongue to tell." A proxy for the tongue, blood and tears translate her "Inexpressless Greif" into intelligible signs: "My bleeding Heart, shall Dictate to my Tongue, / . . . My artless lines shall flow—my anscious heart shall bleed."[37] Like blotting paper or pounce that absorbs the pen's excess ink, Griffitts's memory not only permanently absorbs her mother's image but also "blots" her own excessive tears and perennially bleeding wound.

Such corporeal and handwritten characters recall female memory's genesis in Mnemosyne's maternal gift of wax to the Muses. As one consolationist posits, mourning "is a tender time, while the soul is more susceptible of impression, and turns more easily, as the softend wax to the seal."[38] Susceptible to grief's legible marks, the mourner analogously receives the "never-fadeing Characters." Memory impressions eulogize the dead and serve as a memento mori to the mourner. As the "remains," memory comprises a singular image of the self and other. Scanning her memory, Griffitts thus "finds the mourner's Image on my soul, / While Life & Memory Last." At the same time, however, she discovers her mother's image, insisting that nothing "Can her Dear Image, from my Soul Efface."[39] The complementary memory impressions of the mourner and mourned, she insists, are reciprocal: memory "shall seal her mine, / . . . Till Perfect freedom Seals me Thine."[40] What was originally the "suffering stroke" of death that "Seal'd various sorrows—mine" gradually changed into the seal of their "sacred union, "restored, / And seald secure, & sanctified—in God."[41] Memory's impressionable wax seal embodies grief, weds bodies, and preserves hope. Past pain substantiates future bliss.

The mutual images of self and other sealed within their respective hearts suggest another mode of early American women's collective memory. More than preserving ties between the living and the dead, these wax seals initiate the female elegist into a community of sympathetic mourners, who share both her memories of and grief for the dead:

Come, all the Sacred Mourners—Join with me.
In this my Grief—and emit your Gushing Tears,
Your Pious Tears with mine—and help to bear,

My weight of woe—This sympathetick kindness,
Shall meet a Due Return of Love—from me.[42]

Sending copies of her elegies to intimate friends, Griffitts incorporates the mourners into the sympathetic bond she shared exclusively with her mother. Death's singular body (i.e., Griffitts as the body, her mother as the soul) thus becomes a collective body of grief. Left behind by death, the friends, too, are part of her mother's remains. Rather than identify with the corpse or the resurrected soul, however, the communal mourners turn to the living remains of "Sympathizing Souls."

An ethical stance much like mourning, sympathy challenges a person to imagine herself in the position of the other.[43] Tears mingle. Pain subsides. And the "weight of woe" is lessened. The "Sacred Mourners" not only feel the same pain of separation from Mary Norris Griffitts but also lessen grief's burden by internalizing, each in her turn, another's anguish:

Those that have, felt it, only Can reveal,
Then let—here Real mourning Come

. . . .

Ive felt the Stroke & with Your Souls can mourn
Such mutual Sympathy—may Give releise.[44]

Unlike the counterfeit mourners described by John Weaver, sympathy promises the sincerity of "Real mourning"; it authorizes women's lamentations; and it offers unconditional support. Telling her sorrows to like-minded companions thus frees Griffitts to unleash her grief. As experts conceded, "Grief must have a vent: sorrow must express itself. I may sigh and weep, and tell my mournful story to God and [wo]man."[45]

Turning to other experienced mourners, Griffitts finds the poetic voice she lost to grief, as "Ideas fail, nor Language Can Convey" her feelings. "The Muse herself," she complains, "Deny'd Releif," leaving her with "Speechless Anguish, & the bursting Tear."[46] Because elegiac poetry requires sympathy, Griffitts solicits inspiration from the female mourners, who effectually become her Muses:

Come every weeping-muse—In Sable drest,
and paint the mighty-woe that pains my breast
Let Funereal numbers and the pensive Lay,
Unite Together on this Gloomy day,
Heedless of form and negligent of art,
And Speak the Real anguish of my heart.[47]

Such improvisation rejects the stifling strictures imposed by the male-authored consolation manuals, at the same time reappropriating the pose of the experienced mourner.

If experience (rather than reason) warranted the right to mourn, as some consolationists acknowledged, then women were more than qualified.[48] As Grosvenor contends: "It is somewhat necessary to have been acquainted with grief, in order to address suitably to the tenderness of its nature." Intimately acquainted with grief, women shared their sorrow as part of their Christian duty, for as one consolationist notes, "the opening of the heart to an experienced, tender Christian, is some relief."[49] Mourning was neither excessively indulgent nor unreasonably feminine; it was godlike. Creating a collective and experienced voice, women found a literary outlet for their culturally muted grief. Together they could "Speak the real anguish" of Griffitts's heart.[50]

Dutifully written for more than fifty years, Griffitts's elegy cycle provides a provocative glimpse into women's mourning rituals in the early Republic. Its careful negotiation of life and death, corpse and mourner, body and soul, underscores women's participation in the intimate, material practices of death. Women watched, cleansed, anointed, and wrapped the corpse in a winding sheet, laying it in the coffin for public burial. The elegies, moreover, complicate my ongoing argument in this book about women's bodies as a vehicle for and embodiment of memory. The female mourner's richly textured associations with both the decaying corpse and the communal body of mourners—the "remains"—establish a corporeal and collective form of reminiscence. The body of mourners, longing for reunion with the beloved's soul, collaboratively enact the separation of the singular body and soul after death. They not only imagine the eventual consolation given by their eternal reunion with the dead but also satisfy their nostalgic longing by looking momentarily to the past. Thus they fuse the work of memory and mourning into something resembling Platonic recollection: "When that which has been experienced by the soul in common with the body is recaptured, so far as may be, by and in the soul itself apart from the body, then we speak of 'recollecting' something."[51]

In addition, Griffitts's elegy cycle negotiates the cultural ambivalence that at once invited and prohibited women's mourning in postrevolutionary America. The Protestant call to moderation in mourning was theologically based in the requisite hope for resurrection.[52] But it was also part of the larger mistrust of female sensibility as potentially pathological. Uncontrolled by reason, grief was neurotic, disorderly, and excessive, and therefore notoriously feminine: "Come not near [Grief's] cell; her breath is contagious," warns Robert Dodsley in *The Oeconomy of Human Life* (1798); "she will blast fruits and wither the flowers, that adorn and sweeten the garden of life."[53] Similarly domesticating death in *A Friendly Visit to the House of Mourning* (1830), Cecil complains that continued lamentation is "a *temptation . . .* and it unfits the mourner for the pressing duties of his station." Equally dangerous, temptation and contagion required suppression. The male mourner, he advises, must control his grief and grief's feminine body. Cecil suggests the "conscience should rather be concerned to repress such a disposition," but Grosvenor asks: "But is there any harm in prescribing bounds to it? By what rules of common sense should grief be left unlimited, more than any other passion?"[54] Defining common sense as masculine reason rather than shared sensibility, consolationists reduced women to their corporeality. No better than a decaying corpse requiring quick burial to avert contamination, the sensate female body exemplified mortality's limitations.

Such limitations, critics further argued, instigated protracted or repeated bouts of mourning. Imagining grief as a meddling gossip recklessly spreading mourning by invoking the beloved's memory, consolationists (mis)quoted graveyard poet Robert Blair's famous poem *The Grave* (1743).[55] As Cecil remarks, mourners employ "a 'busy meddling memory to must up past endearments' and personate a vast variety of tender and heart-rending circumstances." Grosvenor agrees: "They shall tear it open again, and make it bleed afresh, by the help of certain 'mementos,' that seem to be kept on purpose for that cruel service; a lock of hair, a picture, a relick of wearing apparel; or such like memorandum."[56] In their gendered allusions to female gossips and collectors, Cecil and Grosvenor ironically reinforce the female sensibility they attempt to subdue; they draw their readers' attention directly toward rather than away from death's sensuality. In both cases they accentuate the material culture of death. A graveyard meditation over the rotting, buried corpse, *The Grave* addresses death's physicality: the corpse and its spirit haunt the graveyard; death destroys the countenance; the arts of embalming and undertaking restore it. Domesticating the grave as the "mansion of the dead," finally, Blair's poem stages the soul's sensual reunion with the body. Glossing Cecil's admonition against repeated mourning, women would have readily identified with "busy meddling memory" and her material practices.

Though Cecil and Grosvenor depict death's physicality as effeminate signs of spiritual corruption, Griffitts and her coterie created a specifically material aesthetic of mourning that preserved their corporeal connection to the dead. Embodying grief in tangible artifacts that represent the absent body, women highlighted the importance of the mourner's body in both lamentation and memory. Since she could no longer see or touch the deceased, a woman relied on "a lock of hair, a picture, a relick of wearing apparel" and other "memorandum" to ignite her memory. Like the *reminiscentia* discussed in chapter 3, mourning objects were metonyms for the heart. Because they embodied the absent other, these objects, when opened, figuratively bled. Recalling the beloved contained in the heart, mourning required a slight incision to make memories "bleed afresh." Neither excessive nor indulgent, bleeding revived the dead through the mourner's feeling heart.

It is this connection between the mourning body and the body of death—in its uniquely collective form of memory—that this chapter recapitulates. Using Griffitts's elegy cycle as a template for women's somatic experiences of grief, I look at the crucial moments that shape women's mourning and its cultural expressions in the early Republic: the deathbed scene, the preparation of the corpse, the wake, the funeral procession, and the tomb. I reconstruct the material practices surrounding death at a historical moment when women were thoroughly involved in both the mundane and aesthetic duties of mourning. Like the elegy, these rituals neither permanently dispose of the dead nor bring satisfactory consolation. They reenact the moment of separation and incorporate the memory of the dead into individual and cultural memory.

FACING DEATH: THE ART OF DYING WELL

Surrounded by her closest female companions in August 1817, Hannah Griffitts prepares to die. "She has been most kindly and affectionately nursed," writes her cousin Deborah Logan, "and nothing omitted that we thought would contribute to her comfort and the alleviation of her sufferings."[57] Despite their loving care, Griffitts quietly speaks "of her approaching change with longings for her release," comforting her attendants by stressing their continued friendship in death: "We have lived for many years in unity & love, let us part in it, & oh if favour'd to meet in his kingdom who is the fulness of love . . . may our friendship be perfected in the kingdom of Love." She then gives explicit directions for her funeral, staging her death in verse:

No show nor luscury gild my last retreat
Nor vain parade by seeming mourners trod,
But tender friendship balm my humble seat,
And the freed spirit centre in its God.

4.2. Thomas Rowlandson, *Mourning Figures around a Coffin,* pen and ink and wash, no date. Courtesy of the Victoria & Albert Museum Picture Library. © The Board of Trustees of the Victoria & Albert Museum.

Forbidding mourning, Griffitts asks to be embalmed in their memory.

Watching for physical signs of death, "the harbingers of that release for which she longed," the attendants, like those in figure 4.2, focus particularly on Griffitts's face, "whose sensible irradiation of divine love melted and tendered all present." They mark her words and await her soul's departure: "Her countenance became animated & she appear'd raised above herself; she bless'd & bid many of us farewel in a most solemn & impressive manner, & uttering many precious escpressions." Delirious the day before, Griffitts temporarily recovered: "She knew all of us upon presenting ourselves & speaking to her, & she escpress'd herself with great force & energy." Her face, they conclude, maintained its telling physiognomy at the hour of death. Though Griffitts laments that "it is impossible for tongue to espress, or thought to conceive the unutterable Love of God in Christ, Jesus," her friends readily translate her final thoughts through her face's articulate expressions.

Hannah Griffitts expired in silence: "Her close was quiet & serene as the sleep of an infant," according to Logan. "She suffered much—at times extreme Agony, yet at the last the dismissal was gentle and easy." Giving a fuller account of Griffitts's death in her diary, Logan writes:

> She died in the evening of the 24th at about 20 minutes before nine o'clock. Cousin S. Dickinson, Polly Griffitts, and myself, with her kind friend and neighbor Hannah Harry, Peggy Jones, Sarah Hooper, and Betsy Morris were present; I closed her dying eyes, and we sat for a time in solemn Silence, each, I believe, contemplating the joyful landing of her Soul upon the celestial Shore, a sweet evidence of her happiness resting with us.—The appearance of her Face after Death would by no means have indicated the great age to which she had attained, but might readily have been taken for that of a person of 70 or even less.[58]

After closing the corpse's eyes, the women stare at the empty face, looking for "sweet evidence" of the soul's arrival in heaven. Though they would soon begin cleaning and wrapping the body in its burial shroud, Logan suspends their material contact by fixating on the face. She ignores the classic admonition that the "Beautifull face must be converted into Rottenness; and the Pampured and well fed Body must become the food of Worms" by preserving the inanimate countenance in her memory: "I am consoled for the unnatural composure of my mind at the time [she was] taken, by the firmness and tenderness with which [her] memories are retained in my mind."[59] Through the art of memory, Logan aestheticizes death and denies its repugnance. Originally describing "the appearance of her Corpse after Death," she emends her manuscript, crossing out the word *Corpse* and replacing it with its antonym, *Face*. The corrected text reads, "the appearance of her Face after Death." Exchanging one for the other, Logan gives textual permanence to her cousin's face as the body quietly begins to rot.

Logan's deliberate focus on the face is not surprising, however, given the coterie's physiognomic understanding of architecture, handwriting, and collective *reminiscentia*. The expressive countenance—before and after death—provided a map for the living. It embodied either the dying person's sinful hesitance or her unwavering faith in the face of death. And it taught the attentive mourners how to die well. Since the soul escaped through the mouth, the face was a particularly liminal site between life and death. "Prayers that breathe / Forth from a lip," waxes Logan, soon "fade with coming death."[60] Consolation writers accordingly explained that a man's face "is a Dial of his Transitory Age, and the manifold Changes" indicating his mortality. The physiognomic differences between men, they concluded, "justly serve for a Memorial of Man's changeable Estate" between life and death.[61] Appreciating the dead as "a new subject for study," the physiognomist John Caspar Lavater hypothesizes that without the body's variable influences, death tellingly "stops and fixes what was before vague and undecided. Everything rises or sinks to its level; all the features return to their true relation."[62] Surrounding Griffitts's deathbed, the mourners memorize her face, for the postmortem face—"without one passions trace"—is most honest in death.[63]

Logan's interpretation of Griffitts's face in death compensates for her failure to record Griffitts's dying words, as "she uttered many more pious & tender escpressions which have escaped me for want of being immediately committed to paper." Arresting death, women sought textual manifestations of the dying, in faces and manuscripts alike. As *The Mourners Book* (1836) suggests: "If we could draw from the last hours and death-beds of our ancestors, all the illuminations, convictions, and uncontrollable emotions of the heart, with which they have quitted it; what a far more affecting history of man should we possess!"[64] Women accordingly supplemented their frequent experience with death by reading consolatory literature of exemplary deathbed scenes.[65] Griffitts, for instance, read a selection of Quaker ministers' accounts in *A Collection of Memorials* (1787).[66] She vicariously witnessed the demise of Sarah Pleasants, who offered "good expressions and advice" for others as they observed "her blooming youth, how changed and likely in a short time to bid adieu to the world." She admired Elizabeth Shipley, who "appeared filled with divine power, and spoke in a lively manner." She also noted those who specifically requested that their words be recorded in writing. Thomas Priestman "asked for pen and ink," writing "something to be inserted in his journal," and Sarah Millhouse wrote an admonition that "was found, wrote in her own hand . . . after her decease."[67] Moved by what she has read, Griffitts writes a poem in 1785, "On Transcribing, some Memorials of the Pious Dead," translating the exemplary faces into a handwritten memorial.[68] She thus likens the ministers' faces to tombstones as she etches them in her memory. With the poem as living testament of their good deaths, they would no longer need "the Sculptur'd lines,—or Marble bust, / To keep them from the oblivion of the dust." Committed to memory, the face memorialized the dead.

Just as women memorized the face and its accompanying expressions before death, so they emphasized the countenance after death when words are no longer possible. The dying face anticipates the soul's exit whereas the postmortem face acts as a mirror for the mourner as well as a reflection of God's face in heaven. " 'Tis sweet, 'tis soothing to the mourner's mind," suggests one consolation writer, "when called to stand by the dying-bed of much loved friends to witness such composedness and tranquility in the hour of death."[69] Witnessing leaves "a deeper Impression upon the Soul," keeping the beloved alive in memory while reminding us of our own mortality.[70] Mourners eventually look past the fading countenance, making a visual "Covenant with our Eyes." As the blood slowly drains away from the cheeks, the disembodied soul makes "vast improvement in knowledge" of God.[71] At this moment the veil is lifted, and we see God's face, realizing: "Now we see darkly, as through a glass; but then face to face." Face to face with God, the mourner gazes on the divine reflection "in a perpetual Vision for evermore."[72] Though the Bible professes that God's face is "such as eye hath not seen, nor ear heard, nor ever entred into the heart of man," women could see divinity in the face of death.[73] The most intimate memento mori, on the one hand, and a promise of resurrection, on the other, the posthumous reflection affords consolation.

Seeking a more material and permanent alternative to memory, many women commissioned postmortem portraits, which provided "gestures of *countenance* designed to stay oblivion."[74] The portraits arrest the moment of death, offering continuance until the living and dead are reunited.[75] Inviting a local artist to Stenton after the death of her son Algernon at age forty-four, Deborah Logan desired a lasting memento of "his most beautiful Remains, for never did Death leave less traces of its Iron power on a victim." Algernon died on 19 December 1835 at 3:15 in the morning, and "his dear Remains lay on his Bed undisturbed, untill after 10 oclock looking as if composed in a sweet sleep—I think I never saw any Countenance in death so lovely." Sometime between that morning and his burial three days later on 22 December, the portrait was painted: the artist "took my beloved son's likeness as he lay a beautiful Corpse, . . . taken from the face as first seen in death." Refusing to mourn "because she should see his face no more," Logan paid for two portraits. The posthumous portrait, then, not only memorializes the moment of death but also delays the final moment before the closed coffin hides his face forever. Viewing the portrait, she later explains, indelibly engraved Algernon "on my imagination and on my heart." Thus she relies on her memory to "accurately furnish the melancholy particulars."[76]

Painting beautified as well as preserved the dead. It alone can "preserve these bodies in that high perfection of form," according to Charles Wilson Peale, for it captured the countenance at its most sublime moment. Likening postmortem portraiture to embalming, Peale considers forestalling "the actual remains" from "corruption and being the food of worms" through "powerful anticepticks."[77] Though he decides that painting is preferable to embalming, his analogy aptly highlights the material and aesthetic nature of death's remains. Painting manuals accordingly created a distinctive palette to effect the most lasting resemblance on canvas: "To make a Colouring to represent Death, you must first clap in White, Orpiment, and Oaker, very pale, and then proceed with Vermillion. . . . work thereon with a Green Mixture, in which is more Blue than of any other Colour, that the Flesh may be livid. . . . The Mouth must be almost Purple . . . and for the strong Strokes you take Bistre and Lake, which are used also for the Eyes, Nose, and the Ears."[78] Unlike the portrait miniature's transparent, ivory surface, which "naturally" reflected the skin, the postmortem complexion required a thick combination of color to approximate the inanimate face and hide the ensuing signs of decomposition. Because fleeting passions no longer enlivened the countenance, posthumous paintings expressed a markedly different physiognomy. The corpse's likeness reflected both the soul's absence and its new life outside the body. A kind of disembodied physiognomy, death's face exemplifies the nostalgic rift between mortality and immortality that sustains a mourner's lament.

When Logan memorized Griffitts's face after death, she performed an act of memory much like portraiture. A gesture of incorporation, memory begins the process of mourning marked by cumulative and assimilative rituals that not only sustain female grief but also metaphorically keep the body alive after burial. As the poet Samuel Rogers writes in *The Pleasures of Memory* (1796), memory, like painting, is specular: "We gaze on every feature till it lives! / . . . And the lost friend still lingers in his shade!"[79] Lingering in the mourner's heart, the deceased assumes a new body.

THE BODY OF DEATH

Though Griffitts's body, like all corpses, "is left behind, as a Pledge of our Corruption," according to consolationists, "to imprint into our minds the horrour of Death, through that putrefaction which soon invades it, when it is deprived of the Souls presence,"[80] Logan says very little about her cousin's remains. Once the soul has fled, the body is instantly devalued. She details the physical deterioration leading to Griffitts's death ("a Parylitic stroke, as her left side was nearly motionless") and the lifeless physiognomy that followed. She sends out funeral invitations, coordinates burial preparations, arranges the funeral procession, and delivers modest bequests (see figure 4.3). But Logan noticeably glosses over washing, anointing, and wrapping Griffitts's lifeless body: "I staid at her house and endeavoured to order every thing according to her directions and what I knew would have been her mind. untill after her interment, which took place on the 26th in the evening, my brother and I following as her nearest relations. She lays buried in the East Side of Friends Grave yard in Arch Street opposite the first door of the meeting House, and not far

and Family are particularly requested to attend the Funeral of

DEBORAH LOGAN,

From her late residence, at Stenton, near Germantown, on THIRD-DAY next, the 5th inst., at 3 o'clock, P. M.

2d Mo. 3d, 1839.

4.3. Funeral invitation of Deborah Logan, 1839. Photograph by author. Courtesy of The National Society of The Colonial Dames of America in the Commonwealth of Pennsylvania at STENTON, Philadelphia.

from the Spot where her parents and the numerous branches of our family are laid."[81] Portraying the time between death and burial as a series of social ceremonies, Logan suppresses the unpleasant reality of preserving a corpse at a time without effective embalming methods.

In the intervals between mourners' visits, Logan and her assistants took turns sitting wake, covering Griffitts's face with a wax- or alum-soaked cerecloth to diminish death's telltale marks. As the soul quietly expired from the mouth, the other orifices grotesquely leaked. "Spirits coming from Putrefaction of Humours bred within the Body," for decomposition suffocated the "Natural Heat," causing "the Humours, Flesh and Secondary

Spirits [to] dissolve and break as it were into an Anarchy."[82] Accelerated by a hot Philadelphia summer, decomposition of Griffitts's corpse began quickly. Just a few days before her death "the Thermometer is in the Open Air, but shaded from the Sun, was at 91." Mercifully, "the change of the weather on the 24th was most remarkable, it was said the Thermometer fell 20 degrees." Unlike the body of her cousin Hannah Peale—"they could not keep her to send Invitations to the funeral"—Griffitts's corpse remained intact long enough for the ceremonial rites.[83] Carefully washed, wrapped in cerecloth, packed in bran, and perhaps even surrounded with ice, Griffitts's body was laid on a beautiful white pall.[84] Finally, the attendants sprinkled aromatic herbs such as rosemary around the corpse.[85] A symbolic token of remembrance, rosemary conveniently masked death's putrid odors.

Despite these preparations, decomposition was inevitable—and swift. Two to four hours after Griffitts's death, livor and rigor mortis aggressively set in. Lasting six to ten hours, livor mortis is the permanent purplish discoloration of the skin that occurs when circulation ceases. Additional chemical changes harden the body's muscles over the next twelve hours. Receding within sixteen to forty-eight hours, rigor mortis ends and the rigid corpse resumes its formerly limp posture. During this time putrefaction begins: gases from bacterial activity are released throughout the body. The body becomes distended; the skin color changes from green to purple to black; and the tongue and eyes protrude. At the same time, the abdominal organs may protrude through the vaginal and rectal openings, excreting foul-smelling, bloodstained fluids. Within twelve to eighteen hours the advanced stages of decomposition are often visible: facial features are no longer recognizable, the hair falls from the scalp, and the entire body becomes swollen to at least twice its normal size. As the body swells, enzymes cause it essentially to digest itself through autolysis, making body tissues soften and eventually liquefy. Bacteria in the body's moist areas (e.g., eyelids, nose, mouth) accelerate decomposition.[86] As Logan "endeavoured to order every thing according to [Griffitts's] directions," her cousin's corpse decayed in the parlor.[87]

Awaiting the predictable decomposition, the women also took extreme measures to ensure that Griffitts had, in fact, died. More than seeking evidence of the soul's sweet passage, they carefully watched for any residual signs of life. Women gleaned methods from a variety of sources. As one mourning manual explained, one should first check the respiration: "This House of Clay is to be Supported by a puff of Ayr continually breathed in and out. . . . another instrument of human frailty is the Pulse, which ariseth from the Heart, and the Arteries or beating Veins; and this by a double motion of Contraction and Dilation."[88] Because it was difficult to discriminate between death and other comatose states, women took every precaution to avoid burying someone alive.[89] Quoting a local doctor's instructions, Logan notes that a funeral "should not take place till unequivocal signs of Death appeared." Meanwhile, the body should be kept in a room "where the Thermometer would rise to 70."[90] Should revival fail to occur, women could resort to more vigorous measures.

As Mary Cole's *Lady's Complete Guide* (1791) illustrates, there are many "Directions for recovery of the Apparently Dead."[91] Though most successful when applied to people who "died of convulsions, suffocations, intoxication, hanging, intense cold, and struck by lightning," her methods were used "with vigor" for approximately three or four hours after death. To restore heat, women rubbed the corpse (especially the hands and feet) with spirit-soaked flannel. They grabbed the legs and arms and violently shook the body for six-minute intervals. And they bundled the corpse between two people, whose friction induced a heart massage. Reviving the dead thus demanded close contact with the living body. Even more personal were the slightly invasive techniques for restoring respiration: mouth-to-mouth resuscitation bellowed air between bodies, and fumigation reanimated the viscera through the bowels. Unlike passively watching the Christian soul's departure from the corpse, reviving the dead was an intensely physical act.

Such assiduous care of the corpse placated both the dead and the living: resuscitation prevented the seemingly dead from being buried alive and justified the mourner's reluctance to release the dead. Consolationists consequently worried "that if the resurrection power were lodged in our hands for one day, we should immediately run to the graves of our dear departed, and fetch them back again."[92] Effecting resurrection on earth, the argument went, women manifest an impatient lack of faith in God's promise of immortality. Patience—especially when dealing with what the early moderns called the "apparently dead"—was indeed a virtue. Resuscitation, like postmortem portraiture, brought the dead to life. But at the same time, it raised questions about the propriety of intimacy with corpses.

Transforming Mary Cole's "Directions for recovery of the Apparently Dead" into an ironic, necrophilic fantasy, Elizabeth Fergusson explores the ethical dangers of resuscitation in her poem "Cadavera's Ghost, or A Visit to Tomboso," written under the pseudonym Hecate (the goddess of ghosts) for her friend the scientist Francis Hopkinson. The poem shows her support for the scientific value of anatomical dissections, on the one hand, while feeding the cultural paranoia about anatomists' liaisons with the dead, on the other. Though Cole suggests an innocent ménage a trois (to "excite

the motion of the heart"), Fergusson recounts the illicit coupling of charnel doctor Tomboso and his beloved Cadavera.[93] The poem begins with
Tomboso taking his "Anatomical Venus" from her tomb and directly into
his bed:

> The Bones they Shook! each *Socket* wondrous movd,
> And all the Form a living motion provd.
> The Listening Mourner, sounds connected heard,
> He hopd alternate, and alternate feard.

Reconsidering what he wished for, the "Listening Mourner" sees the telltale
signs of life. Tomboso then flounders between his commitment to science
and the popular mistrust of anatomy and embalming. As "the Form a living
motion provd," Cadavera had shown "appearances of Death Equivocal."

She suddenly speaks, confounding the body used in anatomy theaters
with the romantic blazon.[94] Unlike a typical blazon, in which a male
speaker rhetorically dissects his love object in an attempt to appreciate and
control her body, Cadavera watches her own loving deconstruction:

> Each *Spiket* fitted to its *Fosset* Bone
> Was plain, and pleasing to Cadavera known
> When the *Vertebraes* to the *Ribbs* you strung
> I saw delight on all your features hung.

Unlike the mourner who patiently watches over the corpse, Cadavera reverses the spectacle and watches herself, assuming a virtually omnipotent
place in the anatomy theater. And unlike the corpse, whose eyes are manually closed at death, she startlingly returns Tomboso's gaze. As both subject
and object, Cadavera views her resuscitation, as "First from a Ribb was female beauty formd / With Life and Elegance supremly warmd." Improving
God's handiwork, the charnel doctor imitates the British painter William
Hogarth's "Line of Beauty" so the "Most Charming Curve" "shines conspicuous" on Cadavera's serpentine figure.

Since death's remains incorporate the mourner and the corpse, Cadavera's reconstructed body finds completion only in its union with Tomboso's: "Tho another may be markd as thine!" she says, "Then let thy
Bones incorporate with mine!" Sexually entwined in death with her
beloved, Cadavera envisions their apocryphal children as a lasting tribute to
her beauty and their love. With such beautiful (though imaginary) progeny, she thumbs her nose at death, for "Death from Thee Could not my
Image draw!" Where other scientists "Meanly diserted as the Flesh De-
cayd" and "left their Partners in the mouldring Tomb," Tomboso permanently engrafts Cadavera in his memory. But as immortal reunion follows a

long separation between the body and the soul, mourner and mourned, Tomboso is left alone again at the poem's end. The "Anatomical Venus" "sought her Pine case as her destind Grave" while "Lone *Tomboso* pressed his widowd Bed."

Separating the body and the face in her descriptions of Griffitts's death, then, Logan displays a distinct but culturally representative ambivalence toward the mortal remains. Preparing the corpse for burial, she and her companions readied themselves for the next, more permanent, separation. Without the help of professional undertakers to ease the process of detachment, their first moment of separation occurred when the cabinetmaker or underbearers closed the coffin. Excluding Griffitts's physical remains from her narrative, Logan began weaning herself from the body for which she so tenderly cared. Whereas contemporary funerary practices protect the living by effacing the reality of death, early American women repeatedly witnessed what the anatomist Thomas Greenhill called the "dismal Accidents and Calamities that befall the Dead."[95]

EMBALMED IN MEMORY

In *The Art of Embalming* (1705) Greenhill posits that the soul leaves the body only when the latter is "corrupt and putrified, as abhoring so loathsome an habitation."[96] Domesticating death, women transformed mourning into an embalming art that revived the living and preserved the dead.[97] Sealed in her heart, the other remains figuratively alive. Since embalming was not yet practiced in the early Republic, however, women could have only a metaphorical relationship to the balsamic art.[98] Likening embalming to their well-practiced arts of memory, they could, as Greenhill says, "*Embalm* the *Dead,* and keep their *Friends* alive" through ritualized mourning.[99]

Different from the material mode of collective memory discussed in chapter 3, in which objects served as metonyms for an absent other, mourning required a more complex set of substitutions. Like embalming, which entailed draining the corpse's blood and injecting preserving fluids, mourning first emptied the body of grief, replacing feelings of loss with lasting memories. In other words, the mourner, rather than the corpse, expires. Death fatally wounds the mourner whereas the immortal dead live, explains Annis Stockton: "The dead we mourn but the survivor dies."[100] While the peaceful corpse dreams of resurrection, she notes, "left behind the hapless mourner dies." The female mourner is emptied, eviscerated, and spiritually dead, "bereav'd of all [her] inmost soul held dear."[101] Fergusson similarly describes the decomposing mourner, quoting English poet James Thomson:

As those we love Decay, we die in part,
String after String is sever'd from the Heart;

. . . .

Draggd lingering on from partial Death to Death,
Till dying all [this] can Resign is Breath.[102]

Gradually dying with each successive death, the mourner withers to nothing but a puff of air. A kind of transference between the dead and the living, mourning is "vented only, as a change of pain."[103] Embalming the dead
in memory, the mourner dissolves into tears.

Like the liquefying corpse, the mourner approximates autolysis through
her perpetual weeping. As the Philadelphia coterie's poetry suggests, tears at
once anoint the corpse, perfume the grave, and embalm the corpse's memory. Like a "soft perfume," tears bring the "sweet remembrance" of the
dead to mind.[104] Standing over a friend's coffin, Griffitts muses, "How oft
have I,—the painful Portion prov'd / To pour the funeral Rite—on friends
belov'd, Weep Bosem Darling tyes."[105] A sweet balsam, her tears quietly
soak the body. Stockton, too, invokes "Sweet pity [to] Come with mois-
tened eyes / And shed the embalming drop."[106] Anointing the body, her
tears gush and soothe her anguish: "*Drop fast* my tears, and mitigate my woe
/ *Unlock* your springs, and *never cease* to *flow.*" Her pain temporarily lessened, the tears return to fragrant drops, for "drops like these can only yield
relief."[107] Once the funeral rites are complete, the tears stop and the
mourners internalize their grief once again. Unshed tears pool around the
heart and sustain the dying mourner, as they "pour [their] balm [and] give
the wish'd supply."[108] The aromatic tears, however, cannot revive the heart,
for the "heart is dead, to all its boast."[109] Virtually emptied of tears, the
mourner experiences the loss of the beloved as a physical hole where her
full heart once rested.

In order to incorporate the memory of another, the mourner must
transplant the deceased's heart into her own. Like ancient embalming practices, which excised and separately preserved the brain, heart, and viscera,
memory required an emotional dissection. Philibert Guibert explained car-
diac embalming a century earlier in *The Charitable Physician* (1639): "The
Heart being washed and the said Vinegar compounded, shall bee put to infuse in the said Vinegar in a pipkin being plaistered round the lidde, that the
aire enters not the space of five or six dayes, then take it out and make an
incision in it, and fill it with balme and pieces of Cotton balmed, and sowe
it up again, and sew it well into a little bag made of Searecloth, and put it
into a case of Lead, Silver, or Pewter, fashioned in the forme of a Heart,

and cary it whither you please."[110] Like the residual tears surrounding a mourner's heart, vinegar saturates the severed organ, which was then stuffed with cloth-soaked balm. Pierced by grief, her heart mends the fissure by transplanting the beloved's image into the resulting emotional cavity. Her heart—like a lead, silver, or pewter casket holding a relic or a coffin housing an intact corpse—encloses the other.

Such embalming does not end with memory's incorporation of the beloved, however; the mourners wrap the memory image, like a corpse, in an imaginary burial garment to forestall its obliteration. Just as the alum-soaked winding sheet enfolds the body, so the mourner's "sable-clad" heart wraps its grief. Virtually indistinguishable, the white death shroud and black mourning cloak join the two bodies of death. As Peter Stallybrass explains, "Cloth is able to carry the absent body, memory, genealogy, as well as literal material value."[111] Since cloth encodes both material and immaterial presences, the mourner (embodying the dead in her heart) makes herself, as Greenhill says, "*Immortal* by the *Dead.*"[112] As the sheet makes the corpse's literal body invisible, women fix its image in their minds. Griffitts explains the transference by envisioning her soul clothed in grief. She "wears the Sable weed of Blackest hue / . . . Cloathed with Grief and Cover'd O'er with Sadness." Mourning "Cloathes [her] Soul—with Unaffected woe," as her "Soul shall ever wear / The deepest grief."[113] Logan similarly says that "everything mournfull and tender seems in union with my mind, and all past scenes of that description croud my memory so that I am internally cloathed with Sackcloth, and set, as it were, in the dust."[114] While the winding sheet retains the corpse's shape, the mourner enfolds the deceased's memory in her heart.

The winding sheet, moreover, is an emblem of women's collective mourning and memory. Though the *Pennsylvania Gazette* indicates as early as June 1751 that "professionals intending to follow the business of an Undertaker, have got a large assortment of mourning . . . Muslins for winding sheets," women's private writings through the first decades of the nineteenth century suggest that they made rather than purchased both shrouds and mourning garments.[115] When Elizabeth Powell died, for instance, Logan remarked that "the Girls had their own and their mothers mourning to make up for the funeral, which will not take place until sixth day, and Sarah kindly stay'd to assist them, as did her sister."[116] Similarly, when "Margaret Patton died[, she] hoped Elizabeth Keppele and Sarah Walker would make a shroud for her, which they accordingly did."[117] Planning her funeral in advance, Elizabeth Fergusson's sister, Jane Graeme Young, had woven her own burial linen by 1752, chronicling her eventual death in 1759 by writing on the shroud: "The Lord hath mercifully guided me by his Council, and I humbly hope through the merits of my Dear Redeemer will Raise me up to Glory. This is the Hour the joyful Hour I have waited for and long very long wished for to be disolved and to be with Christ which is best of all."[118] The telling conflation of the present (*I hope*), present perfect (*I have waited*), and future (*will raise*) tenses highlights the liminal nature of the corporeal remains: as the body resting in the grave awaits reunion with the soul, the mourner is left behind to remember the past and anticipate her own death. Young narrates her impending death in the present tense so that her shrouded body might speak to the mourners in the future as they prepare her for burial.

Implicating the female mourners as readers, moreover, Young's burial cloth inspires collective mourning. As cloth exchanges hands, it binds people in networks of obligation. A type of currency and a means of incorporation, cloth has the ability to be permeated and transformed by maker and wearer alike and to endure over time.[119] Because women were expected to both wrap and mourn the dead, the burial cloth—as a memorial text—offered consolation to the living. Materially wrapping her corpse, Young's words decompose with her body. But as the mourners traced her imprint on the cloth, they felt her continued presence. Ultimately transcribed into a commonplace book and embalmed in her sister's memory, the words outlive her. The burial cloth, then, mediates the present and the future, the living and the dead. Just as Young desires "to be disolved," so the cloth dissolves into more lasting paper.[120]

Since people were buried in winding sheets, their clothes, like paper, were left behind to the mourners' assiduous care. An antonym for the buried shroud, clothes wrapped the living in the memory of the dead. Wearing the deceased's clothes evokes her presence and comforts the mourner. After her son Algernon's death, for example, Logan describes the mnemonic importance of cloth: "We had a fire in the stove of my dear Algey's own chamber and proceeded to put away his cloaths and to arrange things a little for the future.—The Past was brought vividly before us from many circumstances. . . . Maria and Sarah—had been employed in putting away the dear Creatures cloaths and papers that were about his chamber and antichamber."[121] Organized by devoted mourners, clothes and papers—as material memory objects—personify the dead. Like Young's shroud, which narrated her passage to the grave, Algernon's clothes outlive and embody him. His shape, his scent, and other marks signify his lingering presence.

Writing both practical and sentimental directions to be followed after her own death, Logan accordingly makes provisions for her clothes. After directing that "my common things of wearing apparel [be] divided between the 3 old neighbours," she ensures that her finery will be given as an intimate remembrance of herself: "My Sally is near of age and should have a handsome suit of cloaths at my expense, I have given her my silk Boat [hat] and one of my Gowns—If Sally Logan, my kind and suffering niece, will please to accept some of my best linen and best Black silk gown, and also a pretty piece of plate as a remembrance of me, let them be given."[122] Though the silver might retain a smudge of Logan's fingerprint, the contours left by her body more permanently shape the custom-fitted gowns. Slipping into the dress and placing the hat on her head, Sally not only assumes the shape of her revered predecessor but also embodies her memory. The mourner literally assumes the place of the other.

The antecedent to paper, cloth—as burial shroud and mourning dress—materializes the art of memory. Literally and figuratively enclosing the body, it binds the corpse and mourner together. Women envision their grief-stricken hearts as clothed in sorrow and assimilate the deceased's memory within that cloth. The mourner's body, in effect, entombs the dead. Conversely, when women put on their inherited clothes, they invert the process of incorporation, finding comfort in the material's loving embrace. As the mourner's body animates the vacant clothes, the clothes seem to reciprocate, recalling the shape of the absent body and accommodating its current inhabitant to the remembered form. Mingling the two bodies in a single garment, as Stallybrass says, "cloth *is* a kind of Memory."[123]

Cloth's mnemonic significance continues with the coffin. "Chesting" a corpse before interment, the wooden coffin descends from seventeenth-century caskets (small boxes housing intimate objects) and chests (storage places for clothing and blankets). The chest that once held intimate textiles for living bodies evolved into the ultimate enclosure for the linen-wrapped corpse. As "the safe resting place for all of a person's worldly belongings, all that gave him or her a sense of separate identity," according to the furniture historian Gerald Ward, the chest—as coffin—emphasized the shared identity between corpse and mourner as death's remains.[124] To make death seem less permanent and more bearable, many late-eighteenth-century coffins had a sliding partition or glass window in the top, allowing the mourners' constant surveillance over and gradual weaning from death's face until burial.[125] Logan recalls "the wish of the Greek Girl who would have a Casement made in her tomb that she might see the morning Star, and the Rose, and that the Birds might come to tell her of Spring."[126] In contrast to the Greeks' flesh-eating sarcophagi that quickly destroyed the corpse, the imagined casement provided an annual resurrection, as the girl rose from the dead each spring like Persephone. Exemplifying the continu-

4.4. Toy coffin, c. 1790–1850. Courtesy, Winterthur Museum.

ity between life and death, the child's toy coffin in figure 4.4 mimics both an actual coffin and the human chest with its characteristic portal and engraved heart. Superimposed over the face when the lid closes, the heart announces the finality of the corpse and its subsequent incorporation into the mourner's memory. For as Grosvenor says, "the living saint in Heaven should have a little of our heart; it should not always dwell in a coffin, and in a grave."[127]

Replicating a coffin and enfolding a corpse, the series of images in figures 4.5–4.8 textualizes the coffin's finality. Made from a single sheet of paper with two contiguous folds, the images enact the consecutive rituals of winding and burying a corpse on the one hand and reading a text on the other. The poetic directions accompanying death's body recall Jane Young's instructive shroud. Whereas Young merges the present and future in the moment of death, these liminal images display the body before and after death. Double-voiced, the poem's speaker addresses the viewer from his prime of life, through his physical decline, and finally from the grave.

The initial, unopened image presents an eighteenth-century gentleman in all his finery, and the verse betrays his false confidence in material comfort:

Now I have gold and Silver Store
All Worldly Cares Shall flee
What then on earth shall fright me more
Turn down this leaf and see

Turning down the lower leaf, the viewer learns conflicting lessons. Though conspicuous wealth meliorates life's cares, it depreciates in the face of death.

In an apostrophe to the gold and silver, the speaker acknowledges the shimmering stockpile's limited value:

> Sickness is come and Death draws nigh
> Help gold and silver or I die
> It will not do it will not last
> Turn up and see mans life is past.

As sickness wrecks his frame, the speaker admits that death is inevitable. Neither the gold nor the silver (nor his body) will last. Unlike a windowed coffin displaying the face and obscuring the rotting viscera, the folding card's final image shows the body in an advanced state of decomposition. The viewer thus folds up the remaining tab, confronting his or her own death. Breaking the rules of exhumation, the card invites a prurient peek into the coffin:

> Now see o man thou art but dust
> Thy gold and silver is but rust
> Thy time is come thy glories spent
> What Worthy cares can death prevent.

The morbid skeleton, rather than the more popular winged cherub, wields death's dart and foreboding hourglass. Heeding the consolationist's advice that "Carnal Men there be, whose Spiritual Eyes are dazled, or rather blemished, with Terrestrial Objects, and can extend their Intellectual Sight, no farther than the exterior Object of Sense guides 'em," this composite figure of life and death urges both corpse and viewer to look heavenward.[128]

Real or metaphorical, the coffin signifies women's last intimate experience with the dead. Once the body was arranged for public viewing, women would relinquish their control over the remains and begin the more public work of mourning. At this time there was a notable shift away from death's natural body to the social protocol designed to pacify the mourners. Though women internalized mourning through metaphorical sackcloths covering the soul, they now dressed themselves in the expected mourning attire, "replacing the physical obligation of caring for the deceased," as one critic says, with a "decorative exhibition of emotion."[129] As John Weaver suggests in *Ancient Funerall Monuments* (1631), "The procuration of funerals, the manner of buriall, the pomp of obsequies, bee rather comforts to the living, then helpes to the dead."[130] With each successive remove from the corpse, women surrendered their attachment to the physical remains and aestheticized the social trappings of death: from the "collecting hour" and funeral procession to the distribution of mourning objects, women sustained their material connection with the dead.

4.5–4.8. Metamorphosis paper toy, c. 1750. Viewing the images from left to right, one sees the folded card in its closed and opened positions: the unopened cover (4.5), the cover with the bottom flap open (4.6), the cover with the top flap open (4.7), and the card's interior fully revealed (4.8). Courtesy, The Winterthur Library: Joseph Downs Collection of Manuscripts and Printed Ephemera, no. 69x209.4.

4.5

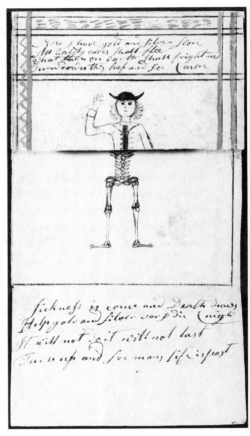

4.6

Now see o man thou art but dust
Thy gold and silver is but rust
Thy time is come thy glass is spent
What wordly cares can death prevent

4.7

Now see o man thou art but dust
Thy gold and silver is but rust
Thy time is come thy glass is spent
What wordly cares can death prevent

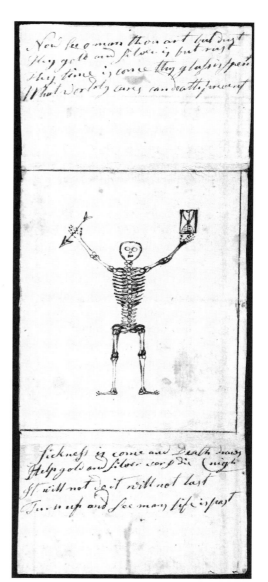

Sickness is come and Death draws nigh
Help gold and silver cease die
It will not be it will not last
Turn up and see man life is past

4.8

THE COLLECTING HOUR

At the "collecting hour" public mourners arrived at the "house of mourning" for one last look before the coffin was closed. The ceremonial pomp began with the delivery of funeral invitations to relatives and friends. Mass-produced by local printers, the black-bordered invitations detailed the appointed time for gathering at the house of mourning. Paid inviters delivered the invitations to select guests, and family members passed the information to their intimates by word of mouth. Often funeral gloves rather than paper invitations were given, serving as memorial tokens of the deceased. This done, the family prepared the best parlor to receive the parade of mourners, staging death as a caesura to life. They stopped the clock at the hour of death, turned the mirrors toward the wall, draped black cloth over the pictures, and drew the curtains. Logan vividly portrays the scene:

> Her corpse was brought down stairs and laid in the north west Parlour . . . on a small Bedstead entirely covered with a white Pall. the window curtains let down to the floor. it seemed like a Tomb. . . . Her attendants, and a number of Young Girls were in the room all bathed in tears. when the heart rending scene was over the Coffin was put in the hearse and we proceeded slowly. . . . followed the Hearse down to the little burial Ground, which has been newly walled round and there we deposited the mortal remains of my poor sufferer in a very deep Grave, that in no future chance they may ever be disturbed.[131]

Displaying the Logan family's finest furniture, textiles, and silver to its guests, the best parlor also exhibited the corpse on its white pall as people gathered around the sad spectacle.

Men and women alike attended the corpse, but most accounts of the "collecting hour" underscore women's predominant role at the house of mourning. Although their importance to the funeral rites diminished as the moment of burial approached, women's domestic responsibilities for the material preparations of death—from dressing the corpse to making food for the guests—continued until the mourners arrived. Typically, two or three o'clock was the appointed time for gathering, but women often arrived early to assist with any last-minute details. "We went over early in the morning . . . a few of their friends had collected to accompany the Corpse to Philadelphia to be interred," writes Logan. Arriving before the other invited guests, women "went to the House . . . and sat there the hour of collecting. . . . It was a tribute of Respect, which we willingly paid to the remains."[132] Paying their respects to the dead, women more importantly took care of the living. In addition to providing much-needed emotional support, they helped prepare the ritual repast. Following standard recipes from such popular cookbooks as *The Compleat American Housewife* (1776), they made "funeral bisquits," "ryaninjun," cornbread, lobster soup, "peas porridge," "beaf steak pies," boiled hare, baked beans, hasty pudding, flummery, and broiled pork and venison. While "our kind neighbours, men and women, came in crowds to offer their assistance," forming "a solemn procession" to view the corpse, the family retired to the dining room for dinner.[133] As the corpse silently decayed, the living would eat and drink—a testament to their mortality.

Illustrating women's designated role to mourn the dead and support the bereaved, Logan recalls the collecting hour at the funeral of her cousin Charles Thomson at his Harrington estate: "A very large collection of Respectable People Attended. Many of the Ladies sat in the Room with Maria and myself, it had been his own chamber and was that in which he had died." Occupying his bedchamber while the "corpse lay in the little Parlour to the Right as you enter, very neatly laid out in his Coffin," the women revisit the place of death. Rather than focus on the corpse's "most venerable and placid countenance," however, Logan notices the architecture of death, appreciating the room's design. Her eyes move from the small recess where Thomson expired to the impressive library that gave him pleasure for almost a century. A memory place, the room embodied Thomson's presence and provided the mourners with a palpable image by which to remember him. "Bent with great interest" on the books, Logan begins the necessary process of detachment that initiates the grieving process. Thus she merges her role as a mourner with her antiquarian interest in collecting books, papers, and other historical artifacts. Materializing death, "collecting" assists mourning and strengthens the memory.[134]

No longer responsible for Thomson's corporeal remains, the women return to the parlor and assume their duty to mourn. Displacing their affection for the corpse onto the synecdochic objects that fill his chamber, they experience a process of mortification, which necessitates grief. "The house of mourning," consolationists explained, "is the School for mortification." Since mortification (from Latin *mors* "death" and *facere* "to make") at once signifies the corpse's submission to decay and the mourner's requisite asceticism, it defines the public etiquette for lamentation, for "submission is a grace that reaches to the behaviour, the features, and the outward postures of the body."[135] Memorizing the deceased's face and monitoring their grief by watching one another's expressions, women are "*made better* in their hearts, by the Consideration of the dead, and by the *Sadness of the Counte-*

nances." Averting their eyes from the living, mourners rest their downturned faces in their hands and internalize the beloved's face: "There is the end of all men, and the living will lay it to his heart."[136] In this way they authorize their lamentation through traditional Christian iconography. Like the weeping daughters of Jerusalem, who followed Jesus to the grave, women accompanied the dead from the house of mourning to the burial ground.[137]

Despite consolation literature's admonition against immoderate grief, mourning was explicitly gendered as feminine in postrevolutionary America. Hannah Griffitts accordingly characterizes the house of mourning by its array of disconsolate women strewn about the coffin:

> In the sad Chambers of retir'd distress
> The scenes of speechless woe; where widow's mourn
> The Tender Husband lost; where orphan's weep
> The Indulgent father, and sustaining friend.
>
> . . . .
>
> Where the sad Sister, faints beneath the stroke
> That rent the Associate Brother from her heart.[138]

Cataloging a similar throng of mourners in "Ill penserosa, an ode," Annis Stockton chronicles: "Some maiden whose lover had died"; "Some widow the prop of whose age / Dire disease had resign'd to the grave"; "Some mother whose daughter like mine / Had gone to a far distant shore"; and "The matron friend with sympathetic heart— / With the lov'd Mother shall at eve repair."[139] As matrons, mothers, and maidens, widows, daughters, and sisters, women performed the lachrymose gestures of lamentation. Weeping, fainting, and moaning, they succumbed to grief, trading the submissive postures of consolation for the more expressive, and culturally legitimate, language of sympathy.

THE PROCESSION

In many ways concern for women's intemperate grief was secondary to the censure of the material affectations marking the funeral procession. Linking women with conspicuous consumption and femininity with luxury, colonies and states passed sumptuary laws that limited mourning attire to ornamental flourishes: only hats, gloves, ribbons, and fans were acceptable signs of grief.[140] A funeral procession, writes one consolation writer, "naturally strikes us [as] the undistinguishing blow with which that common enemy levels all. We behold a great promiscuous multitude all carried to the same abode; all lodged in the same dark and silent mansions."[141] Reverend George Whitefield agrees, asking, "If the wearing of black tends to keep alive the esteem we have for our friends, why will not tying a piece of crape round the arm, or some such external badge of mourning, answer this purpose?"[142] Whereas the former statement creates a homogeneous class of female mourners by effacing the signifiers of socioeconomic status with the mark of gender, the latter predicts that such an "external badge of mourning" would restore common sense (i.e., reason) and corset female sensibility (i.e., excessive grief).[143] As Susanna Wright eloquently echoes, "All different Paths but to one Center tend."[144]

Unaffected by sumptuary legislation or the "new established Method" of funerals, Philadelphians continued their luxurious displays. In 1765 Whitefield challenged "those inhabitants of Philadelphia, whose fortunes admit, and whose stations seem to require this expence," to curtail funerary extravagance, "especially when they consider how much their example will affect their inferiors." Funerals at all social levels, however, continued to be lavish. Whitefield repeatedly criticized "the momentary show," arguing that "it excites no superior veneration for the memory of the deceased; it communicates no happiness to the departed spirit, . . . [and] it affords no consolation to the relatives." Repeating Whitefield in her poem "Monumental Vanity," Griffitts suggests that materialism is not only wasteful but insincere:

> Of what avail, to Happiness,—or woe,
>   Is all the vain Parade of empty state,
> The Muffled knell, That Tolls the funeral show,
>   The sable train, attendant on the great,
> The Mourning Equipage, drag'd steps along,
>   Where form, to form, unfeeling griefs repeat,
> The Proud Inscription of a flattring tongue
>   The enquiring Rabble, & the gazing street—[145]

Such displays, she contends, are not the expressions of "Real Grief." Just as she dismisses consolation manuals' stayed conventions, which silence female lamentation, Griffitts repudiates false theatricality. Indulging life's temporal pleasures, funeral pomp obscured the appropriate message of mortal dissolution and resurrection. It was an ineffectual memento mori.

Appalled by expensive theatrics, members of the Philadelphia coterie left explicit directions for their own modest funerals. Elizabeth Fergusson stipulated "that Funeral expences may not exceed 15 pounds; a Coffin of plain Cherry boards, to be taken to Town & laid at the feet of my Parents."[146] Hannah Griffitts requested that "No show, attend my Nature's last retreat, /

But Decent, Rest beneath its grassy Clod." And Deborah Logan explained, "I do not approve of Pomp and Parade at a funeral—neither do I covet such a private one, by stealth as it were, and as if the survivors wished for no witnesses of the interment."[147] They preferred what Logan considered the eighteenth century's "old fashioned manner," exemplified by Elizabeth Willing Powel's funeral:

> The funeral of Mrs. Powel took place in the morning: it was ordered in the old fashioned manner. The Corpse borne on mens shoulders and covered with a Pall was followed by her Relations and Friends and Domestics, and then by Citizens. About four and twenty Coaches attended. she was buried in her husbands Grave in the Arch Street burial Ground, not in the vault belonging to the Francis family. I was told an invitation had been sent to me tho' I have not recd it, and had I have known how consonant with the "Olden time" things would have been, I surely would have attended.[148]

Missing the funeral because her invitation had not arrived on time, Logan carefully records the details narrated by her friends. The processional order, one immediately notices, is distinctly gendered: the male underbearers carry the corpse, and women closely follow, taking precedence over the general citizens. Since family, friends, and female domestics make up this group, gender rather than class determines its constituency. Compared with men's funerals, in which the female mourners either fall back in the processional order or forgo the parade altogether, women were highly visible at Elizabeth Powel's funeral. Wearing the mourning clothes prepared by the young girls mentioned earlier, they were living symbols of grief.

Women were well trained in funeral and mourning etiquette since girlhood. Ten-year-old Anna Greene Winslow mentions attending funerals several times in her diary. On 14 December 1771 she notes: "I went to Mrs. Whitwell's to see Madm Storers funeral, the walking was very bad except on the sides of the street which was the reason I did not make a part of the procession." A month later, on 18 January, she mentions mourning etiquette once again: "My aunt thought it proper (as our family had an invitation) that I should attend a neighbor's funeral yesterday P.M."[149] Sarah Eve likewise makes a reference to funeral attendance in her diary but specifies her gendered relationship to the corpse: "In the evening B. Rush, P. Dunn, K. Vaughan and myself carried Mr. Ash's child to be buried; foolish custom for Girls to prance it through the streets without hats or bonnets!"[150] A young girl's burial required other girls to carry the white pall while male underbearers carried the coffin beneath it. Much like the train of virgins in figure 4.9, a group of young girls formed the funeral procession of Fanny Durden on 19 December 1813: "Six young ladies of her intimate acquaintance, of which I was one, were asked to be pall bearers. We were all dressed in white with long white veils."[151] Dressed in white, like the virginal corpse, girls attended the sexually untainted body to the grave. Their funeral garb, rather than the customary black, marked their shared chastity with the corpse.

The white dresses, moreover, link the girls to the textual and textile traditions of female mourning, as their diaries and needlework attest. Unlike adult females, who aestheticized the corpse into beautiful, or at least palatable, memory images, eighteenth-century girls understood death in grossly corporeal terms. They accordingly covered their the samplers with antiquated Puritan imagery of skulls, crossed bones, and rotting bodies. More than material evidence of their literacy or able stitching, the textiles display their institutionalized training in the feminine arts of mourning. As a result, samplers typically include such stock phrases as "when I am dead and laid in my grave" and "greedy worms my body eat" and "this mortal frame decay." Facing death on a daily basis, children were keenly aware of their mortality. The sampler, with its vertically rectangular form and inscribed letters, thus resembles a tombstone. Twelve-year-old Martha Taylor's sampler in figure 4.10 illustrates the ascending journey from our earthly home (the tree-lined Georgian estate at the bottom) to heaven's eternal abode (the turret of hearts at the top). Though the accompanying text elaborates that Lancaster is her "Habitation" and Christ her "Salvation," the sampler's final message is a passionless memento mori: "When I'm dead & in my Grave & all my bones are rotten when this you see remember me. Adieu." Contrasting the light-colored ground with black thread, Taylor emphasizes *grave, bones, rotten, remember,* and *adieu.* She does not passively await death but rather accepts it as life's natural conclusion. Since girls did not yet care for the dead, they lacked the metaphors that mnemonically embalmed the dead in a perfected rather than decayed state, retaining only a connection to the putrid corpse in the ground.[152]

More involved in funeral rites as adults, women were still prohibited from full public participation. They walked in processions for deceased females but were often excluded from men's funerals. As Logan explains, she received invitations to the funerals of both George Fox and Spencer Sargeant but did not join in the processions. In the first instance "only Sally and Betsy Roberts and ourselves of Womenkind were there and consequently we did not go to the ground, but after the Procession had passed on near half an hour we got into Cousin's carriage and came to her house." Women apparently attended the house of mourning, but only after the men

4.9. Paul Sandby, sketch, *Pallbearers Accompanying the Coffin at a Spinster's Funeral*. Courtesy of the Victoria & Albert Museum Picture Library. © The Board of Trustees of the Victoria & Albert Museum.

paid their last respects and carried the corpse to the burial ground. Similarly, at Fox's funeral: "As no woman joind the Procession we waited at the House untill the return of the Carriages . . . I was glad I paid the only mark of Respect in my Power to the memory of this good and much-regretted man."[153] Logan's rhetoric of disempowerment is curious. Was she unable to join the procession for practical reasons—a dearth of carriages, bad weather, or poor health? Or does her expected visit to the house of mourning suggest the only social gesture of mourning available to her?

Unsure how to definitively answer the question of female presence at funerals, I momentarily reframe them around the related issue of female speech. Though women attended Elizabeth Powel's funeral, for example, they had only physical visibility; their grief was otherwise muted. As Logan recalls: "The particulars of Mrs. Powels funeral, were of a distressing, or rather I should say 'annoying' nature to me:—Cousin H. Smith was there, and on attempting to speak was stopd by Edward Bued who acted as a master of ceremonies, and on a second attempt he ordered the mourners to advance on. I felt mortified that Hannah should have done this, or intruded at all upon their order, and was sincerely glad I was not present."[154] Since Quakers were egalitarian, allowing both men and women to speak at meeting, Logan's anecdote suggests that women could, in fact, speak at funerals at a particular time and in a particular order. Still, one might expect that female speech, if sanctioned at all, would be limited to funerals of other

4.10. Girlhood sampler by Martha Taylor of Lancaster, Pennsylvania, c. 1797. Courtesy, Winterthur Museum, gift of Elizabeth Oat Rockwell.

women. But there is no apparent place for Smith's voice in Elizabeth Powel's well-attended and highly public funeral. Each time she attempts to speak, Smith is not only stopped by Edward Bued but also ignored by other mourners as he instructs them to move on. As "master of ceremonies," Bued represents a social rather than religious hierarchy, in which funeral etiquette overruled sectarian privilege. In such cases men publicly silenced women. Twice "intruding" on the procession's order, Smith shows either a surprising ignorance of funeral decorum or a blatant disregard for its gendered constraints. But given women's acculturation in mourning practices since childhood, it is difficult if not impossible to read her "intrusions" as accidental.

From the collecting hour to the burial that punctuates the funeral procession, women gradually receded from the corpse. Their distinctly domestic responsibility of preparing the dead and organizing the burial ended at the house of mourning. Although they selectively participated in the processions, women faced more blatant forms of sexism in the public (rather than private) displays of grief.[155] Once the body was buried, however, they resumed their intimacy with the dead by caring for the grave. Looking at a gravestone so forcibly stimulated the memory, according to Logan, "that I felt almost as if at a funeral—it is now near four years since her decease, but the time seems a mere point, her form, her patient cheerfulness, and endearing manners will never be forgotten by me."[156] As the "Repositories of the remains of all we held Dear," the grave, Elizabeth Fergusson agreed, offered consolation.[157]

THE GRAVE

Interred in the grave, the body rests in its final repository: wrapped in a winding sheet, encased in a coffin, and enveloped in the mourner's heart, the remains are invisible, existing only in memory. Such concentric enclosures, however, initially bewildered the mourner. Though Hannah Griffitts's heart "Entombs the Relics" of her mother's "humble Dust," and though filial memory survives "the Ravage of the Tomb," the metaphors leave her cold, wondering what actually happens to the physical body after burial.[158] Susanna Wright shares Griffitts's frustration, asking:

How shall I plunge amidst the numerous Dead?
What, shall I be unbodied?—how & where?
Instant—will those tremendous Scenes appear?
Or must I sleep unnumber'd Ages o'er?[159]

Her litany of questions elicits only inadequate answers. Abstract images of disembodiment yield further unanswerable questions:

To that boundless Space where Matter ends,
Passes the mighty Void, that separates
Invisible—and visible Abodes:

. . . .

But far above where all Conceptions rise,
Beyond the utmost Stretch of human Thought.[160]

Beyond our comprehension, heaven is utterly immaterial. In this other world, consolationists preached, the body becomes ephemeral as the soul flourishes in divine materiality. All will be "substance" rather than "shadow." Confounded by the irony, Wright gives up, conceding, "Since only Death these Mysteries can explore, / O! thou enquiring Mind, enquire no more."[161]

Wright returns to the empirical world, domesticating the boundless afterlife into the more familiar space of the Georgian country house.[162] Along
with the rest of her coterie, she adopts the common iconography of the
tomb as "a Lodging," "an eternal Home," "a resting place," "an eternal
habitation," "a residence for eternity," and "a house for life."[163] They follow
the graveyard poet Robert Blair's architectural metaphors in *The Grave:*
"The House appointed for all the Living" and the "appointed Place of
Rendevous," where "Doors creak, and Windows clap" in the "Mansions of
the Dead."[164] Given women's intimate knowledge of domestic topoi, the
house provided both material images and convenient rhetoric to explain the
otherwise abstract space of the grave. Women represented the tomb, then,
not only as rooms in their houses but also as places in their minds, for as
Locke argues: "Our minds represent to us those tombs to which we are approaching: where though the brass and marble remain, yet the inscriptions
are effaced by time, and the imagery moulders away."[165] But refreshed by
memory, the dead linger.

A precursor to the heavenly mansion, the Georgian house was an accessible prototype for the grave. Its vertical form not only mimics the human
body from head to foot but also enacts the soul's upward ascent at death.
The lower floors characterize corporeality (from the cellar's base functions
to the parlor's more polite social body), and the upper floors signify the soul
(in its exit from the bedchamber into the garret's lofty memory spaces). The
horizontal organization alternately represents the soul's intimate return to
the grave in its homecoming with the resurrected body, as Blair explains:

> . . . Nor shall the conscious *Soul*
> Mistake its Partner; but amidst the Croud
> Singling its other Half, into its Arms
> Shall rush, with all the Impatience of a Man
> That's new-come Home, who having long been absent
> With Haste runs over ev'ry different Room.[166]

The resurrected body, like the Georgian house, is elegantly balanced. Its
perfected form celebrates the proportionate beauty of interdependent parts
as they meet in a nostalgic embrace. When death "conducts us to our
Home, and lands us safe / On the long-awaited Shore," the soul rushes from
room to room, seeking shelter in the uninhabited body.[167]

Because Georgian architecture inaugurated the spatial configuration of
privacy, it also structurally reinforced the personal relationship between the
corpse and the mourner. As expressly feminine spaces, the parlor and best
chamber exemplify the protracted intimacy of death on the one hand and
the social protocol that effaced this bond on the other. As Allestree writes in

Whole Duty of Mourning, "the Grave itself is but a withdrawing Room to re-
tire in for a time; it is going to Bed to take rest, which is sweeter than
Sleep."[168] But marking the end of women's physical contact with the corpse
and the commencement of public mourning, the withdrawing room (or
parlor) muted women's collective mourning. It ceremoniously resigned the
body to its impending grave and confounded the previous intimacy between corpse and mourner. Longing for a sustained connection, women recalled the moment of death, when the soul's traces still warmed the body.
In other words, the drawing room—with its drawn curtains, cloth-lined
coffin, and accompanying pall—roused memories of the death chamber
above.

Whereas the parlor obscured the mundane realities of death, the best
chamber accommodated women's intimate ministrations to the corpse. In
its corporeal associations with sex, birth, and death, the bed and its elaborate textiles naturally received the mortal remains. At the same time, it offered tangible continuity between the living and the dead.[169] With yards
upon yards of curtain material enveloping its frame, the bed seemed "a
room in itself, with four carved posts, flowered curtains for walls, a chintz
tester for ceiling, and steps conducting one into an acre of billowy bolstered
bliss."[170] A room within a room, the bed imitated the corpse's layered en-
casement in a winding sheet and coffin beneath a white pall on what Logan
calls "this side of our blue Canopy." Each layer, moreover, anticipated the
grave's unfathomable depths. A straw-filled tick was the substratum. On top
of this layer was the feather bed, mattress, and bolster. Above this downy region was the bottom sheet, two pillows (propped up against the bolster), a
top sheet, several blankets, and a crowning counterpane. Like a bed, the
grave was a place of rest. As Griffitts imagined it, the "Grave, the Peaceful
Chambers of their rest," with "the Pillow smooth," would "ease the Bed of
Pain" and "Seal their Slumbers Sweet."[171]

Repeatedly admonished "by sight of our Bed to remember our Grave,"
Christians in the early Republic considered the bed a nightly memento
mori. It was "a Tomb or Sepulchre, and every Night before we go into it,
[we] labour for reconciliation with God."[172] Death is not a conclusion, consolationists preached, but rather a temporary sleep: "Why do you mourn as
if they were extinct; as if they were annihilated, and utterly lost?"[173] Heeding their persistent warnings, Fergusson's niece, Anna Young Smith, imagines death as a sweet sleep:

> Ordaind by Fate to give you to the Tomb
> Kind Angels shall your Dying hours attend
> And Sister Spirits oer your Shade shall bend

. . . .
> Their balmy Breaths shall blow your Cares away,
> Their Wings shall waft you to the Realms of Day.[174]

Instead of passively waiting for the body's failed respiration, Young envisions eternal sleep as angels breathing over her still remains. At the song's denouement the angels fan their wings until the fading notes and vanishing breath "sink on the Breeze and melt at Last away." Like a lullaby, death's touch hushes her anguish.

John Keats's lovely ode "To Sleep" similarly paints the moment of death as a seductively calm sleep. Its tactile imagery of death's gentle hands unwittingly personifies the female mourner, who performs the same physical tasks at the deathbed: closing the eyes, embalming the body, and wrapping the corpse in the coffin. The poem begins at the moment of death, when sleep's "benign" and "careful fingers" shut "our gloom-pleased eyes." The eyes close, the breath slows, and everything quietly ceases. The "soft embalmer of the still midnight," sleep wraps the corpse and then turns the coffin's "key deftly in the oiled wards, / And seal[s] the hushed casket of my soul."[175] The body houses the soul, the coffin encloses the body, and the grave envelops the coffin. But stripping away the effacing layers of burial, the poem ultimately returns to the face—the singular manifestation of the soul. Just as women watch the face for the soul's concluding expression, so sleep preserves the countenance in death.

The soothing poetics of death's eternal sleep also illuminated gravestone art until the early nineteenth century. Whereas horizontal body stones map the body buried below (see figure 4.11), and foot stones mark the feet that once trod the earth, vertical headstones not only enact the soul's upward flight from the mortal body but also inscribe the soul's face on their surface. Typically shaped like the human head and shoulders, these rounded stones display the requisite name and dates of the deceased along with the popular soul effigy, which dominated funeral art by 1760.[176] The fashionable effigies, cherubic faces with wings, symbolize the resurrection and recall the corpse's sleeping countenance. Just as death's physiognomy manifests the otherwise internalized soul, so the tombstone externalizes the soul by prominently etching it on the headstone's face.

Though most eighteenth-century gravestones have lost their inscriptions to centuries of unforgiving Philadelphia winters, women nonetheless considered these epitaphs to be an extension of their own elegiac practices. The inverse of an elegy written by the living for the dead, the epitaph is a message from the dead to the living. Like the parting words recorded at the deathbed, or like Jane Young's engraved shroud that spoke to the mourners

4.11. Deborah Logan's tombstone in the Stenton burial ground, now paved over by Germantown's urban sprawl. Courtesy of The National Society of The Colonial Dames of America in the Commonwealth of Pennsylvania at STENTON, Philadelphia.

as they wrapped her body, tombstones textualize death. Remarking on Fergusson's body stone at Christ's Church, Logan writes: "I have heard that the good and talented Mrs. Ferguson would not suffer any eulogium to be inscribed on her tombstone, but that she was a sympathizer with the distressed; and for myself I may truly say that when any affliction attends the families of my connections or Friends, my mind takes its portion with them and feels for the grief and bitterness which is their allotment."[177] A voice from the grave, Fergusson's chosen epithet, "the true sympathizer with the afflicted," speaks to Logan, inviting her to examine her own life. Internalizing Fergusson's message, she too empathetically feels another's grief. Much as mourners have a duty to memorialize the dead, the dead assume responsibility for those they leave behind.

Popularized by *Friendship in Death: Letters from the Dead to the Living*

(1782), by the British bluestocking Elizabeth Singer Rowe, literary epigraphs promised the hope of resurrection. Passing Rowe's book among themselves, members of the Philadelphia coterie circulated poetic imitations, such as Hannah Griffitts's "Copy to Sylvania—from her Freind Fellicia lately Deceas'd,—being a Poetical Imitation of Mrs Rowe's Letters from the Dead, To the Living."[178] The letters beautifully describe the heavenly mansion that mortals can only imagine: Fellicia dwells in "feilds of Light— and Pure Ambrosial air, / (Where I am Safe arrived my Mortal friend)." Recalling moments when she, too, "shiv'ring stood, / Anscious and doubt-full for my future—Rest," Fellicia goes on to describe her soul's "Swelling-flood . . . In Everlasting Glory." She uses her omnipotence to warn Sylvania and offer an experienced model:

> Ten Thousand Dangers now Surround your head,
> Unseen Temtations now beset your way,
> And o, my friend, The Path you Resent tread,
> Will lead you Everlastingly-Astray.

Seeing what is dangerously invisible to Sylvania, Fellicia maps an alternate route to salvation:

> But if Perhaps—(as far as leave To Tell)
> I now discribe This Ever-blooming-Place,
> And hint the Joys, which In our Bosoms dwell,
> I may urge you forward In the Glorious Race.

Fellicia seduces her friend heavenward, ensuring Sylvania's deliverance and their eventual reunion. Envisioning a similar resurrection among friends, Logan is moved by the poem, writing to Griffitts: "I think it is not worthy our time to form friendships that do not look beyond the grave for a continuance, since we have such frequent instances of uncertainty of our stay here."[179]

Gravestone inscriptions thus embody the lasting connection between the living and the dead. They collapse the initial (death) and final (burial) moments of separation and anticipate the amalgamation of the soul and corporeal remains in the afterlife. And finally, they epitomize the material importance of memory. As the writing master George Bickham explains in *The Universal Penman:* "Inscription is the Language of a Tomb; / Art can by Letters speak when Nature's dumb." Annihilating time, letters, he suggests, allow "the Living and the Dead to converse together." Through postmortem conversations we may "learn from the Admonitions of the Dead."[180] A kind of living memory, therefore, gravestone inscriptions recall

Mnemosyne's ancient wax tablet, stylus, and impressionable molds. Epitaphs are "the Muses workes," which "are of all monuments the most permanent."[181]

The gravesite thus regenerates the mourner's intimate attachment to the dead. Rehearsing the private moment of death through its tactile associations with the bedchamber, the grave compensates for the funeral procession's alienating rituals. It ensures that the dead, as Susanna Wright feared, do not "lie forgot, the Trifle of a Day."[182] After the burial, women resumed their guardianship over the dead. Keeping "wakeful sad vigils," mourning "o'er the dust that I love," and singing "the soft dirges at her tomb," as Annis Stockton notes, women devotedly attended the grave just as they did the deathbed.[183] Their tears continued the metaphorical embalming begun in the bedchamber, offering renewal to the mourner and the promise of eternal reunion with the dead. Tending the grave and repeatedly reading the stone's inscription, women enacted another form of resuscitation that kept the deceased's memory alive. As Logan suggests, "Our words yet live on other lips / . . . And such speaking dust / Has more of life than half its breathing molds."[184] The dead speak to and through us.

RELICS OF THE HEART

After reading "Cicero's Offices ('Places of Burying')," Logan desired her grave to be a lasting monument for her progeny. She asked to be laid at her husband's left side with a small marble headstone crowning each grave. "Tho,' I hate Flattery," she writes, "there is surely none in a small stone with the name of the Person interred beneath, with the Date of their birth and death." Inscriptions perpetuate genealogy. Bound by a stone wall in 1821, the "Inclosure" (as Logan fondly called the family graveyard) was "the most beautiful spot of Interment I ever saw."[185] Today, however, its rolling bank of cherry trees, romantic cave, and brightly colored roses, dahlias, and balsams are forever buried under layers of twentieth-century asphalt. Concerned about its future preservation, Logan signed a deed in 1828 to secure Stenton's "Inclosure" for her descendants. Undoubtedly a reaction to the public controversy over Quaker burial grounds in Philadelphia, the deed also anticipated the next decade's rural cemetery movement.[186] Resisting the impersonal public cemetery, Logan laments that for many Quakers the "last resting place [is] that ugly Cemetary that friends have out of town where they bury in Rows and you lie by Strangers."[187] With successive generations of families scattered in various burial grounds, the grave no longer resembled the domestic resting place of the previous century.[188]

Seeking a more permanent connection between the living and the dead,

Logan ensured that her loved ones would receive personal bequests after her burial. "I leave no will," she writes in her diary, "what little property I have the Law will divide between my dear children only I shoud like a piece of Plate or an article of furniture given as a remembrance to each of my Grandchildren." As particularly domestic memory objects, furniture and silver would surpass the grave in intimate associations with home and heritage. Given "with my dear love," these objects would "stand as a small remembrance" of Logan.[189] Such a remembrance was a cherished synecdoche that intentionally contained her heart. Like the mourners' successive incorporation of the beloved into their memories at the deathbed, collecting hour, and burial, treasured bequests were complementary—and intimately corporeal—means of containment. They filled the hole death left in the family's perpetually bleeding hearts, and they survived the publicly vulnerable grave.

Though Logan stipulates, "I want no mourning for myself when I put off this mortal body" but "should like sometimes to be remembered with a feeling of affection (not grief) by those I have loved," she had beautiful mourning jewelry distributed at her funeral.[190] A more personal relic than the furniture or silver, the mourning ring and brooch in figure 4.12 literally contain her physical remains. The glass-enclosed face holds a remnant of Logan's elaborately plaited hair; the reverse side bears the inscription, "D. Logan Ob.t Feb. 2. 1839."[191] Unlike the stock iconography of most early republican mourning jewelry (emphasizing the female mourner leaning on a monument surmounted by a plinth or urn beneath a cypress or willow tree), Logan's rectangular mourning ring and brooch, displaying hair that once framed her face, effectively remembers her coffined corpse. But worn on the mourner's body, the jewelry connects the mortal remains severed at the moment of death. It touches the mourner's skin, reminding her of their eventual commingling in the afterlife. Holding the object in her hand, wearing it close to her heart, and affectionately touching it to her lips, the mourner revisits her intimate proximity to death's body. Since touch is a reciprocal sense, the dead palpably respond as the caressed object returns the sensation in its undeniable physicality. As Sir Thomas Browne writes in *Urne Buriall* (1658), "Teeth, bones, and hair, give the most lasting defiance to corruption."[192]

The popularity of hairwork in mourning jewelry highlights the corporeal nature of female memory and the nostalgic necessity of touch. As the bodily substance that outlives the body, hair, Marcia Pointon suggests, "instantiates continuity and acts as a material figure for memory."[193] It enacts the metaphorical incorporation of the dead illustrated in Griffitts's elegy cycle. A material rather than imaginative link to the absent other, Pointon

4.12. Mourning broach and ring containing a plait of Deborah Logan's hair. Photograph by Laura K. Stutman. Courtesy of The National Society of The Colonial Dames of America in the Commonwealth of Pennsylvania at STENTON, Philadelphia.

says, hair initiates a "chain of connections through which bodily traces become transcendent corporeality."[194] Like the mourner, whose acute sense of touch prompts her memory, the corpse's hair relies on the nervous system for its persistent vitality. As James Stewart argues in *Plocacosmos, or the Whole Art of Hairdressing:* "Every hair does properly and truly live, and receives nutriment to fill and distend it." The hair "shall thrive very well," he notes; "it will grow even on dead carcasses."[195]

Going on to describe the hair's collective properties, Stewart explains the intimate connection between mourner and corpse sustained through memorial hairwork: "Each hair is found to consist of five or six lesser ones, all wrapped up in one common tegument; they are knotted."[196] Twisted together and permanently knotted, hair signifies the mourner's duty to remember the dead and her own mortality. Like individual strands of hair, Stewart says, "we are only several members of one great body; nay, we are of a consanguinity, formed of the same materials, and designed for the same end; this obliges us to a mutual tenderness, converse, and the other to live with regard to equity and justice."[197] The consanguinity that links us in life likewise connects us in death, Stewart suggests, for "this life is only a prelude to eternity, where we are to expect another original, and another state of things."[198] The dead and living are eternally entwined.

Popular in Philadelphia by the later eighteenth century, hairwork was done by professional artisans and taught as a polite art for young women. In 1793 Samuel Folwell opened an academy in Philadelphia where he offered instruction in "the curious Art of working Devices in human Hair." Hair was braided, plaited, and twisted as thread in needlework; encased as a relic in mourning jewelry; and pulverized into paint for mourning portraits. Naturalizing the corpse as part of life, Folwell prepared young women for their eventual duty as mourners, instructing those with "a natural Propensity to this polite Art" to "delineate Nature in every striking Form."[199]

In order to capture a person's unique nature, women borrowed copiously from published pattern books such as John Lockington's *Bowles' New and Complete Book of Cyphers* (1771, 1791).[200] In the book of ciphers, for instance, each page had twenty-five designs, one letter of the alphabet in combination with every other letter. The pattern books thus resembled commonplace books in their variety of adaptable and universal "types." Mottoes, ciphers, and designs were combined, reused, and reframed in a new context. Collected, preserved, and displayed in cabinets, hairwork punctuated the funeral rituals and marked the commencement of mourning.

Keeping the dead for future remembrance, mourning objects are personal memorials that prohibit forgetting. They foster a kind of prospective memory, linking the past and the future, the dead and the living. As a literal relic, the encased hairwork in early federal mourning jewelry replaced the metaphors of incorporation that marked women's participation in public funeral rites: "embalming" the dead in mnemonic images, wrapping these memories in "internal sackcloth," "chesting" the wrapped images in the coffin, and finally interring the coffin in the heart's "tomb." As Elizabeth Fergusson explains, "[Laid are] the ashes and the dear remains / Of sweet associates on these earthly plains / A kind of *Relic* which the *Heart* retains."[201] Retained by the mourner's heart, which in turn contains her grief, the beloved lives.

Restoring death's materiality, which the funeral customs have erased, mourning relics embody the link between corpse and mourner as the mortal remains. As a synecdoche, or a part of the whole, the relic moreover sustains what consolationists prescribed as a kind of proportion in grief. As Robert Dodsley admonished, "Let not thy mirth be so extravagant as to intoxicate thy mind; nor thy sorrow so heavy as to depress thy heart." Death "should not raise thee far above, or sink thee much beneath, the balance of moderation."[202] Though critics argued that mourning tokens encouraged

4.13. William Blake (1757–1827, British), illustration to Blair's *The Grave* (1808), "The Reunion of Soul and Body," etching and engraving, 23.5 × 17.4 cm. Purchased, 1954, National Gallery of Victoria, Melbourne, Australia. Reproduced with permission.

immoderate and unending lamentation, the women of the Philadelphia coterie sought ways to make death more contiguous with life. "These mementos of departed friends," Logan suggests, "are but a melancholy pleasure, some will perhaps say. And I answer that our best pleasures are almost always mellowed by [death's] softening shade." Mourning relics and other accidental artifacts left behind by the dead are another type of remains, which anticipate the mourner's eventual reunion with the beloved in the afterlife. A kind of promise, a mourning relic preserves "the sacred and indisoluble tie" between the dead and the living.[203]

Lovingly writing annual elegies for her mother for more than fifty years, Hannah Griffitts inherited the female duty to mourn the dead. Reliving the pain of separation each year, she continually incorporated her mother's memory into her ongoing life. The elegy cycle's recursive pattern repeats the initial rupture between mortal and immortal remains, at the same time anticipating their reunion in the afterlife, as figure 4.13 so beautifully illustrates. Though cultural rituals alternately demanded that women intimately handle the grotesque corpse on the one hand and distance themselves from the remains through muted lamentation on the other, Griffitts's elegies provided continuity and hope. A form of consolation, the poems are decidedly inconclusive: they neither seek control over the dead nor suppress the grief of the living. Blurring the distinction between corpse and mourner as death's "remains," moreover, the elegies metaphorically enact and reverse the material process of death. The mourner dies while the dead lives. Griffitts's heart completes the successive enclosures of her mother's corpse: the soul in the body, the linen-wrapped body in the coffin, the coffin in the grave. Embalmed in our hearts, the dead are always with us. Though death's "mortal shock" tore the "Dear Idol" from her daughter's heart, Mary Norris Griffitts lived through filial memory.[204] Looking heavenward, Hannah Griffitts rested in the knowledge that a "joy too high for Angels tongues to paint, / Is the blest Portion of the embodied Saint."[205]

CONCLUSION

The Ruins of Time

At the sight of a ruin, reflections on the change, the decay, and the desolation before us, naturally occur; and *they introduce a long succession of others, . . .* which we see, not perhaps as they were, but as they are come down to us, venerable with age and magnified by fame.

—Thomas Whately, *Observations on Modern Gardening* (1770)

Remembering the expansive western view from the old Norris house parlor in her 1827 essay "The Bank of the United States," Deborah Logan narratively strolls through the famed garden, situating her forlorn family estate among the city's prominent, public buildings. The same parlor in which Isaac Norris convened the Pennsylvania Assembly and Constitutional Congress afforded the pleasant prospect of pasture lots bounded by the "Proprietors woods," the Loganian Library and the Pennsylvania Hospital on Sixth Street, the Alms House on Spruce Street, and the prison at Sixth and Walnut. Above the garden's remarkable willow trees she could see the imposing State House steeple, "then much higher than its present Substitute," whose clock punctuated her view of the expanding cityscape.[1] But as the city grew, the Norris garden contracted. Once separated from the "pavement & graveled lane, by a palasade adorned with scarlet honeysuckle, sweet briars & roses, & shaded by fine spreading Catalpa's," the garden enclosure was gradually divided into lots to accommodate the young nation's proliferating buildings.[2]

By 1789 the southwest corner of the beautiful grounds was sold and encompassed by the new Library Hall. Home to Benjamin Franklin's Library Company of Philadelphia from 1790 to 1880, Library Hall maintained the country's oldest subscription library.[3] Also opening its doors to the public that year, the American Philosophical Society's new residence at Philosophical Hall fulfilled Franklin's dream for a cultural institution that would "improve the common stock of knowledge." Founded in 1743, the society was a moveable feast, relocating from one site to another until 1785, when Congress allotted part of the State House yard for its growing library and artifact collection. A prestigious repository for the fine arts and sciences, the society housed Charles Willson Peale's museum from 1794 to 1811 and Thomas Sully's Gallery of Pictures from 1812 to 1822.[4] Along with the construction of Library and Philosophical Halls came additional changes to the Norris garden, which was further apportioned along the western end of Chestnut Street for the construction of five beautiful houses on Norris Row.[5] At the same time, the State House yard (figure C.1), which formerly shared a wall with the Norris garden, was landscaped "in the new romantic taste, with artificial mounds and declivities, serpentine paths, informally disposed clumps of elms and willows, and benches for the enjoyment of the public."[6] Like its razed house, which was replaced by the Second Bank of the United States, the Norris garden was eventually subsumed by a constellation of public archives and faded out of public memory.

Independence National Historical Park maintains only a remnant of a generic eighteenth-century garden, but the Norris garden remains an important metaphor for American cultural memory, both private and public. Like the other memory places described in this book, the garden was both the repository of and inspiration for remembrance. Following the symmetrical and geometric plan of early Tudor gardening, early republican gardens displayed the order and regularity requisite to mnemonic storage and display.[7] With the exception of the irregular, western corner containing the hotbeds and seed house, the Norris garden was laid out in square parterres and beds, regularly intersected by graveled and grass walks and alleys. As Logan recalled, a walk in her family's garden was considered "by the more respectable citizens as a treat to their friends from a distance, and as one of the means to impress them with a favourable opinion of the beauties of the city."[8] A green bank with flights of stone steps led the way into the garden with its profusion of flowers and shrubs. It was here on the garden steps that the young Deborah Norris listened excitedly as the Declaration of Independence was read aloud for the first time. Viewing the ample garden as she contemplated the nation's promise, she undoubtedly remembered her family's illustrious contributions to the colonial and later federal city.

A common topos for memory, the garden thus offered resonant perspec-

C.1. William Birch, *Views of Philadelphia* (1800), plate 23, "State House Garden." Courtesy of the Print & Picture Collection, Free Library of Philadelphia.

tives from which to recollect the past. Because the country house garden nostalgically suspended historical time by merging the past and present in a pastoral stasis, it deferred the real to the symbolic. It introduced universal images—irrespective of local topography—that offered spectators an invitation to escape. This common language read the landscape as a "Publick Manuscript," connecting the arts of gardening and rhetoric. Viewing a landscape was like recalling written commonplaces, according to the essayist Joseph Addison: "The Sett of Ideas, which we received from such a Prospect or garden, having entered the Mind at the same time have a Sett of Traces belonging to them in the Brain, bordering very near upon one another . . . and the whole Prospect or Garden flourishes in the Imagination." Smells and colors record themselves for later pleasure; images and ideas fill retrievable places in the memory which "heighten the Delightfulness of the Original."[9] Gardening was thus a form of associationism, which prompted and recorded contiguous memory images. A naturalistic commonplace book, the garden inspired Logan's memory and imagination. Transferring these pleasures to her own garden at Stenton, she muses, "I love my own sex and think them and flowers to be the most embellished part of the creation."[10]

Given a garden's ability to invoke human thought and emotion, its prospect was to be as "extensive as possible." However, when the "Views cannot be extended," according to one eighteenth-century landscape architect, the garden should ideally lead viewers' eyes toward something awesome—and consequently memorable: "mishapen Rocks, strange Precipes . . . old Ruins, grand Buildings."[11] Since Logan's prospect from the parlor window was eclipsed by the towering State House, she was left staring at the gradually dismantled garden. A kind of ruin, or the residue left behind by the past in the face of the irrepressible present, the Norris garden amplifies the complexity and incompleteness of memory, for "the past is always a ruin." It is shaped just as much by what remains as by what has been worn away from it, as Didier Maleuvre suggests: "Its standing there is a staging of loss, unapproachability made into a monument."[12] Lamenting what she could no longer see, Logan necessarily let her eyes rest on the spectacular profusion of willow trees that remained along the garden's horizon. The trees, she notes, were "the first species here," taken "out of a hamper on a wharf at Boston, by Dr. Franklin, who brought them to Philadelphia and presented them to my Aunt Debby Norris, as one of the most successful cultivators that he knew." The trees grew. Grafts were taken and transplanted. And more trees grew.

As a synecdoche for cultural memory, a cultural ruin challenges us to imagine and preserve what no longer exists. It is the part left behind, representing the whole, literally maintaining its "place" in history. The ruin stands its ground, keeping its original habitation. The remnants of the Norris garden—and even the generic eighteenth-century garden now kept by Independence National Historical Park—remind us of the pastoral enclosure before its diffusion into public archives. Remembering her family's forlorn garden in parts, Logan writes:

> I knew each walk and every valley green,
> Parterre, or shaded spot of this sweet garden,
> With every haunt for sports from side to side,
> My daily walks, and ancient neighbourhood.[13]

At the same time, the ruin's contiguity with the equally fragmented archives ironically preserves the memory of the now forgotten Norris house and garden. Rent from its original context and placed in an artificial collection of similarly displaced objects, an archive is the happy accident of transplantation. Much like the willow sprig given by Benjamin Franklin to Debby

Norris, Logan's archived essay is all that remains of the house and garden today.[14] Grafted together by proximity and necessity, the ruin and archive perform the imperfect work of memory.

Tracing the willow tree's transatlantic genealogy from Benjamin Franklin (a scientist, philanthropist, diplomat, and politician who would forever remain in our cultural memory, on the one hand) to Debby Norris (an otherwise forgotten spinster whose garden rivaled John Bartram's on the city's west end, on the other), Logan continues the genealogical project with which this book begins. In focusing on the willow tree's roots, transplantation, and flourishing display, she not only portrays her aunt as a vital contributor to American cultural memory but also sees this horticultural talent as an inherited gift. The willow tree, she well knew, traditionally symbolized feminine creativity. Called *helice* in Greek, the willow gave its name to Helicon, the abode of the nine Muses—the daughters of Mnemosyne. The willow, then, welcomed aspiring poets beneath its soft branches to gain inspiration and eloquence. A potent metaphor for Logan and her literary coterie, the willow was a resonant image for their poetic ambitions. More than lining their gardens, the willow tree symbolized their contributions to American memory through literary history.

Like Logan, both Annis Stockton and Elizabeth Fergusson adopted the willow as a metaphor for women's poetic contributions to cultural memory. Sometime during the late nineteenth century, for example, one of Stockton's female descendants contemplates the impressive willow trees lining Morven's historic walkway. Picking up on the mythical resonance of Pope's Twickenham in the New Jersey garden, she writes: "Willows in our European gardens [were] brought in a basket from the Euphrates by Mr. Vernon, sent by Lady Mary Wortley Montague to Pope, who planted it with his own hand."[15] This story might be as apocryphal as the famed garden's history, but it was very much in the memory of the women, who planned and tended these neoclassical gardens.[16] At the very least, it provided the reusable topoi for Franklin's identical gesture to Debby Norris: the sapling, the basket, the sea voyage, the transplantation.

Undoubtedly hearing this account from her friends, Fergusson laid the groundwork for the much-repeated tale in her companion odes to the willow tree. Having completed her "Ode to the Litchfield Willow," where she celebrates the famed Litchfield group of artists—including the painter William Hogarth, the actor David Garrick, and the litterateurs Samuel Johnson and Anna Seward—Fergusson considers the willow tree a transatlantic emblem of enlightenment.[17] She traces the willow's transatlantic influence from her contemporaries John and Samuel Fothergill as far back as Shakespeare:

From the Grand Willow too we boast;
A Charming social Train,
Whose Parent Born on *Albions* Coast;
On *Litchfields* favord plain.

Wishing that "Some thriving blooming verdant sprig, / Yet may be wafted Here," she sees the Litchfield group as a model for American arts and letters. Inspired by their genius, she begins "Ode the Second, A Tribute to American Genius and Friendship."

Lauding Benjamin Franklin as the catalyst for the willow's literal and symbolic transplantation to American soil, Fergusson annotates the poem's third stanza with the following anecdote, telling Logan's story almost verbatim:

> About thirty years past a Basket made of Willow came from England and lay a Winter in a damp Cellar belonging to Dr. Franklin; And in the Spring swelld and Budded Showing strong Marks of Vegetation. Dr. Franklin gave it to Miss Deborah Norris, a lady who had a particular taste for Gardening. She had it planted in her Garden near the State House in Philadelphia. It was by her Cherishd and with what Success all in that City know But perhaps they don't know that by much the great part of the Willows which now are so plentifully planted over the State of Pennsylvania took Rise from this Emigration. The Garden which contain the American Parent Stock is now in the Possession of Widow Norris wife to Charles Norris Esquire.

Like Logan, Fergusson praises the willow tree's impressive lineage. In both the poem and the footnote she uses the discourse of genealogy, connecting the willow tree's "Parent Born on *Albions* Coast" to its "American Parent Stock," which continues in a "Charming social train" across the state of Pennsylvania.

Treating the much-repeated willow anecdote as a cultural commonplace, Fergusson uses it to initiate her female coterie into British-American literary history. After a sustained eulogy on her male contemporaries and habitués, she goes on to enumerate the women of her coterie: "We boast too Nymphs as well as Swains / Who Chaunt Harmonious Verse."[18] Not surprisingly, first mention goes to Annis Boudinot Stockton, her lifelong friend and correspondent. "Emilia," she notes, "in Brilliant Rays Reflected back, / Thro' her illumind Pen" graced the salon and found her way into several of Fergusson's commonplace books. Fergusson mentions sculptor Patience Wright, who "with Passion grac'd / And Sculptor's Skill displayd . . . innate Genius." Regretting Wright's departure to pursue her career in England, she moves on to the young artist Betsy Pyle, who moves her pencil with "Elegance and Ease" over "Our Fields she Skims; Our Woods she Roves / While all her Landscapes please!" Pyle's landscape paintings not only highlight the garden's significance to women's literary merits but also remind Fergusson of her beloved niece, poet Anna Young Smith. "Thou soon Cropt Rose Bud of the Muse," Smith was among "the smoothest of Parnassian Maids!" Dying young, Smith never saw her poetry come to fruition. But copied and annotated in several of Fergusson's commonplace books, her poems posthumously flourished through the coterie's scribal mode of publication.

The Philadelphia coterie's shared interest in transplantation (both literal and metaphorical) underscores these women's understanding of the garden as an inspired model for the modern archive. Transplantation—rather than destruction and replacement—effectively preserves memory. "Transplanted thence," Fergusson writes, the willow "flourish'd Fair." Copied into Fergusson's assiduously kept commonplace book, the "Willow Odes" have been kept for more than two centuries. Lovingly preserved by Graeme Park's eventual owner, Lady Martha Strawbridge, the poems were bequeathed to the family estate at her death. Though Fergusson was effectively evicted from her house, dying among relative strangers, it seems fitting to have her manuscripts returned home. The archive, after all, presents a kind of homesickness, a pain or longing to return home or to some lost past where one remembers a sense of wholeness and belonging. It is contemporary culture's most lasting link to the past.[19]

By way of conclusion, let us return once more to the old Norris house. In describing the garden view from the parlor's western window, Logan brings the verdant prospect inside the house, fondly remembering its reflected beauty in the mirrored door of an old escritoire that once stood in the room's corner: "How the rays of the Sun at Some Seasons of the years, fell on the Cut edge of a looking glass in the [desk's] door." Though tellingly deleted from the published version of her essay, this "Phenomenon of Nature" not only brought her great pleasure during childhood but also directed her impressionable thoughts to nature's universal lessons. Like a magic lantern that projected her secreted memories onto a visible screen, the mirror reflected a "beautiful display of prismatic colours" on the white wall. Replicating the garden's universal manuscript, the desk finally brought the archive home. Sitting at her makeshift desk in Stenton's dining room in 1817, Logan nostalgically revisits these former scenes in her memory: "It is truly recording an old womans dreams to set down my sleeping cogitations, but last night transported me to places that now are not—to the old house in Chestnut Street and to Fairhills Groves and Gardens."[20]

NOTES

INTRODUCTION

1. Deborah Logan, manuscript diary, 12:269, 3:156, 6:110, Historical Society of Pennsylvania (HSP), Philadelphia. Hereafter cited by volume and page number. Seventeen volumes (1815–39) are located at the HSP. Logan's earlier diaries (1808–15) were recently acquired by the Library Company of Philadelphia (LCP). I refer to these diaries by date only, following Logan's organizational method. I thank Jim Green for allowing me to peruse them.

2. Kenneth Burke, *Attitudes toward History* (Berkeley, 1984), 179.

3. Constance Greiff traces the bank's architectural history in *Independence: The Creation of a National Park* (Philadelphia, 1987), 109.

4. Though ample evidence of structural deterioration necessitates the bank building's current restoration (to be completed by the fall of 2003), we are also witnessing the preservation of—and perhaps reversion to—an earlier symbol of national (rather than global) power and economic promise in the aftermath of the destruction of the World Trade Center towers on 11 September 2001.

5. See Benedict Anderson, *Imagined Communities: Reflections on the Origin and Spread of Nationalism* (New York, 1991); David Waldstreicher, *In the Midst of Perpetual Fetes: The Making of American Nationalism, 1776–1820* (Chapel Hill, 1997); and Gary Nash, *First City: Philadelphia and the Forging of Historical Memory* (Philadelphia, 2002).

6. One example is the Tammany Club of Philadelphia, which reinforced the founders' use of symbols and ideological concepts indigenous to North America. The club took the name of a Delaware chief, Tamanend, who is said to have welcomed William Penn and to have signed with him the Treaty of Shakamaxon. Known as the "Constitutional Sons of St. Tammany," the Philadelphia chapter dedicated itself to the preservation of the "native Constitutional American Liberties" as early as 1772. On 1 May 1783 members organized a parade with "thirteen sachems" dressed as Indians to celebrate the revolution's end. A cannon was fired, "Yankee Doodle" was played, and a six-foot peace pipe with thirteen feathers and thirteen stars was ceremonially smoked by several hundred people in attendance. I thank David Shields for bringing this fascinating club to my attention.

7. Plymouth Rock was reinvented as a versatile template for national fantasy and identity throughout the eighteenth and nineteenth centuries. See John Seelye, *Memory's Nation: The Place of Plymouth Rock* (Chapel Hill, 1998); David S. Shields, "Moving the Rock," in *Finding Colonial Americas,* ed. David Shields and Carla Mulford (Newark, 2001), 387–402; and Sargent

Bush, "America's Origin Myth: Remembering Plymouth Rock," *American Literary History* 12, 4 (2000): 745–56.

8. Paul Ricoeur, "Memory and Forgetting," in *Questioning Ethics: Contemporary Debates in Philosophy* (New York, 1999), 9.

9. The Bank of North America (1781) occupied a three-story brick house on Third and Chestnut Streets; the First Bank of the United States used Carpenter's Hall from 1791 to 1797 while its new building was constructed. See Kenneth Hafertepe, "Banking Houses in the United States: The First Generation, 1781–1811," *Winterthur Portfolio* 35, 1 (2000): 1–52.

10. *Narratives of Nostalgia, Gender, and Nationalism,* ed. Jean Pickering and Suzanne Kehde (New York, 1997), 10.

11. Karin Wulf, " 'Of Old Stock': Quakerism and Transatlantic Genealogy," in *The British Atlantic,* ed. Carole Shammas and Elizabeth Manke (forthcoming from Johns Hopkins University Press).

12. Logan diary, 10 June 1814, LCP.

13. *The Norris House* (Philadelphia, 1867); *The Bank of the United States* (Philadelphia, 1900); and an excerpt, "Before Our Time," *American German Review* 17 (April 1951): 6–7. I quote from and discuss the 1827 manuscript at Stenton, the Logan family's country house, courtesy of The National Society of The Colonial Dames of America in the Commonwealth of Pennsylvania at STENTON, Philadelphia.

14. It is difficult to draw conclusions from the titles alone. Although the manuscript title, "The Bank of the United States," seemingly privileges the public building, at least one of the published versions, simply titled *The Norris House,* pays homage to the demolished house. In manuscript and printed form Logan's essay highlights the textual moments when public and private memory overlap.

15. Assuming an audience of shared taste, knowledge, and interest, republican print culture effaced difference and underscored the "imaginary" nature of public memory, argues Michael Warner, *Letters of the Republic: Publication and the Public Sphere in Eighteenth-Century America* (Cambridge, Mass., 1990).

16. Here I refer to Foucault's genealogical project, which challenges traditional history's search for origins, continuity, and coherence. See Michel Foucault, "Nietzsche, Genealogy, History," in *Language, Counter-Memory, Practice,* ed. and trans. Donald F. Bouchard and Sherry Simon (Ithaca, 1977); Kathy Ferguson, "Interpretation and Genealogy in Feminism," *Signs* 16, 21 (1991): 322–39; and Lee Quimby, ed., *Genealogy and Literature* (Minneapolis, 1995).

17. H. D. Harootunian, "Foucault, Genealogy, History: The Pursuit of Otherness," in *After Foucault: Humanistic Knowledge, Postmodern Challenges,* ed. Jonathan Arac (New Brunswick, N.J., 1988), 110–37.

18. Isaac Norris to Prudence Moore by Captain Lloyd, Fairhill, 2 November 1747, Isaac Norris wallpaper book, Historical Society of Pennsylvania. I thank Karin Wulf for this reference.

19. For more details on the house's architecture, see Jeffrey A. Cohen, "Early American Architectural Drawings and Philadelphia, 1730–1860," in *Drawing toward Building: Philadelphia Architectural Graphics, 1732–1986,* by James F. O'Gorman, Jeffrey A. Cohen, George E. Thomas, and G. Holmes Perkins (Philadelphia, 1986).

20. John Dickinson married Mary ("Polly") Norris at the old Norris estate on 19 July 1770.

21. Logan presumably found some of the letters beneath the attic eaves of Stenton. The house, in this case, is a literal archive.

22. Logan, 11:66. Watson sketched the eastern view "of our old habitation in Chestnut Street drawn from my description and recollection," but the drawing's scale was inaccurate, minimizing the house's grandeur.

23. Logan, 1:3; Logan diary, 1 August 1808, LCP.

24. Thomas Osborn, "The Ordinariness of the Archive," *History of the Human Sciences* 12, 2 (1999): 51–64.

25. Richard Harvey Brown and Beth Davis-Brown, "The Making of Memory: The Politics of Archives, Libraries, and Museums in the Construction of National Consciousness," *History of the Human Sciences* 11, 4 (1998): 17–32.

26. Jacques Derrida, *Archive Fever: A Freudian Impression,* trans. Eric Prenowitz (Chicago, 1996), 1–2.

27. Michael Lynch, "Archives in Formation," *History of the Human Sciences* 12, 2 (1999): 67; Harriet Bradley, "The Seductions of the Archive: Voices Lost and Found," *History of the Human Sciences* 12, 2 (1999): 110.

28. Carolyn Steedman, "The Space of Memory: In an Archive," *History of the Human Sciences* 11, 4 (1998): 65–83.

29. Pickering and Kehde, 11.

30. On museum aesthetics, see Susan Stewart, *On Longing: Narratives of the Miniature, the Gigantic, the Souvenir, the Collection* (Durham, 1993); Didier Maleuvre, *Museum Memories: History, Technology, Art* (Palo Alto, 1999); Susan Pearce, *Museums, Objects, and Collections: A Cultural Study* (Washington, D.C., 1992); and Mieke Bal, "Telling Objects: A Narrative Perspective on Collecting," in *The Cultures of Collecting,* ed. John Elsner and Roger Cardinal (Cambridge, Mass., 1997).

31. Like all literary periods, these dates are a convenient time frame for presenting the writings of this intergenerational coterie. Though Wright was already writing in the 1720s, I begin my study when the group generally becomes prolific and end it just after Logan's death in 1839. Most important, this range of years enabled me to record the surviving women's retrospective glances from the nineteenth century, a perspective required of all remembrance. For an introduction to this literary circle, see Susan Stabile, " 'Trifling Performances': Letters, Belles Lettres, and the Philadelphia Culture of Performance, 1760–1820" (Ph.D. diss., University of Delaware, 1996).

32. On commonplace practices, see Susan Miller, *Assuming the Positions: Cultural Pedagogy and the Politics of Commonplace Writing* (Pittsburgh, 1998); Ann Moss, *Printed Commonplace Books and the Structuring of Renaissance Thought* (New York, 1996); Joan Marie Lechner, *Renaissance Concepts of the Commonplaces* (New York, 1963). Work on early American commonplace books includes Kenneth Lockridge, *The Sources of Patriarchal Rage: The Commonplace Books of William Byrd and Thomas Jefferson and the Gendering of Power in the Eighteenth Century* (New York, 1992), and *The Commonplace Book of William Byrd of Westover,* ed. Kevin Berland, Jan Kirsten Gilliam, and Kenneth Lockridge (Chapel Hill, 2001).

33. See Marion Reninger, "Susanna Wright," *Lancaster County Historical Society Publications* 63, 4 (1959): 183–90; "The Bartons in Lancaster in 1776," *Papers of the Lancaster County Historical Society* 52 (1948): 213–17; and "Benjamin Franklin in Lancaster County," *Journal of the Lancaster County Historical Society* 61, 1 (1957): 1–26; and Mrs. Henry Heistand, " 'Samuel Blunston': The Man and the Family," *Lancaster County Historical Society Papers* 26 (1922): 191–204.

34. Quoted in Edmund Morgan, *Inventing the People: The Rise of Popular Sovereignty in England and America* (New York, 1988), 193.

35. See Pattie Cowell, "Hannah Griffitts," in *American Writers before 1800: A Biographical and Critical Dictionary,* ed. James A. Levenier and Douglas R. Wilmes (Westport, Conn., 1983), 684–85; Samuel Hazard, *Register of Pennsylvania* 8 (17 September 1831): 178; and Karin Wulf, "A Marginal Independence: Unmarried Women in Colonial Philadelphia" (Ph.D. diss., Johns Hopkins University, 1994), 286–328.

36. Logan, 7:108.

37. See Martha C. Slotten, "Elizabeth Graeme Fergusson: A Poet in 'The Athens of North America,' " *Pennsylvania Magazine of History and Biography* 108 (1984): 259–88; Simon Gratz, "Some Materials for a Biography of Elizabeth Fergusson, née Graeme," *Pennsylvania Magazine of History and Biography* 39 (1915): 257–409, and 41 (1917): 385–89; and Anne Ousterhout, *The Most Learned Woman in America* (University Park, Pa., 2003).

38. For Elizabeth Fergusson's relationship with Benjamin Franklin, see Susan Stabile, "Sa-

lons in the Era of Revolution: From Literary Coteries to Epistolary Enlightenment," in *Benjamin Franklin and Women,* ed. Larry Tise (University Park, Pa., 2001), 129–48.

39. On her salon and literary career, see Susan Stabile, "Translatio Literati: Elizabeth Fergusson and British-American Literary History," in Ousterhout, 1–42.

40. See Carla Mulford, ed., *"Only for the Eye of a Friend": The Poems of Annis Boudinot Stockton* (Charlottesville, 1995); Carla Mulford, "Political Poetics: Annis Boudinot Stockton and Middle-Atlantic Women's Culture," *New Jersey History* 11 (1993): 66–110, and "Annis Boudinot Stockton and Benjamin Young Prime: A Poetical Correspondence, and More," *Princeton University Library Chronicle* 52 (1991): 231–66.

41. Alfred Hoyt Bill, *A House Called Morven: Its Role in American History,* rev. ed. (Princeton, 1978), 31.

42. Mulford, *Only for the Eye of a Friend,* 24.

43. Quoted from *The Writings of George Washington, from Original Manuscript Sources, 1745–1799,* ed. John C. Fitzpatrick, 39 vols. (Washington, D.C., 1931–44), 30:75–77.

44. Miller, 32.

45. James Beattie, *Dissertations Moral and Critical* (London, 1783), 177.

46. See Tamara Thornton, *Handwriting in America: A Cultural History* (New Haven, 1996); Harold Love, *Scribal Publication in Seventeenth-Century England* (New York, 1993); and Margaret Ezell, *Social Authorship and the Advent of Print* (Baltimore, 1999).

47. Beattie, 51.

48. Osborn, 57.

49. Stewart, ix–xi.

50. Much important recovery work on British-American women's literary manuscripts has been done in the last two decades, including the following groundbreaking editions: Pattie Cowell, *Women Poets in Pre-Revolutionary America, 1650–1775* (Troy, N.Y., 1981); Mulford, *Only for the Eye of a Friend;* Sharon Harris, *American Women Writers to 1800* (New York, 1996) and *Selected Writings of Judith Sargent Murray* (New York, 1995); and Catherine Blecki and Karin Wulf, eds., *Milcah Martha Moore's Book: A Commonplace Book from Revolutionary America* (University Park, Pa., 1997). On women's literary salon culture, see David Shields, *Civil Tongues and Polite Letters in British America* (Chapel Hill, 1997).

51. Recently, feminist scholars in philosophy, geography, and critical theory have emphasized the connection between the female body and real or imagined space. See especially Elizabeth Grosz, *Architecture from the Outside: Essays on Virtual and Ideal Space* (Cambridge, Mass., 2001), and *Volatile Bodies: Toward a Corporeal Feminism* (Bloomington, 1994); and Gillian Rose, *Feminism and Geography: The Limits of Geographical Knowledge* (Minneapolis, 1993). This new direction in body studies might complicate debates among feminist historians about "separate spheres," reinvigorated in the 1990s by Habermasian readings of public and private space. See, for instance, *Feminists Read Habermas: Gendering the Subject of Discourse,* ed. Johanna Meehan (New York, 1995).

52. Situating the commonplace book as a material "site," I follow the expertise of the architectural historians and folklorists Dell Upton (*Common Places: Readings in American Vernacular Architecture* [Athens, Ga., 1986]), Bernard Herman and Gabrielle Lanier (*Everyday Architecture of the Mid-Atlantic: Looking at Buildings and Landscapes* [Baltimore, 1997]), and Robert Blair St. George (*Material Life in America, 1600–1860* [Boston, 1988]).

53. See Susan Bordo, *Flight to Objectivity: Essays on Cartesianism and Culture* (Albany, 1987); Londa Schiebinger, *The Mind Has No Sex? Women in the Origins of Modern Science* (Cambridge, Mass., 1989); and Thomas Lacquer, *Making Sex: Body and Gender from the Greeks to Freud* (Cambridge, 1990). My phenomenological approach to women's embodied subjectivity is indebted to the philosophers Maurice Merleau-Ponty (*Phenomenology of Perception,* 2d ed., trans. Colin Smith [New York, 2002]) and Edward S. Casey (*Remembering: A Phenomenological Study,* 2d ed. [Bloomington, 2000]).

54. Marius D'Assigny, *The Art of Memory* (London, 1699), 24–25.

55. Though the definition is now obsolete, the museum's initial association with

Mnemosyne and the Muses would have resonated with Logan as she witnessed both the destruction of her family home and the official inception of the public museum near the turn of the nineteenth century. According to the *Oxford English Dictionary,* 2d ed. (1989), as late as 1783 the word *museum* connoted a private study, library, or apartment for scholarly work. Only by the nineteenth century did it become an official repository for the collection, preservation, and exhibition of historical objects. At this point the archive and museum become distinctly different repositories—the former a collection awaiting interpretation, the latter an exhibition of objects.

56. Logan diary, 1 August 1808, LCP.

CHAPTER 1. THE ARCHITECTURE OF MEMORY

1. François Poulain de La Barre, *De l'égalité des deux sexes*, translated into English by A. L. (London, 1677), 33; Hannah Robertson, *The Young Ladies School of Arts* (York, 1777), 9–13, 22. Courtesy, The Winterthur Library: Printed Book and Periodical Collection.

2. Educated women during the Enlightenment were taught drawing, mathematics, and surveying. By the eighteenth century, building design was seen as an extension of female "accomplishments," displayed in shellwork rooms and grottoes. See Lynne Walker, "Women and Architecture," in *A View from the Interior: Feminism, Women, and Design History*, ed. Judy Attfield and Pat Kirkham (London, 1989), 90–105.

3. See Laura Keim Stutman, "Two Philadelphia Shadow-Box Grottoes," *Antiques* (March 2002): 104–7. See also Hazel Jackson, *Shell Houses and Grottoes* (Buckinghamshire, 2001), and Clare Graham, "Beauties of Shellwork," *Antique Collector* (August 1989): 42–48.

4. Samuel Rogers, *The Pleasures of Memory*, 2 vols., 9th ed. (London, 1796), 1:12.

5. Gaston Bachelard, *The Poetics of Space: The Classic Look at How We Experience Intimate Places* (Boston, 1969; rpt. 1994), 107.

6. Despite the association of knowledge with place during the eighteenth century, particularly in the dictionary and encyclopedia movements, which attempted to universalize knowledge, I would argue that the single dwelling or memory palace (rather than the globe or world map) remained an appropriate, local image for female epistemology. See Sylvia Lavin, "Re-reading the Encyclopedia: Architectural Theory and the Formation of the Public in Late-Eighteenth-Century France," *Journal of the Society of Architectural Historians* 53 (June 1994): 184–92.

7. Sarah Morris Buckley, manuscript no. 68x186.6 (original emphasis). Courtesy, The Winterthur Library: Joseph Downs Collection of Manuscripts and Printed Ephemera.

8. William Hogarth, *The Analysis of Beauty* (London, 1753). Jonathan Prown and Richard Miller, "The Rococo, the Grotto, and the Philadelphia High Chest," in *American Furniture*, ed. Luke Beckerdite (Hanover, N.H., 1996), 105–36; John Bennett, *Letters to a Young Lady on a Variety of Useful and Interesting Subjects* (Boston, 1798), 99; John Gregory, *A Father's Legacy to His Daughters*, in *Lady's Pocket Library* (Philadelphia, 1797), 95; Robertson, 9.

9. William Chambers, *A Treatise on Civil Architecture* (London, 1759), iii.

10. Here I adapt and diverge from the groundbreaking work of the architectural historian Henry Glassie in vernacular architecture and applied structural linguistics, using rhetorical topoi rather than grammar. See Glassie, "Eighteenth-Century Cultural Process in Delaware Valley Folk Building," *Winterthur Portfolio* 7 (1972): 29–57. See also Gabrielle Lanier with Bernard Herman, *Everyday Architecture of the Mid-Atlantic: Looking at Buildings and Landscapes* (Baltimore, 1997).

11. Dell Upton, *Common Places: Readings in American Vernacular Architecture* (Athens, Ga., 1986), 432.

12. On mnemonics from the classical period through the Renaissance, see Frances Yates, *The Art of Memory* (Chicago, 1966; rpt. 1992), and Mary Carruthers, *The Book of Memory: A Study of Memory in Medieval Culture* (Cambridge, 1990).

13. Respectively adapting their mnemonic metaphors to their period architectural styles, Aristotle (*De memoria*), Cicero (*De oratore*), and Quintilian (*Institutio oratoria*) imagined the

human brain not only as divided by arches and columns but also as composed of interior spaces (i.e., vestibulum, atrium, thalamus, aibile, recess). Revived in the thirteenth century by Albertus Magnus, Thomas Aquinas, and John of Garland, the memory house was markedly medieval in its flat, two-dimensional, diagrammatic, and gridlike church, cloister garden, and hospital. Given humanism's expansion of knowledge, Renaissance mnemonics favored libraries, gardens, and theaters as alternative structures to the memory palace. By the eighteenth century in British America, memory palaces were created by the elite class in the "local habitations" of their Georgian country houses.

14. Quoted in Ann Moss, *Printed Commonplace Books and the Structuring of Renaissance Thought* (New York, 1996), 5, 9, 108.

15. James Beattie, *Dissertations Moral and Critical* (London, 1783), 28–29, 48.

16. On women, property, and material culture, see Laurel Thatcher Ulrich, "Furniture as Social History: Gender, Property, and Memory in the Decorative Arts," in *American Furniture*, ed. Luke Beckerdite and William Hosley (Hanover, N.H., 1995), 39–68.

17. *The Guardian* 165 (8 September 1713).

18. Dell Upton, "Vernacular Domestic Architecture in Eighteenth-Century Virginia," *Winterthur Portfolio* (1982): 95–119; Mark R. Wenger, "The Central Passage in Virginia: Evolution of an Eighteenth-Century Living Space," in *Perspectives in Vernacular Architecture*, vol. 2, ed. Camille Wells (Columbia, Mo., 1986), 137–60.

19. Drawing on the architectural analogy to the commonplace book, I describe a prototypical Georgian plan. Each of the houses in this study, however, is a unique adaptation of this style. Women's memory palaces reflected these stylistic innovations but particularized them, creating what rhetoricians called "local habitations" for universalized topoi.

20. Marius D'Assigny, *The Art of Memory*, 2d ed. (London, 1699), 20, 21. Theorists disagreed over the exact place of memory, alternately relegating it to the cerebellum, cerebrum, medulla, cortex, and even the pineal gland, as I discuss in chapter 2.

21. D'Assigny, 21. On the novel and its creation of privacy, see Ian Watt, *The Rise of the Novel* (Berkeley, 1957). See also Annik Pardailhé-Galabrun, *The Birth of Intimacy: Privacy and Domestic Life in Early Modern France*, trans. Jocelyn Phelps (Philadelphia, 1988), and Philippe Ariès and Georges Duby, gen. eds., *A History of Private Life*, vol. 3: *Passions of the Renaissance*, trans. Arthur Goldhammer (Cambridge, Mass., 1989).

22. Horace Walpole, *Anecdotes of Painting in England . . . collected by the late Mr. George Vertue . . . by Mr. Horace Walpole*, 4 vols. (London, 1786), 4:vii.

23. Inigo Jones, 20 January 1615, cited in Hanno-Walter Kruft, *A History of Architectural Theory from Vitruvius to the Present*, trans. Ronald Taylor, Elsie Callander, and Antony Wood (New York, 1994), 231. Though recent feminist scholarship on architecture challenges the idea that "man builds and woman inhabits," I recuperate these rhetorical categories to illustrate how architecture was understood as gendered in the eighteenth century. See *The Sex of Architecture*, ed. Diane Agrest, Patricia Conway, and Leslie Kanes Weisman (New York, 1996); *Architecture and Feminism*, ed. Deborah Coleman, Elizabeth Danze, and Carol Henderson (Princeton, 1996); *Design and Feminism: Re-Visioning Spaces, Places, and Everyday Things*, ed. Joan Rothschild (New Brunswick, N.J., 1999). See also *Gender Space Architecture: An Interdisciplinary Introduction*, ed. Jane Rendell, Barbara Penner, and Lain Borden (New York, 2000).

24. Richard Neve, *The City and Country Purchaser and Builder's Dictionary* (London, 1703), 84.

25. Such passivity clearly reflected the empirical distinction of sexuality based on the visibility or invisibility of genitalia. In what historian Thomas Lacquer calls the "one-sex body," man was celebrated as more complete and perfect in his nature whereas woman was reduced to an incomplete and inverted man. Laqueur, *Making Sex: Body and Gender from the Greeks to Freud* (Cambridge, Mass., 1990). Contemporaneous with and eventually superseding the one-sex theory, biological complementarianism ushered into the eighteenth century what we know as modern sex and gender configurations. Sex was based on discernible, biological difference. The female body, considered a lesser version of the male's in the one-sex theory, now

became its opposite in the two-sex model. Female organs that were seen as derivative and interior versions of the male's exterior organs were now construed to be of an entirely different nature. For an alternative view of premodern sexuality, see Joan Cadden, *Meanings of Sex Difference in the Middle Ages: Medicine, Science, and Culture* (Cambridge, 1993).

26. Women's relegation to domestic life was conveniently justified by biology from the classical period through the Enlightenment (and later, of course, in the Victorian "cult of true womanhood").

27. Hester Mulso Chapone, *Letters on the Improvement of the Mind Addressed to a Young Lady* (Boston, 1783), 160; Lady Pennington, *An Unfortunate Mother's Advice to Her Daughters* (London, 1790), 83–84; Chapone, 163.

28. D'Assigny, 38, 50.

29. Erasmus, D., *De duplici copia verborum ac rerum*, ed. B. I. Knott, in *Opera omnia*, I, 6 (Amsterdam, 1988), 112; D'Assigny, 69.

30. Vitruvius wrote the earliest (surviving) treatise on architecture, *Ten Books on Architecture*, between 33 and 14 B.C.E. Although they had little influence in antiquity, Vitruvius's theories were popularized during the Renaissance and were revived by the British Palladians in the eighteenth century. On Vitruvian influence on architectural theory, see Kruft, 23–29, 229–56.

31. John Evelyn, dedication to "Sir John Denham, Knight," in Roland Freart, *A Parallel of the Antient Architecture with the Modern* (London, 1664), n.p.; D'Assigny, 31–32.

32. Pierre Roussel, *Système physique et moral de la femme*, 5th ed. (Paris, 1775; rpt. 1809), 9.

33. Nicolas Le Camus de Mézières, *The Genius of Architecture; or, The Analogy of That Art with Our Sensations* (1780), trans. David Britt (Chicago, 1992), 88; George Saville Halifax, *Lady's New Year's Gift*, 6th ed. (London, 1699), 90; Robert Morris, *The Art of Architecture, A Poem. In Imitation of Horace's Art of Poetry* (London, 1742), 9; William Kent quoted in Peter Ward-Jackson, *English Furniture Designs of the Eighteenth Century* (London, 1958), 3; Deborah Logan, letter dated 26 October 1834, Logan Family Papers, Historical Society of Pennsylvania (HSP), Philadelphia.

34. D'Assigny, 68.

35. Excepting perhaps Amelia Lanier's house and poem "Cooke-ham" (c. 1609–10), the country-house tradition—from architecture to literature—was a decidedly masculine one. See Mark Girouard, *Life in the English Country House: A Social and Architectural History* (New York, 1978). See also Alistair Fowler, "Country House Poems: The Politics of a Genre," *Seventeenth Century* (1986): 1–13; and Barbara K. Lewalski, "The Lady of the Country-House Poem," in *The Fashioning and Functioning of the British Country House*, ed. Gervase Jackson-Stops, Gordon J. Schochet, Lena Cowen Orlin, and Elisabeth Blair McDougall (Hanover, N.H., 1989), 261–75.

36. In constructing the early modern female as an inhabitant or spectator of architecture, I draw on feminist architectural and film theory's shared concern with "the gaze." Feminist studies of the public and masculine gaze include Laura Mulvey, "Visual Pleasure and Narrative Cinema," *Screen* 16, 3 (1975): 6–18, and Kaja Silverman, "Fassbinder and Lacan: A Reconsideration of the Gaze, Look, and Image," *Camera Obscura* 19 (July 1991): 54–85.

Architectural studies include Alice T. Friedman, "Architecture, Authority, and the Female Gaze: Planning and Representation in the Early Modern Country House," *Assemblage* 18 (1992): 40–62, and Mark Wigley, "Untitled: The Housing of Gender," in *Sexuality and Space*, ed. Beatriz Colomina (Princeton, 1992), 327–89. Neither exclusively oriented by the male gaze nor limited to its visual properties, architecture creates instead an interpretative frame for female inhabitants, which coincides with the eighteenth century's formulation of aesthetics as a wholly sensual—rather than strictly visual—perceptual scheme (via sensibility, neurology, faculty psychology, and associationism).

37. What I describe as proprioception, the philosopher Edward Casey describes as the phenomenon of "inhabitation," "at once an effectuation and culmination of bodily being-in-

space," in *Remembering: A Phenomenological Study*, 2d ed. (Bloomington, 2000), 194. I thank Bernie Herman for our discussions on proprioception.

38. In addition to Bachelard's influential *Poetics of Space*, see Yi-fu Tuan, *Topophilia: A Study of Environmental Perception, Attitudes, and Values* (Englewood Cliffs, N.J., 1974), 247.

39. Elizabeth Graeme Fergusson, "An Old Woman's Meditations On an old Family Piece of Furniture," in "Selections 1797–1799" (Am .0670), HSP.

40. Deborah Logan, manuscript diary, 17 vols., 1:23–24, HSP. Subsequent references to Logan's diaries (1815–39) at the HSP are by volume and page number. I cite her earlier diaries (1808–14), recently acquired by the Library Company of Philadelphia (LCP), by date only, following Logan's organizational scheme.

41. Influenced by faculty psychology, Scottish moral philosophy, and British aesthetics, architectural associationism amplified the spectator's creative role in architecture. As a building's design prompted memories and sensations in the viewer, theorists contended, it also manifested the inherent relationship between inhabitant and habitation. Associationism thus advocated an empirical apprehension of spatial knowledge and memory through sensory perception rather than reason. See, for example, Alexander Gerard, *An Essay on Taste* (London, 1759); Archibald Alison, *Essays on the Nature and Principle of Taste* (Edinburgh, 1790); Lord Kames, *Elements of Criticism*, vol. 3 (Edinburgh, 1765); and William Gilpin, *Three Essays* (London, 1808). See also John Archer, "The Beginnings of Association in British Architectural Esthetics," in *The Past as Prologue: Essays to Celebrate the 25th Anniversary of ASECS* (New York, 1995), 115–34.

42. Rogers, 1:vii; Logan diary, 1:24, HSP; Richard Payne Knight, *An Analytical Inquiry into the Principles of Taste*, 2d ed. (London, 1805), 102, 301; D'Assigny, 26.

43. Quoted in James Sambrook, *The Eighteenth Century: The Intellectual and Cultural Context of English Literature, 1700–1789* (New York, 1986), 6–7.

44. By the eighteenth century theorists disagreed about whether the nerves were hollow or solid: the former provided the labyrinth through which animal spirits moved; the latter moved by repeated vibration. The notion of animal spirits moving through the nerve channels persisted well into the nineteenth century. See John Sutton, *Philosophy and Memory Traces: Descartes to Connectionism* (Cambridge, 1998).

45. Casey, 196.

46. Fergusson, "Old Woman's Meditations."

47. Walter Benjamin, "Paris, Capital of the Nineteenth Century," in *Reflections*, trans. Edmund Jepincott (New York, 1986), 155–56.

48. Excepting the estate inventories for Graeme Park, Stenton, and Wright's Ferry and the historic structures report for Morven, I rely on documentary evidence from the coterie's unpublished commonplace books, diaries, and letters.

49. Logan diary, 1 August 1808, LCP.

50. My descriptions of Fairhill draw on Mark Reinberger and Elizabeth McLean, "Isaac Norris's Fairhill: Architecture, Landscape, and Quaker Ideals in a Philadelphia Colonial Country Seat," *Winterthur Portfolio* 32, 4 (1997): 243–74.

51. Karin Wulf, *Not All Wives: Women of Colonial Philadelphia* (Ithaca, 2000), 53–83.

52. Susanna Wright, "To Eliza Norris," Hannah Griffitts Papers, LCP.

53. Wright, "To Eliza Norris."

54. Deborah Logan, "Reminiscences," Logan Family Papers, vol. 60, HSP.

55. Logan, 12:156, 8:85.

56. Logan, 1:220.

57. Francis Daniel Pastorius's manuscript commonplace book, "Bee Stock or Hive," is in Special Collections, Van Pelt Library, University of Pennsylvania, Philadelphia.

58. Francis Bacon, "Of Empire," in *The Works of Francis Bacon*, 14 vols., ed. James Spedding, Robert Leslie Ellis, and Douglas Denon Heath (London, 1858), 2:419.

59. Logan, "Lines Suggested by a Passage in Lord Bacon's Works," commonplace book, 110, HSP.

60. The manuscript is in the archive collection at Stenton.

61. Thomas Whately, *Observations on Modern Gardening* (London, 1801), 86.

62. Hannah Griffitts to Susanna Wright, 6 February 1763, Fairhill, Norris Family Papers, HSP.

63. See Yates, 118–20, on visual alphabets. Like mnemonic treatises, architectural manuals such as William Salmon's *Builder's Dictionary*, in *Palladio Londinensis* (London, 1734), employed an anthropomorphic vocabulary.

64. Richard Neve, *The City and Country Purchaser* (London, 1726), 254–55.

65. Beattie, 34.

66. Logan, 7:105. My description of Stenton's architecture is indebted to Raymond Sheperd, "James Logan's Stenton: Grand Simplicity in Quaker Philadelphia" (M.A. thesis, Winterthur, 1968). I thank Margo Burnett and Laura Stutman at Stenton for generously opening Stenton's doors and files to me.

67. Logan, 15:200, 7:122.

68. Logan, 15:200, 5:78, 6:180.

69. Logan, 13:285, 1:24.

70. Logan, 12:197–99, 15:50, 6:108.

71. Logan, 6:120, 59, 172.

72. Logan, 9:93, 7:139.

73. Logan, 9:145.

74. Logan, 16:284, 15:346, 1:191–92.

75. Logan, 7:202.

76. Logan, 11:10, 145–46.

77. Logan, 11:91, 8:121. According to James and Sarah Logan's estate inventories in 1752 and 1754, this was the most elegantly appointed chamber, containing an expensive mahogany bed covered with lavish yellow wool damask bed hangings, curtains, and upholstery. The room also contained twelve maple chairs with the same upholstery, a maple chest of drawers, and an old tea table, where Deborah and her friends drank tea.

78. Logan, 7:120.

79. Logan, 7:97–98, 8:60, 5:92, 13:254, 5:94.

80. Logan, 7:120–21, 11:11, 10:2, 5:97.

81. Logan, 7:120–21. For the gendered significance of windows, see "Wrote extempore by P. D. L[ ]y on the Governors appearing much pleased with some new fashion'd large Panes of Glass he had got for his new House," in Catherine Blecki and Karen Wulf, eds., *Milcah Martha Moore's Book: A Commonplace Book from Revolutionary America* (University Park, Pa., 1997), 190.

82. Logan, 1:prefatory pages.

83. Obituary in Stenton manuscript files.

84. Elizabeth Graeme (Fergusson), "Some Lines upon my first being at Graeme Park; after my return from England," in "Poemata Juvenilia," LCP.

85. Blecki and Wulf, 204.

86. Elizabeth Graeme, "A few Extracts from E.G.'s Journal," in Blecki and Wulf, 207.

87. I rely on Mark Reinberger, "Graeme Park and the Three-Cell Plan: A Lost Type in Colonial Architecture," *Perspectives in Vernacular Architecture*, vol. 4, ed. Thomas Carter and Bernard Herman (Columbia, Mo., 1991), 146–54, and Nancy Woostroff, "Graeme Park, an Eighteenth-Century Country Estate in Horsham, Pennsylvania" (M.A. thesis, University of Delaware, 1958), for my architectural descriptions. For an eighteenth-century description to which Fergusson may have contributed, see the advertisement for the estate's sale in the *Pennsylvania Packet*, 29 August 1787.

88. The difficulty of reconstructing the rooms at Graeme Park from the three inventories of September 1772, September 1778, and 8 October 1778 is their variable room designations. The first inventory, for instance, mentioned only two rooms (the front and back parlors on

each floor) whereas the second inventory listed nine living areas: the northwest, middle, and east rooms on the second and third floors but only the east and west rooms on the first floor. Combining the information, I reconstruct these rooms as they were before the American Revolution. Reprinted in Woostroff, the inventories are in the Office of Wills, Philadelphia City Hall.

89. Elizabeth Graeme (Fergusson), "Some Lines upon my first being at Graeme Park," LCP.

90. Fergusson, "Old Woman's Meditations."

91. Benjamin Rush, "An Account of the Life and Character of Mrs. Elizabeth Fergusson," *The Port Folio* 1 (1809): 523; John Young to Elizabeth Fergusson, 22 March 1775, rpt. in T. W. Bean, *History of Montgomery County, Pennsylvania* (Philadelphia, 1884), 895.

92. From the estate inventory after Thomas Graeme's death in 1772, one assumes that formal dining occurred in the east parlor and that the designated "dining room" was a more informal living space—much like the seventeenth-century hall—where families congregated, cooked, ate, and slept. As the parlor began to take on the more public functions of the tea table and salon, the family moved into the back dining room. At least until 1772 the dining room was furnished for family retirement: a couch, easy chair, chest of drawers, a small looking glass, and a bedstead occupied one part of the room. It also held nine chairs, a china table, and tea board (with a yellow teapot) for dining and an old desk for reading and writing. Despite the eclectic furniture, the other inventoried items were exclusively the province of dining: octagonal and round dishes, both Queensware and delftware china, decanters and tumblers, chafing dishes, bread baskets, slop bowls, butter plates, mustard pots, glasses, and china candlesticks.

93. Elizabeth Fergusson, "Il Penseroso, An Ode," 1780–82, manuscript in Benjamin Rush Correspondence, vol. 40, LCP.

94. Fergusson, "Some Lines upon my first being at Graeme Park."

95. "Introduction to Laura's Effusions of Friendship Composed in Solitude at her paternal Seat," commonplace book, HSP.

96. I thank Bernie Herman for his discovery of and research on Graeme Park's writing closet. I assume that the covert writing table is one and the same.

97. Elizabeth Graeme (Fergusson) to unknown correspondent, n.d., in Simon Gratz, "Some Materials for a Biography of Elizabeth Fergusson, née Graeme," *Pennsylvania Magazine of History and Biography* 39 (1915): 387.

98. Jonathan Swift, "The Furniture of a Woman's Mind," in *The Writings of Jonathan Swift*, ed. Robert Greenberg and William Piper (New York, 1973), 529–30.

99. Beattie, 14.

100. 1778 inventory.

101. Elizabeth Graeme (Fergusson), "The Easy Chair," in "Poemata Juvenilia," LCP.

102. Considered one-third of household goods, moveables suggest an economy of kinship, in which a woman on the colonial marriage market, with dowry in hand, was another type of property transferred from father to husband. See Claude Lévi-Strauss, *The Elementary Structures of Kinship*, trans. James Harle Bell, John Richard von Sturmer, and Rodney Needhan (Boston, 1969). For an early but still resonant reading of Lévi-Strauss, see Gayle Rubin, "The Traffic of Women: Notes on the Political Economy of Sex," in *Toward an Anthropology of Women*, ed. Rayna R. Reiter (New York, 1975), 157–210.

103. Elizabeth Fergusson to unknown correspondent, 16 March 1781, Haverford College Library, Quaker Collection, Haverford, Pa.

104. Woostroff, 76.

105. Records of the estate sale are reprinted in Gratz, "Some Materials," 294–96.

106. Elizabeth Fergusson to Rebecca Smith, 6 January 1791, William Smith Papers, vol. 3, University of Pennsylvania Archives and Records Center, Philadelphia.

107. Elizabeth Fergusson's memorandum written on a letter from William Smith, Philadelphia, 9 November 1791, in Gratz, "Some Materials," 315–16.

108. Elizabeth Fergusson to Annis Stockton, 24 December 1793, Rush Correspondence, LCP. She also writes about the disruptive time from 29 December 1793 to 16 January 1794 in her willow odes, in Elizabeth Graeme Fergusson Commonplace Book, c. 1787–88 (created by Elizabeth Graeme Fergusson for the "Five Sisters of the Willing Family"), part of the collections of Graeme Park, Horsham, Pa., administered by the Pennsylvania Historical and Museum Commission.

109. The note is appended to one of the several letters from Christopher Beswick to Elizabeth Fergusson in the Rush Correspondence, 40:158; Elizabeth Fergusson to Annis Stockton, 24 December 1793, Rush Correspondence, 40:16–18, LCP.

110. Eliza Stedman to Mrs. Senior, 6 April 1801, quoted in Chester T. Hallenbeck, "The Life and Collected Poems of Elizabeth Graeme Fergusson" (M.A. thesis, Columbia University, 1929), 177–80.

111. I quote from a transcription of a letter from Susanna Wright to her cousin, William Croudsen Jr., Lancashire, England, 1 May 1714, Chester County Historical Society, West Chester, Pa.

112. Extract of a letter from S. Wright, 22 September 1772, quoted in Blecki and Wulf, 231–32. Elizabeth Fergusson visited Warrington when she was in England in the 1760s, admiring the house, its "genteel" furnishings, and the fine garden. See Anne H. Ousterhout, *The Most Learned Woman in America* (University Park, Pa., 2003), 64.

113. Will of Susanna Wright, 28 January 1782, Lancaster County Historical Society, microfilm at HSP.

114. The description is taken from Bernard Herman's unpublished essay, "Wright's Ferry Mansion," which he generously shared with me. See also Willis S. Shirk, "Wright's Ferry: A Glimpse into the Susquehanna Backcountry," *Pennsylvania Magazine of History and Biography* 120, 2 (1996): 61–87. Though Wright lived in the house of her deceased friend Samuel Blunston from around 1756 until her own death in 1784, I focus on her memories of Wright's Ferry since she was such an active participant in its planning and building.

115. Rhoda Barber manuscript, "Journal of the Settlement of Wright's Ferry on the Susquehanna River" (1830), HSP.

116. Quoted in L. H. Butterfield, "Rush's Trip to Carlisle, 1784," *Pennsylvania Magazine of History and Biography* 73 (1950): 455.

117. Susanna Wright, "The following lines were written in the year 1726 by Susanna Wright on removing from Chester County to the banks of the Susquehenna——the spot where the Town of Columbia now stands," J. Watson Notebook (Am 301), 501, HSP.

118. Benjamin Franklin to Susanna Wright, 11 July 1752, 21 November 1751, in *The Papers of Benjamin Franklin*, 36 vols., ed. Leonard Labaree and Whitfield Bell (New Haven, 1959–), 6:23–24, 4:210–11; Sally Barton to Louisa DeNormandie, undated letter, quoted in "The Bartons in Lancaster in 1776," *Papers of the Lancaster County Historical Society*, 52, 8 (1948): 216–17; and Elizabeth Fergusson, 24 December 1794, quoted in Hallenbeck, "Life and Collected Poems of Fergusson," 45.

119. Herman, 11.

120. See note 87.

121. According to Herman, the parlor entry—gained through a closet in the paneled parlor wall—was probably a secondary entrance for the family to the gardens and other outbuildings (27).

122. See Philip D. Zimmerman, "Queen Anne Chairs at Wright's Ferry Mansion," *The Magazine Antiques* 149, 5 (1996): 736–45, and Elizabeth M. Schaefer, "A Country Seat on the Susquehanna: Wright's Ferry Mansion," *Old Lancaster Antiques Show* (17–20 November 1983): 32–37.

123. See "Benjamin Franklin in Lancaster County," *Journal of the Lancaster County Historical Society* 6, 1 (1957): 1–26.

124. Susanna Wright, "Directions for the Management of Silk Worms," *Philadelphia Med-*

ical and Physical Journal 1, 1 (1804): 103–4, 106–7. Some of Wright's silk samples appear in the Watson Notebook at the Library Company of Philadelphia, and silk fragments from the von Hess Foundation were displayed at the Philadelphia Museum of Art in 1999. See the exhibition catalog, *Worldly Goods: The Arts of Early Pennsylvania, 1680–1758,* ed. Jack L. Lindsey (Philadelphia, 1999), 226.

125. Logan, manuscript sketch of Susanna Wright, 19 March 1822, Stenton; Logan, 12:188. As Wulf points out, some of Wright's poems were transcribed into copybooks by Hannah Griffitts, Mary Flower, Deborah Morris, and Hannah Callender. See *Not All Wives,* 45–47. A selection of Wright's poetry has been published for the first time in *Milcah Martha Moore's Book,* ed. Blecki and Wulf, 119–49, 150–51.

126. Some of Wright's herbal recipes are transcribed in Elizabeth Coultas's recipe book (1759–60), Document 1044, Winterthur Library.

127. Mrs. Henry Heistand in *Journal of the Papers of the Lancaster County Historical Society* 25, 9 (1922) and quoted in Marion Wallace Reininger, "Susanna Wright," *Journal of the Papers of the Lancaster County Historical Society* 63 (1959): 186.

128. Wright, "My Own Birthday—August 4th 1761," quoted in Blecki and Wulf, 147–49.

129. Blecki and Wulf, 135.

130. Wright, "My Own Birthday," in Blecki and Wulf, 148.

131. Logan, 14:101; Rush quoted in "Benjamin Franklin and Lancaster County," 6.

132. Benjamin Rush to Richard Henry Lee, 7 January 1777, *Letters of Benjamin Rush,* 2 vols., ed. Lyman Butterfield (Princeton, 1951), 1:126.

133. I adapt my description of the house from Constance Greiff's unpublished work, "A Documentary History, Prepared for the New Jersey State Museum" (Heritage Studies, N.J., 1989), 171, and Greiff, "The Architecture of Morven," in Alfred Hoyt Bill, *A House Called Morven: Its Role in American History,* rev. ed. (Princeton, 1978), 165–89.

134. Annis Stockton to Julia Stockton Rush, September 1788, Rosenbach Museum and Library, Philadelphia, Pa.; Annis Stockton to Mary Stockton Hunter, September 1791, quoted in Lyman H. Butterfield, "Morven: A Colonial Outpost of Sensibility: With Some Hitherto Unpublished Poems by Annis Boudinot Stockton," *Princeton University Library Chronicle* 6, 4 (November 1944): 6.

135. The latest historic structures report indicates that Morven followed either a center-hall Georgian plan (like Stenton) or an L plan (like Mount Pleasant). Built between 1762 and 1765 by John Macpherson, Mount Pleasant is currently administered by the Philadelphia Museum of Art and Fairmount Park Commission.

136. Charles Thomson to Hannah Thomson, 4 July 1783, in *Congress at Princeton: Being the Letters of Charles and Hannah Thomson, June–October 1783,* ed. Eugene Sheridan and John Murrin (Princeton, 1985), 16.

137. This inventory was published in *New Jersey Genesis* 12 (4 July 1965): 525; Annis Stockton to Julia Stockton Rush, 18 July [1785], Rosenbach Museum and Library, Philadelphia, Pa.

138. Beattie, 27, 28. Beattie's notion is not original. David Hume explains the association of ideas on the three principles of resemblance, contiguity, and causation in *A Treatise of Nature,* ed. L. A. Selby-Bigge (Oxford, 1928), bk. 1, part 2, sec. 5, 60–61.

139. Since these items, along with a pair of large brass andirons, tongs, and brass-topped iron shovel and fender, were the only objects listed in the parlor's 1781 inventory, scholars suggest that the list actually referred to the furnishings of the present hallway to the west wing.

140. Charles Thomson to Hannah Thomson, 3 July 1783, in *Congress at Princeton,* 14.

141. "To Miss Mary Stockton[,] an epistle upon some gentlemen refusing to admit ladies of their circle into the parlour till supper where they met for conversation and business once a week lest the Ladies should hinder by their chit chat the purpose of their meeting," in Carla Mulford, ed., *"Only for the Eye of a Friend": The Poems of Annis Boudinot Stockton* (Charlottesville, 1995), 176–77.

142. Annis Stockton to Mary Stockton Hunter, 15–24 September 1790, Stockton Additional Papers, Manuscripts Division, Department of Rare Books and Special Collections, Princeton University Library; published with permission of the Princeton University Library.

143. Annis Stockton to Elizabeth Fergusson, 24 November 1780, Gratz Collection, HSP.

144. Dated "Morven 1792," the letter appears alongside Stockton's poem, "An Ode," in Elizabeth Fergusson's commonplace book, HSP.

145. Annis Stockton to Elizabeth Fergusson, 10 May 17[ ], Gratz Collection, HSP.

146. J. G. Zimmerman suggests in *Solitude; or, The Effects of Occasional Retirement* (London, 1797) that women are particularly susceptible to the contemplative pleasures of rural life.

147. Stockton to Fergusson, 10 May 17[ ], Gratz Collection, HSP.

148. Thomas Whately, *Observations on Modern Gardening*, 4th ed. (London, 1777), 155–56.

149. A comparison of the plans for the Twickenham and Morven gardens shows a blatant discrepancy between the former's informality and the latter's strict Georgian order. Despite the material differences, Stockton perpetuates the aesthetic—and mnemonic—associations between the two gardens.

150. Richard Stockton to Annis Stockton, January 1767, quoted in Greiff, "Documentary History," 38. On Pope's garden, see Diana Balmori, "Architecture, Landscape, and the Intermediate Structure: Eighteenth-Century Experiments in Mediation," *Journal of the Society of Architectural Historians* (March 1991): 38–56.

151. Quoted in Greiff, "Documentary History," 38.

152. On the difference between history and antiquarianism, see Susan Stewart, *On Longing: Narratives of the Miniature, the Gigantic, the Souvenir, the Collection* (Durham, 1993), 139–45.

153. Karen Bescherer Metheny, Judson Kratzer, Anne E. Yentsch, and Conrad H. Goodwin, "Method in Landscape Archaeology: Research Strategies in a Historic New Jersey Garden," in *Landscape Archaeology: Reading and Interpreting the American Historical Landscape*, ed. Rebecca Yamin and Karen Bescherer Metheny (Knoxville, 1996), 6–31.

154. Annis Stockton to Julia Stockton Rush, 3 May 1797, Rosenbach Museum and Library, Philadelphia, Pa.

155. Deborah Logan, "Recollections Inscribed to my Husband, written in 1820," commonplace book, HSP.

CHAPTER 2. PEN, INK, AND MEMORY

1. Deborah Logan, manuscript diary, 17 vols., 1:2, Historical Society of Pennsylvania (HSP), Philadelphia. I cite her diary by volume and page number for the remainder of the chapter.

2. Deborah Logan, "Morning's Early Prime," commonplace book, Loudoun Papers, Box 46 A, HSP, 105. Also at the HSP is a copy of Logan's commonplace book in Maria Dickinson Logan's hand, dated 25 December 1886.

3. Lady Pennington, *An Unfortunate Mother's Advice to Her Daughters* (London, 1790), 85; Logan, "Morning's Early Prime," 107.

4. Logan, 12:246b, 11:248, 13:322, 9:133. Logan models her simple Quaker style after her aunt and fellow litterateur, Susanna Wright. Remembering a childhood visit to Wright's Ferry, she found that though Wright "was a very sensible, learned, and accomplished woman she dressed very plain and like any other country person. But her dress was of no consequence to her, so it was decent and plain and clean—it was my first practical lesson upon the subject." 11:appendix, 8–9.

5. Logan, 14:189, 13:319.

6. Logan, 11:214, 236.

7. The stool may be one of the four mahogany stools which her father, Charles Norris, commissioned from Philadelphia cabinetmaker John Elliott in 1754 and which she brought to Stenton as part of her trousseau. The stools are now housed at Stenton and the Winterthur Museum and were displayed at the Philadelphia Museum of Art in 1999. See the exhibition

catalog, *Worldly Goods: The Arts of Early Pennsylvania, 1680–1758,* ed. Jack Lindsey (Philadelphia, 1999), 166. See also Philip D. Zimmerman, "Eighteenth-Century Chairs at Stenton," *The Magazine Antiques* (May 2003): 122–29.

8. I quote the first original American penmanship manual, George Fisher, *The American Instructor; or, Young Man's Best Companion* (Philadelphia, 1753), 28. Courtesy, The Winterthur Library: Printed Book and Periodical Collection.

9. Fisher explains the process in detail: "Gum Sandrick Powder (or Pounce as they call it) with a little Cotton dipp'd therein, which rub gently over the Paper, to make it bear Ink the better; particular when full Hands are to be written, and especially when you are obliged to scratch out a Word or Letter. . . . And rubbing the Place with the Pounce, smooth it with the Hast of the Penknife, or clean Paper, and then you may write what is proper in the same Place" (27).

10. Logan doesn't mention her preferred method, but blotting paper was also common by the nineteenth century. Dating at least to fifteenth-century England, it was superseded by dusting sand until about 1800. But because she preferred "old-fashioned" (i.e., eighteenth-century) techniques, including using quills instead of steel pens, Logan probably used pumice to blot excessive ink. Jane Campion's 1999 film adaptation of Jane Austen's novel *Mansfield Park* beautifully re-creates an eighteenth-century woman's careful preparation of her writing paper.

11. Logan, 17:19, 13:322, 16:230.

12. Though such rooms were typically defined as masculine spaces in the eighteenth and early nineteenth centuries, Stenton's dining room and library were gendered by use rather than by architectural form. Architectural theorists from the Renaissance through the eighteenth century considered a man's study, or "withdrawing room" (a small, locked room off his bedroom), an intellectual space, but there is a distinct tension between theory and actual practice. I would argue that domestic spaces are alternately sexed on a day-to-day, room-to-room, and person-to-person basis, according to their occupants and uses. Logan thus negotiated her writing spaces with her husband, family, and domestic help, whose presence changed the gender dynamic of each room at a given time. On gender and space, see *Gender Space Architecture: An Interdisciplinary Introduction,* ed. Jane Rendell, Barbara Penner, and Lain Borden (New York, 2000). See also Elisabeth Donaghy Garrett, "The Dining Room," in *At Home: The American Family, 1750–1870* (New York, 1989), 78–94.

13. Logan, 1:22, 10:99, 1:144, 6:165.

14. Logan, 11:61, 5:92, 7:4, 11:1.

15. Logan, 12:216, 5:92, 7:4, 8:135, 7:105 and 204.

16. Logan, 5:94, 11:9, 8:30, 6:192, 13:194, 7:1.

17. Quoted in Ann Moss, *Printed Commonplace Books and the Structuring of Renaissance Thought* (New York, 1996), 224. Despite the obvious mnemonic benefits of writing, some theorists feared it would replace or irrevocably weaken the memory, repeating Plato's warning in *Phaedrus.* See, for example, William Massey, *The Origin and Progress of Letters* (London, 1763), 7, University of Delaware Library, Newark, Delaware.

18. Logan, 16:65, 10:99; Marius D'Assigny, *The Art of Memory* (London, 1699), 16.

19. Johannes Henricus Alsted, *Consiliarius academicus et scholasticus* (Strasburg, 1610), 238; Joannes Thomas Freigius, *Ciceronianus* (Basle, 1579), 196; and Daniel Georg Morhof, *Polyhistor, literarius, philosophicus et practicus* (Lubeck, 1732), quoted in Moss, 228, 159, 280.

20. Frontispiece of Deborah Logan's commonplace book, HSP.

21. Though writing helps in "reposition," or accumulating memorizable topoi, this chapter focuses on preservation through the reciprocal process of "deposition," the emptying out or copying of memory onto paper. John Willis defines these processes in *Mnemonica; or, The Art of Memory* (London, 1661). Though Willis equates reposition with "memory" and deposition with "recollection," other theorists presented a threefold process: "memory" is the retention of ideas; "remembrance" is recalling ideas stored in the memory; and "reminiscence" recovers lost or forgotten memories, according to D'Assigny, 17.

22. Willis, 30–31; John Jenkins, *The Art of Writing* (Boston, 1791), 62. In the eighteenth century, argues E. Jennifer Monaghan, writing was equated with penmanship rather than composition. See her "Readers Writing: The Curriculum of the Writing Schools of Eighteenth-Century Boston," *Visible Language* 21, 2 (Spring 1987): 7–53, and "Literacy Instruction and Gender in Colonial New England," in *Reading in America: Literature and Social History,* ed. Cathy Davidson (Baltimore, 1989), 53–80. See also Laetitia Yeandle, "The Evolution of Handwriting in the English-Speaking Colonies of America," *American Archivist* (Summer 1980): 294–311, and Tamara Thornton, *Handwriting in America: A Cultural History* (New Haven, 1996).

23. *Ad herennium,* III.xvii.30, quoted in Moss, 8.

24. James Beattie, *Essays Moral and Critical* (London, 1783), 50–51.

25. *The Entertainer; Containing great Variety of Instructive Entertainment, For Persons of Every Age, Rank, or Degree,* collected by Charles Tell-Truth, 2 vols. (London, 1766), 171; Jenkins, 6, 13.

26. I ask the reader to forgive the seeming anachronisms here. Though I cull quotations from Logan's diaries (written between 1808 and 1839), I find them useful precisely because of her focus on eighteenth- rather than nineteenth-century culture. The diaries, full of memories of what she calls "by-past times," are a wonderfully rich record of her life before the turn of the century. As chapter 1 more amply illustrates, Logan persistently acknowledges and prefers her "old-fashioned" house, furniture, and manners.

27. Beattie, 50, 34, 18, 34, 56, 58–59.

28. John Locke, *Essay Concerning Human Understanding,* ed. Peter Nidditch (Oxford, 1975), 77; René Descartes, quoted in David Farrell Krell, *Of Memory, Reminiscence, and Writing: On the Verge* (Bloomington, 1990), 60.

29. Fisher, 305–8; George Bickham, *The Universal Penman* (London, 1743; rpt. New York, 1941), 89; Jenkins, xlvii–xlviii; Massey, 153.

30. William Leekey, "Eudosia, or, the Accomplished Virgin," in *The Young Clerk's Assistant* (London, 1764), 41, University of Delaware Library, Newark, Delaware; Jenkins, 2; Lloyd Reynolds, "Notes on Movement Involving Touch," in *Calligraphy and Paleography,* ed. A. S. Osley (London, 1965), 198. See also Jean-Luc Nancy, "Dum Scribo," *Oxford Literary Review* 3 (1978): 6–20.

31. Logan, 11:27.

32. Jenkins, x, 21.

33. Elaine Scarry, *The Body in Pain: The Making and Unmaking of the World* (New York, 1985).

34. Logan, 9:31, 8:122.

35. Plato, *Philebus,* in *The Collected Dialogues of Plato,* ed. Edith Hamilton and Huntington Cairns (Princeton, 1961), 1118–19.

36. See Richard Cytowic, *Synesthesia: A Union of the Senses* (New York, 1989).

37. Massey, 106–7.

38. For similar synesthetic descriptions of writing, see Bickham, 12; Jenkins, 67; and Fisher, 32.

39. Scarry, 282–85.

40. Thomas Willis, *The Description and Use of the Nerves* (London, 1681), 160.

41. Making private memories perceptible, manuscripts consequently inverted the gendered hierarchy propounded by architectural theories that associated masculinity with exteriority and femininity with interiority. Critics accordingly invoked these convenient stereotypes to censure women's writing. If writing represented exteriority, they reasoned, then it posed the viable threat that a woman would leave both her house and domestic duties (if only in her mind) for the life of a pedant. Metaphorically externalizing (or at least exposing) the female body, writing necessarily "unsexed" a woman. As writing metaphors typically gendered the pen masculine and the paper feminine, a female writer threatened these accepted images, calling her biological sex and requisite chastity into question.

42. George Bickham, *Round Hand: A New Copybook* (Hammersmith, 1750), 8. Courtesy, The Winterthur Library: Printed Book and Periodical Collection. Bickham, *Universal Penman,* 10.

43. Samuel Rogers, *The Pleasures of Memory,* 9th ed. (London, 1796), 20.

44. Kames, Lord Henry Home, *Elements of Criticism* (1762), 2 vols. (New York, 1971–72), 171.

45. Logan, 14:159, 11:236.

46. Though from a French writing manual, the image parallels the rhetoric of British and American penmanship etiquette. See Kip Sperry, *Reading Early American Handwriting* (Baltimore, 1998), and Thornton. See also such exhibition catalogs as David Becker, *The Practice of Letters: The Hofer Collection of Writing Manuals, 1514–1800* (Cambridge, Mass., 1997), and *Calligraphy and Handwriting in America, 1710–1962,* at the Peabody Institute Library, Baltimore (Caledonia, N.Y., 1963).

47. The directions for writing posture are relatively static from the Renaissance through the eighteenth century. Compare, for instance, Edward Cocker's *Magnum in Parvo, or the Pen's Perfection* (London, 1672), 6, with Jenkins's directions in the *Art of Writing* a century later, 21–22.

48. Madame Johnson, "A New and Easy Introduction to the Art of Writing," in *Madame Johnson's Present, or the Best Instructions for Young Women* (London, 1754), 66–67. Courtesy, The Winterthur Library: Printed Book and Periodical Collection.

49. See Laurel Ulrich, "Gender, Property, and Memory in the Decorative Arts," in *American Furniture,* ed. Luke Beckerdite and William N. Hosley (Hanover, N.H., 1995), 39–68, and Deborah I. Prosser, " 'The Rising Prospect of the lovely Face': Conventions of Gender in Colonial American Portraiture," in *Painting and Portrait Making in the American Northeast,* ed. Peter Benes, Dublin Seminar for New England Folklife Annual Proceedings (June 1994): 181–200.

50. William Hogarth defines the "line of beauty" in *The Analysis of Beauty* (London, 1753). For a fuller vocabulary, see Martin Eli Weil, "A Cabinetmaker's Price Book," *Winterthur Portfolio* 13 (1979): 80–192.

51. William Milns, *Plan of Instruction by Private Classes . . . Including Some Remarks on the Cultivation of the Female Mind* (New York, 1794), 15; Fisher, 42.

52. Gerald Ward, "The Intersections of Life: Tables and Their Social Role," in *American Tables and Looking Glasses in the Mabel Brady Garvan and Other Collections at Yale University,* ed. David Barquist (New Haven, 1992), 18.

53. Joseph Addison, *The Spectator* (London, 1711–15).

54. Bickham, *Universal Penman,* 29. American copybooks (and British reprints) consistently used gendered metaphors to describe the practice and rewards of penmanship. Bickham's *Universal Penman,* Jenkins's *Art of Writing,* and Johnson's *Present,* for example, all published identical poems alternately addressed "To Young Gentlemen" and "To Young Ladies." Whereas verse promised literate boys "Fortune," "the Fate of Empires," "Wealth," and "Honour," girls were told that their "pretty Lines and Charms" should aspire to the delicacy of their needlework, as "all shou'd be fair that Beauteous Woman frames."

55. Physiognomy is also connected with memory and handwriting by the face's association with the hand in early modern palmistry. In *Physiognomie and Chiromancie . . . Wherento is added The Art of Memorie* (London, 1653), Richard Saunders describes "*the proper* Language *of the* Brow *and* Hand": "Paraphrase *on each fair written* Grace; / . . . *Observe its* Signatures, *and understand / . . . How* Lines *concur, touch, cut, and range apart,*" 9.

56. Erasmus Darwin, *A Plan for the Conduct of Female Education in Boarding Schools, Private Families, and Public Seminaries* (Philadelphia, 1798), 17–18; Geoffrey Gilbert, *The Law of Evidence* (London, 1726), quoted in Thornton, 35; Johnson, 70; Lavater quoted in Christophe Siegrist, " 'Letters of the Divine Alphabet': Lavater's Concept of Physiognomy," in *The Faces of Physiognomy: Intertextual Approaches to Johann Caspar Lavater,* ed. Ellis Shookman (Columbia, S.C., 1993), 30.

57. On the importance of a woman's "agreeable" countenance to her script, see Johnson, 70, 71; Fisher, 32; Bickham, *Universal Penman,* 24.

58. Logan, 10:133. In addition to her informal desk, Logan preferred a comfortable easy chair to a stiff-backed desk chair. As John Gloag explains in *The Englishman's Chair: Origins, Design, and Social History of Seat Furniture in England* (London, 1964), chairmakers and upholsterers replaced the unyielding, upright bearing of traditional chairs with the easy chair in the late seventeenth century. They increased the standards of comfort and consequently "began to change posture through design, thus unwittingly changing the character of manners, which became less formal, easier" (23). Logan's easy chair, then, represented a more informal mode of behavior, defying writing masters' directions for correct posture.

59. Though Logan's furniture was an amalgam of old and new styles, probably ranging from inherited William and Mary pieces (1700–1725) to items made in Federal or Empire style (1775–1825), most of her furniture, I assume, came from the Queen Anne (1725–50) and Chippendale (1750–75) periods, when she married and accumulated possessions.

60. Some desks were described as having a "full- or half-amphitheater format," imitating the commonplace Renaissance trope of the memory theater. Like the domestic memory palace, the imaginary theater provided rooms on- and offstage as convenient repositories.

61. Erasmus, *De copia,* quoted in Moss, III, 108.

62. In a footnote to *The Art of Writing* Jenkins quotes a signed statement by such well-respected physicians as Benjamin Rush, Samuel Danforth, and James Warren (22). Their medical prescription echoes centuries of advice from writing masters on correct posture. As Edward Cocker suggests in *Multum in Parvo; or, The Pen's Gallantrie* (London, 1660): "Turn not your Head aside, hold in your Arm / Sit from the Desk, to keep your breast from harm" (6).

63. Logan, 9:62.

64. Logan, 14:1, 17:26.

65. Logan, 17:1, 6:117.

66. Logan, 13:145.

67. Locke, 76.

68. Kames, 511.

69. George Cheyne, *The English Malady: or, The Treatise of Nervous Diseases of All Kinds* (London, 1730), 49.

70. Plato, *Theaetetus,* in *Collected Dialogues,* ed. Hamilton and Cairns, 897.

71. John Locke, 2.9:24; Locke, *Some Thoughts Concerning Education,* in *The Educational Writings of John Locke* (London, 1705), rpt. ed. James L. Axtell (Cambridge, 1968), 263–64, 264n. Locke's methods were continued through the eighteenth century. See John Jenkins, "Dialogue on the Use of the Dry Pen," in *Art of Writing,* 56.

72. John Bancks, "A Poem on the Universal Penman," in Bickham, *Universal Penman,* 5.

73. D'Assigny, 58–59.

74. René Descartes, *The Passions of the Soul* (1645–56), in *Selected Philosophical Writings,* trans. Roger Ariew, John Cottingham, and Tom Sorell (Cambridge, 1988), 218–38, and *Treatise on Man,* in *The Philosophical Writings of Descartes,* 3 vols., trans. John Cottingham, Robert Stoothoff, and Dugald Murdoch (Cambridge, 1985), 1:99–108.

75. René Descartes to Père Mesland, 2 May 1644, quoted in Krell, 62. My understanding of Descartes's memory theories is influenced by Krell.

76. Francis Bacon, *De augmentis scientiarum,* quoted in Moss, 269. Since the Renaissance, memory has been likened to a textile. Like Descartes, the contemporary phenomenologist Maurice Merleau-Ponty says that to remember is to immerse oneself in "the horizon of the past and to unfold little by little the perspectives contained there until the experiences bounded by that horizon are, as it were, lived anew in their temporal place." *Phenomenology of Perception* (1945), quoted in Krell, 93.

77. Thomas Willis, *The Anatomy of the Brain* (London, 1681; rpt. Montreal, 1965), 95.

78. Quoted in Krell, 74.

79. Descartes's typography of memory traces continued well into the eighteenth century

in the widespread fascination with neurology. While some upheld the physiology of animal spirits and brain traces, others, such as David Hartley in *Observations on Man* (London, 1749), propounded theories of vibrations to explain how the nerves received and moved sense impressions. David Hume offered an equally corporeal theory in his *Treatise on Human Nature* (London, 1739–40), describing memory in metaphors of physical force, movement, and retention. On materialism and memory, see John W. Yolton, *Thinking Matter: Materialism in Eighteenth-Century Britain* (Minneapolis, 1983), and Timo Kaitaro, "Ideas in the Brain: The Localization of Memory Traces in the Eighteenth Century," *Journal of the History of Philosophy* 37, 2 (1999): 301–22.

80. My description relies on Phillip Gaskell, *A New Introduction to Bibliography* (Oxford, 1972), 57–77; R. J. Lyall, "Materials: The Paper Revolution," in *Book Production and Publishing in Britain, 1375–1475,* ed. Jeremy Griffiths and Derek Pearsall (Cambridge, 1989), 11–31; and Joseph Nickell, *Pen, Ink, and Evidence: A Study of Writing Material for the Penman, Collector, and Document Detective* (Lexington, 1990), 75–76.

81. Immanuel Kant, *Anthropology from a Pragmatic Point of View,* trans. Victor Lyle Dowdell (Carbondale, Ill., 1996), 76.

82. Logan, 17:26.

83. Elizabeth Fergusson, "Lines to a Gentleman Whom Made Laura a Good Pen" (1775), commonplace book, courtesy Archives and Special Collections, Dickinson College, Carlisle, Pa.

84. Massey, 21–22.

85. Edward Cocker, "A New Invented Alphabet of Verses dignified with the choicest Rules of Writings curious Art," in *Magnum in Parvo* (London, 1672), 7.

86. On the mechanization of the writing hand, see Jonathan Goldberg, *Writing Matter: From the Hands of the Renaissance* (Palo Alto, 1990), 60–107.

87. William Leekey, *Discourse on the Use of a Pen* (London, 1744), 4; Jenkins, x.

88. Fisher, 29–30. Although most copybooks include extensive directions for making pens, they ironically insist that actual tactile experience is a better teacher than written directions.

89. Cocker, *Multum in Parvo,* 6; Bickham, *Round Hand,* 8, courtesy, The Winterthur Library: Printed Book and Periodical Collection.

90. Johnson, 65.

91. Logan, 13:322, 6:126, 14:135.

92. Logan, 12:260, 16:105.

93. Jenkins, 27.

94. Jenkins, 5.

95. Quoted in Krell, 70.

96. The pen's opening was often compared to the mouth: "This Image of the Voice did Man Invent," writes Bickham, "To make Thought lasting, Reason permanent," in *Round Hand,* 8. For other examples of eighteenth-century women's adoption of this oral metaphor, see *The Journal of Esther Edwards Burr, 1754–57,* ed. Carol Karlsen and Laurie Crumpacker (New Haven, 1984), 52, 106.

97. Jenkins, 24–25.

98. Fisher, 42–43; prefatory poem by Joseph Dimsdale, "To the Ingenious Author," in Thomas Hawkes, *Art of Writing Geometrically Demonstrated* (London, 1747), 5.

99. Karl Figlio, "Theory of Perception," quoted in Ann Jessie Van Sant, "The Centrality of Touch," in *Eighteenth-Century Sensibility and the Novel: The Senses in Social Context* (New York, 1993), 91. Given Newton's contribution of "opticks" during the Enlightenment, sight was privileged as the supreme sense. Touch, in contrast, was considered the lowest sense, as it required proximity if not actual contact to receive and record sensation. At the same time, touch was all-encompassing and therefore gave information that sight and sound could not, compensating for any deficiency in the other four senses. See Michael J. Morgan, *Molyneux's Question: Vision, Touch, and the Philosophy of Perception* (Cambridge, 1977).

100. Thomas Willis, "Of the Senses in Particular, and first of the touch or Feeling," in *Two Discourses Concerning the Soul of Brutes* (London, 1683; rpt. Gainesville, 1971), 60, 61.

101. David Hartley, *Observations on Man, His Frame, His Duty, and His Expectations,* 2 vols. (London, 1749; rpt. New York, 1971), 1:11, 12; George Berkeley, *A Theory of Vision,* in *The Works of George Berkeley,* ed. A. A. Luce and T. E. Jessop, 9 vols. (London, 1948), 1:233.

102. Bickham, *Universal Penman,* 16.

103. One Renaissance writing manual, for instance, refers to the body of the quill pen as the "channel," which suggests a course or passage through which something (in this case, ink) is directed. Such an image challenges Goldberg's masculine paradigm of the pen's violence in *Writing Matter.* See, for example, Giovanbattista Palatino, *The Instruments of Writing,* trans. Rev. Henry K. Pierce (Rome, 1540; rpt. Newport, R.I., 1953).

104. Jenkins, 2.

105. Jenkins, 14.

106. Hannah Robertson, *The Young Ladies School of Arts* (New York, 1777), 52. Courtesy, The Winterthur Library: Printed Book and Periodical Collection.

107. Massey, 22.

108. On storing ink (including prevention of frost and mold), see Fisher, 44–45.

109. Logan, 16:336.

110. Anna Young Smith manuscript poem, "An Epistle from Damon to Sylvia with the Present of a Small Writing Desk with a Mirror and Letter-Case in it when a Child She had given her on Learning to Write," 1777, in Elizabeth Graeme Fergusson's commonplace book, courtesy Archives and Special Collections, Dickinson College, Carlisle, Pa.; Fergusson quoted in Simon Gratz, "Some Materials for the Biography of Elizabeth Fergusson," *Pennsylvania Magazine of History and Biography* 41 (1917): 389, 407.

111. William Harvey, *The Anatomical Exercises of Dr. William Harvey: Du Motu Cordis,* ed. Geoffrey Keynes (London, 1653); Cocker, "New Invented Alphabet."

112. Willis, *Anatomy of the Brain,* 135–36.

113. Logan, 7:197; 16:105, 308; 12:260.

114. Logan, 17:9.

115. My description of ink relies on Nickell, *Pen, Ink, and Evidence.*

116. Rogers, 20.

117. Jenkins, 14; Logan, 6:160, 11:96.

118. Quoted in Thornton, 14.

119. To the same ends, writers also produced secret, or "sympathetic," ink. Fisher, for instance, promoted several techniques in *American Instructor,* 55–56. Some solutions were applied directly to the paper; others required the heat of a roaring fire to make the script legible; and still others used copperas water to reveal interlinear secrets.

120. Cocker, *Magnum in Parvo;* Jenkins, 1; Leekey, *Discourse,* 10–11.

121. Isaac Ware, preface to *The Complete Body of Architecture,* 4th ed. (London, 1768); Leekey, *Discourse,* 4.

122. Jenkins, 14.

123. Emerging from the Italian Renaissance, the italic hand replaced the English secretary hand in the sixteenth century. It was first used as the official church hand, then adopted for private correspondence, and eventually assimilated as the common vernacular hand until the round hand's evolution during the seventeenth and eighteenth centuries. Many early American women's manuscripts, however, still used the italic or some hybrid version of the italic and round hand. Since women in the Philadelphia coterie were not engaged in business, with its secretary hand, their script, I would say, reflects their elite social status in learning to write as a polite accomplishment as well as their gendered relegation to pursuits of the home.

124. J. Radcliffe, *New British Penman* (London, 1790), 13. See Thornton on the gendered history of penmanship.

125. Logan, 6:124, 11:261.

126. Beattie, 32–33.

127. Johnson, 67; Leekey, *Discourse,* 11; Bickham, *Universal Penman,* 66, 24; Massey, 35.

128. On the eighteenth-century culture of taste and politeness, see David Shields, *Civil Tongues and Polite Letters* (Chapel Hill, 1997), and Lawrence Klein, *Shaftesbury and the Culture of Politeness: Moral Discourse and Cultural Politics in Early Eighteenth-Century England* (New York, 1994).

129. Thomas Sheraton, *Cabinetmaker and Upholsterer's Drawing Book* (London, 1802), frontispiece.

130. Jenkins, 62.

131. Hawkes, 23, 8–9. No study has been done on the shared evolution of architecture and handwriting. I believe the link between architectural and writing manuals goes back at least to the Renaissance. Consider, for instance, Albrecht Dürer's work on geometrical writing and civil building: *Of the Just Shaping of Letters,* from *Applied Geometry of Albrecht Dürer* (New York, 1965). The standard titles and formats in each genre, too, are coterminous: for example, William Halfpenny's *Magnum in Parvo; or, The Marrow of Architecture* (1728) and Edward Cocker's writing manual *Magnum in Parvo* (1672). Like a commonplace book of universal maxims, these texts suggest greatness in a multitude of small parts, propounding a kind of geometric proportion or synecdoche between the whole text and its constituent parts.

132. Hawkes, 8–9.

133. Hawkes, 23–24.

134. William Halfpenny, *The Art of Sound Building,* 2d ed. (London, 1725), 6. Courtesy, The Winterthur Library: Printed Book and Periodical Collection.

135. Hawkes, 5.

136. Asher Benjamin, *The American Builder's Companion* 6th ed. (1827; rpt. New York, 1969), 30.

137. Nicolas Le Camus de Mézières, *The Genius of Architecture; or, The Analogy of That Art with Our Sensations,* trans. David Britt (Paris, 1780; rpt. Chicago, 1992), 79.

138. Mézières, 49, 117; John Shute discusses the genders of architecture in *The First and Chief Groundes of Architecture* (London, 1563). On the masculine orders, see James S. Ackerman, "The Tuscan/Rustic Order: A Study in the Metaphorical Language of Architecture," *Journal of the Society of Architectural Historians* 42, 1 (1983): 15–34.

139. An architectural commonplace, italic script followed the English adaptation of the geometric Georgian style of architecture and gardening. As Cocker remarks in *Multum in Parvo:* "This is proved by the rare Accomplishments of the Italians, from whose flourishing Gardens, we have transplanted the choicest of our Flowers of this kind. . . . our Secretary Hands have lately borrowed their lustre and Gallantry from Italian, . . . and though we make their Letters descend to a Compliance with ours for Celerity and Ornament, yet still they must retain very much of their Original Forms" (3).

140. Cocker, *Multum in Parvo,* 5. The round hand, he intimates here, is later formed by the combination of the italic and secretary.

141. Such voluptuous images of women were appreciated until the nineteenth century, as Logan illustrates: one woman reminds her of "Vandyke and Sir Peter Lely's style of Ladies (which is great praise)"; another "always looks to me like one of Sir Peter Lely's 'Ladies' whose Beautiful Portraits are so capable of commanding attention" (11:235, 12:164).

142. Benjamin, 31–32.

143. Johnson, 63–64.

144. Yeandle, "Evolution of Handwriting."

145. Colonial printers favored the Caslon type. The first printed version of the Declaration of Independence, like other official copy, was set in Caslon. On calligraphical and typographical design, see Thornton, 24–35; Alexander Lawson, *Anatomy of a Typeface* (Boston, 1990); Stanley Morrison, *Selected Essays on the History of Letter-Forms in Manuscript and Print,* ed. David McKitterick, 2 vols. (Cambridge, 1981); and David Berkeley Updike, *Printing Types: Their History, Forms, and Use: A Study in Survivals,* 2 vols., 3d ed. (Cambridge, 1962).

146. On architecture's influence on the evolution of print, see Mario Carpo, *Architecture*

in the Age of Printing: Orality, Writing, Typography, and Printed Images in the History of Architectural Theory, trans. Sarah Benson (Cambridge, Mass., 2001).

147. Quoted in Lawson, 185, 187.

148. Henry Wotton, *Elements of Architecture* (London, 1624; rpt. Charlottesville, 1968), 38. On England's adaptation of Roman architecture, see *Paper Palaces: The Rise of the Renaissance Architectural Treatise,* ed. Vaughan Hart and Peter Hicks (New Haven, 1998).

149. Mézières, 85.

150. Sheraton, 98.

151. Mézières, 84. Though he focuses on the French nobility's town house, or *hôtel,* Mézières's interest in the Renaissance and eighteenth-century revivals of classical architectural aesthetics is relevant to the vernacular Georgian style in the early Delaware Valley. Mézières tellingly feminizes the dining room and bedchamber, the spaces where Logan writes: the former is used "for a pleasant repast those present must number no fewer than the *Graces* and no more than the *Muses,*" and the latter is the "palace of sleep" and "the sanctuary of sleep."

152. The same argument, I imagine, would hold true for those critics of women's round hand. A amalgam of the secretary (business) hand and italic (approved for women's purposes), the round hand could raise questions about women's "unfeminine" ambitions beyond the house. Writing for or in a public venue, a woman would not only destabilize the prescribed bounds of the domestic sphere but also, in eighteenth-century parlance, "unsex" herself and become a man.

153. One could easily read Logan's Stenton for its physiognomic character. Just as the face reflected the hidden secrets of the soul, the house's exterior—with its windowed eyes, decorative dentils or teeth, protective skin of brick or wood, and gaping door or mouth that granted entry—provided portals to the intimate spaces inside. Without exterior shutters (to act as eyelids or lashes), Stenton's bottom-floor windows and sidelights (crowned by segmental arches resembling eyebrows) open a convenient "prospect" of the memory places inside. Rationality (i.e., the parlor and library, associated with the head) presumably inhabited the front and upper regions above the stairs (or waist) whereas appetitive desires animated the lower rooms (i.e., the kitchen and privy). Although some vernacular houses used the cellar for food storage and disposal, Stenton had separate buildings for the kitchen, icehouse, smokehouse, and privy, further distancing the impolite smells of food preparation and elimination from the more polite spaces of the parlor and the intellectual space of the dining room. On architecture's anthropomorphism, see Robert Blair St. George, *Conversing by Signs: Poetics of Implication in Colonial New England Culture* (Chapel Hill, 1998).

154. The following definitions are from William Salmon, "Builder's Dictionary," in *Palladio Longinensis* (London, 1734); and Jacques-François Blondel, *Cours d'architecture,* 6 vols. (Paris, 1771–77).

155. Johann Caspar Lavater, *Essays on Physiognomy,* trans. C. Moore, 4 vols. (London, 1787), 4:200; Cocker, *Multum in Parvo,* 4.

156. Moss, 45.

157. Mézières, 72; Adam quoted in David C. Huntington, "Robert Adam's *Mise-en-Scène* of the Human Figure," *Journal of Architectural Historians* 4 (1968): 260. See also Damie Stillman, *The Decorative Work of Robert Adam* (New York, 1966).

158. Beattie specifically describes the virtues of intercolumnation in writing: "Upon this principle, I must blame, in the fashionable hands, all those flourishes, that either require time, or mix with any other part of the writing; all those heads and tails of letters, which are so long as to interfere with one another; all those hair-strokes (as they are called) which are so fine as to be hardly visible, or which require too great nicety in cutting the pen. Letters, that rise and fall obliquely, are not so distinct as those of an erect form" (33–34).

159. Logan, 14:121.

CHAPTER 3. AMONG HER SOUVENIRS

1. Deborah Logan, manuscript diary, 17 vols., 5:100, 8:45, 8:53, Historical Society of Pennsylvania (HSP), Philadelphia. I cite Logan's diary by volume and page number through-

out the chapter. Note: The chapter title is taken from Vera Lynn's World War II musical hit "Among My Souvenirs," one of my paternal grandmother's favorite songs.

2. Inserted note in front of volume 8 of Logan's diary, signed Maria Dickinson Logan, 1934.

3. Though first-generation Quakers eschewed sitting for portraits, their descendants sat in relatively large numbers after 1760. See Anne Verplanck, "Facing Philadelphia: The Social Functions of Silhouettes, Miniatures, and Daguerreotypes, 1760–1860" (Ph.D. diss., College of William and Mary, 1996); and Diane Johnson, "Living in the Light: Quakerism and Colonial Portraiture" (M.A. thesis, University of Delaware, 1991).

4. Logan, 8:22, 15:200; undated manuscript obituary at Stenton transcribed from *The Friend*, a Quaker periodical published in Philadelphia from 1827 to 1955. Courtesy of The National Society of The Colonial Dames of America in the Commonwealth of Pennsylvania at STENTON, Philadelphia.

5. Thomas Cole, "Oedipus and the Meaning of Aging," in *Aging and Ethics: Philosophical Problems in Gerontology*, ed. Nancy Jeeker (Clifton, N.J., 1991), 93–111.

6. Sir Richard Bulstrode, *Miscellaneous Essays . . . XIII. Of Old Age* (London, 1715), 387.

7. Quoted in Terri Premo, *Winter Friends: Women Growing Old in the New Republic, 1785–1835* (Chicago, 1990), 141.

8. John Caspar Lavater, *The Pocket Lavater* (New York, 1817), 2. Courtesy, The Winterthur Library: Printed Book and Periodical Collection. Reading faces is a common practice among the Philadelphia litterateurs. Logan remembers Susanna Wright's "penetrating, sensible countenance . . . excellent memory and a clear and comprehensive judgment," and Eliza Stedman describes Elizabeth Fergusson's complexion as "remarkably fair, the texture of her skin like an infants. Her eyes were quick and piercing the soul . . . expressive of what passed within, her lips plump & a fine line, and her hair yellow. The general cast of her Countenance pensively thoughtful, but when animated by Conversation every feature spoke. Latterly time had made great ravages, sorrow had marked her for her own, its traces were deeply indented." Logan, Sketch, Stenton, courtesy of The National Society of The Colonial Dames of America in the Commonwealth of Pennsylvania at STENTON, Philadelphia; Eliza Stedman to Mrs. Senior, 6 April 1801, quoted in Chester T. Hallenbeck, "The Life and Collected Poems of Elizabeth Graeme Fergusson" (M.A. thesis, Columbia University, 1929), 177–80.

9. Logan, 8:22.

10. Lavater, *Pocket Lavater*, 20–21, 25, 26.

11. *The Mirror of the Graces; or, The English Lady's Costume*, by a Lady of Distinction (London, 1811), 49. Courtesy, The Winterthur Library: Printed Book and Periodical Collection.

12. Lavater, *Pocket Lavater*, 27, 28–29, 31.

13. Marchioness de Lambert, *Essays on Friendship and Old-Age* (London, 1780), 130, 132.

14. Logan, 17:7.

15. J. G. Zimmerman, *Solitude; or, The Effects of Occasional Retirement* (London, 1797), 18, 228; Logan, 12:177, 10:98.

16. See Kathleen Woodward, *Figuring Age: Women, Bodies, Generations* (Bloomington, 1999); Edward Casey, *Remembering: A Phenomenological Study*, 2d ed. (Bloomington, 1989); and Edmund Sherman, *Reminiscence and the Self in Old Age* (New York, 1991).

17. Sara Ruddick, "Virtues and Age," in *Mother Time: Women, Aging, and Ethics*, ed. Margaret Urban Walker (Lanham, Md., 1999), 45–60.

18. Quoted in Premo, *Winter Friends*, 141.

19. Quoted in Simon Gratz, "Some Materials for the Biography of Mrs. Elizabeth Fergusson," *Pennsylvania Magazine of History and Biography* 41 (1917): 390. Like Logan, Fergusson begins "collecting" during the last twenty years of her life, copying her poems and those of others into commonplace books, thus reframing her memories through the creative process of reminiscence.

20. Cicero, *On Old Age and On Friendship*, trans. Frank O. Copley (Ann Arbor, 1967), 20.

21. Logan, 12:109.

22. Elizabeth Fergusson to Mrs. Smith, 21 April 1792, quoted in Gratz, "Some Materials," 393.

23. Marius D'Assigny, *The Art of Memory* (London, 1699), 17; Susan Pearce, *Museums, Objects, and Collections: A Cultural Study* (London, 1992), 47. The elderly in particular project meaning onto aesthetic objects that survive individual extinction, according to Harry Moody in "The Meaning of Life in Old Age," in *Aging and Ethics*, 51–92.

24. Elizabeth Graeme Fergusson, "An Old Woman's Meditations On an old Family Piece of Furniture," in "Selections 1797–1799" (Am .0670), HSP.

25. Johann Heinrich Cohausen, *Hermippus redivivus: or, The Sage's Triumph over Old Age and the Grave*, 3d ed. (London, 1771), 95. On the changing iconography of aging, see Thomas Cole, *The Journey of Life: A Cultural History of Aging in America* (Cambridge, 1992). See also *The Book of Health, Beauty, and Fashion* (London, 1837), 34–35, and *The Toilette of Health, Beauty, and Fashion* (Boston, 1834), 30–31, on the theory of humors and aging that circulated in the early Republic.

26. Susan Stewart, "Prologue: From the Museum of Touch," in *Material Memories*, ed. Marius Kwint, Christopher Breward, and Jeremy Aynsley (New York, 1999), 35.

27. Quoted in Stewart, "Prologue," 31.

28. Maurice Halbwachs, *On Collective Memory*, ed. Lewis A. Coser (Chicago, 1992), 168–69. I adapt Halbwachs's useful concept of collective "memory" to "reminiscence" since mnemonic objects are matters of recall rather than memory formation for the women in this book.

29. Halbwachs, 53.

30. Logan, 12:272.

31. For a fuller description of an identical dressing table, see Gerald W. R. Ward, *American Case Furniture in the Mabel Brady Garven and Other Collections at Yale University* (New Haven, 1988), 218–19. See also Benno Forman, "Furniture for Dressing in Early America, 1650–1730," *Winterthur Portfolio* (1987): 149–64, and *Vanity and Elegance: An Exhibition of the Dressing Table and Tall Chest in America, 1685–1785* (New York, 1992).

32. Logan, 10:128.

33. Logan, 1:255.

34. Barbara McLean Ward, *A Place for Everything: Chests and Boxes in Early Colonial America* (Winterthur, Del., 1986); William C. Ketchum, Jr., *Boxes* (New York, 1982). Sometimes small boxes were worn on the body close to the heart. Comfit boxes and etuis held toilet or sewing implements, and vinaigrettes (disguised as watches, books, or purses) hid an aromatic sponge.

35. Patches were particularly popular for concealing pox scars. Stylized into an elaborate semiotics by the French, patches could connote a woman's character: passionate, majestic, vivacious, wanton, caressing, forward, flirtatious, discreet, or light-fingered. See Serge Roche, Germain Courage, and Pierre Devinoy, *Mirrors,* trans. Colin Duckworth and Angus Munro (New York, 1985), and Antoine Le Camus, "Library of the Toilet," in *Abdeker: The Art of Preserving Beauty* (London, 1754), 230.

36. Logan, 12:118–19, 243; 14:154. She pasted these same scraps into her diary.

37. French for "little cloth," *toilette* referred to the dressing table, the decorative textile (made of satin, velvet, or tissue) beneath the dressing box, the hygiene accoutrement, and the act of cleansing and beautifying itself. The textile, moreover, was removed from the dressing table and wrapped around a woman's shoulders when she performed her toilette.

38. See John Stalker and George Parker, *Treatise of Japanning and Varnishing* (Oxford, 1688).

39. See Nicholas Lemery, *New Curiosities in Art and Nature; or, A Collection of the Most Valuable Secrets in all Arts and Sciences* (London, 1711). Courtesy, The Winterthur Library: Printed Book and Periodical Collection.

40. Hannah Robertson, *The Young Ladies School of Arts* (New York, 1777), 49. Courtesy, The Winterthur Library: Printed Book and Periodical Collection.

41. *The Toilet of Flora: A Collection of the Most Simple and Approved Methods of Preparing Baths, Essences, Pomatums, Powders, Perfumes, and Sweet-scented Waters,* 2d ed. (London, 1784). Courtesy, The Winterthur Library: Printed Book and Periodical Collection.

42. Richard Corson, *Fashions in Makeup: From Ancient to Modern Times* (New York, 1972), 248; *Mirror of Graces,* 55, 50–51.

43. James Stewart, *Plocacosmos; or, The Whole Art of Hairdressing* (London, 1782), 254. Courtesy, The Winterthur Library: Printed Book and Periodical Collection.

44. *Toilette of Rank and Fashion* (London, 1837), 67. Courtesy, The Winterthur Library: Printed Book and Periodical Collection.

45. *Toilette of Rank and Fashion,* 67–68, 34.

46. *Mirror of the Graces,* 50.

47. *Mirror of the Graces,* 42–43.

48. Elizabeth Fergusson, "A Paraphrase on the 12 Chapter of Eclesiastes The Contrast of Youth and Old Age (adrest to the rising generation)," commonplace book, 1796, HSP.

49. *Mirror of the Graces,* 229.

50. Corson, 189–90.

51. Two centuries old, this recipe was repeated in *Mirror of the Graces* (1811), 224, and *Toilette of Rank and Fashion* (1837), 73.

52. Women were told to avoid all dark colors, caps with ribbons, and any new fashions; maintain a cheerful yet contemplative countenance; conceal any peevishness or discontent; and avoid levity and other "counterfeits" of youth. See Premo, *Winter Friends,* 113–14. Logan frequently remarks on looking and acting one's age. See Logan, 1:255, 3:57, 7:103.

53. Lambert, 109.

54. *Mirror of the Graces,* 32.

55. *The Female Aegis; or, The Duties of Women from Childhood to Old Age* (London, 1798), 173–74.

56. Lambert, 112.

57. Logan, 8:121.

58. Sidney George Fisher remembers that Logan's "old age was indeed 'like a lusty winter, frostly but kindly,' as she herself used to say," in *A Philadelphia Perspective: The Diary of Sidney George Fisher* (Philadelphia, 1967), 72.

59. Quoted in Lambert, 98.

60. Fergusson, "A Paraphrase."

61. On bodily fluids, aging, and remedies, see *Toilette of Rank and Fashion,* 34–35, 67–68, 70, 226; and Stewart, *Plocacosmos,* 172, 175.

62. Manuscript 68.2.29, Stenton. Courtesy of The National Society of The Colonial Dames of America in the Commonwealth of Pennsylvania at STENTON, Philadelphia.

63. Transcribing Annis Stockton's manuscript poem "An Ode on the Advances of Old Age" into her commonplace book (HSP), Elizabeth Fergusson copies an "Extract of a Letter from Mrs. Stockton with the above," also dated Morven 1792.

64. "S. W. to Fidelia. In answer to the foregoing," in *Milcah Martha Moore's Book: A Commonplace Book from Revolutionary America,* ed. Catherine Blecki and Karin Wulf (University Park, Pa., 1997), 151. See also Hannah Griffitts's response, 149–50.

65. Quoted in "The Bartons of Lancaster in 1776," *Papers of the Lancaster County Historical Society* 52, 8 (1948): 216.

66. Griffitts, "The Query," Hannah Griffitts Papers, Library Company of Philadelphia (LCP).

67. Griffitts, "The Query."

68. Logan, 2:67, 3:20.

69. Griffitts, "A Glance of Character," Hannah Griffitts Papers, LCP.

70. Deborah Logan, "Twilight Musings," commonplace book, 1808, HSP.

71. Thomas Sheraton, *The Cabinet Maker's and Upholsterer's Directory* (London, 1802; rpt. New York, 1970), 403. Architecturally transitive, dressing and writing tables were often hybrid structures.

72. Logan, 12:60.

73. *Mirror of the Graces,* 52; Zimmerman, *Solitude,* 13, 68–69, 102.

74. Cohausen, *Hermippus redivivus,* 37–38.

75. Cohausen, *Hermippus redivivus,* 38.

76. Quoted in Premo, *Winter Friends,* 89.

77. Susan Stewart, *On Longing: Narratives of the Miniature, the Gigantic, the Souvenir, the Collection* (Durham, N.C., 1993), 150. See also Mieke Bal, "Telling Objects: A Narrative Perspective on Collecting," in *Cultures of Collecting,* 97–115. For another view, see Esther Leslie, "Souvenirs and Forgetting: Walter Benjamin's 'Memory Work,'" in *Material Memories.*

78. Here I diverge from Jean Baudrillard, who contends that "while the object is a resistant material body, it is also, simultaneously, a mental realm over which I hold sway, a thing whose meaning is governed by myself alone. It is all my own, the object of my passion." "The System of Collecting," in *Cultures of Collecting,* 7.

79. Elizabeth Fergusson to Mrs. Frazer, 20 April 1796, in Gratz, "Some Materials," 397.

80. Her poem, "Upon the Pleasures convey'd to us by writing; wrote on receiving Letters when in England from my Friends," dated from London, 25 February 1765, appears in her commonplace book, "Poemata Juvenilia," LCP. Graeme originally transcribed it in her travel journal, as Milcah Moore's extract illustrates (Blecki and Wulf, 207).

81. Elizabeth Fergusson to Mrs. Campbell, 14 June 1795, Gratz Collection, 1796, HSP.

82. Elizabeth Fergusson to Ann Ridgley, 25 December 1785, quoted in *What Them Befell: The Ridgleys of Delaware and Their Circle in Colonial and Federal Times, 1751–1890,* ed. Mabel Lloyd Ridgley (Portland, Maine, 1949), 42–43.

83. Hugh Blair, "On Epistolary Writing," Lecture 37 in *Lectures on Rhetoric and Belles Lettres,* 3 vols., 2d ed. (London, 1785), 2:67.

84. *Female Aegis,* 44–45.

85. Annis Stockton to Elizabeth Fergusson, 1769, quoted in Lyman Butterfield, "Morven: A Colonial Outpost of Sensibility," *Princeton University Library Chronicle* 6 (November 1944): 3.

86. Stewart, *On Longing,* 127. On the significance of the enclosed heart, see also Orest Ranum, "The Refuges of Intimacy," in *A History of Private Life,* vol. 3, *Passions of the Renaissance,* ed. Roger Chartier (Cambridge, 1989), 207–63.

87. Sarah Barton to Elizabeth Fergusson, 15 February 1794, in Gratz, "Some Materials," 317.

88. Sally Norris Dickinson to Deborah Logan, undated, Logan Family Papers, HSP.

89. Elizabeth Fergusson to Mrs. Campbell and Mrs. Fraser, 1 October 1798, in Gratz, "Some Materials," 407.

90. Hannah Griffitts Papers, LCP.

91. Logan, 16:361.

92. Elizabeth Fergusson, "An Advertisement," November 1774, Benjamin Rush Correspondence, LCP, 40:131–32.

93. My description of the mirror stages is indebted to Kathleen Woodward, "The Mirror Stage of Old Age," in *Memory and Desire: Aging, Literature, Psychoanalysis,* ed. Kathleen Woodward and Murray M. Schwartz (Bloomington, 1986), 97–113. See also Sally Gadow, "Recovering the Body in Aging," in *Aging and Ethics,* 113–20; and Ruddick, "Virtues and Age."

94. Elizabeth Graeme Fergusson, "The Four Stages of Life," in "Poemata Juvenilia," 152–59, LCP.

95. Secularized by the Renaissance, this life-stage motif lasted until the nineteenth century. By the eighteenth century, however, there was a distinct shift from the "ages" of man to the "stages" of life, condensing the seven ages into four discrete stages: childhood, youth, maturity, and old age. See Cole, "Oedipus and the Meaning of Aging" and *Journey of Life;* and James Burrows, *The Ages of Man* (New York, 1986).

96. Haim Hazan, *Old Age: Constructions and Deconstructions* (Cambridge, 1994). Though women were added to the visual iconography of the life stages by the seventeenth century, these stages were still inherently masculine: early modern theories that previously subsumed women under the category of men or ignored them altogether were replaced by Enlightenment concepts of sexual difference conveniently based on biology and domesticity in the eighteenth century.

97. *Female Aegis,* 27; Lambert, 95, 111.

98. The poems are copied into Elizabeth Fergusson's commonplace book, 1796, HSP. Both are published in *"Only for the Eye of a Friend": The Poems of Annis Boudinot Stockton,* ed. Carla Mulford (Charlottesville, 1995), 172–74.

99. Lambert, 54, 61.

100. Stewart, *Plocacosmos,* 358.

101. David Hume, *Essay on Human Nature,* ed. L. A. Selby-Bigge (Oxford, 1967), 365.

102. Diane Tietjens Meyers, "Miroir, Memoire, Mirage: Appearance, Aging, and Women," in *Mother Time,* 23–24.

103. *The Entertainer; Containing great Variety of Instructive Entertainment, For Persons of Every Age, Rank, or Degree,* collected by Charles Tell-Truth, 2 vols. (London, 1766), 83–84.

104. Charles Le Brun, *A Method to Learn to Design the Passions* (London, 1734), 13. Courtesy, The Winterthur Library: Printed Book and Periodical Collection.

105. Zimmerman, *Solitude,* 55.

106. Lambert, *Essays,* 42.

107. Zimmerman, *Solitude,* 39.

108. Logan, 1:7.

109. William Cowper, *Poetical Works of William Cowper* (London, 1872), 449–50.

110. Elizabeth Fergusson, "On the Minds being engross'd by one leading pursuit," in "Poemata Juvenilia" (LCP) and commonplace book (HSP).

111. Zimmerman, *Solitude,* 61, 19.

112. Elizabeth Fergusson, "Wrote to a Lady on the Back of a Fan," in "Poemata Juvenilia," 199–200, LCP.

113. Although my discussion describes the fan as a typical accoutrement of the eighteenth-century woman's dressing table, it became an indispensable part of her toilette by the next century's end. By the 1890s a "dressing case fan" included the entire toilet in the fan. Mounted on sticks, the center mask allowed a woman to apply her makeup while maintaining a polite view of her surroundings. The guards housed a small mirror on one side and a receptacle for hairpins, scissors, and the like on the other. At the fan's end, finally, was a small, silver powder box. See Bertha de Vere Green, *Fans over the Ages: A Collector's Guide* (New York, 1975), 94.

114. *Spectator* no. 102, quoted in *The Language of the Fan: An Exhibition at Fairfax House* (York, 1989), 32.

115. Printed in Gratz, "Some Materials," 279, the poem appears in Fergusson, "Poemata Juvenilia," LCP.

116. It is not clear, however, to what extent fan language was actually used. A faster alternative language was developed in Spain by Fenella and translated into German by Frau Bartholomeus and into English by the Parisian fanmaker Pierre Duvelleroy. In this system whole sentences rather than individual words were manually indicated. Fan language, critics believed, was known by men and women alike and was sometimes used between women, but

more typically men were the recipients. The number of courtship fans existing from the revolutionary and early national period suggests a predominantly heterosocial discourse. See de Vere Green, 84.

117. Le Brun, 21, 23.

118. Matthew Towle, *The Young Gentleman and Lady's Private Tutor* (London, 1770), 194–95.

119. Formal etiquette's imposition on whimsical fanology may have resulted from the increasing availability of inexpensive printed (rather than hand-painted) fans for women in Europe and British America. What was once the privilege of the courtly was now a sign of the middle class. Presented in etiquette books, fans marked idealized and stereotypical images in a kind of visual shorthand that signified the well-bred woman.

120. Similarly rejecting the imposition and expectation of courtship onto fan use, Hannah Griffitts writes a satiric poem, "To Sophronia"—on the back of a fan—to defend her choice of spinsterhood. Hannah Griffitts Papers, LCP. On single women, see Karin Wulf, *Not All Wives: Women of Colonial Philadelphia* (Ithaca, 2000).

121. Annis Boudinot Stockton, "The Restoration of a Stolen Fan," in *Only for the Eye of a Friend,* 250; Joseph Addison, *Spectator* no. 102, quoted in de Vere Green, 84–85.

122. Emblematic of the rococo craze for naturalistic ornament, shells were valued for their delicacy and variegated hues. Jean Baptiste Pillement, *Ladies Amusement,* 2d ed. (London, 1762), mentions fan decorating as a woman's pastime, and Robertson's *Young Ladies School of Arts* (1777) provides extensive directions for "Fan-Mounting." Her method emphasizes its similarity to arranging commonplace books (48–49).

123. Logan, 12:243.

124. Unlike the brise, or broken, fan (comprised of rigid sticks joined by interwoven ribbon at its top and a rivet at its base, and folding up between outer guards in a slightly overlapping position), the pleated fan bears a resemblance to a commonplace book. Opening, folding, and closing like a book, the pleated, or folding, fan evolved from small writing tablets used by court officials in China and Japan as early as the seventh century A.D. See Anna G. Bennett and Ruth Berson, eds., *Fans in Fashion* (San Francisco, 1981).

125. Quoted in David Farrell Krell, *Of Memory, Reminiscence, and Writing* (Bloomington, 1990), 62.

126. Anna Gray Bennett, *Unfolding Beauty: The Art of the Fan: The Collection of Esther Oldham and the Museum of Fine Arts, Boston* (New York, 1988), 23. Like mass-produced copybooks or printed images, fan leaves were made by copper engraving.

127. See *Folding Fans in the Cooper-Hewitt Museum* (Washington, D.C., 1986); Helene Alexander, *Fans* (London, 1984); Herbert Coutts, *The Indispensable Fan: The Story of the Fan in Society* (Edinburgh, 1984); Lady Charlotte Schreiber, *Catalogue of the Collection of Fans and Fan-Leaves* (London, 1803).

128. John Gay, *The Fan: A Poem in Three Books* (London, 1714), 3:30.

129. Elizabeth Fergusson, "Lines on Returning a Miniature Picture to the Lady that Desired It," in Gratz, 407–9.

130. Stewart, *On Longing,* 46.

131. Quoted in Ruel Pardee Tolman, *The Life and Works of Edward Greene Malbone, 1777–1807* (New York, 1958), 62.

132. Stewart, *On Longing,* 69.

133. Women were also taught the arts of miniature painting. In *The Spectator* for 1712, for example, Addison claims the arts of fan making and portrait miniatures as the domain of women: "Limning, one would think is no expensive Diversion, but . . . she paints fans for all her female acquaintance and draws all her relations in miniature." The *American Herald* for 7 March 1785 similarly argues: "Young Ladies, it is obvious, cannot accurately delineate with their needles sprigs, flowers, birds, or landscapes, without a regular initiation into this art."

134. Though the miniature's small size and delicate detail were first determined by the size of the book page, the word has come to mean all things small in its misleading association

with the Latin prefix *min* (expressing smallness). As a result, it has sometimes been disregarded by archivists as "trifling," "insignificant," and "scarcely worth arranging." See Katherine Coombs, *The Portrait Miniature in England* (London, 1998), 7, 12. See also Roy Strong, *The English Renaissance Miniature* (New York, 1983); and *The English Miniature,* ed. John Murdoch, Jim Murrell, Patrick Noon, and Roy Strong (New Haven, 1981).

On American portrait miniatures, see Robin Bolton-Smith, *Portrait Miniatures in the National Museum of American Art* (Chicago, 1984); Susan Strickler, *American Portrait Miniatures: The Worcester Art Museum* (Worcester, Mass., 1989); Martha Severens, *The Miniature Portrait in the Collection of the Carolina Art Association* (Charleston, 1984); Harry B. Wehle, *American Miniatures, 1730–1850* (New York, 1970); and Robin J. Frank, *Love and Loss: American Portrait and Mourning Miniatures* (New Haven, 2000).

135. First liberated from the manuscript page by artists at the courts of Henry VIII and Elizabeth I, these tiny portraits were designed as intimate, personal documents not kept by the subject of the likeness but rather given as mementos to loved ones. Housed in finely wrought "portrait boxes," they were worn around the neck on a ribbon, kept close to the heart on a lapel, or worn on the hand as a ring or bracelet. See Patricia Fumerton, " 'Secret' Arts: Elizabethan Miniatures and Sonnets," *Representations* 15 (1986): 57–97.

136. William Camden, *Remains* (London, 1607), quoted in Murdoch et al., "From Manuscript to Miniature," *English Miniature,* 68. As Camden explained: "There is required an Impress . . . a correspondency of the picture, which is as the body; and the Motto, which as the soul giveth life. That is the body must be of fair representation, and the word in some different language . . . most commended when [it is] a parcel of verse."

137. Camden, quoted in Fumerton, 69.

138. Painting miniatures is much the same as commonplacing, according to *The School of Miniature* (London, 1733). The method of combining parts to create a whole recalls the moveability of commonplaces: "Divide the whole Piece into many small and equal Squares, . . . we observe what is contain'd within each Square of the Piece we would Copy, as a Head, an Arm, a Hand . . . and where each is plac'd; all which you must punctually follow on your Paper, and having thus obtain'd the Situation of each part, we join the whole together" (7). Each square contains a memory image, which, rearranged and assembled, forms a complete countenance. Courtesy: The Winterthur Library: Printed Book and Periodical Collection.

139. William Byrd to John Perceval, 12 July 1736, *The Correspondence of the Three William Byrds of Westover, Virginia, 1684–1776,* 2 vols., ed. Marion Tinling (Charlottesville, 1977), 2:487.

140. Jonathan Richardson, *An Essay on the Theory of Painting,* 2d ed. (1725; rpt. Yorkshire, 1971), 74, 80.

141. Quoted in Margaretta M. Lovell, "Mrs. Sargent, Mr. Copley, and the Empirical Eye," *Winterthur Portfolio* 33, 1 (1988): 27. On stock or formulaic faces, see T. H. Breen, "The Meaning of 'Likeness': American Portrait Painting in an Eighteenth-Century Consumer Society," *Word and Image* 6, 4 (October–December 1990): 325–50. David Slotkin, *Painting for Money: The Visual Arts and the Public Sphere in Eighteenth-Century England* (New Haven, 1993), argues that stock faces helped forge class solidarity and friendship, much like my contention about portrait miniatures and collective memory.

142. Joshua Reynolds, Discourse 6, *Discourses on Art,* ed. Robert R. Wark (New Haven, 1981), 200. John Dryden similarly argues: "The imitation of nature is therefore justly constituted as the general and indeed the only, rule of pleasing, both in poetry and painting," in "A Parallel of Poetry and Painting" (1695), in *Selected Prose and Poetry of John Dryden,* ed. Earl Miner (New York, 1985), 480–500. His emphasis on pleasure elucidates mnemonic theories that suggest familiar and pleasurable images as the only proper and effective tools of memory.

143. Samuel Johnson, *Selected Poetry and Prose,* ed. Frank Brady and W. K. Winsatt (Berkeley, 1977), 90.

144. Reynolds, *Discourses on Art,* 200. The miniature concentrated on the face, shoulders,

and perhaps the hands, but in the 1790s a new kind of miniature came into vogue, depicting the single human eye, usually framed by part of the forehead and the curvature of the nose. These "eye miniatures," as they were called, were the ultimate refinement of "ideal presence" since the viewer had to supply not only the "expression" but also the rest of the face. My overview is indebted to Lance Bertelsen, "Jane Austen's Miniatures: Painting, Drawing, and the Novel," *Modern Language Quarterly* 45, 4 (1984): 350–72.

145. William Gilpin, *Observations, Relative Chiefly to Picturesque Beauty, Made in the Year 1772,* 2 vols. (London, 1786), 2:11–13.

146. Reynolds, *Discourses on Art,* 259.

147. Nicolas Hilliard, *The Art of Limning,* ed. R. K. R. Thornton and T. G. S. Cain (Manchester, 1981), 87. This edition is bound with Edward Norgate's treatise *A More Compendious Discourse Concerning the Art of Limning* (1648).

148. *School of Miniature,* 5–6.

149. Hilliard, 62.

150. Stewart, *On Longing,* 48.

151. My descriptions rely on Murdoch et al., "The Craft of the Miniaturist," 2.

152. John Payne, *The Art of Painting in Miniature* (London, 1820), 11. Courtesy, The Winterthur Library: Printed Book and Periodical Collection.

153. Payne, 12.

154. Emma Kendrick, *Conversations on the Art of Miniature Painting* (London, 1830), 14. Courtesy, The Winterthur Library: Printed Book and Periodical Collection.

155. Claude Boutet, *The Art of Painting in Miniature,* 6th ed. (London, 1752), 138. Courtesy, The Winterthur Library: Printed Book and Periodical Collection.

156. Payne, 19.

157. *The Complete Drawing Book* (London, 1740), 5–6. Courtesy, The Winterthur Library: Printed Book and Periodical Collection.

158. Wehle, 2–3.

159. Payne, 16.

160. Payne, 17.

161. *School of Miniature,* 36.

162. David Rosand, "Remembered Lines," in *Memory and Oblivion,* ed. W. Reinink and J. Stumpel (Boston, 1999), 811–16.

163. *The Literary Remains of Albrecht Dürer,* trans. William Martin Conway (Cambridge, 1889), 177, 247, quoted in Rosand, 812.

164. Quoted in Giovanni Perini, "Hogarth's Visual Mnemotechnics: Notes on Abstraction as an *aide-memoire* for Figurative Painters," in *Memory and Oblivion,* 837.

165. Charles F. Adams, Guernsey Jones, and Worthingon C. Ford, eds., *Letters and Papers of John Singleton Copley and Henry Pelham, 1739–1776* (Boston, 1914), 302–3.

166. *Art of Painting in Miniature,* 137.

167. This mnemonic transference seems to have continued into the nineteenth century, as Kendrick illustrates: "In painting, indeed, the mind requires two things to engage it at once, and the merely mechanical part should be relieved by something which will rouse the imagination into force" (102).

168. Painted in oil on vellum, tin, and copper, early miniatures probably used the identical cerulean white found in women's cosmetics. Recipes for paint and cosmetics appear in the same manuals. The *Young Ladies School of Arts* (1777) suggests "equal quantities of common water and vinegar, with the yolk, white, and shell of an egg, well beaten, . . . all its colours, then void of lustre, may be seen in all kinds of lights, which colours in oil, or covered with varnish cannot" (23–24), and the *School of Miniature* explains: "All the colours are temper'd in small ivory cups or in sea shells, with water, in which have been previously dissolv'd Gum-Arabic and Sugarcandy. The last prevents the Colours from scaling when applied, which they commonly do without it" (12). Similarly, Nicholas Lemery offers recipes for face and paint "varnishes" alike in *New Curiosities in Art and Nature,* 40–41, 108.

169. Some eighteenth-century miniaturists reportedly breathed on a painting after various color applications, mingling layers and giving it a smoother finish. See Murdoch et al., "Craft of the Miniaturist," 20.

170. Undated notation accompanying silhouette of Mary Ladd Parker, HSP, cited in Verplanck, 92–93 n. 43.

171. The silhouettes appear in a copy of Logan's commonplace book transcribed by Maria Dickinson Logan, wife of Albanus Charles Logan of Stenton, 26 December 1886. The silhouettes are of Mary Norris Logan and Elizabeth Logan (wife of J. Betton), daughters of Albanus Charles and Maria Dickinson Logan.

172. Rosand, 811.

173. See David Piper, *Shades: An Essay on English Portrait Silhouettes* (New York, 1970); Alice Van Leer Carrick, *A History of American Silhouettes: A Collector's Guide, 1790–1840* (Rutland, Vt., 1968); Helen and Nel Laughon, *Auguste Edouart: A Quaker Album: American and English Duplicate Silhouettes* (Richmond, 1987); and Victor Stoichita, *A Short History of the Shadow* (London, 1997).

174. Unlike the portrait miniature's liberation from the illuminated manuscript, however, silhouettes were preserved in books in a museumlike fashion, whereby viewers discreetly looked without touching. Unlike portrait miniatures, which invited human touch, silhouettes, warned the profilist Auguste Edouart in *A Treatise on Silhouette Likenesses* (London, 1835), are ruined by appreciative hands: "The practice [is] injurious to cuttings, in asmuch as they are too liable to be handled, and even destroyed by the rubbing of fingers" (14). Courtesy, The Winterthur Library: Printed Book and Periodical Collection.

175. According to Verplanck, from 1790 to 1850 Philadelphia-area Quakers largely eschewed oil portraits and miniatures for the simpler and less expensive silhouette. Quakers exchanged profiles within their intimate social circles and carefully assembled them into albums, reinforcing ties of friendship, kinship, and community (102).

176. Verplanck, 90.

177. Quoted in Edouart, 26.

178. *Aurora,* 13 August 1803. Unlike the personal process followed by women, Peale employed the African-American profilist Moses Williams in 1803 to cut profiles with the physiognotrace, saving the center cutouts in an album. Although "it would be too great a task for Mosis to write the Name on each, all are deserving of being remembered, for truly a great many of them are all block heads." *Charles Willson Peale: The Artist as Museum Keeper, 1791–1810,* in *The Selected Papers of Charles Willson Peale and His Family,* 3 vols., ed. Lillian Miller (New Haven, 1988), 2.2:916. Remembrance, as I have argued, depends on intimacy and proximity.

179. Other than images quickly produced by a physiognotrace, as discussed later, the cut-and-paste and hollow-cut methods were the most frequently used in late-eighteenth- and early-nineteenth-century America. From 1750 to 1860 some profilists painted in watercolor on card. After 1800 they used gold (called *bronzing*) to show detail on black profiles. Others painted on flat or convex glass, still others painted on ivory, and a few painted with pine soot (for color) and beer (as a fixative) on plaster. Sometimes called *composition,* this last method echoes the silhouette's distinctive textuality. See Sue McKenchie, *British Silhouette Artists and Their Work, 1750–1860* (Totowa, N.J., 1978). See also Peter Benes, "Machine-Assisted Portrait and Profile Imaging in New England after 1803," in "Painting and Portrait Making in the American Northeast," *Dublin Seminar for New England Folklife Annual Proceedings* 19 (Boston, 1996), 138–50, and Wendy Bellion, "The Mechanization of Likeness in Jeffersonian America," 19 December 1999, available online at http://web.mit.edu/comm-forum/papers/bellion.html. Some artists used printed lithograph bodies that were cut out, painted with watercolor, and pasted to paper on which a profile had been produced, as Blume J. Rifken illustrates in *Silhouettes in America, 1790–1840* (Burlington, Vt., 1987).

180. Quoted in Barbara Stafford, *Body Criticism* (Cambridge, Mass. 1991), 98.

181. E. Nevill Jackson, *Silhouette: Notes and Dictionary* (New York, 1938), 46.

182. Edouart, 18, 20. On the silhouette's indebtedness to neoclassicism, see Ellen Miles, *St. Memin and the Neoclassical Profile Portrait in America* (Washington, D.C., 1994).

183. Edouart, 25. Samuel Folwell (who painted George Washington's silhouette in India ink in 1791) and Major André (who cut profiles of Washington and Benjamin Franklin, among others, from 1773 to 1778) rank among other prominent Philadelphia profilists.

184. Logan, 3:119.

185. John Caspar Lavater, *Essays in Physiognomy,* vol. 3 (London, 1797).

186. John Jay Smith, *Recollections of John Jay Smith,* 3 vols. (Germantown, Pa., 1892), 1:292.

187. See Blecki and Wulf.

188. Charles Willson Peale to Rembrandt and Rubens Peale, 1 April 1803, in *Charles Willson Peale and His Family,* vol. 1 of *Selected Papers of Charles Willson Peale,* 517. The physiognotrace made silhouettes so popular, in fact, that Peale threatened legal action to preserve his copyright two months later: "Various are the attempts to take advantage of the rage for profiles, by our sundry Citizens, and I suspect that I shall be obelged to punish some by making them pay the penalty provided by the Patent act, which will amount to a large sum, being three times the Value of my right in the use of such a Machine exclusively in the City of Philadelphia and the Liberties." *Charles Willson Peale,* 537.

189. David R. Brigham, *Public Culture in the Early Republic: Peale's Museum and Its Audience* (Washington, D.C., 1995), 71–72.

190. The advertisement, reprinted in *Selected Papers of Charles Willson Peale,* 2.1:478, was originally published in the *Aurora,* 28 December 1802.

191. Edouart, 22.

192. Cicero, *Cato Major, or His Discourse on Old Age,* trans. James Logan (Philadelphia, 1744), 15.

193. Reiterating Cicero's gendered omission, most theorists of aging throughout the eighteenth and early nineteenth centuries exclusively considered men in their treatises. See, for example, Bulstrode, *Of Old Age:* "None can imagine how green and vigorous some Mens Minds are in Old Age. . . . It is certainly a particular Happiness to preserve the Force of the Mind in the Decay of the Body" (383).

194. Elizabeth Fergusson, "Il Penseroso, or The Deserted Wife," 1780–82, in Rush Correspondence, vol. 40, LCP.

195. Bulstrode, 383; Lambert, 93–94.

196. Logan, 11:144.

197. Logan, 11:1–2.

198. Logan, 8:164.

199. Fisher, *Philadelphia Perspective,* 72.

200. *Gentleman's and London Magazine* (1792), quoted in Corson, *Fashions in Makeup,* 265.

201. Susanna Wright, untitled poem, July 24 1722; quoted in Blecki and Wulf, 125.

CHAPTER 4. IN MEMORIAM

1. John Locke, *An Essay Concerning Human Understanding,* ed. A. S. Pringle-Pattison (Oxford, 1924), bk. 2, chap. 10, 80.

2. Hannah Griffitts Papers, 24 February 1803, Library Company of Philadelphia (LCP). The entire elegy cycle is in the LCP's collection. Hereafter I refer to the elegies by author and date.

3. Embalming (of the upper classes) was practiced in England during the eighteenth century but began in the United States only during the Civil War. According to Virginia Russell-Remsberg, doctors initially performed the task, given their training in specimen preservation and anatomy, but undertakers trained at embalming schools took over the practice by the 1880s, although even then preservation was the exception rather than the rule. "From Coffin-Making to Undertaking: The Rise of the Funeral Directing Industry in the 1880s" (M.A. thesis, Winterthur, 1992). See also Robert Habenstein and William Lamers, *The History of American Funeral Directing* (Milwaukee, 1955); Gary Laderman, *The Sacred Re-*

mains: *American Attitudes toward Death, 1799–1883* (New Haven, 1996); and Christine Quigley, *The Corpse: A History* (Jefferson, N.C., 1996).

4. Griffitts, 1775.

5. William Kenrick, *The Whole Duty of Woman* (Exeter, 1794), 54. Courtesy, The Winterthur Library: Printed Book and Periodical Collection.

6. Griffitts, 1756.

7. For standard readings of death in early America, see Jessica Mitford, *The American Way of Death* (New York, 1963); David Stannard, *The Puritan Way of Death: A Study in Religion, Culture, and Social Change* (New York, 1977); Philippe Ariès, *The Hour of Our Death* (New York, 1982) and *Death in America,* ed. David Stannard (Philadelphia, 1975); Margaret Coffin, *Death in Early America* (Nashville, 1976); and *Mortal Remains: Death in Early America,* ed. Nancy Isenberg and Andrew Burnstein (Philadelphia, 2003).

8. *Oxford English Dictionary.*

9. William Alexander, *The History of Women* (Philadelphia, 1796), 296. Courtesy, The Winterthur Library: Printed Book and Periodical Collection.

10. In *The English Elegy: Studies in the Genre from Spenser to Yeats* (Baltimore, 1985), Peter Sacks describes the pastoral elegy's masculine method whereby the male mourner, trying to overcome or conquer his grief, uses traditional conventions: the sexualized vegetation deity, repetition and refrains, reiterated questions, violent outbursts, the procession of mourners, the movement from grief to consolation, and standard images of resurrection.

11. Here I agree with the feminist critic Celeste Schenk's conceptualization of the female elegy in *Mourning and Panegyric: The Poetics of Pastoral Ceremony* (University Park, Pa., 1988). See also Melissa F. Zeiger, *Beyond Consolation: Death, Sexuality, and the Changing Shape of Elegy* (Ithaca, 1997), and Juliana Schiesari, *The Gendering of Melancholia: Feminism, Psychoanalysis, and the Symbolics of Loss in Renaissance Literature* (Ithaca, 1993).

12. The Protestant Reformation's replacement of Purgatory with *memoria* stressed the didactic potential of the lives and deaths of the virtuous, as Nigel Llewellyn argues in *The Art of Death: Visual Culture in the English Death Ritual, 1500–1800* (London, 1991), 28. Llewellyn discerns three bodies of death: the corpse's natural, decaying body; the social body sustained in postmortem artifacts; and the monumental body of portraits serving as a memento mori and promise of resurrection. On death's natural and metaphysical bodies, see Robert St. George, "Embodied Spaces," in *Conversing by Signs: Poetics of Implication in Colonial New England Culture* (Chapel Hill, 1998), 116–203.

13. Griffitts, 1762.

14. Griffitts, 1781.

15. Richard Cecil, *A Friendly Visit to the House of Mourning* (New York, 1830), 37, LCP. Other consolation writers similarly describe excessive mourning as engulfment. Benjamin Grosvenor, for instance, writes in *The Mourner: or, The Afflicted Relieved* (Philadelphia, 1791), LCP, that grief is "ready to devour" the mourner; we may be "entirely swallowed up in our private griefs" (4–5). Courtesy, Library Company of Philadelphia.

16. Griffitts, 1798.

17. Griffitts, 1758.

18. Griffitts, 1752.

19. Grosvenor, 53–54.

20. John Weaver, *Ancient Funerall Monuments* (London, 1631), 15. Logan was still reading from Weaver's text in 1815, as she transcribed a prototypical memento mori in her diary:

> Time was, I stood where thou dost now
> And view'd the Dead as thou dos't me,
> E'er long thou'lt lie low as I
> And others stand and look on thee.

Deborah Logan, manuscript diary, 17 vols., 1:103, Historical Society of Pennsylvania (HSP), Philadelphia. I cite Logan's diary by volume and page number throughout the chapter.

21. Cecil, 19, 21.

22. Margaret Urban Walker, "Moral Understanding," in *Explorations in Feminist Ethics,* ed. Eve Browning Cole and Susan Coultrap-McQuin (Bloomington, 1992). I thank Marian Eide for this helpful reference.

23. Griffitts, 1759. Griffitts approaches heavenly proportion as her laments subside with her growing proximity to death and reunion with her mother, following Grosvenor's suggestion that "the measures of mourning are represented to lessen in proportion as men are nearer to God" (7). Richard Allestree explains in *The Whole Duty of Mourning* (London, 1695) that the "our Faith to God-ward is demonstrated." Framing grief's proportions in geometric space makes mourning another mnemonic art.

24. Allestree, 8.

25. Griffitts, 1759.

26. Griffitts, 1751.

27. Griffitts, 1783.

28. Griffitts, 1763.

29. Allestree, 6.

30. Griffitts, 1778.

31. Grosvenor, 66–68.

32. Griffitts, 1753.

33. Griffitts, 1794.

34. Freud's letter to Binswanger, 12 April 1929, in *Letters of Sigmund Freud,* ed. E. L. Freud (New York, 1961), 386. Though criticized for its goal-oriented emphasis on displacing the dead, achieving consolation, and returning to the reality of living, Freud's masculine model of mourning in his classic essay "Mourning and Melancholia" offers a useful frame for my discussion of female mourning and memory. Freud might read Griffitts's resistance to consolation as the feminine descent from grief into melancholy, but his language resonates with my ongoing argument about nostalgia and collective reminiscence: there is an inherent gap between experience, the memory of that experience, and the recollection of that memory. But this gap is precisely what initiates and sustains our desire to look back. Detachment does not defer mourning; it makes it possible. See Sigmund Freud, "Mourning and Melancholia," in *The Standard Edition of the Complete Psychological Works of Sigmund Freud,* 24 vols., ed. James Strachey (London, 1953), 14:243–58. See also George Hagman, "The Role of the Other in Mourning," *Psychoanalytic Quarterly* 65 (1996): 327–40.

35. Grosvenor, 99.

36. Griffitts, 1751.

37. Griffitts, 1753, 1758. As the common lexicon in eighteenth-century sentimental novels, tears find their antidote in consolation literature. "Moderate weeping is most highly Commended, for it expresseth a natural affection we had to the departed, but with a Christian-like moderation of our Grief, whereby our Faith to God-ward is demonstrated" (Allestree, 155). Rev. John Flavel similarly contends in *A Token for Mourners* (Boston, 1729): "Ah, cease to weep longer for your deceas'd relation, and weep rather for your dead heart" (16–17).

38. Grosvenor, 6–7.

39. Griffitts, 1777.

40. Griffitts, 1776.

41. Griffitts, 1791 (written in 1792), 1789. The image of wax seal impressions recurs throughout the elegy cycle, also appearing in 1761, 1774, and 1781.

42. Griffitts, 1751.

43. Here I paraphrase the moral philosophers of the Scottish school (including Adam Smith, David Hume, and Francis Hutcheson), whose works were widely read by Griffitts and her circle. Responding to Smith's queries in his *Theory of Moral Sentiments,* for example, Elizabeth Fergusson composes a poem, "Lines Written in the Margins of Smith's Theory of Morals," in "Poemata Juvenilia," LCP.

44. Griffitts, 1754.

45. Grosvenor, 9.

46. Griffitts, 1794, 1763.

47. Griffitts, 1753.

48. My thoughts on female epistemology and experiential knowledge have been influenced by many feminist critics, among them Elizabeth Grosz, *Volatile Bodies: Toward a Corporeal Feminism* (Bloomington, 1994); Diana Fuss, *Essentially Speaking: Feminism, Nature, and Difference* (New York, 1989); and Linda Alcoff and Elizabeth Potter, eds., *Feminist Epistemologies* (New York, 1993).

49. Grosvenor, 4; Flavel, 8–9.

50. Griffitts, 1755. She sends a copy of the elegy to Elizabeth Norris at Fairhill.

51. Philebus to Socrates, in *The Collected Dialogues of Plato,* ed. Edith Hamilton and Huntington Cairns (Princeton, 1961), 34b, 1112.

52. Consolation literature from the Renaissance through the nineteenth century argued for moderate grieving practices. See Patricia Phillippy, *Woman, Death and Literature in Post-Reformation England* (New York, 2002).

53. Robert Dodsley, *The Oeconomy of Human Life* (London, 1798), 41. Courtesy, The Winterthur Library: Printed Book and Periodical Collection.

54. Cecil, 39; Grosvenor, 5–6.

55. Robert Blair, *The Grave* (London, 1743).

56. Cecil, 39; Grosvenor, 27–28.

57. Logan writes two accounts of Griffitts's death, which I combine here. The first, from which I initially quote, appears in Logan's manuscript diary at the Historical Society of Pennsylvania. This version is mostly narrative and interrupted (in typical diary fashion) by Logan's daily obligations; the second account is more dramatic, interpolating direct quotations by Griffitts. The second version, "Some account of the last illness of my dear Cousin Hannah Griffitts who departed this life the 24th 8th month 1817. in the ninety first year of her age," is from the Haverford College Library, Quaker Collection. Explaining her intentions for future readers, Logan writes: "My beloved cousin H. Griffitts having been much favour'd in her last illness, I have thought the following account of some of her expressions might not be unacceptable to some of her friends." Perhaps afraid that her diary would be neither preserved nor read by posterity, Logan ensured her cousin's memory with an additional essay.

58. Logan, 3:28.

59. Allestree, 16; Logan, 6:12.

60. Logan, 13:287.

61. Allestree, 31.

62. Quoted in Barbara Stafford, *Body Criticism: Imagining the Unseen in Enlightenment Art and Medicine* (Cambridge, Mass., 1994), 100.

63. Logan, 13:288.

64. *The Mourners Book: By a Lady* (Philadelphia, 1836), 19. LCP.

65. In 1802, for instance, the Philadelphia Quaker Elizabeth Drinker perused the tenth edition of Charles Drelincourt's *The Christian's Defence against the Fears of Death, with Seasonable Directions how to Prepare ourselves to Die well* (1721), translated into English by Marius D'Assigny, the celebrated author of *The Art of Memory* (London, 1699). *The Diary of Elizabeth Drinker,* 3 vols., ed. Elaine Forman Crane (Boston, 1991), 2:1604 (hereafter cited by volume and page number).

66. *A Collection of Memorials Concerning Divers deceased Ministers and others of the People called Quakers in PA, NJ, and Parts adjacent, from nearly the first Settlement therof to the Year 1787* (Philadelphia, 1787). Courtesy, The Winterthur Library: Printed Books and Periodical Collection.

67. *Collection of Memorials,* 373, 316, 313, 331–32.

68. There are at least two extant copies of this poem: one in the Hannah Griffitts Papers (LCP) and the other in Deborah Logan's (1808) commonplace book, HSP. The shared tran-

scription illustrates how women textually reinforced their status as experienced mourners. In addition, Griffitts wrote an undated poem, "Wrote on Reading Some Memorials of [Susanna] Lightfoot, in her last Illness," Hannah Griffitts Papers.

69. *Mourner's Book,* 21. Logan fills her diary with physiognomic descriptions of the "beautiful death." Whereas she remembers her husband George Logan's "Look of 'still calm majesty,'" she depicts her niece as an angel, whose "countenance serene, and her lips a little parted as if her Soul had escaped in a gentle aspiration thro their portal, her cheek rested upon her hand, and her whole appearance indicated that the final dismissal had been without a pang." Logan, 7:74, 5:88–89.

70. Allestree, 58.

71. Grosvenor, 100–101.

72. Allestree, 65.

73. Allestree, 60, quotes 1 Corinthians 2.9.

74. Susan Stewart, "Death and Life, in that Order, in the Works of Charles Willson Peale," in *The Cultures of Collecting,* ed. John Elsner and Roger Cardinal (London, 1994), 295. Here she refers to E. Levinas's work on countenance and oblivion in *Totality and Infinity: An Essay on Exteriority,* trans. A. Lingis (The Hague, 1961; rpt. Pittsburgh, 1969).

75. Some artists took plaster casts (much like ancient death masks) as a model from which to paint; others expeditiously painted the corpse as it lay in state; and still others painted from the recital of a relative's memory. Describing postmortem silhouettes, Auguste Edouart explains in *A Treatise on Silhouette Likenesses* (London, 1835) that family members of the deceased would memorize and then narrate the corpse's face to him, and he, in turn, would translate those verbal memories into more permanent, visual images: "I have had some who were so touched when I had finished, that they were nearly fainting; it would seem by the effect it produces, those scenes are not without making strong impressions upon my mind, from the recollection it brings forward of my own losses" (19). Affected by his patrons' responses to the completed silhouette, Edouart himself begins a process of recollection, reliving past bereavement.

76. Logan, 15:257, 256, 346, 254. For a scandalous example of postmortem portraiture, see Logan's diary, 13:9, describing Elias Hicks's covert exhumation by friends (who desired a cast of his head) and again by the angry Hicks family (who found residual plaster in his hair).

77. *Charles Willson Peale: Artist in Revolutionary America, 1735–1791: The Selected Papers of Charles Willson Peale and His Family,* 3 vols., ed. Lillian B. Miller (New Haven, 1983), 1:380.

78. *School of Miniature* (London, 1733), 40. Courtesy, The Winterthur Library: Printed Book and Periodical Collection.

79. Samuel Rogers, *The Pleasures of Memory,* 9th ed., 2 vols. (London, 1796), 1:253–60.

80. Allestree, 49.

81. Logan, 3:28.

82. Thomas Greenhill, *Nekrokedeia, or the Art of Embalming* (London, 1705), 13.

83. Logan, 3:28. Eighteenth-century midwife Martha Ballard similarly comments on the seasonal difficulties of preserving corpses, in *The Diary of Martha Ballard, 1785–1812,* ed. Robert R. McCausland and Cynthia Mac Alman McCausland (Camden, Minn., 1992), 13 April 1790, 157.

84. If I read Ballard's diary correctly, laying out the body took two to four hours: "I Left home about three O Clock PM," she writes, and "went as far as Daviss Store. was Calld to Colon Howards to asist Mrs Pollard & Bisby Lay out the Corpse of his wife just now Deceast. . . . I returnd home a Little after Sun Set." 28 October 1785, *Diary of Martha Ballard,* 19.

85. Teresa Flanagan, *Mourning on the Pejepscot* (Lanham, Md., 1992), 43. In her diary Elizabeth Drinker alludes to the practice of stuffing bran around the coffined body: "There was some little change, and it was thought best to screw it up with a quantity of bran" (2:1324).

86. Russell-Remsberg, "From Coffin-Making to Undertaking"; Quigley, *Corpse.*

87. They may also have hired a professional woman, as Elizabeth Drinker's diary entry for July 1800 suggests: "Molly Humphries who attends on funerals, was here this forenoon"

(2:1325). Women were involved in the business of funerals as early as 1752, as the *Pennsylvania Gazette* for 17 March indicates: "Mary Leech, is moved from her house in Coomb's alley, to a house in Market street, next door to Samuel Grisley's; where any person may be supply'd with mourning, & c. for funerals, as usual." By 1810 *The Philadelphia Directory* listed about a dozen women as "Layers Out of the Dead."

88. Allestree, 19.

89. A complement to her anecdote of Elias Hicks's exhumation is Logan's story about Quaker George Fox's premature wake and near burial in France. After apparently eating a child's half-baked cake, Fox lapsed into a coma. He was washed and laid out in white satin as the funeral preparations were made. A medical friend paying his respects moved him from the coffin into a warm bed, where he revived (and lived forty more years). Logan, 12:62.

90. Logan, 16:193.

91. Mary Cole, "Directions for the recovery of the Apparently Dead," in *The Lady's Complete Guide* (London, 1791), 439–40. Eighteenth-century Americans read many sources on the topic of resuscitation, including the physician Benjamin Rush's *Essay on Vital Suspension: Being an Attempt to Investigate and to Ascertain Those Diseases, in which the Principles of Life are Apparently Extinguished, by a Medical Practitioner* (London, 1741). Benjamin Franklin advertises another (somewhat salacious) text in the *Pennsylvania Gazette* for 9 October 1746: *The Uncertainty of the Signs of Death, and the Danger of Precipitate Interments and Dissections Demonstrated.*

92. Grosvenor, 104.

93. Cole, 439–40; Elizabeth Fergusson, "Cadavera's Ghost; or a Visit to Tomboso," in Benjamin Rush Papers, HSP.

94. See Nancy Vickers, "Blazing Beauties: Marot's Poetic Anatomies," in *The Body in Parts: Fantasies of Corporeality in Early Modern Europe*, ed. Carla Mazzio and David Hillman (New York, 1997), and Jonathan Sawday, *The Body Emblazoned: Dissection and the Human Body in Renaissance Culture* (New York, 1997). Though not technically considered embalming, dissection often accompanied autopsies in eighteenth-century America, as Martha Ballard's diary suggests (526). Laurel Thatcher Ulrich amplifies this point in *A Midwife's Tale: The Life of Martha Ballard, Based on Her Diary, 1785–1812* (New York, 1991), 235–61.

95. Greenhill, 9.

96. Greenhill, 105. Since Protestants rejected the idea of Purgatory, believing instead in the immediate deliverance of the soul to its immortal resting place, embalming was a sacrilege. For more on early modern embalming, see Ariès, *Hour of Our Death,* 361.

97. There is scattered evidence of disembowelment in seventeenth-century New England, but it seems to be the exception rather than the rule. Whereas eighteenth-century embalming practices in England entailed draining the body's blood through several incisions, making arterial injections of preserving fluid, and packing cavities with camphor, Americans kept the corpus whole, treating exterior symptoms of decay with fragrances and waxed cerecloth. Even when Victorian funeral directors advocated arterial embalming in the late nineteenth century, according to Russell-Remsberg, Americans remained resistant to chemical preservation, opting for more expensive refrigeration (34), reflecting the mainstream Protestant reluctance to tamper with nature.

98. Trying unsuccessfully to acquire an embalmed body to display in his natural history museum, Charles Willson Peale shows an explicit interest in embalming practices as early as 1793. "The preservation of human bodies has for many years engaged the thoughts of some of my leisure hours," he writes, "& I have devised various means to effect it, some more perfectly than others as well as more or less expensive." See *Peale: The Artist as Museum-Keeper,* 2.2:945–48.

99. Greenhill, prefatory poem, n.p.

100. Annis Boudinot Stockton, "An Elegy on the death of Mrs. Wilson," 19 April 1786, in *"Only for the Eye of a Friend": The Poetry of Annis Boudinot Stockton,* ed. Carla Mulford

(Charlottesville, 1996), 133–34. Hereafter poems from this volume are cited by title and page number.

101. Stockton, "An elegiack Ode on the 28th day of February [1782]," 112–13.

102. This poem is by James Thomson. Elizabeth Graeme Fergusson, commonplace book, 232–33, HSP.

103. Stockton, "To Doctor Rush," 1782, 114.

104. Stockton, "Fragment on the death of a minester," 249.

105. Griffitts, "To the Memory of my Valued friend Reb[ecca] Steel who died at Phila[delphia], Dec. 27th 1783," Hannah Griffitts Papers, LCP.

106. Stockton, "Lines on the Death of Mrs. Petit of Philadelphia," 137–38.

107. Stockton, "A Short Elegy to the Memory of Her Husband," 99.

108. Griffitts, "Pestilence—the awful 1798," 17 November 1798, Hannah Griffitts Papers, LCP.

109. Griffitts, "The (Only) safe Restoring Peace," May 1801, Hannah Griffitts Papers, LCP.

110. Philibert Guibert, *The Charitable Physician,* trans. I. W. (London, 1639), 143–44. I thank Patricia Phillippy for this source.

111. Peter Stallybrass, "Worn Worlds: Clothes, Mourning, and the Life of Things," in *Cultural Memory and the Construction of Identity,* ed. Dan Ben-Amos and Liliane Weissberg (Detroit, 1999), 36–37.

112. Greenhill, prefatory poem, n.p.

113. Representative of the other elegies to her mother, these images are taken from the 1751, 1753, and 1757 poems.

114. Logan, 6:105.

115. According to funerary advertisements in local newspapers, corpses were buried in cotton or linen winding sheets or shrouds until sometime in the mid-nineteenth century. In the October 1754 *Pennsylvania Gazette* British upholsterers James White and Thomas Lawrence announced, "Funerals furnished, and shrouds ready made, as in London," and another advertisement said, "Funerals furnished, and shrouds ready made, pink'd as in London, or plain and plaited, and sheets." According to Margaret Coffin, shrouds were typically rectangular with drawstrings at the top. *Death in Early America,* 73, 101. Both Martha Ballard's and Deborah Logan's diaries provide evidence that female corpses were sometimes buried in plain white shifts. Though Ballard typically uses the generic term "Grave Cloaths," she also mentions receiving "a pair of Sheets for 2 Do & 2 Shifts which I Carried to Lay out the [Dead]" (699). The shifts, I imagine, were either an option to the winding sheet or worn over the tightly wrapped body for an angelic effect, as in Logan's description of Sally Johnson: "She was setting in the easy chair dressed in a loose dress of white dimity with her hair fancifully arranged in full curl—the effect discordant and indeed something shocking, it seemed like dressing up a victim of Death, her chamber was as nice as possible—a white Bed and curtains and made very comfortable by a stove" (12:150).

116. Logan, 12:262.

117. Logan, 4:84.

118. Quoted in Anne H. Ousterhout's biography of Elizabeth Graeme Fergusson, *The Most Learned Woman in America* (University Park, Pa., 2003).

119. Stallybrass, 30.

120. See chapter 2 for more on eighteenth-century paper's derivation from cloth.

121. Logan, 15:266, 269.

122. Logan, 11:3–4.

123. Stallybrass, 30.

124. Gerald Ward, *American Case Furniture in the Mabel Brady Garvan and Other Collections at Yale University* (New Haven, 1988), 7–8.

125. Both the Cooperstown Museum and the Museum of American Mourning (Drexel, Pa.) have coffins with viewing windows.

126. Logan, 9:10.

127. Grosvenor, 23.
128. Allestree, 157.
129. Flanagan, 39.
130. Weaver, 17.
131. Here she recounts the death of her niece, Debby Norris Logan (5:28–29).
132. Logan, 1:86, 13:168.
133. Logan's description of her husband's funeral just a few months earlier (4:63–64). Although her accounts of other funerals always include a meal (sometimes before, other times after burial), I suspect that participation in dining practices was dictated by one's intimacy with the deceased. In George Logan's case, she explains that "according to his often expressed desire we designed it to be private and only for our relatives and particular friends" (4:63–64). This is a marked divergence from the earlier European tradition of hiring a male sin-eater for a sixpence to eat and drink over the corpse, symbolically swallowing the dead's sins and ensuring a pure passage to the afterlife.
134. Logan, 7:80–83.
135. Allestree, 55; Grosvenor, 53–54.
136. Allestree, 55.
137. Luke 23.27–31.
138. Griffitts, "On the Death of John Roberts and Abraham Carlisle," 9 November 1778, Hannah Griffitts Papers, LCP.
139. Annis Stockton, "Ill penserosa, an ode," 238–39.
140. Eighteenth-century mourning etiquette was strict for those who could afford to follow it: widows, widowers, and children wore mourning attire for twelve months; grandparents for nine months; siblings for six months; and aunts and uncles for three months.
141. *Mourners Book,* 60–61.
142. George Whitefield's farewell sermon in St. Paul's Church, printed in the *Pennsylvania Gazette,* 23 May 1765. See Frank Lambert, *Pedlar in Divinity: George Whitefield and the Transatlantic Revival, 1737–1770* (Princeton, 1994).
143. Women's mourning duties, it seems, sometimes defied class boundaries altogether. When her spinner, Mary Kain, died, Logan recorded: "Poor Mary Kain died this afternoon, to my sorrow and regret, a devoted adherent of mine, my best Spinner, the affectionate wife of Old Mickey, who had been a labourer on the farm time out of mind. . . . Thus it is that I here write her Eulogy, the only one she will probably ever have but it is no matter, the most splendid names are only rescued for a brief space from the Gulph of Oblivion. And I doubt not 'the single talent well employed' has gained her a seat in the realms of Peace.—I feel however as if I had lost a friend—a sincere and humble one" (6:112). Identifying with Kain, Logan realizes that they are not only the same age but also linked by a gendered connection to cloth. Kain wove the linen for George Logan's shirts, which Deborah Logan kept as a remembrance after his death.
   Though crossing class boundaries, women typically stayed on their side of the racial divide, according to Drinker. Describing a "Negro funeral" in 1798, she writes: "A Negro burying past our door going up town, in different order from any I have ever before seen, six Men went before the Coffin, one with a book in his hand, they sang aloud, psalms, I suppose, in a very loud and discordant voice: a large concourse follow'd. Methodists, I take them to be" (2:1043).
144. Susanna Wright, "A Meditation," in *Milcah Martha Moore's Book: A Commonplace Book from Revolutionary America,* ed. Catherine Blecki and Karin Wulf (University Park, Pa., 1997), 133.
145. Whitefield, farewell sermon; Hannah Griffitts, undated poem, "Monumental Vanity," Hannah Griffitts Papers, LCP.
146. Elizabeth Stedman to Mrs. Senior, 6 April 1801, quoted in Chester T. Hallenbeck, "The Life and Collected Poems of Elizabeth Graeme Fergusson" (M.A. thesis, Columbia University, 1929), 177–80.
147. Logan excerpts Griffitts's poem in her essay account of her cousin's death, Edward

Wanton Smith Papers, Haverford College Library, Quaker Collection; Logan, 15:147. She also remarks: "I went to the funeral of dear Jane Shoemaker. . . . The funeral was prodigiously large. I think the procession must have been more than a mile in length and the meeting house was crowded with people" (6:111).

148. Logan, 12:263.

149. *Diary of Anna Green Winslow: A Boston Schoolgirl of 1771,* ed. Alice Morse Earl (Bedford, Mass., 1996), 9, 18.

150. "Extracts from the Journal of Sarah Eve: Written while Living near the City of Philadelphia in 1772–73," *Pennsylvania Magazine of History and Biography* 5 (1881): 195.

151. Arthur Singleton in 1814 confounds this tradition, witnessing at a funeral procession "a relick of an ancient custom, now rare, that the deceased youth should be supported to the grave by the opposite sex." Both are quoted in John T. Faris, *The Romance of Old Philadelphia* (Philadelphia, 1918), 199.

152. Genealogy samplers, popularized at the end of the eighteenth century, were continually updated or revised texts, as girls added—in black thread—the dates of death as they occurred.

153. Logan, 12:60, 7:64.

154. Logan, 12:262–65.

155. Female friends, neighbors, or even hired midwives typically assisted families in preparing the corpse, but some evidence exists (Martha Ballard's diary, for example) that men helped by lifting the corpse into the coffin, and the cabinetmaker turned undertaker may have assisted in removing the body from the house. Solely responsible for laying out the dead until the professionalization of funeral directing in the 1880s, American women were barred from this profession, much as male midwives and obstetricians superseded midwives.

156. Logan, 2:133.

157. Simon Gratz, "Some Materials for the Biography of Mrs. Elizabeth Fergusson," *Pennsylvania Magazine of History and Biography* 41 (1917): 391.

158. Griffitts, "To the Worthy Memory of my Valued Friend Benjamin Trotter, who Died March 11, 1768," Hannah Griffitts Papers, LCP.

159. Susanna Wright, "Untitled," in Blecki and Wulf, 131.

160. Susanna Wright, "A Fragment," in Blecki and Wulf, 139.

161. Wright, "Untitled," in Blecki and Wulf, 131.

162. Recent scholars have connected domestic architecture to gravestone art, focusing specifically on the door and its resonant liminality between life and death. For example, see St. George, *Conversing by Signs,* 371–73, 389–95. But since the door likewise signifies the ideological boundary between the private and public spheres, and since women, as chapter 1 argues, are associated with domestic interiors, eighteenth-century American women, I maintain, moved beyond the door and into the house. See *The Comfortable Chambers Opened and Visited* (Boston, 1796), 12.

163. Wright, "A Meditation" and "On Death," in Blecki and Wulf, 133–34, 137–38.

164. Robert Blair, *The Grave: A Poem* (London, 1743).

165. Locke, bk. 2, chap. 10, 81.

166. Blair, 39.

167. Blair, 36.

168. Allestree, 8.

169. As both tombstones and pattern books illustrate, late-eighteenth- and early-nineteenth-century gravestones—with their neoclassical urns, weeping willows, and female mourners—continued to resemble the curtained swags of the bed canopy, but the emphasis was switched from the mortal to the living remains. The mourners, and the responsibility of the living to remember the dead, I would argue, characterize these stones. See Anita Schorsch, "A Key to the Kingdom: The Iconography of a Mourning Picture," *Winterthur Portfolio* 14, 1 (1979): 41–71, and *Mourning Becomes America: Mourning Art in the New Nation* (Clinton, N.J., 1976).

170. Elisabeth Donaghy Garrett, *At Home: The American Family, 1750–1870* (New York, 1990), 109.

171. On the death of Molly Potts Jones on 18 March 1787, Hannah Griffitts writes "Serious Reflections, on the Death of a Young Woman," which quotes John 19.28–30 on death as sleep (Blecki and Wulf, 250–52).

172. Allestree, 25.

173. Grosvenor, 166–67.

174. Anna Young Smith, "Lines Written in Consequence of the Writers walking in the Garden of *Wicacoe Church* And its Burial Ground in the Southern Environs of Philadelphia. This Church Stands on the Banks of the River *Delaware* 1775," Elizabeth Fergusson commonplace book, Archives and Special Collections, Dickinson College, Carlisle, Pa.

175. John Keats, "To Sleep," in *Oxford Book of English Verse,* ed. Arthur Quiller-Couch (New York, 1955), 760.

176. On tombstone iconography, see Michael Ragon, *The Space of Death: A Study of Funerary Architecture, Decoration, and Urbanism,* trans. Alan Sheridan (Charlottesville, 1983), 19, 25; Allan Ludwig, *Graven Images: New England Stonecarving and Its Symbols, 1650–1815* (Middletown, Conn., 1966); Edwin Dethlefsen and James Deetz, "Death's Heads, Cherubs, and Willow Trees," *American Antiquity* 31, 4 (1966): 502–12; and Ruth Little, *Sticks and Stones: Three Centuries of North Carolina Gravemakers* (Chapel Hill, 1998).

177. Logan, 12:266.

178. The poem, though preserved in Griffitts's hand, is composed by "SD," whom I take to be Sally Norris Dickinson. Hannah Griffitts's "Copy to Sylvania—from her Freind Fellicia lately Deceas'd,—being a Poetical Imitation of Mrs Rowe's Letters from the Dead, To the Living," Hannah Griffitts Papers, LCP.

179. Deborah Logan to Hannah Griffitts, undated letter, HSP.

180. George Bickham, *The Universal Penman* (London, 1743; rpt. New York, 1941), 89.

181. Weaver, 3. See Robert Fitts, *Puritans, Yankees, and Gravestones: A Linguistic Analysis of New England Gravestone Inscriptions* (Columbia, S.C., 1990), and Ann Douglas, "Heaven Our Home: Consolation Literature in the Northern United States, 1830–1880," in Stannard, *Death in America,* 49–68.

182. Wright, "A Meditation," in Blecki and Wulf, 133–34.

183. Stockton, "Elegy on the death of Miss Chandler, as if written in her father's church-yard," 1784, 130–31.

184. Logan, prefatory pages to her 1828 diary.

185. Logan, 8:79, 6:78.

186. See James Farrell, *Inventing the American Way of Death: The Development of the Modern Cemetery, 1830–1920* (Philadelphia, 1980); David Sloane, *The Last Great Necessity: Cemeteries in American History* (Baltimore, 1991); and Thomas Bender, "The 'Rural' Cemetery Movement: Urban Travail and the Appeal of Nature," in *Material Life in America, 1600–1860,* ed. Robert St. George (Boston, 1988), 505–18.

187. Logan, 15:210.

188. Though William Penn had granted the land for the Quaker burial ground at Fourth and Arch Streets in 1701, it had become crowded by the end of the eighteenth century. The overuse was compounded by the interment of non-Quakers after the yellow fever epidemic of 1793 and by the plans to build a new meeting house over the graves. In an effort to deter non-Quaker burials the gate was locked and could be opened only by permission of the committee for "Rules of Discipline." But as Logan's diary contends, the gates were routinely forced open, "effecting an entrance for the corpse, a most revolting and uneasy procedure" (12:274). Many bodies, she further notes, were disinterred and moved to other locations. See Logan, 9:150, 13:127–28, 15:210.

189. Logan, 11:3–4.

190. Logan, 6:12.

191. Though earlier mourning jewelry discreetly resigned the hair to the jewelry's back, hair became part of the surface decoration by the latter part of the eighteenth century. See Marcia Pointon, "Materializing Mourning: Hair, Jewellery, and the Body," in *Material Memories,* ed. Marius Kwint, Jeremy Aynsley, and Christopher Breward (New York, 1999), 39–71; Pointon, "Wearing Memory: Mourning, Jewellery, and the Body," in *Trauer Tragen,* ed. G. Ecker (Munich, 1998); Martha Gandy Fales, "Mourning, Love, and Fancy Pieces" and "Hairwork" in *Jewellery in America, 1600–1900* (Woodbridge, Suffolk, 1995), 23–28, 98–107; and Davida Tenenbaum Deutsch, "Jewelry for Mourning, Love, and Fancy, 1770–1830," *The Magazine Antiques* (April 1999): 567–75.

192. Thomas Browne, *Urne Buriall* (1658), ed. J. Carter (rpt. Cambridge, 1967), 33.

193. Pointon, "Materializing Mourning," 45.

194. Pointon, "Materializing Mourning," 46.

195. James Stewart, *Plocacosmos; or, The Whole Art of Hairdressing* (London, 1782), 172–73. Courtesy, The Winterthur Library: Printed Book and Periodical Collection.

196. Stewart, 174–75.

197. Stewart, 358.

198. Stewart, 426, 427.

199. Dunlap's *American Daily Advertiser,* 6 March 1793; Robert Fulton (1765–1815) was also a "Miniature Painter & Hair Worker" in Philadelphia at this time. *Pennsylvania Packet and Daily Advertiser,* 5 June 1786. See Deutsch, "Jewelry for Mourning."

200. John Lockington, *Bowles' New and Complete Book of Cyphers* (London, 1771, 1791).

201. Elizabeth Fergusson, "Il Penseroso, An Ode," written in four parts, Hope, Doubt, Solitude, and Adversity, 1780–82, Benjamin Rush Correspondence, LCP.

202. Dodsley, *Oeconomy of Human Life,* 39–40.

203. Logan, 6:176, 1:26.

204. Griffitts, 1774.

205. Griffitts, "To the Memory of Margt Mason who died 29th March 1775," in Blecki and Wulf, 250–52.

CONCLUSION

1. Built in 1732, the State House (Independence Hall) was renovated at the time of the Norris mansion's construction in 1753, when its cupola was removed and a new tower was added at the south end. The steeple was removed in 1781, and the stair tower was capped by a low, hipped roof. The State House tower is best known as the original home of the Liberty Bell. See Constance Greiff, *Independence: The Making of a National Park* (Philadelphia, 1987), and Jeffrey A. Cohen, "Pennsylvania Statehouse," in *Drawing toward Building: Philadelphia Architectural Graphics, 1732–1986,* ed. James F. O'Gorman, Jeffrey A. Cohen, George E. Thomas, and G. Holmes Perkins (Philadelphia, 1986), 33–35.

2. Deborah Logan, "The Bank of the United States: Formerly the Norris House and Garden" (1827), manuscript at Stenton. Courtesy of The National Society of The Colonial Dames of America in the Commonwealth of Pennsylvania at STENTON, Philadelphia.

3. The Library Company now resides at 13th and Locust Streets in the center of Philadelphia; its original site is occupied by the American Philosophical Society's faithful reconstruction of Library Hall.

4. Notoriously private for a public archive, the American Philosophical Society recently opened its doors with its first ongoing public exhibit in almost two hundred years. Opening in 2001 and displayed until March 2003, the exhibit highlights the society's impressive scientific collections: "From the Laboratory to the Parlor: Scientific Instruments in Philadelphia, 1750–1875." In many ways the society exemplifies the inverted development of the archive from private to public space discussed in the introduction.

5. Jeffrey A. Cohen, "The Norris Album (c. 1740–1790)," in *Drawing toward Building,* 35.

6. Greiff, 32.

7. Stephen Bending, "Re-Reading the Eighteenth-Century English Landscape Garden," in *An English Arcadia: Landscape and Architecture in Britain and America,* ed. Guilland Sutherland (San Marino, Calif., 1992), 379–99; John Dickson Hunt and Joachim Wolschke-Bulmahn, eds., *The Vernacular Garden* (Washington, D.C., 1995); David Jacques, *Georgian Gardens: The Reign of Nature* (London, 1983); Salim Kemal and Ivan Gaskell, eds., *Landscape, Natural Beauty, and the Arts* (New York, 1993); Guilland Sutherland, ed., *An English Arcadia: Landscape and Architecture in Britain and America* (San Marino, Calif., 1992); Tom Williamson, *Polite Landscapes: Gardens and Society in Eighteenth-Century England* (Baltimore, 1995).

8. Logan, "Bank of the United States."

9. Joseph Addison, *Spectator* no. 417, 28 June 1712, in *The Spectator* (London, 1711–15).

10. Deborah Logan, manuscript diary, 17 vols., 11:187, Historical Society of Pennsylvania (HSP), Philadelphia.

11. Batty Langley, *New Principles of English Gardening* (London, 1728; rpt. New York, 1982), 195.

12. Didier Maleuvre, *Museum Memories: History, Technology, Art* (Stanford, Calif., 1999), 61.

13. Logan concludes her essay "The Bank of the United States" with this poetic extract.

14. In addition to the Stenton manuscript discussed in this book's introduction, copies of Logan's handwritten and published essay are preserved at the Historical Society of Pennsylvania, the American Philosophical Society, and the Library Company of Philadelphia. See also Cohen, "Pennsylvania Statehouse."

15. Katherine Gauss, "Two Hundred Years of Morven I Record," *House Beautiful* 62 (July 1927): 50–51.

16. See chapter 1 for more details on the Morven and Twickenham gardens.

17. The two odes are in the Elizabeth Graeme Fergusson commonplace book, c. 1787–88 (created by Elizabeth Graeme Fergusson for the "Five Sisters of the Willing Family"), part of the collections of Graeme Park, Horsham, Pa., administered by the Pennsylvania Historical and Museum Commission.

18. Tracing American arts and science back to England's long-standing and rich traditions, Fergusson toasts the president and military hero George Washington, the interdisciplinary genius Benjamin Franklin, the scientist and clockmaker David Rittenhouse, and the painter Benjamin West, claiming that through them, the willow "May to perfection Rise / If we the Metaphor pursue / Symbolic of the Wise." She then acknowledges the male habitués of her famed literary salon: Thomas Godfrey, Nathaniel Evans, Thomas Coombe, Jacob Duche, William Smith (president of Philadelphia College and head of the "Schuylkill Swains"), and the musician James Bremnar. Fergusson commonplace book, Graeme Park.

19. See *Narratives of Nostalgia, Gender, and Nationalism,* ed. Jean Pickering and Suzanne Kehde (New York, 1997), 10–11.

20. Logan diary, 2:162, HSP.

INDEX

Adam, Robert, 67, 124, 161
Addison, Joseph, 90–91, 156, 160, 230
Aging, 15, 49; and ages-of-life motif, 143, 151–53, 175; and associationism, 133; and beauty, 133, 144, 176; and cosmetics, 139–40, 142–44; and Elizabeth Ferguson, 141, 143–44, 150, 153, 155; and Hannah Griffitts, 145–46; and Deborah Norris Logan, 142–44, 147–48, 150, 154–55, 176–78; and mirror stage, 150–51, 153–55; and nostalgia, 135, 144, 147, 163, 177; and proportion, 131–32, 144–45, 147, 154, 176, 177; and reason, 132, 144, 146; and reminiscence, 132–36; and solitude, 132–33, 135, 176; and Annis Stockton, 144–45, 151–53; and tactile sense, 134–36, 144–48; and wisdom, 131, 136; and Susanna Wright, 145–46. *See also* Dementia; Gender; Physiognomy
Allestree, Richard, 183, 217–18
Alphabet: and anthropomorphism, 124; and architecture, 33, 37–38, 67–69; and characters, 81–82, 84, 95–96, 104–6; and cipher books, 215; and fan language, 157–58; and memory, 104–5; and painting, 168–69; Roman, 37–38, 117; as topos, 37, 122.
Amnesia, 1–2, 83, 149. *See also* Dementia; Forgetting
Animal spirits, 32, 83, 85–86, 96–97, 99, 104; and ink, 106–7, 109; and *reminiscen-*

tia, 134, 148. *See also* Humors; Nervous system; Respiration
Anthropomorphism: and alphabet, 124; in architecture, 117–21, 124, 217; in furniture, 88–90; and gravestones, 219; in handwriting, 86, 117–21, 124
Antiquarianism, 72, 78–79, 131, 165, 209
Architects: William Chambers, 22; Inigo Jones, 26; William Kent, 29; Robert Morris, 29; Richard Neve, 26, 37; Vitruvius, 46. See also Adam, Robert; Halfpenny, William
Architectural orders, 67, 117–24; and handwriting, 110–25
Architecture: and caractère, 122–24; and death, 217–19; physiognomy of, 122–24, 255n153; and proportion, 20, 29, 46, 111–20; and rhetoric, 22–23, 30, 122, 217; sex of, 26–27, 29–30; use and beauty of, 110–15, 122, 124. *See also* Alphabet; Anthropomorphism; Decorum; Floorplans; Gender; Handwriting; "Local habitation"; Memory palaces; Rooms; *names of individual buildings*
Archive, 8–9, 13, 16, 78–80, 131, 228–29, 231–32, 234; versus museum, 238–39n55
Artificial memory, 12–13, 22–25, 27–29. *See also* Commonplace books; Memory palaces; Topoi
Associationism, 30–32, 48, 55–56, 58, 69, 136; and gardens, 71, 230–31; and manuscripts, 80. *See also* Recollection; Topophilia

Bachelard, Gaston, 20
Bacon, Francis, 35–36, 96
Balstrode, Richard, 176
Barton, Sally, 59, 146, 149
Beattie, James: on artificial memory, 12–13, 23, 53; and associationism, 69; on writing and memory, 38, 74, 82
Beauty: and aging, 133, 144, 176; and death, 191, 193; and physiognomy, 122–24; and script, 86, 91–92, 109–15, 117–19, 122; and women, 119, 122, 175. *See also* Cosmetics
Benezet, Anthony, 77, 101
Benjamin, Walter, 32
Berkeley, George, 104
Blair, Hugh, 149
Blair, Robert, 188, 217
Blood: circulation of, 144, 147–48, 166; and complexion, 141–42; as epistolary metaphor, 149, 163–64; and ink, 106–9, 185; as metaphor for mourning, 182–83, 185, 189
Body. *See* Anthropomorphism; Architecture; Death; Decorum; Ergonomics; Gender; Handwriting; Phenomenology; Proprioception
Body parts. *See* Blood; Brain; Face; Hands; Heart; Humors; Nervous system; Respiration
Brain, 240 n20; cerebellum, 25, 41, 103; medulla, 32, 103; pineal gland, 96–97, 102. *See also* Closets; Topoi
Browne, Thomas, 223
Buckley, Sarah Morris, 20–22
Burial shrouds. *See* Cloth
Byrd, William, 165

Cartesianism, 16, 24–25, 132–33, 136, 240–41 n25
Cecil, Richard, 182, 188
Cicero: on burial, 222; on old age, 175–76
Closets: for manuscript storage, 41–42, 44, 79–80; and writing, 52, 92. *See also* Topoi
Cloth: and burial shrouds, 191, 201–3, 216–20; and funeral palls, 208, 212; and memory, 96–97, 201–3; and paper, 97–98, 202–3; as text, 201–2, 204–7, 213
Clothing, women's, 64, 74–75, 80–90, 92, 117–18, 132; and memory, 201–3; mourning clothes, 201, 205, 210–13
Cocker, Edward, 106–7, 117–19
Coffins, 201, 203–6, 218

Cohausen, Johann, 134
Collecting: as feminine art, 12–15; and mourning practices, 192, 209; of shells, 13–14, 19–20, 72; and silhouettes, 171–72. *See also* Commonplace books
Commonplace books, 54, 63–64, 87, 93; and architecture, 22; and collecting, 8–10, 12–14; and fans, 161–63; and feminine knowledge, 12–16; and literary history, 233–34; and mirrors, 155; process of creating, 80–82, 133–34; and rhetoric, 22–23; and silhouettes, 171–72. *See also* Topoi
Consolation literature, 179, 181–86, 192, 196, 205, 209–11, 216–18. *See also* Allestree, Richard; Cecil, Richard; Dodsley, Robert; Grosvenor, Benjamin; Weaver, John
Contiguity, 69, 83, 230–31. *See also* Associationism
Corpses, 179–80, 188–89, 194–99. *See also* Death
Correspondence. *See* Epistles
Cosmetics, 136, 175; and aging, 139–40, 142–44; and handwriting, 147; and health, 139–42; and paint, 170, 263 n168; and physiognomy, 139–41; recipes for, 139, 141–42
Coterie. *See* Philadelphia coterie

D'Assigny, Marius, 16, 25, 28, 30, 96, 134
de Mézières, le Camus, 124
Death: and architecture, 217–19; and deathbed, 51, 189–94, 218–19; iconography of, 51, 205, 210, 213, 219–23; and remembrance, 178–89; and resurrection, 179–81, 187, 217, 221, 226–27; and resuscitation, 184, 196–98, 222; textualization of, 204–7. *See also* Cloth; Coffins; Corpses; Domesticity; Embalming; Funerals; Gravestones; Graveyards; Mourning; Physiognomy
Decorum: architectural, 27–29, 110; in handwriting, 90–92, 110; in mourning, 187–88, 209–10
Dementia, 65, 94, 136, 143–45, 149, 175. *See also* Amnesia; Forgetting
Descartes, René, 83; and corporeal memory, 96–99, 102, 104, 161–66
Dickinson, John, 7, 35, 50, 93
Dickinson, Sarah Norris, 129–30, 149, 191
Diderot, Denis, 88, 161–62
Dodsley, Robert, 187–88, 225

Domesticity: and death, 188, 208–10, 215–16; as impediment to writing, 74–78, 92, 111; as mnemonic aid, 30, 132; and woman's mind, 24–32

Edouart, Auguste, 172, 175
Embalming, 15, 178, 195, 200–201; and anatomy theater, 198; as mnemonic metaphor, 178–79, 182, 188, 190, 199–201, 213, 222, 227; compared with portraiture, 193–94; and tears, 200–201
Emlen, Anne Reckless, 20, 72
Epistles: circulation of, 52 148, 149–50; and gender, 90–91; poetic, 136, 155–56, 163–64, 166
Erasmus, Desiderius, 23, 28
Ergonomics: and fans, 158–60; and pens, 102–3; and script, 114; and writing desks, 84, 86–90
Escritoires, 52, 87–93, 234. *See also* Writing Desks
Etiquette. *See* Decorum

Face: and aging, 143–44, 150–51, 153–55; and cosmetics, 139–40, 143; in death, 179, 188, 189–94, 195–96, 219; and handwriting, 87–92, 103; and memory, 131, 158. *See also* Physiognomy
Fairhill, 33–38, 41, 69, 234
Fans, 14, 136–37, 147, 148; and commonplace books, 162–63; and Elizabeth Fergusson, 155–57; language of, 157–60, 163; making of, 161–62; and memory, 163; and physiognomy, 157–58
Feeling, 94, 104, 133. *See also* Phenomenology; Synesthesia; Touch
Fergusson, Elizabeth Graeme, 9, 11, 70–71; aging of, 141, 143–44, 150, 153, 155; and American Revolution, 53–55; on architecture, 45–46; commonplace books of, 45–46, 52, 57, 234; and coverture, 48, 51–56; and death, 157, 163, 4, 197–99; epitaph of, 220; funeral directions of, 211; and literary history, 49–50, 56, 232–34; and mourning, 51, 199–200; at Wright's Ferry, 59; on writing, 99, 106. *See also* Associationism; Epistles; Fans; Graeme Park; Life review; Portrait miniatures; *Reminiscentia*
Fergusson, Hugh Henry, 51, 54–55, 164
Fisher, George, 76, 83, 100–101
Floorplans: 3–cell, 24, 48, 60–61; center passage, 24, 32, 38–45; H-shaped, 33,

37–8, 69; L-shaped, 67–69; medieval-hall, 69; T-shaped, 67, 69. *See also* Architecture; Rooms
Forgetting, 27, 48, 74, 82, 94; and aging, 15, 65; antidote for, 84, 144; as cultural amnesia, 2, 4, 5; and letters, 149–50; and mourning objects, 225. *See also* Amnesia; Dementia
Fothergill, Samuel, 58–59, 232
"Founding Fathers," 2–3, 7, 11–12, 59, 61–62, 65
Franklin, Benjamin, 59, 51–52, 65, 229, 231–32, 233
Friendship, 129; and collective reminiscence, 145–46, 148–50, 153–57, 160–61, 163; and death, 189–90, 220–21; and genealogy, 164; and silhouettes, 175
Funerals, 194; ceremony of, 205; instructions for, 211–12; invitations to, 194–95, 208, 212; materialism of, 210–12; procession, 189, 210–16; and social class, 211–13, 215, 272n143; and wakes, 189, 208–10. *See also* Gender; Graveyards
Furniture: beds, 51, 53, 54; cabinets, 51; chairs, 40 49, 53, 54, 69, 70; chests of drawers, 43, 53, 54; Chippendale style, 6, 92; desks, 42, 52, 62, 70; dressing furniture, 51, 70, 136–38, 146–47, 149, 170; and japanning, 138–39; Queen Anne style, 6, 88, 92; sideboards, 49; sopha, 44; stools, 43–44; tables, 43, 49, 51, 53, 69, 70. *See also* Escritoires; Writing desks

Gardens: at Fairhill, 34–35, 234; grottoes in, 20–2, 71–2; and memory, 229–31; as metaphor for literary history, 232–34; at Morven, 71–72, 232; at Norris house, 228–29, 231, 234; at Stenton, 49, 76, 79
Gender: and aging, 132, 134, 143–44, 151–53, 175–77; and architecture, 24–31, 59–60, 80, 117–24, 217–18; and female knowledge/memory, 16, 20, 29–33, 50, 64–65, 124–25; and funerals, 212–16, 273n151; handwriting, 87–92, 104–5, 109–11; and mourning, 181–82, 185–89, 206–9, 211, 212–14, 216; and property, 47–48, 54–57, 58–60, 65. *See also* Ergonomics; Phenomenology
Genealogy, 4–9, 12, 16, 33; and cloth, 201, 203; and collective reminiscence, 145–46; and death, 178–89; and Fairhill, 33–34; and Graeme Park, 48; and literary history, 232–34; and remembrance,

Genealogy (*continued*)
223, 227; and Stenton, 40, 42, 44–45,
170–71, 175; and Wright's Ferry, 57–58,
62
Geometry, 113–17, 121, 124. *See also* Architecture; Proportion
Girls, 151–53, 212–13
Graeme, Ann Diggs, 45, 49–51
Graeme, Thomas, 47–49, 51
Graeme Park, 11, 45–57, 233–34
Gravestones, 192, 205; inscriptions on,
219–22; of Deborah Logan, 222
Graveyards, 213, 216–22; and live burial,
197; of Quakers, 194–95, 212, 222,
274 n188; at Stenton, 131, 208, 222
Griffitts, Hannah, 10–11, 72; aging of,
145–46; death of, 189–91, 194–96; and
elegy cycle, 178–89, 223, 227; at Fairhill,
33, 36–38; on friendship and death, 221;
and funeral directions, 189–90, 194–95;
on memorialization, 192, 211; and
mourning, 200–201, 210; physiognomy
of, 191; and *reminiscentia*, 150.
Griffitts, Mary Norris, 10, 178–89, 227
Grosvenor, Benjamin, 182, 184, 187–88,
204

Halfpenny, William, 113–16
Hand, 84, 99–100, 103, 158; and fan language, 155–60. *See also* Handwriting;
Pens and quills; Script; Touch, sense of
Handwriting: and architecture, 14, 80–82,
87; 110–25; and beauty, 110–15; corporeality of, 79, 83–92, 101–2, 124; and legibility, 77, 82–83, 86, 91, 96, 101–2, 106,
109–10, 121; as materialization of
thought, 96, 109; and memorization, 82,
84, 95, 101–2; and memory, 14, 74,
80–87, 91–92, 101–2, 106; and mourning, 184–5; and nervous system, 84–86,
94–97, 102–4, 106–7; and permanence,
74, 82, 85, 93–94, 96, 104, 111; and portraiture, 165–69; versus print 63, 65, 80,
82; and transparency, 83, 86; usefulness
of, 110–15. *See also* Decorum; Gender;
Physiognomy; Proportion; Script
Hawkes, Thomas, 113–16
Heart, 106–7, 147–49, 176; and embalming,
199, 200–201; and incorporation of the
other, 154, 157, 201, 204, 223, 227; and
mourning, 189, 199; as synecdoche,
223–25
Heirlooms, 4, 39–40, 149–50, 202–3

Historic preservation, 2–4, 13–14, 39,
63–65
Hogarth, William, 22, 88, 169, 198, 232
Hume, David, 32, 53, 153
Humors, 27, 29, 141, 148, 195–96. *See also*
Animal spirits; Blood; Nervous system;
Respiration

Imitation: in handwriting, 95, 104, 113; and
portrait miniatures, 165–66, 167, 169;
and silhouettes, 172. *See also* Neoclassicism
Inhabitation, 48, 64. *See also* Associationism; Phenomenology; Topophilia
Ink, 70–71, 76–77, 87, 105–9, 145–47; and
mourning, 184–85
Inkstands, 76–77, 107–8

Jenkins, John, 81–82, 83, 102, 104–5
Johnson, Madame, 91–92, 101, 119–20
Johnson, Samuel, 166, 232

Kames, Lord, 87, 94
Knowledge, spatial metaphors for, 20,
24–25. *See also* Gender; Phenomenology

Lambert, marchionesse de, 143, 151,
153–54, 176
Lavater, John Caspar, 92, 131–32; and postmortem physiognomy, 192; and silhouettes, 172–73
Library, as public archive, 228–29. *See also*
Rooms; Topoi
Life review, 135–36, 147, 155, 163, 175;
Elizabeth Fergusson on, 133–34
Limning. *See* Portrait miniatures
Literary history, transatlantic, 50, 53,
232–34, 276 n18
"Local habitation," 1, 12, 14, 20, 23, 30, 56,
176. *See also* Topoi
Locke, John, 81–83, 94–95, 178, 217
Logan, Algernon, 192, 202
Logan, Debby, 43, 208
Logan, Deborah Norris, 9–10, 72; aging of,
142–44, 147–48, 150, 154–55, 176–78; as
anachronism, 39, 43, 45; "The Bank of
the United States," 4–8, 228, 232,
236 n14; and clothing, 74–75, 92, 132,
201–3; commonplace book of, 39, 74,
170; on death, 189–91, 193–96, 202; and
diaries, 39, 45, 74, 93; dressing table of,
136–38, 146–47; on Fairhill, 33–36, 38,
234; on Elizabeth Fergusson, 220; on fu-

nerals, 201, 208–9, 212–16; on gardens, 40, 230–31; on graves/graveyards, 131, 208, 216, 222; and Hannah Griffitts, 189–91, 194–96; and historic preservation, 4–8, 39–40, 63–65, 222; on memory, 31, 94, 132–33, 136, 142–43; and mourning, 201, 222, 226; mourning jewelry for, 223; on Norris House, 1–2, 4, 6–8, 228–31, 234; physiognomy of, 132; and portraiture, 129–33, 135, 177, 193; and recollection, 63, 133, 136; and silhouettes, 170–71, 173–75; on Susanna Wright, 63–65; on writing, 109–11, 125; writing practices of, 74–81, 84–85, 87–88, 91–94, 98–99, 101, 105, 107–9

Logan, George, 7, 39, 41, 78, 80, 93–94

Logan, James, 7, 38, 44, 78, 138; and *Cato Major*, 175–76; correspondence with William Penn, 8, 80; and Susanna Wright, 58, 60, 61

Logan, Maria Dickinson, 130, 135, 170, 177

Manuscripts: and commonplace books, 9–10, 52; at deathbed, 192; as gardens, 230; as heirlooms, 39, 41, 45; legibility of, 82, 93, 109–10; material culture of, 76–77, 108–9; and memory, 67, 72–73, 74, 80–82, 93; and painting, 165, 168–69; and print culture, 63, 65, 80, 82, 84, 95, 97; as scribal publication, 13, 15, 221. *See also* Epistles; Handwriting; Script

Memento mori, 183, 185, 193, 211, 224

Memorization, 67; of death's face, 192, 194; in handwriting, 82, 84, 95, 101–2, 104, 115; and painting, 169; and silhouettes, 172–73

Memory: as deposition, 81–82, 87, 96, 169–70; and nationalism, 2–3, 4–8, 13–14, 69; as reposition, 64–65, 80–81, 88, 92, 94, 96. *See also* Alphabet; Artificial memory; Cloth; Clothing; Face; Fans; Gardens; Gender; Handwriting; Logan, Deborah; Manuscripts; Memory palaces; Memory traces; Nervous system; Nostalgia; Pens and quills; Physiognomy; Print culture; Silhouettes; Stockton, Annis; *Reminiscentia*; Topoi

Memory palaces, 6, 14, 20, 24–25, 29, 34, 38, 57, 131, 239n6; and commonplacing, 45–46. *See also* Topoi

Memory traces, 30, 32, 64, 72, 94, 97, 103–4, 115; and reminiscence, 133, 155, 167

Mirrors, 14, 49, 52, 64, 136, 147, 148, 150–55, 234; and commonplace books, 155; and death, 208

Mnemonic theorists: Halbwachs, Maurice, 135; Willis, John, 81. *See also* Beattie, James; D'Assigny, Marius; Descartes, René; Erasmus, Desiderius; Locke, John

Mnemosyne, 45, 64; and genealogy, 13, 15, 83, 232; and wax impressions, 13, 82–83, 87, 95, 185, 222

Moore, Milcah Martha, 63, 173–74

Morven, 11–12, 65, 72, 232

Mourning: and collective reminiscence, 179, 184–87, 201–4, 209–10, 218; as death's reversal, 181, 183–84; and detachment, 181, 189, 205, 209, 216, 222; and incorporation, 181, 189, 200–203, 205, 209–10, 223–27. *See also* Decorum; Gender; Proportion

Mourning objects, 189, 202, 205, 209; hairwork, 223–25; jewelry, 222–27

Mythology, Greek: Callimachus, 119; Corinthia, 119; Dibutades, 170; Hecate, 197; Korinthia, 170, 172, 175; Persephone, 203; Philomela, 63; Procne, 63

Nationalism, 2–3, 4–8, 13–14, 69, 235–36n7

Neoclassicism: in architecture, 67, 124, 161; in painting, 165–66, 169, 172; in poetry, 179. *See also* Imitation

Nervous system: and architecture, 32, 40–42, 67; and handwriting, 83–84, 86, 95–97, 99, 102–4, 106–7; and memory, 94, 106; and reminiscence, 147–49. *See also* Brain; Humors

Norris, Deborah, 7, 231–32, 233

Norris, Elizabeth, 33–34, 37

Norris, Isaac, 7, 33, 37, 61, 228

Norris house, 1–8, 16, 228, 234; and garden, 228–29, 231, 234

Nostalgia, 1–8, 9, 79, 234; and Fairhill, 34–38; and Elizabeth Fergusson, 45–46; and mourning, 184, 187, 223–24; and portrait miniatures, 164, 170; and Susanna Wright, 57–60. *See also* Aging

Paper, 52, 70–71, 76–77, 93–96, 108, 145–46; and cloth, 202–3; and fan-making, 163; and portrait miniatures, 165; production of, 97–98; and silhouettes, 171–72

Peale, Charles Willson: and embalming, 193; and Deborah Logan's portrait, 129–32, 135; portrait gallery of, 2, 229; and postmortem portraits, 193–94; and silhouettes, 172–73, 174–75

Penmanship. *See* Handwriting

Penmen: Bickham, George, 83, 221; Massey, William, 83. *See also* Cocker, Edward; Fisher, George; Hawkes, Thomas; Jenkins, John; Johnson, Madame

Penn, William, 8, 80; and Tammany Club, 235n6

Pennington, Lady, 74

Pens and quills, 70–71, 76–77, 87, 93, 95, 99–105, 145; making of, 77, 100–101, 105, 107; and memory, 101; and nervous system, 99

Phenomenology, 134–35; and architecture, 124–25; and body memory, 101–2, 104; and handwriting, 79, 81–87, 124; and reminiscence, 134–35. *See also* Associationism; Gender; Inhabitation; Proprioception; Topophilia

Philadelphia coterie, 9–15, 23–24, 72–73, 110, 237n31; and aging, 142–44; on death/mourning, 179, 191, 189; epistolary communication, 147–50; and manuscript circulation, 221, 232–34; and reminiscence, 136, 161

Physiognomy: and aging, 131–32, 135–36, 142–44, 154, 170; and cosmetics, 139–40, 146–47; and death, 179, 188–94, 196, 199, 209–10, 219, 269n69; and handwriting, 87–92, 103, 122–24, 146–47, 192; and fans, 157–58; and memory, 135–36; and portrait miniatures, 167–70; and silhouettes, 170, 172. *See also* Architecture; Beauty; Face

Physiognotrace, 173–75

Plato, 85, 95, 187

Pope, Alexander, 71–72, 149, 232

Portrait miniatures, 14, 136, 147, 148, 172, 194; and commonplacing, 169; and Elizabeth Fergusson, 163–64; and intimacy, 166–67; and memory, 169–70; methods of, 167–69; and physiognomy, 167–70; and reminiscence, 165, 167, 169; textuality of, 165, 169

Portraitists: Boutet, Claude, 168; Fraser, Charles, 164; Hilliard, Nicholas, 166–67; Kendrick, Emma, 168; Le Brun,

Charles, 154, 157; Payne, John, 167–68; Reynolds, Joshua, 166. *See also* Hogarth, William; Peale, Charles Willson

Portraiture, 40–42, 49, 69, 88, 129–31, 135; and commonplace books, 169; and cosmetics, 138–41, 170; and proportion, 168; theories of, 165–66. *See also* Portrait miniatures

Pounce, 76–77, 147, 185

Powell, Elizabeth Willing, 201, 212, 214

Print culture, 63, 65, 95–96; and anonymity, 121–22; and memory, 83, 97, 236n15; Roman versus manuscript, 80, 82, 84; Roman block prints, 38, 69

Proportion: and handwriting, 90, 99, 104, 110–14, 117, 124–25; and mourning, 181–83, 185, 187–89, 210–11, 217, 225–26; and painting, 168; and typefaces, 121. *See also* Aging; Architecture

Proprioception, 30–33, 57, 65, 104; and "bodily situation," 104. *See also* Associationism; Inhabitation; Phenomenology; Topophilia

Quakers, 58–60, 131, 171; and funerals, 213–15; graveyard of, 194–95, 212, 222; and materialism, 64–65

Quills. *See* Pens and quills

Recollection, 45, 49, 63, 71, 74, 87, 94, 133, 135, 179, 187

Relics, 71–72, 80, 137, 176, 189, 201, 216, 223, 225–27

Remembrance, 14, 178–79, 196, 203, 229

Reminiscence, 134; and friendship, 145–46, 148–50, 153–57, 160–61, 163–64, 175. *See also* Mourning; *Reminiscentia*

Reminiscentia, 134–36, 144, 147–48, 150–57, 163–67, 170–72; and mourning objects, 189, 191, 223. *See also* Fans; Heirlooms; Mirrors; Mourning objects; Portrait miniatures; Silhouettes

Respiration, 32; and aging, 142; and death, 183–84, 196–97, 219, 222; and painting, 170; and reminiscence, 147–50, 164; and writing, 84, 92, 102, 106–7, 109

Rhetoric: ekphrasis, 75, 79, 94, 166; metaphor, 232; metonym, 88–90, 136, 155; personification, 49, 56, 134; synecdoche, 223, 225. *See also* Topoi

Ritchie, Juliana, 155–57, 160, 163–65, 167

Robertson, Hannah, 19, 105

Rogers, Samuel, 19, 20, 87, 194

Rooms: attic, 53; bedroom, 42–45, 51–52, 70–71, 217–18; dining room, 42–43, 48, 69–70, 74–77, 80–81, 92, 108; hall, 34, 40, 48, 61, 67–68; kitchen, 6, 42; library, 35, 44, 77–81, 108; parlor, 40–41, 48–51, 54, 61–62, 69, 208–9; piazza 6, 41–42, 67. *See also* Architecture; Closets; Floorplans; Topoi

Rowe, Elizabeth Singer, 50, 220–21

Ruins, 36–38, 54, 72, 228; archive as, 231–32; as synecdoche, 231

Rush, Benjamin, 11, 50, 59, 65, 66

Rush, Julia (Stockton), 67, 70, 72

Scribal publication, 9–10, 13, 15, 52, 63, 65. *See also* Commonplace books; Epistles; Handwriting; Philadelphia coterie

Script, 109–25; italic hand, 52, 90–91, 110, 117–23; roman, 121; round hand, 52, 91, 110, 117–23; secretary (running) hand, 109–10, 117. *See also* Handwriting

Second Bank of the United States, 1, 5, 229; architecture of, 2–4; and national memory, 3–4; and portrait gallery, 9

Shells, 72, 109; and commonplacing, 23; and inhabited shell, 20, 24; shellwork houses, 19–22, 105, 239 n2

Sheraton, Thomas, 113, 147

Silhouettes, 14, 131, 147, 148, 176–77; and commonplace books, 171–72; and genealogy, 170–71; and Lavater, 172–74; and Deborah Logan, 170–71, 173–75; and memory, 172–73; and methods of, 172; and Charles Willson Peale, 172–73; and physiognomy, 170. *See also* Physiognotrace

Smith, Anna Young, 52, 55, 106, 218–19, 234

Smith, Hannah, 214–15

Smith, Rebecca (Moore), 50, 54–55

Smith, William, 50, 52, 55, 56

Solitude, 78–79, 132–33, 135, 176

Souvenirs. *See* Mourning objects; *Reminiscentia*

Stenton, 20, 38–45. *See also* Architecture: physiognomy of

Stewart, James, 139–40, 224–25

Stockton, Annis Boudinot, 9, 11–12; aging of, 144–45, 151–53; and American Revolution, 65–66; and associationism, 71–72, 232; children of, 67, 70, 72; death of, 72; and Graeme Park salon, 50, 233; and letter-writing, 67, 70–71, 149; and mourning, 199, 200, 210, 222. *See also* Morven

Stockton, Richard, 66, 69–72

Synesthesia, 79, 86, 94, 103. *See also* Phenomenology

Textiles. *See* Cloth

Toilette, 136–47

Topoi: alphabet, 37, 81–82; attic, 53; beekeeping, 35; closets, 24–25, 41, 52; digestion, 80–81; furniture, 23, 53, 87, 131; gardens, 229–30; library, 36, 81; pigeonholes, 92; storerooms, 80–81. *See also* Memory palaces

Topophilia, 30–33, 49–51, 58, 63, 72–73, 176. *See also* Associationism; Inhabitation; Proprioception

Touch, sense of, 94, 103–4, 134–36, 144, 156, 166–67; and mourning objects, 189, 223–24. *See also* Reminiscentia

Towle, Matthew, 158–60

Typefaces, 121–22. *See also* Print culture

Ward, Gerald, 90, 203

Wars: American Revolution, 33, 36–37, 53–55, 65–66, 70; Civil War, 179; Seven Years' War, 58, 62; War of 1812, 3

Washington, George, 3, 11–12, 66, 69–70

Washington, Martha, 69–70

Watson, John Fanning, 8, 11, 80

Weaver, John, 182, 186, 205

Whately, Thomas, 36, 38, 228

Whitfield, George, 210–11

Willis, Thomas, 86, 96, 103, 107

Willows, 223, 228, 232–34

Winding sheets. *See* Cloth: and burial shrouds

Wright, Susanna, 9–10, 72; aging of, 145–46; in cultural memory, 63–65; on death, 211, 216–17, 222; on Fairhill, 33–34, 36, 38; memory of, 65; and nostalgia, 57–59, 65; on painting, 177; as property owner, 58–60; and proprioception, 57; silk manufacture, 62–63. *See also* Wright's Ferry

Wright's Ferry, 10, 57–65

Writing desks, 42, 51, 52, 62, 74–75, 79, 136; and architecture, 87, 92; and

Writing desks (*continued*)
dressing tables, 146–47; lap desks, 90; as mnemonic topos, 92. *See also* Escritoires
Writing materials. *See* Ink; Paper; Pens and quills; Pounce

Young, Edward, 53, 70
Young, Jane (Graeme), 52; burial shroud of, 201–2, 204, 219–20

Zimmerman, J. G., 132–33, 154